DATE DUE

Severely Handicapped Young Children and Their Families

Research in Review

Severely Handicapped Young Children and Their Families

Research in Review

Edited by

Jan Blacher
School of Education
University of California
Riverside, California

With a Foreword by James J. Gallagher

1984

ACADEMIC PRESS, INC.
(Harcourt Brace Jovanovich, Publishers)
Orlando   San Diego   San Francisco   New York   London
Toronto   Montreal   Sydney   Tokyo   São Paulo

ACADEMIC PRESS, INC.
Orlando, Florida 32887

United Kingdom Edition published by
ACADEMIC PRESS, INC. (LONDON) LTD.
24/28 Oval Road, London NW1 7DX

Library of Congress Cataloging in Publication Data

Main entry under title:

Severely handicapped young children and their families.

  Bibliography: p.
  Includes index.
  I. Handicapped children--Family relationships--
Addresses, essays, lectures. I. Blacher, Jan.
[DNLM: I. Handicapped--Psychology. 2. Child,
exceptional. 3. Family. WS 105.5.F2 S498]
HV888.S46 1984   362.8'2   83-21469
ISBN 0-12-102750-3 (alk. paper)

PRINTED IN THE UNITED STATES OF AMERICA

84 85 86 87   9 8 7 6 5 4 3 2 1

To Mom,
In Memory of My Dad, Leo

Contents

6. Severely Handicapped Children and Their Brothers and Sisters

Thomas M. Skrtic, Jean Ann Summers, Mary Jane Brotherson, and Ann P. Turnbull

7. The Severely Handicapped and Child Abuse

John H. Meier and Michael P. Sloan

III. Family Involvement in the Educational Process

8. Clinical Research and Policy Issues in Parenting Severely Handicapped Infants

Crystal E. Kaiser and Alice H. Hayden

Contributors

Numbers in parentheses indicate the pages on which the authors' contributions begin.

Bruce L. Baker (319), Department of Psychology, University of California, Los Angeles, California 90024

Jan Blacher (3), School of Education, University of California, Riverside, California 92521

Marie M. Bristol (91), Frank Porter Graham Child Development Center and Division TEACCH, Department of Psychiatry, School of Medicine, University of North Carolina at Chapel Hill, Chapel Hill, North Carolina 27514

Gene H. Brody (179), Department of Child and Family Development, University of Georgia, Athens, Georgia 30602

Mary Jane Brotherson (215), Research and Training Center on Independent Living, University of Kansas, Lawrence, Kansas 66045

Roberta D. Granger (51), Institute for the Study of Developmental Disabilities, Department of Psychology, University of Illinois at Chicago, Chicago, Illinois 60608

Alice H. Hayden (275), Department of Special Education, University of Washington, Seattle, Washington 98195

Crystal E. Kaiser (275), Wichita State University, College of Education, Wichita, Kansas 67208

Marty Wyngaarden Krauss (143), Eunice Kennedy Shriver Center for Mental Retardation, and Brandeis University, Waltham, Massachusetts 02154

John H. Meier (247), Research Division, CHILDHELP, U.S.A./INTER-

NATIONAL, Beaumont, California 92223; and Neuropsychiatric Institute, University of California, Los Angeles, California 90024

Arnold J. Sameroff (51), Institute for the Study of Developmental Disabilities, University of Illinois at Chicago, Chicago, Illinois 60608

Eric Schopler (91), Division TEACCH, Department of Psychiatry, School of Medicine, University of North Carolina at Chapel Hill, Chapel Hill, North Carolina 27514

Marsha Mailick Seltzer (143), Research Department, School of Social Work, Boston University, Boston, Massachusetts 02215

Thomas M. Skrtic (215), Department of Special Education, University of Kansas, Lawrence, Kansas 66045

Michael P. Sloan (247), The Village of CHILDHELP, U.S.A., Beaumont, California 92223; and Department of Psychology, University of California, Riverside, California 92521

Zolinda Stoneman (179), Department of Child and Family Development, The University of Georgia, Athens, Georgia 30602

Jean Ann Summers (215), Kansas University Affiliated Facility at Lawrence, and Department of Special Education, University of Kansas, Lawrence, Kansas 66045

Ann P. Turnbull (215, 377), Bureau of Child Research and Department of Special Education, University of Kansas, Lawrence, Kansas 66045

Pamela J. Winton[1] (377), Carolina Institute for Research in Early Education for the Handicapped, Frank Porter Graham Child Development Center, University of North Carolina at Chapel Hill, Chapel Hill, North Carolina 27514

Judith Sewell Wright (51), Institute for the Study of Developmental Disabilities, University of Illinois at Chicago, Chicago, Illinois 60608

Regina Yando (401), Judge Baker Guidance Center/Children's Hospital, and Harvard Medical School, Boston, Massachusetts 02115

Edward Zigler (401), Department of Psychology, Yale University, New Haven, Connecticut 06520

[1]Present address: Atlantic Center for Research in Education, 604 West Chapel Hill Road, Durham, North Carolina 27701.

Foreword

This book provides an impressive state-of-the-art summary of research conducted on severely handicapped children and their families. In scope and in detail, the individual chapters show an impressive increase in sophistication achieved in less than two decades by the variety of professional fields represented here. The book also provides reassurance that we will never return to the professionally embarrassing situation of the 1940s and 1950s, when many professionals tended to either blame parents for the handicapping situation, as in the case of infantile autism, or had totally unrealistic expectations of how parents should behave with their severely handicapped child. We hardly need reminding that the help that the professional could or did offer the family was indeed limited in that time period. At the same time, the unfinished nature of many of the questions and issues revealed in the chapters show how far we still have to travel before obtaining a clear portrait of the family with a severely handicapped child and, above all, in the discovery and implementation of effective ways of intervening in a constructive fashion with these families.

It is clear that the present research interest and developmental activities have been based largely upon a series of federal initiatives. Federal legislation to support research, development, demonstration, and leadership training for the handicapped began with a series of legislative efforts in the mid-1960s. It was not until the mid-1970s, when Public Law 94–142, the Education for All Handicapped Children Act, passed with an emphasis on the support of professional activities designed to create a better education for the handicapped child, that the federal government significantly joined the already active local and state governments in providing for direct services. Embedded in this landmark legislation itself was a statement of priorities requiring that local and state programs provide special educational services to handicapped children who had not previously been served. Those affected by this requirement were mostly moderately to severely handicapped children who had not traditionally been seen as an educational, as opposed to a health, responsibility.

Accompanying this increased pressure to develop service programs for severely handicapped children was the establishment of a series of research centers and institutes financed by special education programs in the U.S. Department of Education, which provided the resources for teams of trained research and development personnel who were able to focus a significant amount of their professional time on concerns surrounding the education of severely handicapped individuals. While many other professionals have also made significant contributions to our research knowledge, the focus of these efforts has and can be expected to continue to yield a steady flow of concepts, ideas, and materials in the years to come.

The significant pressures and stresses upon the family that are triggered by the arrival of a severely handicapped child are only beginning to be understood. Growing evidence of marital dissolution, child abuse, and other negative indicators underlines the major task of service personnel in assisting these families to adapt without a major negative impact on all of the family members. It should be recalled that this family adaptation problem is also relatively new. It was not until after World War II that the expectation that the family of a severely handicapped child would institutionalize such a child was reversed. However great the burdens of guilt and stress that such institutionalization created, it did remove the day-to-day responsibilities of coping with a child who revealed minimum responsiveness to adult stimulation. The current strong movement toward deinstitutionalization has presented families with a new type of potential stress. Previously families had to deal with the symbolic death of the "child-who-would-never-be" (the expected normal child), and possibly the guilt feelings associated with the decision to institutionalize the child, but they now have to face a continuing care problem that stretches as far into the future as the family can project.

One of the most difficult problems with which the family of a severely handicapped child must cope is the permanency of the handicapping condition. One of the traditional strategies for coping with stress, whether it is associated with visits to a dentist's office, a final examination, or the presence of a preschool child in the home, has always been the knowledge that the stressor is not permanent. Adults can comfort themselves with the notion that it will eventually disappear, which allows them to endure the discomfort for a measured period of time, after which they can go on to a new and, hopefully, less aggravating environment. But the family of a severely handicapped child can offer themselves no such reassurance. Instead, there is often a lifelong responsibility to cope with someone who, even under the best of circumstances, will always be a dependent individual.

The importance of a warm, personal relationship with a counselor that will allow the parents to express their concerns and anxieties can hardly be overestimated. These opportunities for emotional expression should not just be provided to the mother—the role of the father in these families has been receiving belated attention, and it is clear that the entire family unit, including the siblings, deserves sustained attention regarding how each member copes with the realization of the permanence of the handicapping condition. The siblings, as they grow older, may begin to wonder what their eventual role will be in caring for their dependent brother or sister when their parents retire or die. This requires some additional coping skills, together with recognition of the potential guilt feelings for their almost inevitable resentment that the severely handicapped child received so much care and parental attention, often to the partial neglect of the normal sibling.

It seems quite clear that professionals have underestimated two serious adaptation problems for families. We have always tended to be too pessimistic about the capabilities of even the most severely handicapped child, and we have placed too little emphasis on the treatment and continuing support of the family unit. This volume is one of a growing number of milestones marking the increased concern and sophistication of professionals, and it provides the basis for hope that our work with families of handicapped children will become even more constructive and effective in the near future.

James J. Gallagher
Frank Porter Graham Child Development Center
University of North Carolina at Chapel Hill

Preface

There are many general books available on living with a severely handicapped child that "tell it like it is." However, one is likely to find that reports of data or of the research literature relevant to this population are spotty and uncoordinated. Particularly lacking are comprehensive up-to-date reviews of the literature in relevant research domains: family adjustment, family dynamics, and family involvement in schooling. Issues of development, schooling, or family dynamics among severely handicapped children differ from those of mildly handicapped or high-risk children, and thus merit treatment in a separate research volume. Furthermore, studies related to the development of severely handicapped children cut across the disciplinary boundaries of developmental and clinical psychology, special education, sociology, social work, and pediatrics. Hence, this volume is intended to serve as a collection of research reviews from several disciplines, providing guidelines for future research directions and applications.

It is our hope that this volume will generate new interest and ideas for research among students of normal development as well as students, researchers, teachers, clinicians, and parents interested in the effects of severely handicapped young children on families.

Part I of this volume pertains to issues of family adjustment to the arrival and rearing of a child with a severely handicapping condition. Chapter 1, in which Jan Blacher reviews the theoretical and methodological perspectives represented in the literature on family functioning and adjustment vis-à-vis a handicapped child, serves as a framework for the entire book. This chapter also presents a model for researching the effects of a severely handicapped child on the family. The remainder of Part I explores more specific effects such a child may have on families. Chapter 2, by Judith Sewell Wright, Roberta D. Granger, and

Arnold J. Sameroff, delineates aspects of acceptance or rejection in families; and Chapter 3, by Marie M. Bristol and Eric Schopler, focuses on stress in families with autistic children, viewing autism as a very specific type of severely handicapping condition. In Chapter 4, Marsha Mailick Seltzer and Marty Wyngaarden Krauss cover an issue of great importance to families of all severely handicapped children: alternative placement options. Perhaps the single most critical variable determining family adjustment to a young severely handicapped child is whether the family can cope with living with the child, or whether some alternative placement out of the natural home is required.

Part II focuses on the severely handicapped child's influences on family dynamics. Such influences include child and parent characteristics, such as those believed to influence parent–child interactions, explored by Zolinda Stoneman and Gene H. Brody in Chapter 5. In Chapter 6, Thomas M. Skrtic, Jean Ann Summers, Mary Jane Brotherson, and Ann P. Turnbull present a model for studying relationships between a severely handicapped child and his or her siblings, as well as other family relationships. Other adverse child influences on family dynamics are presented by John H. Meier and Michael P. Sloan in Chapter 7, which reviews the literature on the relationship between severe developmental disabilities and child abuse.

Part III of this volume centers on family involvement in the educational process. Chapter 8, by Crystal E. Kaiser and Alice H. Hayden, focuses on clinical and research issues in parenting severely impaired infants. Bruce L. Baker provides a thorough review of behavioral interventions in families with young handicapped children in Chapter 9, with particular emphasis on unique problems in early intervention with families who have a severely impaired child. Chapter 10, contributed by Ann P. Turnbull and Pamela J. Winton, reviews current models and issues surrounding parent involvement policy and practice. Due both to legal requirements inherent in educational legislation and to the elaborate interdisciplinary effort required to educate many severely handicapped children, the education of this population has become a "family affair."

The concluding chapter, by Regina Yando and Edward Zigler, is a synthesis of the entire book, a state-of-the-art interpretation of research related to parents and families of severely handicapped children, and a forum for exploring policy recommendations.

The contributors to this volume have collected data, either from their own or other projects, that elaborate, extend, or illustrate the perspectives inherent in previously published works on severely impaired individuals. In addition, all chapters contain potential applications of the research amassed to date. The intended result of this volume is a more comprehensive picture of severely handicapped children at home and at school.

This book was completed while the editor was a Visiting Assistant Professor of Psychology in the Division of Psychiatry at Harvard Medical School, and coordinator of "Parent Place," a new educational program for parents at the Judge Baker Guidance Center. I thank Sunny Yando, Chief of Psychology at the Judge Baker Guidance Center and Children's Hospital Medical Center, for allowing me time to work on this manuscript and for sharing her own expertise in working with parents and families. I am also grateful to Beth Germanotta for her help in manuscript preparation and to the School of Education, University of California–Riverside, my home institution, for the administrative, financial, and secretarial support provided.

I extend special thanks to my mentor, friend, and colleague, C. E. Meyers, for providing input and counsel throughout preparation of this volume. And I offer multitudinous thanks to Bruce L. Baker for helping me to overcome by "terminal anxiety" at the word processor, and for all the good sense, constructive criticism, humor, and relaxing moments he provided during my work on this book.

I am fortunate to have worked with some outstanding professionals at Academic Press who patiently provided conscientious feedback, meticulous editing, and moral support.

Finally, I would like to thank each of the contributors of this volume for acknowledging my reminders, tolerating my prodding, working with a sense of humor, and turning in an excellent product.

$=$ PART I $=$

Perspectives on Family Adjustment

A Dynamic Perspective on the Impact of a Severely Handicapped Child on the Family*

Jan Blacher

Introduction

This chapter focuses on the severely impaired child who, ironically, has been essentially neglected in previous studies of parent–child interactions. As pointed out by Sameroff and Chandler (1975), not all caretakers respond to a helpless and dependent infant the same way. The caretaking response may actually be negative if particularly adverse or aggravating factors are present (e.g., physical handicap or temperamental characteristics such as crying or restlessness). Indeed, physical ab-

* This chapter was completed while the author was a Visiting Scholar at the Judge Baker Guidance Center, Boston, Massachusetts, and Visiting Assistant Professor of Psychology in the Department of Psychiatry, Harvard Medical School. Preparation of this chapter was supported in part by grant No. RO1 HD14680 from the National Institute for Child Health and Human Development.

3

normalities such as extreme hyper- or hypotonicity resulting from complicated births have been shown to markedly influence mother–child relationships (Prechtl & Stemmer, 1962). It is no small wonder, then, that children who are considered severely handicapped have, at the very least, a distinct effect on their parents and families. It is ironic that previous studies of parent–child interaction have rarely included this population, for the severely handicapped child may disrupt family harmony and produce such extraordinary financial burden or stress that the child is ultimately placed out of the natural home.

Moreover, as this entire volume suggests, the severely handicapped child affects relationships other than the parent–child dyad. Part I of the book describes some major aspects of family adjustment to a severely handicapped child. Part II focuses on other ways in which a severely handicapped child influences the family and covers the development of sibling relationships and the underlying dynamics of child abuse. Part III describes the extent of family involvement in educating this child. It includes a detailed review of the literature on parent training as well as discussions of relevant research and policy issues.

In describing the ways that a severely handicapped child may impact on the family, the authors of the chapters in this volume present a variety of theoretical and methodological perspectives. Thus, the purpose of this introductory chapter is to provide some conceptual "glue" for the reader and to preview some of the major issues explored in subsequent chapters. This chapter begins with a brief introduction to the population of severely handicapped children, with emphasis on the diversity within this group. There follows a discussion of some methodological approaches used in the past to study the impact of a severely handicapped child, with mention of some limitations and advantages of each approach.

The remainder of the chapter builds toward the presentation of a research model that identifies variables either shown or hypothesized to be important in considering the impact of a severely handicapped child. Three topics receive considerable treatment in the sections that follow the discussion of methodology. One is attachment, proposed here as a unifying theoretical concept and a critical factor in understanding family adjustment to a severely handicapped child and family decision making regarding placement of that child. A second related topic of heuristic interest is the relationship between handicapping conditions and child abuse. The third topic is parent–child dynamics in families with a severely handicapped child. Other chapters in this volume will be cited, where appropriate, to guide the reader to more detailed reviews.

Who Is the Severely Handicapped Child?

The term *severely handicapped* describes a wide range of children including those who are autistic, severely emotionally disturbed, developmentally disabled, and severely or profoundly retarded. While the Association for the Severely Handicapped currently has no official definition of this population, the term *severely handicapped* generally includes those individuals who are severely and profoundly mentally retarded but also those whose handicap (e.g., emotional disturbance, health impairment, orthopedic impairment, blindness, deafness) is so severe as to render them functionally retarded. Severely handicapped individuals thus represent a heterogeneous group with respect to central nervous system functioning, physical growth and development, and adequacy of behavioral repertoire (M. Snell, 1982).

Many severely handicapped individuals have mental retardation of biologic origin. As stated in the 1983 American Association on Mental Deficiency classification in mental retardation, "the correlation between intelligence level and biologic retardation is very high. The relationship of biologic retardation to adaptive behavior is less precise; some individuals with IQs in the moderate range can achieve some degree of self-sufficiency with proper training and supervision" (H. J. Grossman, 1983, pp. 59–60). What severely handicapped individuals share is a need for intervention and training to learn basic social and adaptive skills. Most also depend strongly on nonhandicapped adults in their environment for support or survival (H. J. Grossman, 1983). Prevalence rates for severely and profoundly mentally retarded individuals vary according to the definition used. For example, designating those individuals with an IQ less than 50 as severely retarded, Abramowicz and Richardson (1975) reported prevalence rates as 4 out of 1000 persons. More conservative estimates put the prevalence rate of severely retarded individuals at 0.8 per 1000 and of profoundly retarded individuals at 0.5 per 1000, or 1.3 per 1000 for both groups (see Eyman & Miller, 1978).

From an educational or programming perspective, the particular etiology of most severely handicapping conditions is not too relevant (Robinson & Robinson, 1976). Looking more closely at the types of problems that may be present, one sees that many severely handicapped children have problems in learning (e.g., memory and attention), speech and language acquisition, and delays in motor development. While the impact of a severely handicapped child on the family will be greatly affected by whether the child is ambulatory or nonambulatory, motor development in this population is quite variable (Shapiro, Accardo, & Capute, 1979). Significant problems in physical domains may also be apparent and have a daily impact on families: (1) sleeping (too much, too little, night terrors, crying); (2) feeding (underfeeding, with resulting failure to gain weight); (3) overfeeding (characteristic of individuals with Prader–Willi syndrome); (4) bowel and bladder problems (chronic enuresis, chronic constipation, encopresis, fecal smearing); (5) neurological problems (seizures; movement disorders such as tics, hyperactivity); (6) stereotyped behaviors (head rolling, rocking); or (7) self-injurious behaviors. Finally, deficits in social and adaptive behaviors, including extreme withdrawal, aggression, or self-stimulation, can be significant.

Unlike those with mild mental retardation, individuals in the severely handicapped category are likely to appear in all socioeconomic groups (Birch, Richardson, Baird, Horobin, & Illsley, 1970). This seems to be true even though infection and prematurity, both causes of serious retardation, are more prevalent among lower socioeconomic classes and amniocentesis, a procedure that can detect many types of severely handicapping conditions before birth, is more often available to upper socioeconomic class women (M. Snell, 1982).

At the greatest extreme of handicap, severely handicapped individuals may have a combination of perceptual, cognitive, biological and behavioral difficulties. For example, some may not be toilet trained; they may aggress toward others; they may not attend to the most rudimentary stimuli; they may self-stimulate, ruminate, and/or manifest minimally controlled seizures or temper tantrums (Sontag, Burke, & York, 1973). Fortunately, many of these problems can be eliminated or altered by means of behavioral procedures (Berkson & Landesman-Dwyer, 1977; Fink & Cegelka, 1982: Schroeder, Mulick, & Schroeder, 1979). For example, while seizures can often be controlled by anticonvulsant medication, they can also be brought under stimulus or environmental control. Techniques include identifying and modifying preseizure behaviors or employing differential reinforcement of competing behaviors (Gardner, 1967; Zlutnick, Mayville, & Moffat, 1975). Recent instructional and habilitative techniques have also been shown to be successful in decreasing maladaptive behavior, training social skills, and increasing the overall adaptive functioning of such individuals (M. E. Snell, 1978). As pointed out by Sontag, Smith, and Sailor (1977), "Inasmuch as a severe or profound handicap is a matter of degree of disability, it follows that children with such impairments may start out both in life and in education at relatively the same point, but their individual potentials will vary spectacularly" (p. 5).

Thus, many individuals whom we would consider severely handicapped are able to live in their own homes as well as in alternative residential placements.

Methodological Approaches to Studying the Impact of a Severely Handicapped Child

A child with the severe handicaps just described will obviously impact on the family in many ways. Yet the specific nature of that impact has been difficult to study for a variety of methodological reasons. Highlights of several considerations of measurement and design are presented next.

Most studies of families with severely handicapped children have relied on interviews with, or questionnaires completed by, parents. Direct observation is methodologically preferable (Landesman-Dwyer & Sackett, 1978) to gain information on the child's social, behavioral, or intellectual functioning. However, if the goal is to understand child behavior in the context of the family, school, or broader culture, present observational strategies are limited. An alternative not much explored is the use of intensive, qualitative analyses of observations gathered in an ethnographic participant-observer design. This more ecological approach to the study of parent–severely handicapped child dynamics would consider broader influences in the child's social and cultural environment (Whalen & Henker, 1980). Chapter 5 of this volume, by Stoneman and Brody, contains a comprehensive overview of methodological issues raised by observational studies of interactions between parents and severely handicapped children and research questions appropriate for this approach.

The ideal design for many questions about severely handicapped children and their families is *longitudinal*. Measuring the same group of subjects repeatedly over a long period to study changes in behavior or attitudes is a useful procedure for studying issues such as stages of family adjustment or decisions about out-of-home placement. While most desirable, this approach has probably been used least. Longitudinal research is costly, time-consuming, and tedious; that often discourages researchers. Furthermore, the commitment to participate over an extended period of time often discourages parents of handicapped children from undertaking such involvement.

Experimental pre–post designs, most rigorous because of the control the experimenter might have in placing subjects into treatment groups, do assess behavior over time, but they are limited to studies of the effectiveness of intervention. For example, changes in parent and child behavior following training programs can occur, as noted in Chapters 8 (Kaiser & Hayden) and 9 (Baker). Since the goal of most studies of the impact of a severely handicapped child concerns variables over which the research has no control, however, experimental methods are rarely appropriate or possible. For example, severely handicapped children cannot, in most cases, be randomly assigned to homes or institutions.

There are several ways that researchers use data gathered at one point in time to address longitudinal questions. The *cross-sectional* approach, in which individuals in different age groups are assessed at the same time and contrasted, has not been utilized much in studying the effect of a severely impaired child. One reason is that the family is most often the unit of research, and independent variables or categories by which to group families are more difficult to determine than, for example, age or level of intelligence. The *retrospective* design gathers accounts from a sample of parents about their past experiences. In many cases, notably the work of Farber and associates (Farber, 1959, 1960a, 1960b, 1972; Farber, Jenne & Toigo, 1960), retrospective study yielded an initial charting of unexplored territory. However, researchers who ask parents to recall events surrounding the birth or early upbringing of a handicapped child may receive distorted information, for it is well known that memories fade and the significance of events changes over time (Haggard, Brekstad, & Skard, 1960).

Perhaps the least scientifically rigorous method, but one frequently used, is the *case study* approach. This might include gathering retrospective accounts from parents as well as intensive contemporary data obtained via interview, questionnaire, or observation (Mind, Hackett, Killou, & Silver, 1972). Case studies can have heuristic value, and a case example that is selected to illustrate in detail a specific point or issue that has emerged from other research can be descriptively useful. When properly controlled, case studies used to evaluate intervention, that is, single-subject designs, can have internal validity. However, the case study approach does lack external validity.

The most frequently used design is *correlational*, ascertaining the relationship between two or more variables. This approach is useful in identifying factors related to broad constructs such as family adjustment, parent involvement in schooling, or use of social support networks. However, correlation obviously does not imply causation; this approach may be subject to confounding and difficulty in interpretation. In light of debates about the directionality of effect (Bell & Harper, 1977), causal conclusions about changes in families and their severely handicapped children should describe interactional relationships. Simplistically, a gain in child skill acquisition as a result of parent training could enhance loving and care behaviors of the parent, which in turn could produce further child progress.

More sophisticated ways of analyzing correlational data can be used depending on the types of questions under investigation. A few brief examples may be illustrative. If one wished to predict later status from earlier data, as could be done in research on the development of attachment, one could employ stepwise multiple regression analyses. If one wished to predict placing of the child out of the natural home versus not placing, a discriminant function analysis could be appropriate. If one wished to sort families into typologies, cluster analysis could be used (Mink, Nihira, & Meyers, 1983); however, since the number of variables could involve redundancy and covariation making it difficult to sort out relationships, factor analytic procedures could be used to reduce them.

The remainder of this chapter identifies research themes pertinent to studying the effect of a severely handicapped child on the family. The reader will soon see that much of what is known about this topic is inferred from research using a variety of measures and designs and hampered by the many inherent problems already noted.

Attachment: A Unifying Concept

While it may be true that the concepts of attachment and research on attachments have been overblown and faddish and that the word is often employed tautologically, attachment formation between the mother and a mentally retarded or other developmentally disabled child commands special interest. The presence and nature of attachment seems particularly pertinent to parenting a severely disabled child. The quality of the attachment could well relate to family accord or discord, to the early burnout of the parent as care provider, to the level and extent of parent collaboration with schools and services available, to possible abuse or neglect of the child, or to inclination to place the child out of the home.

Blacher and Meyers (1983) reviewed the literature on attachments and related dyadic phenomena for various categories of developmental disability. Two findings emerged. The first was that, despite the popularity of attachment studies with normal, premature, and disadvantaged populations, very little attachment study has been conducted with developmentally disabled children and their care providers under the standardized model of Ainsworth and colleagues (Ainsworth, Blehar, Waters, & Wall, 1978; Ainsworth & Wittig, 1969) (see Appendix).

The second finding was that, with disabled children, attachment

formation seems to be delayed, distorted, or even absent. To put this
finding in perspective, I will briefly consider Bowlby's thesis on attachment formation and several qualifications in adapting it to severely
handicapped children.

On Attachment Formation

Belief in a disturbed development is tenable in view of the Bowlby–
Ainsworth thesis that attachment formation is not an inevitable phenomenon, like locomoting or vocalizing, but is produced through dyadic
interaction of the child and the care provider. Such interaction, involving reciprocal communication of feeling and meaning, presupposes
some cognitive development and sensory intactness in the child.

Bowlby (1958, 1980) considered close emotional attachment as imperative for good adjustment throughout life. Mother–infant attachment
is an adaptive behavior system serving both the infant and the species.
The helpless infant receives physical protection; distress is kept minimal
by the comfort supplied only, or best, by the principal care provider. The
adult, meanwhile, has an impulse to love, protect, and interact. The relationship resembles in its adaptive function the imprinting that occurs in
certain bird species and many other protective phenomena that are
described by the ethologists. Such dyadic bonding serves a role throughout life, as with friends, spouses, and members of the social network.
"Intimate attachments of other human beings are the hub around which
a person's life revolves. . . . From these intimate attachments a person
draws his strength and enjoyment of life and, through what he contributes, he gives strength and enjoyment to others" (Bowlby, 1980,
p. 442). Sundering such an attachment presumably leads to crises in adjustment. However, according to Bowlby (1980), multiple bonding may
occur and new bonds may replace old or lost ones.

The use of the attachment construct for understanding the dynamics
of parent–severely handicapped child interactions requires qualifications. I will note three. First, attachment of parents to children born with
a handicap should be differentiated from attachment to children in
whom the handicapping condition becomes apparent later. In the latter
case, learning that a child is handicapped can be far more traumatic to
parents. According to Lonsdale (1978), "These parents had bonded to a
normal child believing this to be what they had got" (p. 105). Poznanski
(1973) pointed out that the parent "has usually formed a strong attachment to the child; with the newborn the mother's emotional attachment

to the child is still highly tenuous and is more easily arrested or interfered with" (p. 323). The inference is that some parents might become less attached to children diagnosed earlier.

Second, Ainsworth (1973) maintained that the one quality most likely to foster a secure bond between a young child and a caretaker is the mother's sensitive responsiveness, that is, her ability to do such things as discriminate cues provided by the child and return appropriate responses. It is easy to imagine how a severely impaired infant might lack the sensory, motor, and/or cognitive skills to emit any such cues or to respond differentially to the mother. Table 1.1 displays examples of behaviors that promote attachment as well as those that might discourage attachment in handicapped infants.

Third, some may question whether severely impaired children even have innate attachment behaviors. Interestingly, some autistic children (considered severely handicapped in most states) who lack demonstrable attachment to people have been found to show attachments to nonsoft, inanimate objects (Haslett, Bolding, Harris, Taylor, Simon, & Schedgick, 1977; Marchant, Howlin, Yule, & Rutter, 1974). Children with gross physical deformities may be particularly at risk for parental rejection and failure to develop or receive attachment behaviors. Despite this, studies have shown many of their parents to be warm, responsive, and by implication attached (Poznanski, 1973).

TABLE 1.1

Examples of Discrete Behaviors and Characteristics Promoting and Discouraging Attachment, As Observed in Handicapped Infants

Characteristics and behaviors that promote attachment	Characteristics and behaviors that discourage attachment
Smiling	Negative response to being handled
Crying	(stiffening, tenseness, limpness,
Vocalizing	lack of responsiveness)
Visual searching and regarding	Lowered or bland activity level
Eye contact	Bizarre or unpleasant crying
Locomotion around room	Hyperactivity
Demonstrating physical contact	High threshold for arousal
Tactile discrimination	Lack of ambulation
Angry, aggressive behavior	Undifferentiated anger
(related to separation)	No response to any communication
Adaptive hand behavior	Passivity
Gross and fine motor behaviors	Physical deformity

Attachment Studies with Handicapped Populations

Although attachment is conceptualized as a mutual development between mothers and infants, most literature has reported on only the development of the child's attachment to the mother, rarely providing information on how the mother performs. I first consider the child's development and later the mother's behavior.

Table 1.2 summarizes some attachment research that has specifically involved developmentally disabled populations. In general, investigation has not been systematically extended to reveal developmental trends. Most neglected are severely handicapped populations. Most often included in these studies of attachment have been Down's syndrome infants and young children, and the most common assessment procedure has been the use of a set of eight episodes described by Ainsworth and Wittig (1969; see also Ainsworth et al. 1978; and the discussion of Ainsworth's four phases of attachment in the Appendix). Generally, investigations employing the Ainsworth–Wittig procedure or variations of it suggest that infants with Down's syndrome proceed through the same stages of attachment as normal infants, but at a slower pace and with less distress at separation (Berry, Gunn, & Andrews, 1980; Cicchetti & Serafica, 1981). Procedures other than the Ainsworth–Wittig approach have been employed to observe and describe discrete attachment behavior in Down's syndrome groups. Emde and Brown (1978) used clinical interviews, developmental testing, and other systematic observations of social interaction to reveal diminished eye contact, smiling, and overall social responsiveness in Down's syndrome infants.

The literature on children considered developmentally disabled also suggests delays and disruptions in the development of attachment. Greenberg and Marvin (1979) reported that the level of attachment in deaf children with hearing mothers was related to communicative competence of both the mother and the child rather than to the child's age or developmental level. Most severely retarded or delayed young children show sufficiently dulled perception or awareness to affect subsequent mother–child interactions. As aptly stated by Stone and Chesney (1978), "the failure of the handicapped infant to stimulate the mother leads to failure of the mother to interact with the infant" (p. 11).

Although the general literature on attachment in nonhandicapped children is repleted with studies identifying variables believed to be associated with attachment formation, investigators of disabled populations have not studied variables associated with attachment such as family adjustment, marital harmony, or placing the child out of the natural home. The design and implementation of such studies will be ad-

TABLE 1.2

Studies of Attachment and Analogous Behavior with Handicapped Populations[a]

Type of handicap	Procedure	Focus	Subjects N	Subjects Age[b]	Investigators
Down's syndrome	Ainsworth–Wittig	Child	12	33.5 (median)	Serafica & Cicchetti, 1976
Down's syndrome	Observations[c]	Child	14	18	Cicchetti & Sroufe, 1976
Down's syndrome	Observations	Child	60	16	Cicchetti & Sroufe, 1978
Down's syndrome	Ainsworth–Wittig	Child	18	$\bar{X}$, 24; SD, 6	Berry, Gunn, & Andrews, 1980
Down's syndrome	Ainsworth–Wittig	Child	42	30–42	Cicchetti & Serafica, 1981
Down's syndrome	Structured procedures[d] and interviews[c]	Mother	6	4–12	Emde & Brown, 1978
Down's syndrome	Observations	Child and mother	6	13–24	Jones, 1979
Mixed developmentally disabled[e]	Interviews	Mother	36	Not given	Rosen, 1955
Mixed developmentally disabled[e]	Structured procedures	Child	42	$\bar{X}$, 13.5	Greenberg, 1971
Mixed developmentally disabled	Observations	Child and mother	Not given	0–24	Bromwich, 1976
Various handicaps[f]	Structured procedures and interview	Mother	15	Infancy (specific ages not given)	Stone & Chesney, 1978
Various handicaps	Structured procedures	Mother	10	Postnatal	Nix, 1980
Visually impaired	Structured procedures	Child and mother	10	Infancy (specific ages not given)	Fraiberg, 1971
Visually impaired	Structured procedures	Child and mother	10	23 days–11 mo.	Fraiberg, 1974
Auditorially impaired	Structured procedures	Child and mother	28	$\bar{X}$, 52.2; SD, 8.9	Greenberg & Marvin, 1979

[a] Source: Blacher & Meyers (1983).
[b] In months unless otherwise specified.
[c] Nature of attachment (or analogous behavior) inferred from observations or clinical interviews.
[d] Structured procedures, but different from the Ainsworth–Wittig design.
[e] Most are mentally retarded, with various diagnoses.
[f] A combination of handicaps (e.g., epilepsy, Down's syndrome, physical disability).

dressed in the final section of this chapter, in an attempt to achieve a more integrated view of parent–severely handicapped child dynamics.

Few researchers doubt all the positive consequences of bonding or attachment, but some do acknowledge potential negative effects of placing so much emphasis on the attachment phenomenon. Chess and Thomas (1982), for example, asked, "What price is being paid for these [developmentally desirable] gains?" (p. 217). These investigators cited instances in which attachment or bonding between a mother and a new infant is unable to develop, such as the case of a mother who is unable to have skin-to-skin contact with her baby due to illness (in the mother or the child) or to inflexible hospital hours or routines. Their concern is that a mother whose baby is considered "deviant" because the baby does not show the expected reciprocal behaviors necessary for attachment will conclude this to be her fault. Rather, they point out:

> Just as the child's nutritional requirements can be met successfully with a wide range of individual variation, so can his psychological requirements. Once mothers can appreciate this, that the neonate separated from his mother is not permanently damaged by this experience as such, that the child whose signals are not always easy to understand is not doomed to an unhealthy parent attachment, that the infant who appears "insecure" with strangers is not necessarily suffering from poor mothering, they can perhaps relax and actually become better mothers. (p. 221)

Unfortunately, it seems that for every study of very bizarre or impaired children in which attachment has been shown (Haslett et al., 1977; Marchant et al., 1974; Poznanski, 1973) there are others showing delayed, dulled, or complete lack of attachment in handicapped children (see Table 1.2). The concern here is for the mothers of those young severely handicapped children, as well as for the children themselves, as neither is to "blame" if attachment does not take place. Lack of attachment could, however, influence the family's choice to place the child out of the natural home; conversely, a strong attachment could influence the family to keep a severely handicapped child at home longer than they might otherwise (Downey, 1965). The data are unclear as to whether attachment will develop in out-of-home placements, but the issue is an intriguing one.

For institutionalized children, the reality of multiple staff and frequent turnover raises interesting issues and concerns regarding the development of attachment. For example, Sroufe (1979) suggested that attachment is based on reliable patterns of care giver interaction, ones that are familiar to infants or young children so they may utilize the comfort of this familiarity in new situations. Rutter (1979) called into question the innate tendency of the child to form a unique attachment to one figure (known as *monotrophy*). He suggested that there is a hierarchy of attachments that children make and that these multiple attachments have similar functions. Furthermore, Ainsworth (1973) found that attachment to other figures can develop even when these others have no role in routine care of the (normal) infant but simply interact and play with him or her. But what about the infant who, because of more severe retardation, has difficulty recognizing the familiar? What is the impact of substitute or multiple care giving on these children? Tizard and Rees (1975) showed that 4-year-old institutionalized nonhandicapped children showed more attachment behavior (e.g., clinging and following) than family-reared children, but they were less likely to show selective bonding or deep relationships. It is possible, of course, that the development of more meaningful relationships for handicapped children toward their care givers in an institutional setting could be fostered and maintained through intervention. However, the practical and theoretical implications of multiple bonding between an institutionalized severely handicapped child and his or her many caretakers remain largely unexplored.

Dynamics of Child Abuse

Studies of the epidemiology and the dynamics of child abuse contribute to the analysis of the mother–handicapped child relationship. For example, abuse and other maltreatment are more common with handicapped children than with nonhandicapped siblings or peers (Friedrich & Boriskin, 1976; Frodi, 1981).

Epidemiologically, abuse is more commonly found in families with a tradition in the subculture or the extended family in which physical punishment is not only practiced but parents are also expected to employ it. That abusers have had a history of being abused makes sense in light of the finding that preschool-aged abused children are more aggressive toward their peers (George & Main, 1979). However, it appears that childhood aggression is predisposing rather than absolutely causative of abusive behavior in later years.

Not all parents with a predisposition to abuse actually become abusers or neglecters (Belsky, 1980). Most writers (e.g., Belsky, 1980) have suggested that abusive behavior is triggered only if in-family distress and lack of secondary or social network support make the adult vulnerable. It appears that among subculturally likely groups, those experiencing current stress are more prone to be abusers. Abusing parents appear to have fewer psychological resources because they demonstrate less social interaction, including affection and emotional support, than parents in matched control families and they show more threatening and complaining behavior (Burgess & Conger, 1978). Another established epidemiological fact is that abuse occurs disproportionately in large families with closely spaced children and in families that are in economic difficulty. Steinberg, Catalano, and Dooley (1981) listed an abundance of references relating incidence of abuse to economic distress and demonstrated that an increase in reported abuse followed an increase in unemployment. Conditions that overburden either parent (noise, crying, intersibling squabbles, budgetary anxiety, and the like) are contributory or trigger mechanisms for the parent who has reached a tolerance limit for stress (Belsky, 1980; Elmer, 1977).

Thus, the predisposed and distraught parent is provoked by uncontrollable bad behavior or crying in the child. The triggering of abuse in predisposed adults under stress is a favorite theme among the theories, and it reflects the conviction that abuse is by its very nature interactive; the child must contribute by lacking normal qualities, by being a severe bother to rear (or at least perceived as such), or by having an odd or displeasing appearance that does not invite solicitude (Belsky, 1980).

Abuse and Handicapped Children

Frodi (1981) assembled evidence that abuse is disproportionate in the instance of premature, handicapped, and other deviant children. Not all handicapped children are abused, but they are more likely to be the targets. Put another way, it is more likely that handicapped children supply the above-mentioned trigger mechanism. Abusing parents report backwardness of the child, hyperactivity, continual crying, difficulty in being controlled, constant irritation, or failure to be lovable as qualities of the child that bother them.

Of great interest to the study of the dynamics in parent–handicapped child relations are the observed reactions of parents to the birth of a premature or an injured child. The premature or the injured child does not sound or look like other neonates the parent has seen; the child has a different cry, cries more, and may be unattractive, small, and developmentally retarded (Frodi & Lamb, 1980). Frodi (1981) indicated the complexity of relationships among the child's own characteristics and those of the parents in a study of the connection between abuse and handicap. She made a case for an elicited aggression model. Anyone prone to an aggressive reaction may be triggered by the perceived aversive characteristics, appearance, or behavior of the handicapped child. She adduced the Berkowitz (1974) model of impulsive aggression, in which triggering of abuse is more likely in situations of great stress.

Attempts to discern what it is in handicapped babies and children that invites abusive treatment have been made, most notably regarding crying. Crying by its nature invites attention and easily becomes an irritant, especially if it is not easily controlled, is continuous, or is as different from normal as it is in prematurely born infants. Frodi, Lamb, Leavitt, and Donovan (1978) showed videotapes of a crying or smiling infant to parents who were given different identifications of the infant. Those who were told the baby was premature or difficult reacted differently, both behaviorally and autonomically, from those who were told the baby was normal. Crying in the infant labeled premature aroused them more physiologically than did smiling; those viewing both premature and difficult infants were less sympathetic than were parents who were told the baby was normal. This study is interesting in that it may be the parents' "self-talk" (e.g., My baby doesn't love me; I'm no good; I have a defective baby) rather than the crying per se that irritates them. In another study, Frodi, Lamb, Leavitt, Donovan, Neff, and Sherry (1978) demonstrated with dubbed-in sound of a premature infant that this crying caused more physiological arousal and feelings of aversion than the cry of a nonpremature infant. Thus, the investigators were able to demonstrate that, apart from the label received, the premature child's cry itself could be irritating, over and above the arousal character of crying in general.

Comparisons have also been made between the physiological and behavioral responses of abusing, neglecting, and "normal" parents to crying and laughing in infants. Abusers are more aroused and neglecters less aroused on measures of heart rate than are normal parents (Doerr, Disbrow, & Caulfield, Note 7 in Frodi, 1981). In summary, the data reported by Frodi (1981) suggest that parents whose experiences have been with atypical infants show an exaggerated and often negative pattern of responses to aversive infant stimuli (e.g., crying, difficult temperament, unattractiveness).

Attachment and Child Abuse

It has been proposed that parental abuse and neglect of young handicapped children may be related to an interference during the normal bonding process between mother and infant (Helfer, 1975). This interference can take place when an infant is separated from his or her care giver at or immediately after birth. Severely handicapped infants are more likely than "normal" infants to undergo these separations since many are premature, sickly, or have congenital malformations requiring immediate medical attention and prolonged hospitalization.

Thus, severely impaired infants not only may have physical, mental, and behavioral characteristics that may invite abuse (Friedrich & Boriskin, 1976; Frodi, 1981) but also they have fewer early experiences during which bonding could occur. While premature infants frequently experience such early separations from mother, some research findings do not indicate a long-term negative impact of this type of separation (Chess & Thomas, 1982; Grossman, Thane, & Grossman, 1981; Rode, Chang, Fisch, & Sroufe, 1981).

Abuse may occur, of course, in children who do seem to be attached to their mothers. Attainment of Ainsworth's fourth phase of attachment marks a bond that presumably endures even when abuse has occurred. However, severely handicapped children are unlikely to attain this stage. Thus, the complications of a severe handicap in infants or young children may, at the very least, interrupt normal development and predispose some children to other risks such as child abuse. (See Chapters 2 [Wright, Granger, & Sameroff] and 7 [Meier & Sloan] for more in-depth discussion of these issues.)

Studies of Parent-Child-Family Dynamics

Attachment research serves as a unifying construct in understanding both positive (e.g., acceptance) and potential negative (e.g., abuse) effects of a severely impaired child. Parent–child interaction research has also guided our efforts in evaluating the impact of a severely impaired child on the entire family. This section contains a brief overview of trends in traditional parent–child interaction research that have implications for studying parent–severely handicapped child dynamics.

Traditional Study of Parent–Child Dynamics

Investigators have long been interested in how parental attitude and rearing methods are related to the nature of the child's and family's adjustment. Objective information began to accrue in the 1930s. Data came initially from clinical files (Levy, 1943; Symonds, 1939) and later from structured home visits (Baldwin, Kalhorn, & Breese, 1945, 1949; Baumrind, 1968, 1971, 1972; Sears, Maccoby, & Levin, 1957) and even from experimental studies (Meyers, 1944). Many interpretations of these data were, from today's perspective, simplistic. They assumed a causality direction from parental treatment to resultant child personality. It was clear, even as early as Levy's cases on maternal overprotection, that interaction of parent treatment with the child's "nature" had to be considered. Inspection of Levy's protocols, for example, indicated that at the outset all the sons were dominated. However, some (perhaps because of their individual temperamental makeup) rebelled against the domination and their mothers then became indulgent in order to maintain the bond. Integrative summaries of the relation between parent attitude and/or practice and child variables have frequently been proposed (Becker, 1964; Schaefer & Bell, 1958). Bell (1968) and Bell and Harper (1977), for example, voiced concern over the assumption of causality; they reinterpreted some data to show how the child could produce the treatment received, just as we have shown how certain characteristics of a handicapped child may elicit abuse or inhibit the formation of attachment.

Another line of inquiry involved studies of parental rearing methods and qualities of the home environment, often by employing the Caldwell Home Observation for Measurement of the Environment (HOME). There are infant and preschool versions. In both, the home visitor observes the mother or care provider in action with her child noting expression of affection, methods employed to control and redirect the child, stimulation of the child in language and other areas of development, and presence of appropriate materials (books, toys) for child development. Bradley and Caldwell (1979) have shown that these aspects of the child's home environment correlate positively with child IQ (e.g., as measured by the Stanford–Binet test).

More recently, Sameroff (1983) related parents' concepts or levels of understanding of their child's development to their subsequent styles of and competence in child rearing. The way in which parents think about their children should have an impact on the way they will behave toward them and ultimately on the developmental outcomes for those children. For example, parents who see individual differences as rooted in the nature of the child should make less use of remedial or therapeutic programs than should parents who see their child's behavior as being strongly influenced by environmental contingencies. While severely handicapped children have deficiences most often due to nature, many of their bizarre or deviant behaviors may, in fact, be strongly influenced by environmental contingencies. Sameroff's model, with implications for very severely impaired children, is delineated more fully in Chapter 2 of this volume, by Wright, Granger, and Sameroff.

What all this means is that research on family dynamics can no longer proceed meaningfully from studying the effect of the child on the family or the effect of the parent (e.g., of personality, child rearing, or attitude) on the child (e.g., on development, personality, or temperament).

The current zeitgeist favors adopting a more ecological view (Bronfen-brenner, 1977; Whalen & Henker, 1980) or even a perspective derived from general systems theory (Ramey, MacPhee, & Yeates, 1982). In his conceptualization of the whole process of child development, Bronfen-brenner (1977) delineated four levels of analysis, with emphasis on the impact of diverse social settings (e.g., day care) and institutions (e.g., the school or family) on the growing child. Whalen and Henker (1980) adopted a similar approach for conceptualizing the effects of psycho-stimulant treatment on children—one that emphasized mutual impacts on the child, on significant others in the child's environment, on health and education practices, and on society and culture. A modified version of Whalen and Henker's model will be used to discuss parent–child dynamics in families with a severely handicapped child.

Parent–Child Dynamics in Families with a Severely Handicapped Child

Most of the earlier studies involving mentally retarded children and their parents were retrospective and descriptive in nature and focused broadly on the impact of a retarded or handicapped child on the family (Carr, 1974; Cohen, 1962; Dunlap & Hollinsworth, 1977; Farber, 1960a, 1960b, 1972, 1975; Ferguson & Watt, 1980; Fowle, 1968; Gath, 1977; Lonsdale, 1978; McMichael, 1971; Schonell & Watts, 1956). Such a focus often does not clarify the interactive effects of the child, the family, the social environment, and cultural influences on one another. The simple model presented in Fig. 1.1, with its elements described in Table 1.3, shows four widening concentric circles surrounding the individual se-verely handicapped child. The first circle represents specific character-istics of the child (e.g., sensory or motor capabilities) as well as general characteristics that are more likely to affect the relationship with his or her parents (e.g., dependency needs, temperament). These characteris-tics can, in most instances, be directly assessed. The other levels of circles represent what Whalen and Henker (1980) referred to as emana-tive effects. The second circle denotes the mutual impact of the child, caretaker (usually the mother), and family on one another. How do child characteristics influence maternal attitude toward or maternal com-petence in dealing with the severely handicapped child, and vice versa?

The third concentric circle includes the broader social environment of the child and family, such as the child's teacher, professionals who in-teract with the family concerning the child's handicaps, and the social supports available to the family. The fourth circle represents a broad

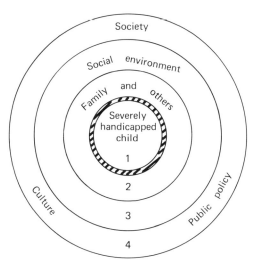

Figure 1.1   Model representing the bidirectional levels of influence of a severely handicapped child. The center of the diagram indicates more pervasive effects and the outer circles represent more diffuse, yet important, influences on family dynamics. (Adapted from Whalen & Henker, 1980.)

focus on society in general, culture, and public policy. A major question concerns the impact of schooling, as embraced by Public Law (PL) 94–142 (the Education for All Handicapped Children Act of 1975), on severely handicapped children, their families, and others included in their social environment.

The remainder of this chapter considers the literature available on the impact of a severely handicapped child within the context of each of these four levels. Moving from the inner to the outer circle, one can see that effects become less specific or defined and more difficult to measure. Nonetheless, each circle or level represents a powerful influence, and all are bidirectional—that is, the severely handicapped child influences all levels, just as the people or institutions represented in Levels 2, 3, and 4 have a profound impact on the child.

Level 1: Child Characteristics

Assessment of the impact of a severely handicapped child on the family can begin at birth: "Remarkable and appealing neonatal capacities and early maternal responsiveness both function to initiate a specific relationship which protects the infant during the precarious neonatal period" (Lozoff, Brittenham, Trause, Kennell, & Klaus, 1977, p. 8). This section will describe some of the deviances and delays in

TABLE 1.3

Summary of Elements in Parent–Child Interaction Research
Critical for Understanding Parent–Severely Handicapped Child
Dynamics

Characteristics of child	Social environment
Temperament	Stability of caretaking
Mobility	environment
Communicative ability	Availability of social supports
(e.g., response mode	Family size and socioeco-
available, smiling,	nomic status
looking)	Stressful life events
Dependency	
(e.g., for caretaking	
needs)	
Social skills	
(e.g., smiling, vocal-	
izing)	Society
"Cuddleability" (hypo-	Cultural norms
or hypertonicity)	Public policy
Physical attractiveness	
(e.g., subtle versus cos-	
metic disfigurement)	
Sensory avenues available	
(e.g., hearing, vision)	
IQ or cognitive competence	
Role-taking ability	
Family: parental attitude	Family: parental competence
Desirability of pregnancy	Education, IQ
Attitude toward newborn	Skill in teaching or handling
Level of acceptance or stage	child (e.g., involvement in
of adjustment	parent training)
Perception of child's	Skill in caretaking of physically
competencies or skills	handicapped child or child
	with medical complications
	Ability to "read" child's signals
	Overall responsiveness (immedi-
	ate and contingent responding
	to child)

capacities of severely impaired infants and young children that may, in turn, lead to differences in maternal responsiveness, attitude, and competence in interactions with such a child.

Particularly salient characteristics of such children include their limited mobility, lack of "normal" communicative ability, possible unattractiveness due to deformity, severe physical handicap, limited sensory awareness due to visual or hearing impairment, and lack of "cuddleability" due to hyper- or hypotonicity. In children who have brain damage, cognitive competence will be limited; hence, learning from infancy on will be delayed, especially so without structured intervention efforts. Fundamental social skills, such as smiling, eye contact, or vocalizing, may not occur, thus inhibiting, delaying, or even preventing the behavioral interchanges or reciprocity that characterize interactions between mothers and nonhandicapped infants. Finally, because these children may have tremendous difficulty learning self-help or caretaking skills, their dependency needs may extend well beyond infancy.

Literature on parent–child interaction with nonhandicapped and premature infants suggests how dramatically these child characteristics affect mother–child or even family–child dynamics. I will again consider the attachment construct because of its important role in the social and emotional development of the child. In a study comparing premature infants who varied in their level of prematurity, medical difficulties, and visual ability, Wright and Zucker (1980) found that lower gestational age or prematurity itself was not an impediment to maternal attachment, as shown in looking, touching during feeding time, or frequency of calls or visits to the hospital. Rather, attenuated attachment or withdrawal of attention by the mother correlated with medical difficulty. It was also found, surprisingly, that medical difficulty was associated with lower maternal distress, as measured by personality and other questionnaires tapping the dimensions of depression, anxiety, hostility, negative attitudes, and marital adjustment. In interpreting this finding, the authors suggested that mothers may minimize their contact with and attachment to infants with medical complications in order to maintain lower distress and anxiety.

When the helplessness of infancy continues without the positive influences of eye contact and smiling, a mother's attitude toward her infant may turn to disenchantment or even anger. In studying the role of eye contact in the development of maternal attachment, Robson and Moss (1970) found that a brain-damaged infant made less eye contact than would be expected from a nonhandicapped infant, and that this led to negative feelings in the mother and subsequent attenuated maternal attachment. Attachment in this case was determined by the mother's answers to questions about her feelings toward her baby. Some of the factors found to contribute to the infant's ability to make eye contact were alertness, sex differences, sensory modality preferences, predisposition to gaze aversion, and maternal disposition to gaze aversion. In addition to eye contact, Robson and Moss found other determinants of attachment: the infant's physical appearance (e.g., "cute" infantile characteristics), the infant's ability to exhibit behaviors that are more characteristic of adult relationships (e.g., smiling, vocalizing), and the mother's feelings of competence.

Studies have also related child temperament to attachment and parent–child interaction. In developing their theory of infant temperament, Goldsmith and Campos (1982) suggested that infant temperamental differences might influence mother's social responsiveness, and conversely mothers' social responsiveness might influence the expression of infant temperament. For example, infants learn from observing their mothers that there are features of the environment to fear (e.g., stairs, stoves, strangers); the mother who models an unusual number of such warnings could influence the development of a fearful infant.

Cognitive impairment in severely handicapped infants may also delay aspects of language, social, and personality development. For example, there is a related body of literature showing that specific linguistic delays in young handicapped children affect subsequent mother–child and family–child interaction patterns. For example, lack of communicative responsiveness in handicapped infants may give mothers fewer opportunities to provide verbal feedback (Jones, 1979) or may elicit more directive responses from mothers (Cunningham, Reuler, Blackwell, & Deck, 1981). Although severely handicapped preschoolers have been shown to demonstrate fundamental social communication skills such as pointing or showing (Blacher, 1982), there is an acknowledged lag in the development of social–cognitive behaviors in many retarded and otherwise handicapped children (Simeonsson, Monson, & Blacher, in press). Similarly, Down's syndrome infants and young children (who may or may not be so retarded as to be "severely" handicapped) show delayed or dulled affective development, notably in the development of fear and smiling (Cicchetti & Serafica, 1981; Cicchetti & Sroufe, 1976, 1978; Emde, Katz, & Thorpe, 1978) or in "maternal referencing," that is, the infant's back-and-forth looking from an ambiguous stimulus to the mother's face (Sorce, Emde, & Frank, 1982). Hence, it is possible that more severely handicapped children may never achieve full reciprocity in social interactions.

The preceding discussion pointed out child characteristics that can affect the development of maternal attachment. A few studies have measured maternal attachment to handicapped infants or young children directly. Some utilized questionnaires or interviews to obtain such information (e.g., Emde & Brown, 1978; Robson & Moss, 1970; Rosen, 1955); in these, mothers were asked directly how they felt about aspects of their infant's behavior. Others incorporated structured interactions or behavioral observations (e.g., Bromwich, 1976; Emde & Brown, 1978; Fraiberg, 1971, 1974; Nix, 1980), focusing on maternal behaviors during natural caretaking activities, such as feeding, or during structured interactions designed to elicit attachment behaviors. While it is a major thesis of this chapter that maternal attachment may strongly influence acceptance of the severely handicapped child and willingness to raise the child at home (at least initially), child characteristics do play an important role in the development and maintenance of parental attitudes and behavior.

Level 2: Emotional Climate in the Family

Child characteristics only partially determine the impact of a severely impaired child on the family. For example, mothers of handicapped children have reported feelings of social isolation (Wahler, 1980) and the parents of a severely handicapped child are not the only family members affected; Chapter 6 (Skrtic, Summers, Brotherson, & Turnbull) delineates the effect of a severely handicapped child on nonhandicapped brothers and sisters. Social isolation is only one of several factors creating stress for families of such children.

The type of family (i.e., as determined by child-rearing attitudes and practices), home environment, and degree of parental adjustment to the child all contribute to what we here refer to as the emotional climate in the family. A few of the major factors included in this level (see Figure 1.1, Level 2) will be discussed. The emotional climate in the family can not only affect the child directly (e.g., in terms of the amount and quality of parent–child interaction displayed), but also indirectly (e.g., by influencing subsequent child developmental gains and school adjustment).

Parenting Skills. Nihira, Meyers, and Mink (1980) and Nihira, Mink, and Meyers (1981) related quality of parenting as measured by the Caldwell HOME inventory to the home and school adjustment of educable and trainable mentally retarded children. As part of the same endeavor, Mink et al. (1983) demonstrated clear typologies of family characteristics that related to the child's adjustment. In these studies good parenting, as judged by the observations made in extensive interviewing with parents (around issues of child-rearing practices, attitudes, and quality of the home environment), was shown to be positively related to the child's scores on the Adaptive Behavior Scale and also to gains in these scores. Parenting was also related to the child's adjustment at school, providing one of the first indications thus far reported on this population that home treatment or the home environment matters in school.

Several laboratories have directed attention to families whose children are at risk for developing mild mental retardation because of the low intelligence of the mother and the extreme disadvantage of the home environment. The Milwaukee Project (Garber, in press; Garber & Heber, 1977), beginning with stimulation early in infancy, succeeded in lifting children's IQs well above those of control children. The gains persisted well into and through elementary school. Treatment consisted of language and cognitive coaching not only of the child but also of the mother and siblings. Earlier similar work was conducted by Gray and associates (Klaus & Gray, 1968), although it did not start with infants in cribs. The results were similar but the gains made over control children tended, as with other studies where treatment terminated on enrollment in kindergarten or first grade, to vanish. The Abecedarian Project of Ramey and colleagues (see Ramey *et al.*, 1982, for an excellent review of data from this project) is similar to the Heber–Garber study in some respects, particularly in that it started with infancy. In addition to the impressive child gains demonstrated in this program, especially in the areas of linguistic and social competence, there have been parental gains. More mothers of the experimental children who were enrolled in the longitudinal day-care project either went back to school or obtained jobs than mothers of control children.

While these intervention studies are impressive in their design, implementation, demonstration of child gains, and positive spillover effects to other family members, they primarily involve mildly handicapped children or those at risk for mental retardation. Major demonstrated risk factors appear to be low maternal IQ and educational status and, consequently, questionable maternal competence in parenting skills. The factor of maternal competence takes on additional meaning in studying the parent–severely handicapped child interaction as shown in Table 1.3. In this case education and IQ are no less important, but a variety of specific parenting skills (e.g., in caretaking, teaching, and communicating with the young child) become even more critical.

The parent of a low-functioning child who is handicapped by cerebral palsy, for example, must learn a unique set of skills for handling or positioning the child. If involved in home teaching activities, this parent would need to learn how to adapt instructional materials so the child could hold them. If the child is nonverbal, the parent must learn to interpret his or her other response modes (eye gaze, head nodding, pointing) of communication. The parent, too, must communicate in a manner understandable to the child, learning to respond immediately and contingently to the child's overtures. The rationale for special training and intervention with the parents of severely impaired children, in addition to the provision of early intervention or schooling for the children themselves, is clear. Chapter 8 by Kaiser and Hayden elaborates on the special parenting required by severely handicapped infants. Chapter 9 by Baker extensively reviews models of parent training and their applications to families with severely impaired children.

Adjustment and Acceptance. The emotional climate in the family is dependent, at least in part, on how the family adjusts to and accepts the severely handicapped child. Adjustment and acceptance here refer to broad descriptive variables and are different in measurement from the developmental construct of attachment. Aspects of acceptance or rejection of severely handicapped children have been discussed in detail by Waisbren (1980) and by Wright *et al.* (Chapter 2). Two fairly behavioral indices of rejection of severely handicapped infants have been mentioned previously in this chapter—abuse and out-of-home placement. Some older literature on counseling parents of severely handicapped children emphasizes institutionalization or finding alternative placements for the child soon after birth (Kozier, 1957). Such actions clearly do not suggest great tolerance for the defective child.

As a result of his extensive study of family adaptations to severely retarded children, Farber (1975) described one adaptation phase as *elimination,* in which a family might elect to institutionalize their handicapped child. Some parents in his study, particularly those from middle-class families, regarded the institutionalized child as "dead or depersoned" and maintained little contact with him or her. Lower-class families, on the other hand, regarded institutionalization as a form of living away from home, and appeared more willing or ready to reincorporate the child back into the family. In a more recent investigation, Lei, Nihira, Sheehy, and Meyers (1981) interviewed 180 biological parents of retarded clients (aged 21 or younger) in foster care regarding their satisfaction with their child's placement; 80% of those interviewed never considered trying to bring their child back home permanently.

More often, issues of acceptance and nonacceptance are couched within a stages model. Conceptualizing parental reactions to the birth of a handicapped child according to stages is not new, and it parallels earlier work on people's reactions to crises or stressful events, such as grief (Lindemann, 1944). The literature on this subject is extensive and reflects the disciplines of education, medicine, psychology, social work, and sociology. The general theme is that there are, at the very least, three stages of adjustment that parents of a handicapped child experience (Turnbull & Blacher-Dixon, 1980). The initial stage is that of shock and denial, in which parents refuse to acknowledge the reality or at least the extent of their child's delay in an effort to believe that a cure or magical intervention will prevent any lifelong problem. Although parents may eventually achieve intellectual awareness of the problem, reactions such as anger, disappointment, grief, or guilt can still subsequently occur. These reactions characterize the second stage of emotional disorganization. The stage of emotional adjustment typically represents a constructive adaptation to the child's handicap and realistic expectations of his or her progress. Great controversy surrounds this third stage; many parents feel the need to adjust continually to the demands and changing needs of their handicapped child (Birenbaum, 1971; Olshansky, 1970; Turnbull & Turnbull, 1978). Furthermore, the literature on these hypothesized stages of adjustment yields an unclear picture as to (1) whether the stages can, in fact, be empirically validated, (2) whether they are experienced in a particular order (3) the amount of time it takes to move through each stage emotionally, and (4) whether ultimate parental acceptance or emotional adjustment is related to the degree of the child's handicap.

Empirical support for the existence of these stages as experienced by parents of young severely handicapped children has been investigated in at least one study (Eden, 1983). Over 70 parents (primarily mothers) of severely handicapped children, aged 3–8 years, were interviewed and completed a questionnaire designed to assess their stage of adjustment. Five hypothesized factors or stages were proposed: (1) shock, confusion, (2) refusal, denial, (3) guilt, anger, (4) despair, depression, and (5) adjustment, recovery, acceptance. While several stages were empirically validated, the final stage of acceptance or adjustment was found not to be a single isolated outcome. Based on analyses to date, it appears that there may actually be a level of acceptance that parents attain within each factor or stage. Also, because acceptance may be a more fluid concept than originally proposed in the literature (i.e., parents do not reach one ideal level of acceptance of their severely handicapped child but, rather, they experience periods of acceptance throughout the years of coping with their child), researchers should be cautious when studying family adjustment at only one point during the many years of child rearing.

The stage model can be utilized with families to help assess their level of adjustment and to propose an intervention based on their emotional readiness to receive additional services (Blacher, in press; O'Hara, Chaiklin, & Mosher, 1980; Thompson & Young, 1977). For example, families who are experiencing shock, denial, or elements of emotional disorganization would not be expected to seek instruction in additional care and teaching for their handicapped child actively. On the other hand, families who have accepted the reality of their child's handicap and limitations may be amenable to suggestions for dealing with the handicap, whether that means treating the handicapped child as a "regular" family member, albeit with some limitations, enrolling in a parent training program to do some home teaching, or placing the child in some other residential setting.

Stress in the Family. Stress can be experienced regardless of stage of adjustment since it relates in large part to daily caretaking realities. Much has been written about stress in families with handicapped children (Bradshaw & Lawton, 1978; Breslau, Staruch, & Mortimer, 1982; Mink, Nihira, & Meyers, 1981) and stress in families with chronically ill children, including those with asthma (Liebman, Minuchin, & Baker, 1974), cystic fibrosis (Kucia, Drotar, Doershuk, Stern, Boat, & Matthews, 1979), and tracheostomies (Aradine, 1983). In nearly all cases, the presence of the handicapped or special needs child required increased parental (usually maternal) involvement with and attention to the child's daily care needs. The type of involvement varies with specific child needs. For example, family members may need to learn how to administer medication and or control the environment of a child with cystic fibrosis, how to control the self-injurious behaviors of a child with profound retardation, or how to use toys to play with a child who is blind and also has severe cerebral palsy. However, it has been proposed that such intensive involvement with a handicapped child will be a stressful task for the family (see Chapter 10 by Turnbull & Winton). For example, Doernberg (1978) reported that some families feel stress when they encounter problems in fulfilling educational or treatment programs recommended by professionals.

The literature abounds with studies of the negative impact of a handicapped—primarily mentally retarded—child on family functioning (Booth, 1978; Carr, 1974; Cohen, 1962; Farber, 1960a, 1960b, 1972, 1975; Fotheringham & Creal, 1974; Fowle, 1968; Friedrich & Friedrich, 1981; Gath, 1977; Jordon, 1962; Lonsdale, 1978; Matheny & Vernick, 1968; Schonell & Watts, 1956). In nearly all cases, the handicapped child is reported as affecting in a negative way some or all of the following: the marital relationship, sibling relationships, finances, relationships with friends and relatives, planning daily activities, or family vacations. Presumably, when the impact of the handicapped child on the above family functions is negative, one outcome is increased stress for the family. (See Chapter 3 by Bristol & Schopler for a review of specific factors that affect stress and coping in families with autistic children.)

Parent and family adjustment are typically assessed via interviews and verbatim retrospective accounts. Some researchers, notably Farber (1959), have developed questionnaires and structured interview formats expressly for the purpose of their study. Farber's seminal research, conducted with 240 families, focused on three broad topics: (1) aspects of living with the child at home, (2) aspects of living with the child at home versus the child in an institution, and (3) relations between the family and community. The main instruments used to gather information were (1) an index of marital harmony or adjustment, (2) a sibling role tension index to assess the effect of the retarded child on siblings, (3) a modified version of the Vineland Social Maturity Scale (Doll, 1947) to obtain a gross measure of social competence, and (4) a neighborliness scale to assess aspects of social support available to families. Summarizing aspects of living with a retarded child at home, Farber found that a severely mentally retarded boy affected marital integration more adversely than did a severely mentally retarded girl, and that this effect was more pronounced in lower-class parents. Mothers' rating of their retarded children's level of dependence did not appear to be related to marital integration, but it was related to sibling role tension, with girls more affected by the dependence of their retarded sibling than boys. Comparisons of family adjustment when living with the retarded child at home versus placing the child out indicated that placement was often beneficial to families. Most relieved by placement were nonhandicapped sisters, who were thus freed of additional caretaking responsibilities. Data pertaining to the third topic, extended family relations, indicated that mothers derived more social support from interaction with their own mothers than from interaction with their husband's mothers. Because Farber's data were gathered in the 1950s, a systematic replication similar in scope to his study is in order.

Evidence of Coping. At this point it is critical to note that all families do not respond negatively and with stress to having a handicapped child. As Hewett (1970) pointed out, much has been written about the problems that beleaguer families with a handicapped child, but little about "families who meet the crisis of a handicap as they meet other crises, with resilience and common sense" (cited in Lonsdale, 1978, p. 101). Since the publication of Hewett's book, however, at least two investigations have yielded more positive findings. Ferguson and Watt (1980) examined aspects of motherhood in 87 families with a retarded child and found that these parents were realistic, adaptable, and resourceful. Although this study involved only a single contact with families, it included mothers of almost equal numbers of severely handicapped, moderately handicapped, and nonhandicapped children from both middle and working classes. Interestingly, analyses revealed that mothers' perceptions of the problems the child could create for the family were not directly related to the level of the child's handicap. Based on interviews with over 400 families in rural Alabama, Dunlap and Hollinsworth (1977) also found that families did not necessarily perceive a negative effect of having a developmentally disabled family member. However, those children who had additional or secondary handicaps, such as epilepsy or cerebral palsy, were viewed as requiring extra time, physical assistance, and financial help.

Some families develop their own effective strategies for coping (Featherstone, 1980), while others even report benefits that accrue to the siblings of the handicapped child (Grossman, 1972). Chapter 5 (Stoneman & Brody) contains pilot data suggesting some positive effects on siblings of severely handicapped children, and Chapter 6 (Skrtic *et al.*) presents a review of studies with siblings of handicapped children.

Level 3: Social Network Supports

According to the model presented in Figure 1.1, the people in the family's social environment comprise Level 3. The current tendency is to refer to a person's or family's relations with relatives, friends, neighbors, co-workers, and other acquaintances as the personal social network or the family social network (Powell, 1980). It should be clear that any systematic study of the effects of a severely impaired child on the family needs to involve examination of social networks, which include extra-family as well as intrafamily interactions. McAllister, Butler, and Lei (1973) examined patterns of social interaction among families of behaviorally retarded children and compared these patterns to those in families who did not have a retarded child. Of particular interest is the fact that families of retarded children interacted significantly less with neighbors and somewhat less with friends and co-workers.

This is particularly unfortunate because some of the literature has suggested that the quality of parent–child interaction may be related to the support provided by the parents' social network (Cochran & Brassard, 1979; Crockenberg, 1981; Powell, 1979; Weinraub, Brooks, & Lewis, 1977). Parents of handicapped children may seek more than mere emotional support from their social networks, including advice, specific guidance or instruction, or feedback on their skills for managing their child. Pearlin, Liederman, Menaghan, and Mullen (1981) pointed out, however, that members of the social network can also inflict pain or unpleasantness (as well as support or aid) by providing feedback that may raise conflicts or question parental practices.

The following vignette may illustrate one type of conflict that a social network member might pose for a family:

Consider the couple in their 30s with two healthy children (aged 5 and 9 years) who give birth to a severely retarded, physically handicapped child. After working through such stages as shock, denial, or anger and having reached some level of adjustment, the parents decide to try to keep the child and raise her as a member of their family. This involves tremendous effort on their part to pursue a home teaching program studiously, to involve their other children actively in the care and training of the handicapped child, and to make sacrifices in terms of vacations, evenings out with friends, and material luxuries. All the while, however, the mother's parents (who have always provided strong emotional and financial support for this family) urge the couple to "put away" the child. With the intent of helping out and easing their burden, the in-laws zealously investigate local institutions for retarded individuals and muster supporting arguments from the media. This advice is particularly disabling for the family because of the parents' own ambivalences regarding their child's severe handicaps and whether the child should remain at home. If they were truly not conflicted, the disagreement by the mother's parents might be annoying and disappointing but easier to dismiss. The mother's parents in this case give words to a voice within them that they perhaps work very hard not to hear.

Such conflicting views from members of one's close personal network can create considerable conflict and stress for the parents, with the result that the severely impaired child has a more negative impact on the family than might otherwise be the case.

Level 4: Cultural Influences

One important cultural influence is the prevailing view of where severely handicapped people should live, with whom they should live, and the structure of their home setting. Such decisions regarding placement of a severely handicapped child are difficult and often complex, involving input or influences from other than family members. Level 4, depicted in Fig. 1.1, represents public policy, culture, and society—all which may have an influence on family decision making regarding a severely handicapped child. For example, the passage of PL 94–142 represents public policy that advocates the education of handicapped children in the "least restrictive environment" possible. The institution, although appropriate for some, is thus viewed as the most restrictive type of placement. Public policy often reflects the views of an interested and vocal minority; in this case, current professional opinion is strongly in favor of deinstitutionalization, community placement, and even maintenance of a severely handicapped child in the natural home whenever possible. (See Chapter 4 by Seltzer & Krauss for an extensive review of placement data and issues; the final chapter of this volume,

Chapter 11 by Yando & Zigler, expands on policy issues affecting severely handicapped children.)

However, not all families may opt to raise a severely handicapped child at home. This point was recognized by a mother of a profoundly mentally retarded, cerebral palsied and epileptic child, who said: "I am not foolish enough to think that every severely handicapped child will be as comparatively easy to take care of as Stephen" (Hosey, 1973, p. 14). Ultimately, if a severely impaired child has too few adaptive behaviors and too many maladaptive behaviors (Level 1), places a heavy burden for care on family members (Level 2), and if the family feels necessary professional and social supports are lacking (Level 3), then that child is at great risk for out-of-home placement, despite public policy or societal expectations (Level 4).

Indeed, at least one survey study in the late 1970s indicated that 32% of severely mentally retarded and 80–90% of profoundly mentally retarded individuals were institutionalized (Eyman & Miller, 1978). Risk of out-of-home placement is also shown in Fig. 1.2; these data are from

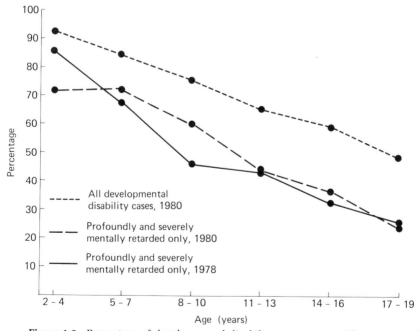

Figure 1.2 Percentage of developmental disability registrants residing in natural home, by age. Data are from complete records of a developmental disabilities regional center in California serving a total population of about 1.25 million. (From Meyers *et al.*, 1981.)

one of about 20 regional centers in California that serve approximately a million handicapped children and their families. The proportion of severely and profoundly retarded children residing in the natural home drops rapidly at school age. However, the addition of services to severely handicapped children and their families (those listed as profoundly and severely mentally retarded on the graph) since 1978 has delayed the rate of placement slightly. It will be interesting to see how the slope of the graph changes after the impact of services under PL 94–142 is truly felt. Hence, a major factor of interest in any study of the impact of a severely handicapped child on the family should include parents' contemplation of finding, or actual steps taken to find, an alternative home or placement for the child.

Previous work of this nature identified some of the variables contributing to a family's decision to institutionalize their child. Stone (1967) interviewed 103 families of Down's syndrome children who were between the ages of less than 1 year and 9 years at the time of interviews. Of these families, 50 had already applied for institutionalization. Parents identified their own early experiences and relationships during the initial birth crisis (i.e., learning that they had a retarded child) as important in reaching this placement decision (see also Farber et al., 1960). Increasing family stresses as the child grew older or stresses in the marital relationship (Gath, 1978) also had a strong influence on the ultimate placement of the child. In a study similar to Stone's, 100 families who had already applied for institutionalization of their Down's syndrome infant received comprehensive services and professional guidance in making informal choices between institutional or home care for their child (Giannini & Goodman, 1963). On the basis of the special services offered, 24 of the 100 families decided to try to keep their child at home; unfortunately, lack of follow-up data does not allow further assessment of this type of intervention. Nevertheless, this study is an exception; the older literature suggests that parents were encouraged to institutionalize their severely handicapped child (Andrew, 1968; Kozier, 1957).

Several investigators have noted that early placement "out of sight" does not necessarily mean "out of mind," as traumatic effects of early separation have been reported (Giannini & Goodman, 1963; Hewett, 1976). One study that examined reasons for placement, age of child, and subsequent parental interest following placement viewed placement as a function of child's age, parents' education, and parents' attachment to the child. Attachment between parent and child appeared to be stronger in older children who had remained at home prior to institutionalization; where a strong bond had been formed, the level of parental interest in the child after institutionalization was high (Downey, 1965).

There is also evidence that institutionalization can affect an already-formed bond between a family and the retarded child, since many institutions tend to discourage family involvement or visitations (Willer, Intagliata, & Wicks, 1981). There are additional, though unpublished, data on frequency of visiting children in one institution in Massachusetts (B. L. Baker, personal communication, October 11, 1982). One of two variables that predicted frequency of family visits was age of child at time of institutionalization, with children older at time of placement being visited more. While attachment per se was not directly measured, this finding does seem consistent with Downey's (1965) report. It is conceivable that families who initially have less attachment to the child placed into an institution may also be less likely and less eager to visit or to arrange for the child to return home. (The other variable predicting frequency of family visits was the amount of programming being implemented on the wards. It seemed that families were more likely to visit knowing that their children were engaged in ongoing, structured activities.)

Research to date has not addressed how attachment develops between an institutionalized handicapped child and his or her caretaker, or whether multiple attachments to the inevitable multiple caretakers develop. Most of us know, through anecdotal reports or personal experiences, of strong attachments that do develop in such settings. Systematic studies of caretaker–child interactions to document caretaker attachment behaviors would be a welcome addition to the literature.

There are other types of placement options than "the institution" available for families of severely handicapped children. Counseling efforts with these families now try to advocate placement options for families (Morse, 1979), many of which are explored in detail in Chapter 4 by Seltzer and Krauss.

Achieving an Integrated View of Family–Severely Handicapped Child Dynamics

The final section of this chapter contains a proposed model for longitudinal study of the effects of a severely impaired child on the family. The elements of this model have been under study as part of a 3-year project at the University of California, Los Angeles, and Lanterman State Hospital Mental Retardation Research Center directed by Meyers and Blacher (1982).

The rationale for this study is the implementation of PL 94–142 (the Education for All Handicapped Children Act). Prior to Public Law

94–142, many severely handicapped children were not even admitted to public schools, and related services often deemed necessary for their education (e.g., physical therapy, occupational therapy, speech therapy) were not provided unless purchased privately by parents. This law has a number of provisions, either explicit or implicit, that promise to impact on the dynamics of families that have a severely impaired child. These include an individualized education program for each child, specialized transportation when required, related auxiliary services, and the involvement of parents in all key phases of the educational program—all at no cost to parents. Hence, this proposed new study incorporates the Level 4 represented in Fig. 1.1; PL 94–142 represents public policy and the broader influence of cultural context.

One major effect of providing schooling and related services to severely impaired children is that parents receive respite from care during the school hours. Presumably, the provision of day education and training programs will relieve stressful pressures on parents (Fink & Cegelka, 1982). As pointed out by Meyers, Zetlin, and Blacher-Dixon (1981), one may surmise that this school-provided respite can affect family plans about continuing care versus placement of the child. As shown in Fig. 1.2, such children have historically been at great risk for institutionalization or other out-of-home placement; the question was not so much whether these children would be placed as when (Carr, 1974). Hence, there is now a unique opportunity to investigate systematically the impact of schooling on the families of severely handicapped children.

The research model proposed in this section is a study of the effect of schooling (Level 4) on severely impaired children and their families and has been designed to address some of the methodological issues raised, explicitly and implicitly, throughout this chapter. First, the study is longitudinal, so that the impact of schooling (which also implies impact of the severely handicapped child himself or herself) on families can be assessed over a 3-year period. There will thus be an opportunity to determine change in parents' manner and extent of involvement with their child's education or training, and changes in how schooling or services offered to the child affect the family. Second, the study involves children in the age range of 3 to 8 years. This age span should cover an early period during which parents may seek or at least contemplate alternative placement for their child. Third, a combination of data collection procedures will be used including interviews with parents, observations of mothers and their severely handicapped children, questionnaires and rating scales to be completed by parents, videotaping, and phone calls to maintain contact and follow-up with families. Fourth, while the study design is primarily correlational, or descriptive, in nature, procedures to study the phenomenon of attachment between young severely handicapped children and their mothers will be developed and validated. It will thus be possible to utilize measures of attachment as both independent and dependent variables.

Approximately 100 children and their parents from a large four-county area of southern California have been invited to participate. All children must be "severely handicapped"; we anticipate that most children will be at the severe or profound level of mental retardation. Families will be interviewed and observations of parent–severely handicapped child interactions will be made twice over a 3-year period. Careful analysis of the content of parental responses should provide information on the three major foci of this study: family adjustment, family involvement in schooling, and family social support networks.

Family Adjustment

As detailed in this chapter, and indeed in this entire volume, family adjustment is a complex variable that directly involves the child and other family members. Several constructs are included for study in the model proposed here. First, the development of parent–child attachment may affect, or be affected by, overall family adjustment. For example, a parent who accepts the severely impaired child (e.g., has reached some stage of adjustment) or who has learned appropriate skills and activities for interacting with the child (e.g., as a result of parent involvement in the child's school program) may more easily interact with the child and thus be more likely to develop an attachment. On the other hand, a parent who has not been able to interact comfortably with a severely handicapped child is unlikely to develop this attachment; adjustment to having the child may thus be more difficult.

Procedures for assessing the development of attachment between mothers and their severely impaired children have been developed (Meyers & Blacher, 1982). Mothers' attachment to their children has been assessed in two ways: (1) by observing behavioral indices of attachment, using a modified version of the Ainsworth (1973) four-phase paradigm (e.g., looking, touching, vocalizing) (see Appendix), and (2) by interviewing mothers, using a series of questions developed to tap issues and incidence of attachment. Observations and subsequent coding will reflect unique needs of these handicapped children; for example, alternative forms of communication may be used with children who are nonverbal (signing, pointing, communication boards, making sounds), and adaptive equipment may be used for positioning the child who is nonambulatory or for allowing mobility.

Family adjustment might also be measured by scaling the degree of marital harmony, intersibling relationship, stress, and the contemplation of or actual placement of the child. Careful, repeated interviews and analysis of content of responses provide additional information. Furthermore, there are published instruments and procedures already developed to assess aspects of family adjustment (Moos, 1974; Nihira et al., 1980) and marital relationship (Locke & Wallace, 1959).

Family Involvement in Schooling

Parent or family involvement in their child's schooling—as educational decision makers, evaluators, participants in the educational programming process—also provides opportunities for research on family dynamics. Research at this level clearly involves others in the larger social environment (see Fig. 1.1). While the school is mandated to invite parents to participate, parents are not compelled to respond. Some interesting individual differences in amount or extent of involvement, in stress produced as a result of involvement, and the degree to which the school program functions as respite should emerge. Again, information on most of these variables may be secured through intensive interviews and school records.

In studying the impact of the school program on families, one should not overlook its differential effect on children and their parents. As the mother of a severely impaired 3-year-old said, "Public Law 94–142 has taken our [severely handicapped] children out of the closet and put the parents in!" (Meyers & Blacher, 1982). This parent was concerned that the increased number of school hours and services for her child would leave her and her husband in a somewhat helpless role. They demonstrated obvious attachment to the child and interest in her development with ongoing home teaching programs. It was their wish to continue in this manner after the school program started. This research aimed to monitor such parental interest and involvement with their severely impaired child's education, both at home and at school.

Most schools that serve severely impaired children also provide some opportunity for parent involvement, perhaps in the form of group counseling, parent workshops for skill training, social activities, or a more formal club such as a PTA. The involvement of parents in these activities can provide emotional support and/or improve parenting skills through training. The empirical issue is the determination of whether involvement with their child's schooling positively affects parents' adjustment to and acceptance of their severely handicapped child and, if so, which types of involvement are effective. Furthermore, it would be instructive to determine whether involvement leads to gains in general parenting, coping, or teaching skills.

Family Social Support Networks

Often parents have resources other than the school and its activities available to them. For example, they may receive social and/or emotional support from participation in a church or synagogue, the Association for Retarded Citizens, or work-related social groups. This study examined the extent to which support from extended family members or extrafamilial contacts reduces stress for parents of severely handicapped children. As shown earlier in this chapter, these various social network influences, comprising Level 3 in Fig. 1.1. may pull parents in conflicting directions and add to confusion and uncertainty (Cochran & Brassard, 1979).

Summary

Table 1.4 displays the three major foci of this investigation, including a description of the variables hypothesized to be related to a family's decision to keep the child in the home or to seek an alternative placement. The table lists variables; it does not suggest interactions between elements in a category or between categories. Some of the methodological techniques presented earlier might permit drawing limited conclusions without implying causality. As an example, path analysis has been used by Eyman, Demaine, and Lei (1979) to show that mentally retarded residents with certain characteristics residing in a specific environment (e.g., natural home or board-and-care home) will show a certain outcome with a given probability; residents with other characteristics living in some other residence and receiving treatment there (e.g., schooling) will show a different outcome, again with a probability range. Summary scores that reflect the three major foci of this study will be examined as correlates of placement.

In conclusion, although prior research has been done on the impact of a severely impaired child on the family (e.g., Farber 1959, 1960a, 1960b) and on parent involvement, the now-mandated schooling for these children should have a pervasive, and as yet unmeasured, effect. A related and intriguing issue is how early education for severely handi-

TABLE 1.4
Variables Hypothesized to be Related to Parents' Keeping versus Placing Child
Out of the Home

Influencing parents toward keeping child	Influencing parents toward placement
Foci: To determine the course of family adjustment, marital integration, parent–child interaction patterns, and tendency to place the child out of the natural home as impacted by the presence of a severely impaired child	
Child is manageable in the household	Child is difficult to manage
Child is less than 10 years old	Child is over 10 years old
Child has older siblings	Child is only or firstborn
Child has no severe medical problems, frequent seizures, frequent doctor calls	Child requires much care, frequent health visits to doctors, shots; has seizures
Child is ambulatory	Child is nonambulatory
Child is nonhandicapped until several months of age	Early onset of handicap
No prolonged hospitalization	Prolonged hospitalization
Temperament: compliant, attentive, responsive, etc.	Temperament: defiance, irritability, erratic behavior, etc.
Parent–child attachment	No apparent attachment
Redefinition of family roles leading to a accommodation and acceptance	Redefinition of family roles leading to family crisis
Stable marriage	New marriage; alienation; divorce; single parent
Burden of child care shared in family	Little sharing of child care
Older mother	Younger mother
Foci: To determine parental response to school's overtures for participation as related to family adjustment and placement tendency	
Active involvement in developing and implementing child's educational plan	No concern with school activities or participation in programming
Views child's school progress as positive	Views school and child's school progress as negative
Sees (or hopes for) gains in child's development	Does not see and has no hope for gains in child's development
Foci: To determine parental utilization of extraschool sources of support and services, including social networks and both extended and immediate family members	
Supportive extended family members	Nonsupportive extended family
Extrafamily networks consisting of parents with handicapped children, school personnel, care providers, counseling groups, etc.	Nonsupportive social networks; involved with non-child-oriented activities (the arts, music, etc.)
Stable life-style	Erratic life-style: frequent relocation, alcoholism, unemployment
Burden of care shared in family	Little sharing of burden of care
Mother close to husband	Husband alienated, divorced or nonexistent

capped children impacts on the development of attachment between mother and child. The model proposed herein will thus allow examination of multiple influences on families of severely handicapped children (see Fig. 1.1): the impact of the severely handicapped child's self (Level 1) on parents and other family members (Level 2), on teachers and professionals (Level 3), and on the public school system (or society, Level 4). Similarly, Levels 2, 3, and 4 will all impact on the development of the child. Embedded within this proposal is a unique study of attachment between severely handicapped children and their parents, a phenomenon essentially unstudied in this population.

Closing Comment

The impact of a severely impaired child on the family appears to be profound, pervasive, and persistent. It is reasonable to assume that parents feel the effects of such a child throughout infancy, early childhood, during the school years, and beyond into adult life. The remainder of this volume explores in detail how a severely impaired child affects the family as well as how various extra familial factors (such as policy, legislation, training, or placement options for families) affect the development of the child and the dynamics of the family.

Appendix

Ainsworth (1973) described four phases of attachment development as originally proposed by Bowlby (1969). The first, includes infants' suckling movements, smiles, cries, and other vocalizations toward environmental objects, as well as their attempts to seek and hold eye contact with people. At about age 3 months, infants appear to differentiate people from inanimate features in their environment and become more selective and enduring in their responses.

In the second phase, infants differentiate the mother and perhaps one or two other individuals for special contact and proximity seeking. This behavior may be observed after age 6 months, when absence of the mother or presence of a stranger leads to distress, best known by the popular expressions "8-month anxiety," "stranger wariness," or "fear of strangers." In the third phase, occurring toward the end of the first year of life, the child has made good progress in the establishment of a mother–object constancy or person permanence (i.e., knowing the mother in her absence and recognizing her voice and other attributes at a distance).

This interdependency between parent and child presumably increases until about age 4–5 years, when a full trust may be established. This marks the fourth phase, which is more cognitive–representational in nature. Delays in achieving this degree of attachment are evident in those 4- or 5-year-olds delivered at school who are distressed at the mother's departure; the secure child accepts her departure, demonstrating trust and an understanding of the mother's right and need to go now, for her own reasons (Blacher & Meyers, 1983).

Procedures described in detail by Ainsworth et al. (1978), Ainsworth and Wittig (1969), and Maccoby and Feldman (1972) are frequently used to assess attachment. To summarize, these methods may be employed with infants in the first 2 years of life, with modifications for older children. The episodes provide for a "strange" situation: the mother leaving temporarily, the child alone, the child alone with a stranger, a reunion between child and mother, and so on. Observations are recorded of child behaviors such as proximity seeking and maintenance of proximity, distress, resisting contact with the stranger, and crying, as well as some positive behaviors. The mother's degree of sensitive responsiveness (touching, looking, vocalizing to the child) is also often recorded.

References

Abramowicz, H. K., & Richardson, S. A. (1975). Epidemiology of severe mental retardation in children: Community studies. *American Journal of Mental Deficiency, 80,* 18–39.

Ainsworth, M. D. S. (1973). The development of infant-mother attachment. In B. M. Caldwell & H. N. Ricciuti (Eds.), *Review of child development research* (Vol. 3). Chicago: The University of Chicago Press.

Ainsworth, M. D., Blehar, M. C., Waters, E., & Wall, S. (1978). *Patterns of attachment.* Hillsdale, NJ: Erlbaum.

Ainsworth, M. D. S., & Wittig, B. A. (1969). Attachment and exploratory behavior of one-year-olds in a strange situation. In B. M. Foss (Ed.), *Determinants of infant behavior* (Vol. 4). London: Methuen.

Andrew, G. (1968). Determinants of negro family decisions in management of retardation. *Journal of Marriage and the Family, 30*(4), 612–617.

Aradine, C. R. (1983). Parents of medically impaired infants. In V. J. Sasserath (Ed.), *Minimizing high-risk parenting.* Piscataway, NJ: Johnson & Johnson Baby Products Company.

Baldwin, A. L., Kalhorn, J., & Breese, F. H. (1945). Patterns of parent behavior. *Psychological Monographs, 58*(3, Whole No. 268).

Baldwin, A., Kalhorn, J., & Breese, F. (1949). The appraisal of parent behavior. *Psychological Monographs, 63*(4, Whole No. 299).

Baumrind, D. (1968). Authoritarian vs. authoritative parental control. *Adolescence, 3,* 255–272.

Baumrind, D. (1971). Current patterns of parental authority. *Developmental Psychology Monographs*, 4(1, Pt. 2).

Baumrind, D. (1972). An exploratory study of socialization effects on black children: Some black-white comparisons. *Child Development*, 43, 261–267.

Becker, W. C. (1964). Consequences of different kinds of discipline. In M. L. Hoffman & L. W. Hoffman (Eds.), *Review of child development research* (Vol. 1). New York: Russell Sage Foundation.

Bell, R. (1968). A reinterpretation of the direction of effects in studies of socialization. *Psychological Review*, 75, 81–95.

Bell, R. Q., & Harper, L. V. (1977). *Child effects on adults*. Hillsdale, NJ: Erlbaum.

Belsky, J. (1980). Child maltreatment: An ecological integration. *American Psychologist*, 5, 320–335.

Berkowitz, L. (1974). Some determinants of impulsive aggression: Role of mediated associations with reinforcements for aggression. *Psychological Review*, 81, 165–176.

Berkson, G., & Landesman-Dwyer, S. (1977). Behavioral research on severe and profound mental retardation (1955–1974). *American Journal of Mental Deficiency*, 81, 428–454.

Berry, P., Gunn, P., & Andrews, R. (1980). Behavior of Down syndrome infants in a strange situation. *American Journal of Mental Deficiency*, 85(3), 213–218.

Birch, H. G., Richardson, S. A., Baird, D., Horobin, G., & Illsley, R. (1970). *Mental subnormality in the community: A clinical and epidemiological study*. Baltimore, MD: Williams & Wilkins.

Birenbaum, A. (1971). The recognition and acceptance of stigma. *Sociological Symposium*, 7, 15–22.

Blacher, J. (1982). Assessing social cognition in young retarded and nonretarded children. *American Journal of Mental Deficiency*, 86(5), 473–484.

Blacher, J. (in press). Sequential stages of parental adjustment to the birth of a handicapped child: Fact or artifact? *Mental Retardation*.

Blacher, J., & Meyers, C. E. (1983). A review of attachment formation and disorder of handicapped children. *American Journal of Mental Deficiency*, 87(4), 359–371.

Booth, I. A. (1978). From normal baby to handicapped child: Unravelling the idea of subnormality in families of mentally handicapped children. *Sociology*, 12(2), 203–221.

Bowlby, J. (1958). The nature of the child's tie to his mother. *International Journal of Psychoanalysis*, 39, 350–373.

Bowlby, J. (1969). *Attachment and Loss: Vol. 1. Attachment*. New York: Basic Books.

Bowlby, J. (1980). *Attachment and loss: Vol. 3. Loss: Sadness and depression*. New York: Basic Books.

Bradley, R. H., & Caldwell, B. M. (1979). Home observation for measurement of the environment: A revision of the preschool scale. *American Journal of Mental Deficiency*, 84(3), 235–244.

Bradshaw, J., & Lawton, D. (1978). Tracing the causes of stress in families with handicapped children. *British Journal of Social Work*, 8(2), 181–192.

Breslau, N., Staruch, K. S., & Mortimer, E. A. (1982). Psychological distress in mothers of disabled child. *American Journal of Disorders of Childhood*, 136, 682–686.

Bromwich, R. M. (1976). Focus on maternal behavior in infant intervention. *American Journal of Orthopsychiatry*, 46(3), 439–446.

Bronfenbrenner, U. (1977). Toward an experimental ecology of human development. *American Psychologist*, 32, 513–531.

Burgess, R. L., & Conger, R. D. (1978). Family interaction in abusive, neglectful, and normal families. *Child Development*, 49, 1163–1173.

Carr, J. (1974). The effect of the severely subnormal on their families. In A. M. Clarke &

44   Jan Blacher

A. D. B. Clarke (Eds.), *Mental deficiency: The changing outlook.* New York: Free Press.

Chess, S., & Thomas, A. (1982). Infant bonding: Mystique and reality. *American Journal of Orthopsychiatry, 52*(2), 213–222.

Cicchetti, D., & Serafica, F. C. (1981). Interplay among behavioral systems: Illustrations from the study of attachment, affiliation, and wariness in young children with Down's syndrome. *Developmental Psychology, 17*(1), 36–49.

Cicchetti, D., & Sroufe, L. A. (1976). The relationship between affective and cognitive development in Down's syndrome infants. *Child Development, 47*, 920–929.

Cicchetti, D., & Sroufe, L. A. (1978). An organizational view of affect: Illustration from the study of Down's syndrome infants. In M. Lewis & L. A. Rosenblum (Eds.), *The development of affect.* New York: Plenum Press.

Cochran, M. M., & Brassard, J. A. (1979). Child development and personal social networks. *Child Development, 50*, 601–616.

Cohen, P. C. (1962). The impact of the handicapped child on the family. *Social casework, 43*, 137–142.

Crockenberg, S. B. (1981). Infant irritability, mother responsiveness, and social support influences on the security of infant–mother attachment. *Child Development, 52*, 857–865.

Cunningham, C. E., Reuler, E., Blackwell, J., & Deck, J. (1981). Behavioral and linguistic developments in the interactions of normal and retarded children with their mothers. *Child Development, 52*, 62–70.

Doernberg, N. L. (1978). Some negative effects on family integration of health and educational services for young handicapped children. *Rehabilitation Literature, 39*, 107–110.

Doll, E. A. (1947). *Vineland Social Maturity Scale.* Minneapolis: Educational Test Bureau.

Downey, K. J. (1965). Parents' reasons for institutionalizing severely mentally retarded children. *Journal of Health and Social Behavior, 6*, 147–155.

Dunlap, W. R., & Hollinsworth, J. S. (1977). How does a handicapped child affect the family? Implications for practitioners. *The Family Coordinator, 26*(3), 286–293.

Eden, G.V.S. (1983). *An instrument to assess parental adjustment to a handicapped child.* Unpublished master's thesis, University of California, Riverside.

Education for All Handicapped Children Act of 1975, 20 U.S.C. §1401.

Elmer, E. (1977). A follow-up study of traumatized children. *Pediatrics, 59*(2), 273–279.

Emde, R. N., & Brown, C. (1978). Adaptation to the birth of a Down's syndrome infant. Grieving and maternal attachment. *Journal of Child Psychiatry, 17*(2), 299–323.

Emde, R. N., Katz, E. L., & Thorpe, J. K. (1978). Emotional expression in infancy: II. Early deviations in Down's syndrome. In M. Lewis & L. A. Rosenblum (Eds.), *The development of affect.* New York: Plenum Press.

Eyman, R. K., Demaine, G. C., & Lei, T. (1979). Relationship between community environments and resident changes in adaptive behavior: A path model. *American Journal of Mental Deficiency, 83*, 330–338.

Eyman, R. K., & Miller, C. (1978). Introduction: A demographic overview of severe and profound mental retardation. In C. E. Meyers (Ed.), *Quality of life in severely and profoundly mentally retarded people: Research foundations for improvement.* Washington, DC: American Association on Mental Deficiency.

Farber, B. (1959). Effects of a severely mentally retarded child on family integration. *Monographs of the Society for Research in Child Development, 24*(2, Serial No. 71).

Farber, B. (1960a). Family organization and crisis: Maintenance of integration in families with a severely mentally retarded child. *Monographs of the Society for Research in Child Development, 25*(1, Serial No. 75).

Farber, B. (1960b). Perceptions of crisis and related variables in the impact of a retarded child on the mother. *Journal of Health and Human Behavior*, 1(2), 108–118.

Farber, B. (1972). Effects of a severely mentally retarded child on the family. In E. P. Trapp & P. Himelstein (Eds.), *Readings on exceptional children: Research and theory* (2nd ed.). New York: Appleton-Century-Crofts.

Farber, B. (1975). Family adaptations to severely mentally retarded children. In M. J. Begab & S. A. Richardson (Eds.), *The mentally retarded and society: A social science perspective*. Baltimore, MD: University Park Press.

Farber, B., Jenne, W. C., & Toigo, R. (1960). Family crisis and the decision to institutionalize the retarded child. *Council for Exceptional Children Research Monograph Series*, (No. 1).

Featherstone, M. A. (1980). *A difference in the family*. New York: Basic Books.

Ferguson, N., & Watt, J. (1980). The mothers of children with special educational needs. *Scottish Educational Review*, 12(1), 21–31.

Fink, W., & Cegelka, P.T. (1982). Characteristics of the moderately and severely mentally retarded. In P. T. Cegelka & H. J. Prehm, *Mental retardation: From categories to people*. Columbus, OH: Merrill.

Fotheringham, J. B., & Creal, D. (1974). Handicapped children and handicapped families. *International Review of Education*, 20(3), 353–371.

Fowle, C. M. (1968). The effect of the severely mentally retarded child on his family. *American Journal of Mental Deficiency*, 73, 468–473.

Fraiberg, S. (1971). Intervention in infancy: A program for blind infants. *Journal of the American Academy of Child Psychiatry*, 10(3), 381–405.

Fraiberg, S. (1974). Blind infants and their mothers: An examination of the sign system. In M. Lewis & L. A. Rosenblum (Eds.), *The effect of the infant on its caregiver*. New York: Wiley.

Friedrich, W. N., & Boriskin, J. A. (1976). The role of the child in abuse: A review of the literature. *American Journal of Orthopsychiatry*, 46, 580–590.

Friedrich, W. N., & Friedrich, W. L. (1981). Psychosocial assets of parents of handicapped and nonhandicapped children. *American Journal of Mental Deficiency*, 85(5), 551–553.

Frodi, A. M. (1981). Contribution of infant characteristics to child abuse. *American Journal of Mental Deficiency*, 85(4), 341–349.

Frodi, A. M., & Lamb, M. E. (1980). Child abusers' responses to infant smiles and cries. *Child Development*, 51, 238–241.

Frodi, A. M., Lamb, M. E., Leavitt, L., & Donovan. W. (1978). Fathers' and mothers' responses to infant smiles and cries. *Infant Behavior and Development*, 1, 187–198.

Frodi, A. M., Lamb, M., Leavitt, L., Donovan, W., Neff, C., & Sherry, D. (1978). Fathers' and mothers' responses to the appearance and cries of premature and normal infants. *Developmental Psychology*, 14, 490–498.

Garber, H. L. (in press). *The Milwaukee Project. Preventing mental retardation in families at risk*. Washington, DC: American Association on Mental Deficiency.

Garber, H., & Heber, F. R. (1977). The Milwaukee Project: Indications of the effectiveness of early intervention in preventing mental retardation. In P. Mittler (Ed.), *Research to practice in mental retardation: Care and intervention* (Vol. I). Baltimore: University Park Press.

Gardner, J. (1967). Behavior therapy treatment approach to a psychogenic seizure case. *Journal of Consulting Psychology*, 31, 209–212.

Gath, A. The impact of an abnormal child upon the parents. (1977). *British Journal of Psychiatry*, 130, 405–410.

Gath, A. (1978). Down's syndrome and the family: The early years. New York: Academic Press.

George, C., & Main, M. (1979). Social interactions of young abused children. Approach, avoidance, and aggression. Child Development, 50, 306–318.

Giannini, M. J., & Goodman, L. (1963). Counseling families during the crisis reaction to mongolism. American Journal of Mental Deficiency, 67(5), 740–747.

Goldsmith, M. H., & Campos, J. J. (1982). Toward a theory of infant temperament. In R. N. Emde & R. J. Harmon (Eds.), The development of attachment and affiliative systems. New York: Plenum Press.

Greenberg, N. H. (1971). A comparison of infant-mother interactional behavior in infants with atypical behavior and normal infants. In J. Hellmuth (Ed.), The exceptional infant, Volume 2: Studies in abnormalities. New York: Brunner/Mazel.

Greenberg, M. T., & Marvin, R. S. (1979). Patterns of attachment in profoundly deaf preschool children. Merrill-Palmer Quarterly, 25, 265–279.

Grossman, F. K. (1972). Brothers and sisters of retarded children. New York: Syracuse University Press.

Grossman, H. J. (Ed.). (1983). Classification in mental retardation. Washington, DC: American Association on Mental Deficiency.

Grossmann, K., Thane, K., & Grossmann, K. E. (1981). Maternal tactual contact of the newborn after various postpartum conditions of mother-infant contact. Developmental Psychology, 17(2), 158–169.

Haggard, E. A., Brekstad, A., & Skard, A. G. (1960). On the reliability of an anamnestic interview. Journal of Abnormal and Social Psychology, 61, 311–318.

Haslett, N. R., Bolding, D. D., Harris, J. A., Taylor, A. L., Simon, P. M., & Schedgick, R. (1977). The attachment of a retarded child to an inanimate object: Translation into clinical utility. Child Psychiatry and Human Development, 8(1), 54–60.

Helfer, R. (1975). The relationship between lack of bonding and child abuse and neglect. In M. H. Klaus, T. Leger, & M. A. Trause (Eds.), Maternal attachment and mothering disorders: A round table. Piscataway, NJ: Johnson & Johnson Baby Products Company.

Hewett, S. (1970). The family and the handicapped child. London: Allen and Unwin.

Hosey, C. (1973). Yes, our son is still with us. Children Today, 2(6), 14–17, 36.

Jones, O. H. M. (1979). A comparative study of mother-child communication with Down's syndrome and normal infants. In D. Shaffer & J. Dunn (Eds.), The first year of life. New York: Wiley.

Jordan, T. E. (1962). Research on the handicapped child and the family. Merrill-Palmer Quarterly, 8(3), 243–260.

Klaus, R., & Gray, S. (1968). The early training project for disadvantaged children: A report after five years. Monographs of the Society for Research in Child Development, 33(4, Whole No. 120).

Kozier, A. (1957). Casework with parents of children born with severe brain defects. Social Casework, 38, 183–189.

Kucia, C., Drotar, D., Doershuk, C. F., Stern, R. C., Boat, T. F., & Matthews, L. (1979). Home observation of family interaction and childhood adjustment to cystic fibrosis. Journal of Pediatric Psychology, 4(2), 189–195.

Landesman-Dwyer, S., & Sackett, G. P. (1978). Behavioral changes in nonambulatory, mentally retarded individuals. In C. E. Meyers (Ed.), Quality of life in severely and profoundly mentally retarded people: Research foundations for improvement. Washington, DC: American Association on Mental Deficiency.

Lei, T., Nihira, L., Sheehy, N., & Meyers, C. E. (1981). A study of small family care for mentally retarded people. In R. H. Bruininks, C. E. Meyers, B. B. Sigford, & K. C. Lakin

(Eds.), *Deinstitutionalization and community adjustment of mentally retarded people*. Washington, DC: American Association on Mental Deficiency.

Levy, D. M. (1943). *Maternal overprotection*. New York: Columbia University.

Liebman, R., Minuchin, S., & Baker, L. (1974). Use of structured family therapy in the treatment of intractable asthma. *American Journal of Psychiatry, 131*, 535–539.

Lindemann, E. Symptomology and management of acute grief. (1944). *American Journal of Psychiatry, 101*, 141–148.

Locke, H. J., & Wallace, K. M. (1959). Short marital-adjustment and prediction tests: Their reliability and validity. *Journal of Marriage and Family Living, 21*, 251–255.

Lonsdale, G. (1978). Family life with a handicapped child: The parents speak. *Child: Care, Health and Development, 4*, 99–120.

Lozoff, B., Brittenham, G. M., Trause, M. A., Kennell, J. H., & Klaus, M. H. (1977). The mother-newborn relationship: Limits of adaptability. *The Journal of Pediatrics, 91*(1), 1–12.

Maccoby, E. E., & Feldman, S. S. (1972). Mother-attachment and stranger-reactions in the third year of life. *Monographs of the Society for Research in Child Development, 37*(1, Serial No. 146).

Marchant, R., Howlin, P., Yule, W., & Rutter, M. (1974). Graded change in the treatment of the behavior of autistic children. *Journal of Child Psychology and Psychiatry, 15*, 221–228.

Matheny, A. P., & Vernick, J. (1968). Parents of the mentally retarded child: Emotionally overwhelmed or informationally deprived? *Journal of Pediatrics, 74*, 953–959.

McAllister, R. J., Butler, E. W., & Lei, T. J. (1973). Patterns of social interaction among families of behaviorally retarded children. *Journal of Marriage and the Family, February*, 93–100.

McMichael, J. K. (1971). *Handicap. A study of physically handicapped children and their families*. London: Staples Press London.

Meyers, C. E. (1944). The effect of conflicting authority on the child. *University of Iowa Studies on Child Welfare, 20*, 31–98.

Meyers, C. E., & Blacher, J. (1982). *The effect of schooling severely impaired children on the family* (NICHD Grant No. HD14680). UCLA/MRRC Group at Lanterman State Hospital, Pomona, CA.

Meyers, C. E., Zetlin, A., & Blacher-Dixon, J. (1981). The effects of schooling on families of severely impaired children: An invitation to research. *Journal of Community Psychology, 9*, 306–315.

Mind, K. K., Hackett, J. D., Killou, D., & Silver, S. (1972). How they grow up: 41 physically handicapped children and their families. *American Journal of Psychiatry, 128*, 104–111.

Mink, I. T., Nihira, K., & Meyers, C. E. (1983). Taxonomy of family life styles: 1. Homes with TMR children. *American Journal of Mental Deficiency, 87*(5), 484–497.

Mink, I. T., Nihira, K., & Meyers, C. E. (1981, August). *Stressful life events in families with retarded children*. Paper presented at the Annual Convention of the American Psychological Association, Los Angeles.

Moos, R. H. (1974). *Family work and group environment scales*. Palo Alto, CA: Consulting Psychologists Press.

Morse, J. (1979). Program for family management of the multiply handicapped child— Tempo as a clinical model. *Rehabilitation literature, 40*, 134–146.

Nihira, K., Meyers, C. E., & Mink, I. T. (1980). Home environment, family adjustment, and the development of mentally retarded children. *Applied Research in Mental Retardation, 1*, 5–24.

Nihira, K., Mink, I. T., & Meyers, C. E. (1981). Relationship between home environment and school adjustment of TMR children. *American Journal of Mental Deficiency, 86*(1), 8–15.

Nix, K. S. (1980). Maternal attachment behaviors with defective versus normal infants. *Monographs: Mother-Infant Studies.* Denton, TX: College of Nursing, Texas Woman's University.

O'Hara, D., Chaiklin, H., & Mosher, B. S. (1980). A family life cycle plan for delivering services to developmentally handicapped children. *Child Welfare, 59*(2), 80–90.

Olshanky, S. (1970). Chronic sorrow: A response to having a mentally defective child. In R. L. Noland (Ed.), *Counseling parents of the mentally retarded. A sourcebook.* Springfield, IL: Thomas.

Pearlin, L. I., Liederman, M. A., Menaghan, E. G., & Mullan, J. T. (1981). The stress process. *Journal of Health and Social Behavior, 22,* 337–356.

Powell, D. (1979). Family-environment relations and early child rearing: The role of social networks and neighborhoods. *Journal of Research in Development and Education, 13*(1), 1–11.

Powell, D. R. (1980). Personal social networks as a focus for primary prevention of child mistreatment. *Infant Mental Health Journal, 1,* 232–239.

Poznanski, E. O. (1973). Emotional issues in raising handicapped children. *Rehabilitation Literature, 34* (11), 322–326.

Prechtl, H. F. R., & Stemmer, C. J. (1962). The choreiform syndrome in children. *Developmental Medicine and Child Neurology, 4,* 119–127.

Ramey, C. T., MacPhee, D., & Yeates, K. O. (1982). Preventing developmental retardation: A general systems model. In L. A. Bond & J. M. Joffee (Eds.), *Facilitating infant and early childhood development.* Hanover and London: University Press of New England.

Robinson, N. M., & Robinson, H. B. (1976). *The mentally retarded child: A psychological approach* (2nd ed.). New York: McGraw-Hill.

Robson, K. S., & Moss, H. A. (1970). Patterns and determinants of maternal attachment. *The Journal of Pediatrics, 77*(6), 976–985.

Rode, S. S., Chang, P., Fisch, R. Q., & Sroufe, L. A. (1981). Attachment patterns of infants separated from birth. *Developmental Psychology, 17*(2), 188–191.

Rosen, L. (1955). Selected aspects in the development of the mother's understanding of her mentally retarded child. *American Journal of Mental Deficiency, 59,* 522–528.

Rutter, M. (1979). Maternal deprivation, 1972–1978: New findings, new concepts, new approaches. *Child Development, 50,* 283–305.

Sameroff, A. J. (1983). Factors in predicting successful parenting. In V. J. Sasserath (Ed.), *Minimizing high-risk parenting.* Piscataway, NJ: Johnson & Johnson Baby Products Company.

Sameroff, A. J., & Chandler, M. J. (1975). Reproductive risk and the continuum of caretaking casualty. In F. D. Horowitz (Ed.), *Review of child development research* (Vol. 4). Chicago: University of Chicago Press.

Schaefer, E. S., & Bell, R. Q. (1958). Development of a parent attitude research instrument. *Child Development, 29,* 339–361.

Schonell, F. J., & Watts, B. H. (1956). A first survey of the effects of a subnormal child on the family unit. *American Journal of Mental Deficiency, 61,* 210–219.

Schroeder, S. R., Mulick, J. A., & Schroeder, C. S. (1979). Management of severe behavior problems of the retarded. In N. R. Ellis (Ed.), *Handbook of mental deficiency: Psychological theory and research* (2nd ed.). Hillsdale, NJ: Erlbaum.

Sears, R. R., Maccoby, E., & Levin, H. (1957). *Patterns of child rearing.* New York: Harper and Row.

Serafica, F. C., & Cicchetti, D. (1976). Down's syndrome children in a strange situation: Attachment and exploration behaviors. *Merrill-Palmer Quarterly, 22*(2), 137–150.

Shapiro, B. K., Accardo, P. J., & Capute, A. J. (1979). Factors affecting walking in a profoundly retarded population. *Developmental Medicine and Child Neurology, 21*, 369–373.

Simeonsson, R. J., Monson, L. B., & Blacher, J. (in press). Social understanding and mental retardation. In P. Brooks, R. Sperber, & C. McCauley (Eds.), *Learning and cognition in the mentally retarded.* Hillsdale, NJ:L. Erlbaum & Assoc.

Snell, M. (1982). Characteristics of the profoundly mentally retarded. In P. T. Cegelka & H. J. Prehm, *Mental retardation: From categories to people.* Columbus, OH: Merrill.

Snell, M. E. (Ed.). (1978). *Systematic instruction for the moderately and severely handicapped.* Columbus, OH: Merrill.

Sontag, E., Burke, P., & York, R. (1973). Considerations for serving the severely handicapped in the public schools. *Education and Training of the Mentally Retarded, 8*, 20–26.

Sontag, E., Smith, J., & Sailor, W. (1977). The severely/profoundly handicapped: Who are they? Where are we? *The Journal of Special Education, 11*, 5–11.

Sorce, J. F., Emde, R. N., & Frank, M. (1982). Maternal referencing in normal and Down's syndrome infants. In R. N. Emde & R. J. Harmon (Eds.), *The development of attachment and affiliative systems.* New York: Plenum Press.

Sroufe, L. A. (1979). The coherence of individual development. Early care, attachment, and subsequent developmental issues. *American Psychology, 34*(10), 834–841.

Steinberg, L. D., Catalano, R., & Dooley, D. (1981). Economic antecedents of child abuse and neglect. *Child Development, 52*, 975–985.

Stone, N. D. (1967). Family factors in willingness to place the mongoloid child. *American Journal of Mental Deficiency, 72*(1), 16–20.

Stone, N. W., & Chesney, B. H. (1978). Attachment behaviors in handicapped infants. *Mental Retardation, 16*(1), 8–12.

Symonds, P. M. (1939). *The psychology of parent-child relationships.* New York: Appleton Century.

Thompson, T., & Young, A. (1977). Behavioral counseling of the parents of retarded children. In T. Thompson & J. Grabowski (Eds.), *Behavior modification of the mentally retarded* (2nd ed.). New York: Oxford University Press.

Tizard, B., & Rees, J. (1975). The effect of institutional rearing on the behavioral problems and affectional relationships of a 4-year old child. *Journal of Child Psychology and Psychiatry, 16*, 61–73.

Turnbull, A. P., & Blacher-Dixon, J. (1980). Preschool mainstreaming: Impact on parents. In J. J. Gallagher (Ed.), *New directions for exceptional children* (Vol. 1). San Francisco: Jossey-Bass.

Turnbull, A. P., & Turnbull, H. R. (Eds.) (1978). *Parents speak out.* Columbus, OH: Merrill.

Wahler, R. B. (1980). The insular mother: Her problems in parent-child treatment. *Journal of Applied Behavior Analysis, 13*, 207–219.

Waisbren, S. E. (1980). Parents' reactions after the birth of a developmentally disabled child. *American Journal of Mental Deficiency, 84*(4), 345–351.

Weinraub, M., Brooks, J., & Lewis, M. (1977). The social network: A reconsideration of the concept of attachment. *Human Development, 20*, 31–47.

Whalen, C. K., & Henker, B. (1980). The social ecology of psychostimulant treatment: A model for conceptual and empirical analysis. In C. K. Whalen & B. Henker (Eds.), *Hyperactive children. The social ecology of identification and treatment.* New York: Academic Press.

Willer, B., Intagliate, J., & Wicks, N. (1981). Factors related to the quality of community adjustment in family care homes. In R. H. Bruininks, C. E. Meyers, B. S. Sigford, & K. C. Lakin (Eds.), *Deinstitutionalization and community adjustment of mentally retarded persons*. Washington, DC: American Association on Mental Deficiency.

Wright, B. M., & Zucker, R. A. (1980). Parental responses to competence and trauma in infants with reproductive casualty. *Journal of Abnormal Child Psychology, 8*(3), 385–395.

Zlutnick, S., Mayville, W. J., & Moffat, S. (1975). Modification of seizure disorders: The interruption of behavioral chains. *Journal of Applied Behavior Analysis, 8*, 1–12.

CHAPTER 2

Parental Acceptance and Developmental Handicap*

Judith Sewell Wright
Roberta D. Granger
Arnold J. Sameroff

Introduction

Research and practice in early childhood development have brought together the disciplines of special education and developmental psychology in new ways. Where previously the relationship had been exclusively devoted to the cognitive development of the child, more recently social and emotional arenas have been added. This addition was not made, however, out of exclusively humanitarian concerns for the child, but rather out of the recognition that the young child's social and emotional condition provide both the support and content of most early learning.

Increasingly, the focus on the social–emotional life of the child has expanded to the social and emotional life of the family because educa-

* Preparation of this manuscript was partially supported by funds from the National Institute for Handicapped Research and the Office of Special Education and Rehabilitation Services, U.S. Department of Education.

51

tion during the first years of life has been almost exclusively in the family context. Moreover, the social and emotional health of the family has come to be seen as an important ingredient in not only the social–emotional growth of the child, but in cognitive growth as well.

Another theme that is playing an important role in current models of early education is that the nature of the child has an impact on the family's attitudes and behaviors toward that child. This impact can be minor, as in the case of temperamental variations, or major, as in the case of children with severe developmental disabilities.

In this chapter we review the effects of a handicapped child on the family. We then discuss the way parents have been involved in intervention programs and the effects such interventions have had on their attitudes and feelings. In the concluding section we describe a model that attempts to identify the characteristics of the family environment that would be most supportive of the development of the child. These characteristics would become the target of early intervention programs designed to enhance the development of handicapped children.

Parents differ dramatically in their reaction to having a child with a handicap. Moreover, very little of the variance in reaction is directly related to the severity of the disability. The first explanation offered for these differences in reaction is such external variables as degree of stress or amount of social support. However, these variables explain only a small part of the parental reaction. What we suggest is that the analysis must also include internal variables: the beliefs, attitudes, and understanding of development that the parents bring to their new situation.

When we examine how intervention programs have dealt with parents, we find that there has been a fragmentation among programs that focus on parents' educational skills, attitudes and emotions, and social–emotional interactions with the child. Each of these aspects has something to contribute to the intervention process, but each taken alone may reduce the parent's competence in other important developmental domains.

Finally, we suggest an approach to understanding the development of handicapped children that permits an appreciation of the many factors that play a role in the outcome. The model contains traditional variables such as the severity of the child's problem, environmental stresses, and availability of family and professional support, but adds new variables of parental perspectives as well as family systems to the mix. We end by offering a model that does not offer simple solutions, but that reflects the complexity of developmental determinants that any intervention program needs to consider.

Acceptance of a Handicapped Child

The birth of a handicapped child is a stressful event for a parent. Researchers who have looked directly at the effects of having a handicapped child on the family agree that the child's birth precipitates major family stress (Cummings, Bayley, & Rie, 1966; Farber, 1960; Hare, Lawrence, Paynes, & Rawnsley, 1966; Johns, 1971; Roskies, 1972). Special strains are placed on the family that affect parental behavior in general and subsequently affect performance in the parenting role. Numerous authors have discussed the need for a better understanding of parental adjustment to this event, pointing out that the manner in which parents deal with this crisis can have long-term consequences for the parents, the family, and the child (Davis, 1975).

Despite reports that parental reaction tends to proceed through typical stages (Drotar, Baskiewicz, Irvin, Kennell, & Klaus, 1975), it is apparent that individual parents respond with varying degrees of stress and debilitation (Roskies, 1972). While a few studies have attempted to account for these differences in individual reaction to the birth of a handicapped child (Offord & Aponte, 1967), most have simply compiled descriptive statements regarding frequently observed patterns. Those few studies that have attempted to show the relationship between the various factors that may play an important role in the parents' ability to cope have looked primarily at social and child factors and less at the interaction of these factors with factors intrinsic to the mother. Social support systems and severity of handicap are the type of variables that have been most frequently explored. These studies, as reviewed elsewhere (Blacher, in press), can be discussed in terms of three general categories: clinical observations, reports based on interviews with parents, and studies using questionnaire data.

Clinical Observations

A large number of the published reports concerning the families of handicapped children are case studies by clinicians who provide services to the children and their families. These studies do not present quantitative data, but rather consist of specific case examples from which generalizations are made (Mackey, 1978). The generalizations made often exceed the methodological and conceptual limitations of the underlying evidence, which is gained primarily from observations of selected populations (Kelman, 1964).

Clinical observations have suggested that the emotional trauma experienced by parents upon discovering that their child is handicapped arouses anxieties, fears, and guilt not generally associated with the birth of a normal child (Sheimo, 1951). Parents' reactions to the frustration associated with the birth of a handicapped child have been found to take several different forms. Strong feelings of anger and rejection may lead the parent to strike out at the child or the environment (Fletcher, 1974; Poznanski, 1973). Parents may blame themselves and subsequently feel guilt, inadequacy, and anxiety. Bryant and Hirschberg (1961) reported from their clinical observations that parents often express anxiety about raising a retarded child, much of which stems from lack of confidence in their ability to meet the child's needs. The parents may also feel frustrated because the child's handicap is felt as a blow to their success as parents and because their aspirations for the child will not be fulfilled. Grebler (1952) has described the handicapped child as a threat to the parents' "narcissistic wish to live on in their children" (p. 476).

Olshansky (1962) described the parent of the mentally defective child as suffering from chronic sorrow. Solnit and Stark (1961) also discussed the mourning process and suggested that, along with mourning, there was a large component of guilt experienced especially by the mother. They suggested that some parents may attempt to ward off the grieving process by forming a guilty attachment to the child, thus neglecting other family members. Clinical writers have noted several forms that parental reaction may take. However, they have paid less attention to those factors that influence the parents' sensitivity to the stressful event. Rather than identifying those characteristics of the event, of the individual, or of support systems that account for differences in individual reactions, they have merely compiled descriptions of frequently observed patterns. Although clinical observations are important in that they suggest hypotheses for further study, they lack the controls necessary to warrant generalizations to the population of parents of disabled children as a whole or to extend our understanding of parental reaction to the birth of a handicapped child beyond descriptive anecdotes.

Studies Utilizing Interviews with Parents

Reports based on parent interviews are subject to some of the same difficulties inherent in case studies: small sample size, subjectivity of interviewer judgment, and a tendency to rely on broad-range interview data to turn up interesting conclusions rather than on the formulation of specific hypotheses to test. Many of these reports are based on samples of interviews, case illustrations, and—at best—tabulations of the number of cases included in support of their conclusions (Mackey, 1978). However, some of the interview research has utilized structured interviews and statistical analysis of the data and thus has provided meaningful information regarding parents' reactions to the birth of a handicapped child. As with clinical reports, the findings primarily describe the overall adjustment process of parents and include lists of the factors that parents have reported as significant to their adjustment, without empirically determining the interrelation of a variety of influences on the parents' ability to cope.

Drotar et al. (1975), in a study based on structured interviews with the parents of 20 children with a wide range of malformations including Down's syndrome, congenital heart disease, multiple physical anomalies, and cleft palate, concluded that many of the parents struggled with common issues and experienced similar identifiable emotional reactions. They found that for most parents periods of initial shock, disbelief, and intense emotional upset were followed by a period of gradual adaptation. Adaptation was characterized by a lessening of activity and an increase in the parents' ability to care for and experience satisfaction with their child.

Other observers of parental adjustment to the birth of a handicapped child have noted similar reactions. Following interviews with mothers whose children's disabilities ranged from Down's syndrome to clubfoot, Johns (1971) reported that while all reacted initially with anxiety, acceptance and adaptation gradually occurred, although the time required for the adjustment process varied for individual parents. Drotar et al. (1975) attempted to elicit some of the factors influencing the extent and rate of adjustment. Several mothers in this study reported that emotional and physical support systems played an important role. The maintenance of a satisfactory relationship between the parents was cited as a crucial aspect of their positive adaptation. The crisis of the birth was found to have the potential for either bringing the parents closer together and establishing mutual support or estranging the parents from one another. Parents who were able to communicate their feelings and provide support for each other during the crisis were able to adapt more successfully to the child's birth than those who could not communicate and who eventually separated. Johns (1971) noted that the degree and extent of adaptation and acceptance seemed in part contingent on the husband's reaction and on the support given to the mother in caring for the child. Several mothers who were faced with caring for the child alone reported it to be a draining and "intolerable" experience.

The type and severity of the disability has also been cited as an important factor in parental reaction. After interviewing 19 mothers of children with congenital heart disease, Offord and Aponte (1967) concluded that the mother's perception of the severity of the child's illness was a critical factor in determining the extent of overprotectiveness exhibited by the mother. Mothers who perceived their child's illness as more severe were likely to be more overprotective than mothers who perceived the child's illness as less severe. Johns (1971) reported that abnormality of the head and neck resulted in greater anxiety about future development than impairment of any other part of the body.

Like clinical observations, these reports generally agree that the event is stressful, leading to a reaction of anxiety that gradually gives way to acceptance and adaptation. Going a step further than clinical reports, these studies have suggested several factors that may influence the nature and extent of the parents' adaptation. Specifically, environmental factors involving the availability of social and emotional support and the nature of the child's disability have repeatedly been cited as critical to the parental reaction.

Studies Using Questionnaire Data

Clinical case reports provide information that can lead to testable hypotheses; these then can be evaluated by studies of larger samples. Interview studies can examine larger samples but are subject to the individual characteristics of the investigator. Studies using questionnaires carry clinical insights into the realm of larger sample sizes and reproducible findings. The use of an objective measure reduces the possibility of bias by the experimenter but also reduces the range of information that can be collected to the items on the scale.

Several studies have used more objective criteria to test the hypotheses generated by clinical observations and studies using parent interviews. The studies discussed in this section include those using objective measures (i.e., questionnaires or standardized personality inventories), reports of numerical data, and a systematic investigation of hypotheses relating to the factors influencing parental reaction to the birth of a handicapped child. This research has generally relied on self-report data from the parents. Bell (1964) emphasized the importance of adequately controlled studies utilizing questionnaire-based data: They often provide more interpretable information than observational studies because factors such as interviewer bias are not as likely to contaminate the results. The evidence from clinical observations and parent interviews that the birth of a handicapped child is a stressful event for the parents has generally been supported by the questionnaire research (Bradshaw & Lawton, 1978; Farber, 1960). Regarding the influence of the nature of the disability and of the availability of support systems, however, contradictory findings have been reported.

Severity of Handicap

An important finding is that not all parents share a common metric of severity of handicap. Barsch (1964), in looking at parental perceptions of the severity of their child's handicap, found that these parents rank-ordered 10 handicapping conditions for severity as follows, from most to least severe: cerebral palsy, mental retardation, mental illness, brain injury, blindness, epilepsy, deafness, polio, heart trouble, and diabetes. Parents of deaf children and parents of blind children tended to view their own child's problems as relatively mild in comparison to their perception of levels of seriousness of other handicaps. Although parents of cerebral palsied, organically damaged, and Down's syndrome children tended to rate other problems as more serious than their own, they still ranked their own problem relatively high in seriousness. This finding seems to indicate that while parents as a whole have a general sense of a rank order of seriousness of disabilities, they tend to soften their perception of seriousness in relation to their own child. It may be that familiarity with a given handicap gained by living in close contact with it tends to normalize the perception of the handicap. On the other hand, it may be that parents are defending against acknowledgment of the seriousness of the problem by changing their perception so that less stress is experienced by the family. Similar findings from a study on parents of children who are severely handicapped, autistic, or have spina bifida were reported by Eden (1983) and discussed in Chapter 1.

For the most part, researchers who have tried to find group differences between mothers of mildly and severely handicapped children have focused on parent attitudes toward child rearing as their dependent variable. The Parental Attitude Research Instrument (PARI) (Schaefer & Bell, 1958) has been the tool most commonly used to measure mothers' attitudes after the birth of a handicapped child. Using the PARI, Cook (1963) found that differences in diagnostic category and severity of the child's handicap correlated with differences in child-rearing attitudes. He reported that a strong authoritarian trend characterized the mothers of the severely handicapped children; for example, mothers of children with Down's syndrome and cerebral palsy tended to be more punitive and strongly authoritarian compared to mothers of children with other handicaps. Parental rejection was more likely to be associated with a mild handicap, while parental overprotection was associated with more severe conditions.

In a study looking at differences in attitudes between mothers of low- and high-functioning Down's syndrome children, Strong (1970) also found that the mothers of the low-functioning children were more overprotective as determined by the PARI. On the other hand, Dingman, Eyman, and Windle (1963) found that mothers of mildly retarded children were somewhat more protective, as determined by their attitudes toward child rearing, than parents of severely retarded children.

While the studies just cited suggest that the nature and degree of their child's disability may influence parents' overall attitudes toward child rearing, the significance of these findings is somewhat unclear due to contradictory findings and methodological problems. For example, in the Dingman *et al.* (1963) study, the differences in attitudes were largely consistent with differences in educational level of the two groups. The mothers of the mildly retarded children were significantly less well educated than the mothers of the severely retarded children, a factor that confounds the evidence because education has been found to be directly related to child-rearing attitudes. In their review of the PARI, Becker and Krug (1965) raised serious question about the usefulness of the instrument, noting the influence of educational level of the respondent and the lack of clear evidence that parent attitudes toward child rearing predict either parental behavior or child development very well.

Researchers interested in exploring the more direct influence of the birth of a handicapped child on maternal behavior have focused on the degree of stress experienced by the mother. These studies have also yielded somewhat contradictory findings and have suggested that the relationship between the birth of a handicapped child and levels of stress experienced by the mother is a complicated one.

Using the Malaise Inventory (Rutter, Tizard, & Whitmore, 1970) to measure stress, Bradshaw and Lawton (1978) found that the level is much higher for mothers of disabled children than for mothers of nonhandicapped children. Within the group of mothers of handicapped children, however, the mothers' level of stress did not vary according to type or severity of impairment. This finding agrees with that of Dorner (1975), who studied the families of 63 teenagers with spina bifida.

Social Support

In addition to looking at the role of the severity of handicap, Bradshaw and Lawton (1978) assessed the relation of the mothers' level of stress to the social and economic circumstances of the family. They concluded that little of the variation in the level of stress could be ascribed

to the external social and physical conditions of the family and child and
that the provision of goods, services, or financial assistance did not appear to have an impact on the level of mental well-being of the mothers.
Thus, the overall conclusion of this study was that neither the severity of
the handicap nor tangible support services and external environmental
conditions were significantly related to maternal stress associated with
caring for a handicapped child. Instead, they found that level of stress
was more closely related to the mother's perception or appraisal of her
situation (e.g., her feeling of satisfaction or dissatisfaction in her role as a
housewife or her feeling that she needed more help than she received)
than to the reality of the situation.

In support of these findings, Waisbren (1980), in a study comparing
Danish and U.S. parents of disabled children, found that the relationship
between use of support systems and coping was a complicated one. Support from informal sources, such as family, was found to be related to
positive feelings toward the child. Despite their more positive feelings
toward the child, these families experienced more symptoms of internal
stress. Formal support services, such as help from professionals or social
agencies, were not found to figure prominently in lessening the internal
strain or facilitating positive adjustment to the birth of a developmentally disabled child. This study does not entirely support common-sense
assumptions regarding the role of support. Waisbren attempted to explain the findings by pointing out that the public services used by the
parents often did not include certain important elements, such as
psychological counseling. If her explanation is a valid one, it again
points to the crucial role of intrapersonal factors in conjunction with
social supports in determining maternal adjustment to the birth of a
disabled child, and suggests that the relation between internal resources
and external support systems is a complicated one. It is also possible that
professional intervention requires parents to acknowledge the seriousness of the problem and to seek new ways of functioning in order to cope
effectively, a situation which may not be compatible with the reduction
of internal stress. Waisbren explained the finding that support from
family and friends correlated positively with an increase in the symptoms of stress as a trade-off: In order to relate better to their handicapped
child, parents internalized some of the strain, resulting in an increase in
anxiety and physical symptoms of stress.

Minimal Adaptation: A Theoretical Approach

Farber (1975) discussed the process of family adaptation to the addition of a handicapped child from a theoretical perspective as a process
of successive minimal adaptations. His underlying assumption holds

that families will make as minimal an adaptation as possible and that there is a temporal progression of adjustment from the simple to the complex, from the least disruptive to the more fully disruptive of family functioning. Usually one family member is affected more than others in a crisis situation and experiences more role changes. In the situation of the birth of a handicapped child, the mother is usually the family member who experiences the greatest impact. As adaptations become more extreme and require more family participation and revision of roles, disruption of established patterns takes place and tension increases.

Farber hypothesized six phases of successive adaptation through which the family of a handicapped child may progress. The first is the labeling phase, in which the basis for the existing role arrangements are removed and there is a realization that major assumptions underlying family relationships may have to be renegotiated. When a child fails to develop according to a normal developmental timetable, the parent usually tries to explain the deviancy by using the least offensive labels first, dreading the most stigmatizing ones. For example, the parent who regards his young son with Down's syndrome as having a slight speech impediment, correctable through speech therapy, does not yet require strategies of pervasive adaptation. While the behavior is not normal, it is not yet considered severe enough to be offensive. The redefinition of the behavior from merely "improper" to "grossly offensive" produces a shock to the parents. Having reached the point of defining the child's failure to develop normally as offensive to them, the parents must now decide how to handle the problem.

In the second phase, normalization, the family tries to handle the deviant child within the existing norms. Farber noted several strategies through which this may be accomplished: (1) some family members may suppress their perceptions about the existence of a problem, (2) some may convince others to change their perceptions (i.e., their labels), or (3) some may pretend that there is no problem. As long as the deviant person and the family can carry off the fiction of normality, there is no need for further adaptations in family roles or norms. While mothers are able to perform roles similar to those performed by mothers of normal children they can carry on as before. When their roles or functions must change, however, an imbalance in the family is created. The mother may be forced to neglect other family members (e.g., the husband or other children), thus increasing the level of stress in the family. It is only when the fiction of normality can no longer be sustained that more complex adaptations must be sought.

In the third phase, mobilization, the family finds that it cannot resolve the problem within existing arrangements; it must make adaptations affecting all family members. Ordinary community relationships do not support the norms and values pertinent to handling their problem.

In the revisionist fourth phase, the family discovers that minor revisions in family roles are not sufficient and there is a general demand for changing the basic role structure of the family. The continuation of family life may be sustained only through a rearrangement of age, sex, and generation roles in the family, and finally even the power structure may be rearranged. One of the organizational problems that occurs with extensive revision of family roles is how to maintain a coherent set of social relationships in the face of a high degree of tension. Major revisions in family roles often occur at great cost for some family members who sacrifice personal goals and extrafamily relationships to fulfill their required responsibilities.

The fifth phase, polarization, occurs as interaction between family members decreases. They coexist with little mutual sharing and often without fulfilling negotiated roles. Eventually, the accumulation of problems generated by the failure of successive adaptations becomes so great that the entire complex of family relationships loses its viability.

In the final phase, elimination, offending persons in the family are eliminated. The handicapped child is frequently blamed for the tension in the family and institutionalization may be the next recourse. The progression of unsuccessful adaptations may have generated so much offensive behavior in the family that other members are expelled as well, resulting in some cases in sending a sibling to live with a relative or in the parents' divorce. Fortunately, the problem escalates to this point for relatively few families.

In summary, Farber (1975) has argued that in response to crisis, families try to make as few changes as possible in roles, norms, and values. As the simpler adaptations fail to produce an acceptable accommodation to the offending problem, however, they go on to more complex solutions. As the more complex solutions fail, they progress to strategies that are still more complex, and so on.

Farber noted that the progression of successive minimal adaptations requires the qualification that all other things are equal. However, numerous factors impinge on family interaction and affect the course of events. Given different conditions, Farber acknowledged that the substance and succession of adaptations may be modified. Some families may skip certain phases of the process, or complex adaptations may precede simpler ones.

While Farber's phases present an interesting theoretical approach, further empirical validation is needed. Nonetheless, the basic principle of moving from minimal adaptation to mobilization, which results in a subsequent increase in stress, is certainly not a new thought. The idea that an individual's response to a critical event is to change as minimally as possible and that mobilization often results in an increased state of stress can frequently be found in the social psychological literature. It is implied in Nisbet's (1969) concept of "priority of fixity," which holds that fixity rather than change is the natural state of social behavior, and in the systems approach to family intervention, which emphasizes family homeostasis and stable equilibrium (Speer, 1970). Applied to families of handicapped children, it raises some interesting questions regarding the conditions that result in variation of response between families and the impact of certain situational factors, such as professional intervention, on adaptation and mobilization.

The purpose of this review is to set the stage for an analysis of how the social service system has attempted to intervene in families with handicapped children. The movement away from institutionalization and toward normalization must take the family as the central unit of concern. To what extent has this been done and to what extent is there recognition of the system characteristics of the family with all the feelings and reactions described above? In the following section we review intervention models that have included some aspect of the family and discuss the relative success or lack of success associated with these models.

Intervening with Parents

Just as the handicapped child impacts on the family, the family system impacts on the handicapped child's development. Parents involvement in the treatment of the handicapped child has become an increasingly more important aspect of the child's education. Historically, therapists took a primarily child or client focus. The professionals involved in special education and allied disciplines were trained with a focus on the child's handicap. Professional responsibility to parents included little more than providing reports of the child's progress.

The more recent emphasis on the importance of parents in the educational process has included three main approaches. Tymchuk (1975) identified two of these: training parents to be teachers of their handicapped children and providing counseling to help parents adjust to and accept their child. A third approach has received recent attention in the literature: providing programming to enhance the interaction between parents and their children with handicaps (Bromwich, 1976; Kogan, Gordon, & Wimberger, 1972; Seitz & Terdal, 1972). Each of these three forms of parent involvement has been demonstrated to be effective in some ways; however, each approach has different effects on the child's development and the family's adjustment. The disadvantages of each approach are especially apparent when implemented in isolation.

Parents as Teachers

Training parents to be teachers of their handicapped children has become the most common approach, especially in early intervention programs. This model will be discussed from the following points of view: the effectiveness of parent training, the effects of parent training on parental adjustment and family relationships, individual differences among parents in implementing training, and difficulties in implementing parent training. Parent training is designed to maximize the effects of special education by providing for therapeutic activities within the home environment on a daily basis. Many programs have been developed to train parents to train their children. While the form and content of training may vary, the common goal is to prepare parents to conduct educational and/or therapeutic activities with their children. These programs are described in more detail in other chapters of this volume.

Training parents to teach their handicapped children has been demonstrated to augment child's developmental progress (Frazier & Schneider, 1975; Fredericks, Baldwin, & Grove, 1975; Hayden, 1975; Watson & Bassinger, 1974). This approach has the added advantage of being cost-effective because parents are able to spend more time implementing therapeutic activities with their children than would be possible with trained professionals.

Parents or Teachers?

While there is little disagreement about the benefits of training parents to teach their handicapped child, there have been unforeseen problems. Parents who became successful teachers may have done so at the cost of becoming less of a parent (Wright, 1982). An additional cost may be a change in the structure of the family system or its overall functioning.

By focusing on the parent as a teacher, professionals influence the parent–child interaction and may change the source of pleasure for parents of handicapped children. For example, Jones (1980) compared mothers of Down's syndrome children with mothers of nonhandicapped children. When asked what they enjoyed most about their children, the mothers of Down's syndrome children tended to refer to successes in teaching situations. The mothers of nonhandicapped children most frequently referred to enjoying their children for themselves or enjoying their company. The mothers of handicapped children were more directive in interaction with their children, and teaching was frequently quoted as an essential part of their child rearing.

Kogan, Tyler, and Turner (1974) compared mother–child interactions of children with cerebral palsy while mother and child played together and while they were engaged in therapy. While performing therapy, the mother and the child showed greater amounts of negative behavior (i.e., control, hostility, intrusion, ambiguous affect, negative voice, and content) than when they were only playing. Mothers were coded as more controlling in the treatment situation. Maternal differences persisted over a 2-year period demonstrating that they were not temporary reactions to a new situation. Friendly, warm, and positive behaviors during play sessions as well as during therapy sessions progressively declined over the intervention period.

Baker (1980) reported that after a parent-training program, mothers perceived themselves in the role of teacher more than they did before the program. Wright (1982) pointed out that in the training situation there can be covert or overt pressure put on the parent to do well, creating an additional source of stress and tension in the interaction with their child. The parent's feeling of being evaluated can alter the interaction. It can be that parents' confidence in interacting with their child is undermined by the emphasis on parents as teachers. They may feel judged and evaluated so they work harder and play less, thus changing their relationship with their child from parent–child to teacher–student.

The adjustment or mourning process that accompanies the birth of a child with a handicap also can contribute to the mother focusing only on teaching. Parents feel guilty and responsible for the child's handicap even when they are clearly not at fault (Featherstone, 1980). They are told that their child will not make maximum developmental progress unless they teach the child regularly. Any minute they are not working with their child may be seen as detrimental. Thus, focusing on teaching the child may help them expiate their feelings of guilt.

Successful training of parents to teach their children requires that the parent attend the program, learn the requisite skills, implement the techniques at home, and generalize the information to other developmental tasks and/or settings. Many parents are able to meet these requirements and contribute to their child's developmental progress; others, however, are not (Wright, 1982). The characteristics of a parent and the family as well as their adjustment and reactions to having a child with a handicap can interfere with meeting these requirements.

One of the least discussed but most important issues in early intervention is the fact that many parents either do not avail themselves of existing services or, if they do, frequently drop out. Although professionals have become proponents of parental training, parents do not universally desire parent training programs (Baker, 1980; MacMillan & Turnbull, 1983). Stile, Cole, and Garner (1979) reported that despite professional encouragement for participation, parent attrition is high but rarely reported. Only 17 reports of attrition were found in 85 sources reviewed. Baker (1980) reported that only 10% of appropriate families join when invited to participate in a parent-training program. The joiners in Baker's program had children who were more severely handicapped. Of those parents who did attend training programs, all did not benefit equally from the same training. Baker reported that 30% of the parents in this program did not reach posttraining criteria. Even when parents adequately demonstrated a teaching skill in the classroom, it did not necessarily become incorporated into routine home life with their child.

Several studies report differences between parents who were highly successful and those who had low success in training their children. Wahler (1980) reported that mothers who did not profit from a parent-training approach were characterized by insularity, that is, they lived within sparsely constructed community social networks. These mothers differed in the functional nature of their social contacts as well. The insular mothers did not initiate social contacts; contacts were made by relatives or helping professionals. In addition, the type of support offered to these mothers tended to be directive and instructive, which was apt to be punishing to the insular mother. The support available to successful mothers was more likely to be facilitative and guided by the mother's wishes and needs. It did not have an implicit demand that the mother perform a desired behavior. Another study in which successful and nonsuccessful parents could be discriminated by parent rather than child characteristics was conducted by Mink, Nihira, and Meyers (1983). They found that few families could combine an active child stimulation program with harmonious family interactions. One or the other suffered.

Baker (1980) reported that those parents who joined his program and completed activities at home had children who were different. They were more retarded and had behavior problems that interfered with teaching. These parents were also more involved in other school programs. Parents who did not participate reported more major disruptive events, lack of time, and daily interruptions.

The process of parents' adjustment can influence the effectiveness of parent training. Parental resistance to attending training programs or to learning and implementing activities with their handicapped child may be part of the mourning or adjustment process (Ross, 1964). The parents' feelings of denial and anger can subvert the educator's or therapist's attempts to work with them. If the parents deny there is a problem, they are not likely to be cooperative in implementing solutions. If parents are experiencing a global response of anger, they may also be resentful of any professional or authority figure who deals with their handicapped child. Further, some parents resent the added burden of learning special skills to teach their child. The need for such training can be seen as one more sign that their child is different and contribute to their feeling of being stigmatized. Depression, ambivalence, and fatigue are other common reactions to having a child with a handicap that can interfere with efforts to train parents (Featherstone, 1980).

Two of the most frequently reported reactions of mothers to the birth of a handicapped child are a sense of incompetence and the loss of self-esteem. All that the parent already knows about child rearing is not enough, and it may be counterproductive. During training the sense of the parents' incompetence can be further heightened. Many compare their initial awkward attempts at handling their child with the seemingly magic hands of the physical therapist or polished skills of the educators. It is not surprising that parents may begin to feel powerless, impotent, and hopeless in this situation. This additional stress placed upon already-burdened parents frequently affects negatively the nature of the parent–child relationship (Wright, 1982).

Another issue that influences the effectiveness of parent training is the frequent apparent conflict between culturally sanctioned child-rearing practices and therapeutic or educational techniques. For example, parents may place their children in a walker, a practice seen by therapists as detrimental to the child's motor development. To the therapist, the parents appear to be noncompliant. To parents the child in the walker appears more normal and the walker allows the child independence. Without attention to the reasons why certain patterns of parental behavior persist, it is far more difficult to replace them with more adaptive patterns.

Some further drawbacks have emerged when parent training is seen from the viewpoint of the structure and function of the family system. Implementing activities at home may have a cost (MacMillan & Turnbull, 1983). Siblings may receive less attention, recreational or other family activities may decrease to create the time and energy for implementing home therapies, the father may have a decreased child-rearing role because the mother is usually the primary target for intervention, and parents have less energy available to support one another, increasing marital stress. In turn, the effectiveness of parent training may be reduced by these stresses on the family system. When parents implement programs at home, normal routines are upset or their child may become more distressed. Again it is not surprising that if parents are not sure why a task is important or do not see immediate results, they often abandon the teaching when it becomes difficult for them.

Skill training for parents is often not fully effective as an intervention technique (Bricker & Casuso, 1979). Considered in the light of Farber's (1975) family adaptation model, the demand on parents to be teachers may have prompted more role revision than the family was ready or able to integrate. The result for the family may be increased stress that is exhibited as resistance to intervention or ultimately attrition from the program. While training parents to train their children is a viable channel for parental involvement, the approach does not work uniformly well and can negatively influence the parent–child relationship and the family system.

Parent Counseling

Parent counseling is another mode of helping parents with handicapped children. The intent and form of parental counseling has differed depending on the provider of counseling, ranging from individual psychotherpy to social gatherings. Few reports of content and effectiveness appear in the literature; the themes that are frequently mentioned include parent support, parent education, and emotional development.

Parent Support

Support for the parents of handicapped children has been a major goal of parental counseling. This often has been provided through groups where parents of handicapped children gather periodically to talk about their experiences and feelings. Support and self-help groups have been demonstrated to reduce the sense of isolation often experienced by parents of handicapped children by providing a setting in which they can discover that others share the same problems (Lieberman & Borman, 1979). Parental support groups also offer a forum for exchange of resources and information and practical advice pertaining to parenting a handicapped child, information that is not otherwise easily available. The group serves as an extended family, providing support and parenting information.

Parent Education

Parent counseling can become educational by focusing on topics such as behavior management, parenting skills, methods for determining child needs, and finding services to meet those needs (Adamson, 1972). Counseling has been demonstrated to increase parental understanding of the educational, social, and psychological processes involved in the child's individual educational plan (McWhirter & Cabanski, 1977) and to facilitate school–home communication (Bricklin, 1977).

Teaching parents problem-solving techniques is another approach to parent counseling. Parents of handicapped children have been found to have difficulties in identifying and solving other family problems (RoTrock, Kostory, Corrales, and Smith, 1981). The counseling approach frequently expands the goals of parent education beyond problems only related to the disabled child.

Emotional Development

The emotional reactions of parents to the birth of a handicapped child have been another focus of parental counseling. Counselors implement interventions to assist parents through the adjustment or mourning process that accompanies the birth or diagnosis of a handicapped child. Counseling directed at facilitating the expression of these feelings provides a forum for nonjudgmental acceptance and reassurance that these feelings are normal reactions. While the content or intensity of these feelings, if seen apart from the precipitating event of having a handicapped child, may seem pathological, they are in fact common reactions of parents of handicapped children (Featherstone, 1980; Roos, 1963).

Parents or Patients?

As with programs that emphasize parents' roles as teachers, there are problems implicit in the provision of parental counseling. One is the assumption that if parents need counseling, they must be unhealthy, maladaptive or pathological. Parents have been labeled as overreacting, overprotective, aggressive, hostile, resistant, or rejecting. Parents have been seen as unrealistic people who either smothered their handicapped child in overprotectiveness or totally rejected their child (Akerley, 1978; Barsch, 1968). Parents also have been accused of being ignorant or of not wanting to hear the truth. Barsch (1968) aptly depicted the bind for parents:

> If the parent is militantly aggressive in seeking to obtain therapeutic services for his child, he may be accused of not realistically accepting his child's limitations. If he does not concern himself with efforts to improve or obtain services, he may be accused of apathetic rejection of his child. If he questions too much, he has a "reaction formation" and may be oversolicitous. If he questions too little, he is branded as disinterested and insensitive. (p. 8)

An additional problem is that parent-counseling groups have been utilized by a select population of parents. They tend to have higher incomes, be older, married, and have more education. They have children with more severe handicaps, have other parents of handicapped children as close friends, and are more likely to use other services such as babysitters and professionals (Keenan & Suelzle, 1982).

Another qualification about parent counseling models emerges from findings that when counseling was effective in assisting parents through mourning stages and toward acceptance of their child, it did not necessarily translate into improved performance in the children (Tymchuk, 1975). That is, counseling to gain resolution of the parents' feelings does not necessarily change their handling skills or enhance their child's development.

Parent–Child Interaction Training

The third trend of parent involvement, in addition to training parents to be teachers and providing counseling, has been to focus on the mother–child interaction. This model will be reviewed in terms of the effects of parental adjustment on interactions with their children and on the effects of intervention on these interactions. Mother–child interactions are seen as forming the basis of cognitive, language, and emotional development (Bakeman & Brown, 1980; Clarke-Stewart, 1973; Tronik & Adamson, 1980). These investigations of the interactions between parents and nonhandicapped children led to the assumption that if interactions could be enhanced then subsequent child development of handicapped children would be improved.

Such interventions are especially important for parents and their handicapped children because of the high risk of unsatisfactory interactions. Stone (1975) elaborated:

When the child's biological dysfunction affects the feedback, the responses he
makes to his mother, their ability to establish a communication channel may be
delayed or prevented. The mothers "doing what comes naturally" may not lead to
the establishment of parenting practices which are helpful to the child. The child
with a low level of activity can be seen as "good and undemanding" and can be left
unstimulated in his crib. The infant who stiffens and is unable to mold his body to
that of the person who is handling him can alienate the most loving mother. (p. 17)

The ways in which a parent of a nonhandicapped child finds
pleasure in interaction are often not available to the parent of a handicapped child. Even feeding a handicapped child—which is normally a
warm, rewarding experience—may be a source of frustration for both
mother and child. The handicapped child may not give out cues that are
easily read by the mother and/or the child may not be able to understand
or respond to the mother's attempts at caregiving (Bromwich, 1981).

The parent's emotional state and reactions to the handicapped child
will also influence the interaction. A depressed mother is not likely to
have the resources with which to respond to the handicapped child or to
interact playfully. An ambivalent mother may feel guilty about her
negative feelings and "force" a strained interaction. A mother frustrated
by a delayed or hypotonic child may overstimulate the child in attempts
to get the child to respond. A number of studies have documented these
differences in interactions between mothers and handicapped children
and mothers and nonhandicapped children (Imamura, 1965; Kogan &
Tyler, 1973; Vietze, Abernathy, Ashe, & Faulstich, 1978).

Intervention with interactions also differs from parent training
because the mother's therapy is integrated with the child's. The child is
seen as a contributor to the mother's effectiveness and not just a passive
recipient of reinforcement. Most of the literature on parent–child interactions has examined the components of interactions. Problems that
have served as targets for intervention have been allowing the child time
to respond, the ability to read behavioral cues, and the ability to avoid
overriding the child's responses (Clark & Seifer, 1983; Field, 1979). This
approach does not focus on parent teaching or doing therapy with the
child, but focuses on the reciprocal relationship of the parent and the
child.

The relationship between a mother and her handicapped child is
less likely to be satisfying for either partner. Even though their interactions can be facilitated, the improved interactions do not necessarily
translate to improved overall child performance. Where the child's play
behavior has been increased, the physical or cognitive development of
the child may not have been demonstrably improved through the intervention. Interaction coaching or teaching is important and effective

in some areas, such as language and emotional development. However, simply facilitating the parent–child interaction is not sufficient to change the course of development.

Broadening the Parental Model

The review of the three main avenues for parent involvement—training parents to train their children, counseling parents, and facilitating the parent–child interactions—has demonstrated the strengths and weaknesses of each approach. One purpose of parent involvement is to maximize the child's developmental progress and each mode of parent involvement must be assessed on the basis of its effect on the child.

Training parents to train their children is effective when the parent has a positive relationship with his or her child and has the resources to implement the training. A danger is that a mother may become focused on teaching her child to the exclusion of enjoying her child. Training parents to train their children cannot be effective unless parents implement the programs, and many parents do not. We suggested that while parent training can be effective, it is not sufficient. Many parents do not participate fully, and some parents find their relationships with their child to be negatively effected.

Counseling parents of handicapped children has been implemented in many different ways and there is little research data available on its effectiveness. It has been shown to reduce institutionalization of handicapped children and to be effective in resolving parents' negative feelings toward their child. Parent counseling has not, however, been shown to have a significant influence directly on the child's developmental progress. Further, it may not necessarily change the way parents interact with or teach their child.

Programs developed to improve mother–child interaction have been shown to be successful in modifying the play behavior of children and increasing the quality of mother–child interaction. The improved interactions may enhance emotional and cognitive development. However, these changes may not directly translate into improved child performance, reduction of other symptoms, or increased parental acceptance of the child.

Efforts at involving parents have not been uniformly effective. Training parents to train their children, counseling parents, and improving mother–child interactions are in themselves not sufficient to influence the child's total development. The shortcomings of each approach can be minimized by integrating all three approaches in a single model that attends to the needs of the family as well as the child. Counseling can improve the parent's attitude toward the child and increase coping skills. Intervention in parent–child interactions can enhance child learning by making the parent more sensitive to the child's communications. Training programs can assist the parent to integrate therapeutic activities into normal daily interactions. The child's competence is improved through a sophisticated holistic approach in which not only are the parts seen as related but are also each diagnosed and improved.

Intervention Program Outcome

While the long-term goal has been child change, programs have attempted to have positive effects on parents as well. However, there has been limited evaluation of the effects of the various types of early intervention programs on maternal behavior and even less evaluation of program impact on the interaction between parent and child behavior. Parental involvement in early education programs for culturally deprived children has been shown initially to have constructive impact on the child (Bronfenbrenner, 1974); however, evaluation of the impact on the mothers has revealed inconsistent findings. Some evidence indicates that desired changes in maternal behavior occur as a result of intervention programs, but there is also evidence that mothers may change in the opposite direction from that intended (Philipp & Siefert, 1979). More specifically, Philipp and Siefert, in a study of families of preschool-aged handicapped children over a 3-month period, hypothesized that programs stressing maternal involvement would result in a greater degree of positive change in maternal attitudes toward child rearing than those minimizing maternal involvement. Using a child-rearing practices report (Block, 1965), they found that mothers' overall attitudes significantly improved along such dimensions as supervision, punishment, and training of the child for mothers involved in intervention programs compared to those not involved. The involved mothers also expressed significantly more feelings of program support and open expression of affect than did the noninvolved mothers. At the same time, however, the involved mothers reported significantly more shame of the child than mothers who were minimally involved. This finding raises some questions that cannot be answered from the available data. It is possible that the mothers' admission of shame is linked to their feeling greater program support, which allows them to express "socially inappropriate" feelings toward their child. Another explanation may be that their high degree of involvement and extensive contact with other handicapped children and their parents forced these parents to confront the reality of their child's handicap and subsequently to deal with their feelings toward the handicapping condition to a greater extent than mothers who had minimal contact with the program and with other children. In a study of culturally disadvantaged children, Chilman (1973) also noted the possibility that parent training may make the mother more anxious or unsure of herself with her child and thus subsequent negative behaviors may be enhanced rather than eliminated. While early intervention programs may result in improved child development, the impact on parents may go either way.

In their review of parental effects on child development and on parent-training programs in general, Clarke-Stewart and Apfel (1978) noted that the parent program movement continues to be based on untested assumptions. This is particularly true with early intervention programs for handicapped children, which are instituting the relatively new concept of parent involvement as a major component of their intervention strategy. Not only is it important to evaluate the overall effect of this type of program on maternal behavior, but it is also necessary to consider the interaction of maternal training with characteristics of individual mothers that may account for differences in behavior.

Despite the strong belief among professionals that parents are important to the education of their children, especially if the child is handicapped, it has become increasingly apparent that many parents do not share this belief or, if they do, their view of their role is different from the view held by many professionals. This discrepancy between the beliefs of professionals and parents is most apparent in the issue of attrition. Getting and maintaining parent participation may depend on the degree to which the program conforms to parental expectations and beliefs as well as on background variables such as socioeconomic status and educational achievement. It is becoming increasingly clear that in order to understand the effects of intervention programs on the parent–child relationship, individual parental variables must be considered along with the more global dimensions on which intervention programs differ.

Individual Factors in Parent Behavior

The birth of a handicapped child has generally been portrayed as a stressful event to which parents react with similar patterns of anxiety and subsequent processes of adaptation. Many studies in the past have focused on the linear relationship between the child's handicap and the reaction of the mother, without considering intervening or mediating variables. Although the reaction of individual parents to the crisis and the extent to which it becomes a debilitating factor to their emotional well-being and their subsequent interaction with the child may depend upon a number of factors, there have been only a limited number of empirical studies attempting to discriminate the specific factors that may influence the parental reaction. These studies have primarily looked at the external circumstances of the parents (e.g., tangible support services and severity of handicap of the child) and have paid little attention to the way in which these environmental factors interact with perceptions and beliefs of the parents. Relatively recent research has indicated that a parent's subjective experience may indeed play an important role and points to the need for further study in this area. This implication is not surprising, as past research dealing with the effect of life stressors in general has indicated that a critical factor in evaluating the impact of stressful events is the individual's perception or interpretation of them. Dohrenwend and Dohrenwend (1969) suggested that the perception of stressful events is mediated by two broad categories of variables, one consisting of personal or internal factors and the other of interpersonal or external ones. Thus far, research evaluating the impact of a handicapped child on the parent has virtually ignored the influence of personal characteristics, and research looking at environmental factors has yielded confusing and conflicting results. Because of the implications for intervention, it is important to understand the role of both external conditions and internal mediating factors.

The importance of considering individual variables in conjunction with situational variables as determinants of behavior has been discussed by numerous theorists (Murray, 1938). Sells (1963) clearly stated that the principle that "behavior represents the interaction of the individual and the environmental situation" (p. 3) implies that the total variance of any response can only be accounted for by considering differences in individual characteristics, environmental characteristics, and the interactions among aspects of each. Vale and Vale (1969) argued also that a successful psychology should have the organism–environment interaction as the locus for study and stressed the interdependence of individual and environment in determining behavior.

One of the most prominent dimensions found to influence an individual's behavior and emotional responses is cognitive, that is, one's belief system and understanding or perception of a situation. Lazarus (1967) alluded to the importance of the cognitive dimension and its interaction with situational variables in describing the personality attributes that bear on the individual's appraisal of stressful situations. He noted that the role of situational variables in coping depends on factors within the psychological structure, specifically the general beliefs of the individual about the environment. Reaction to a situation is determined by the appraisal of the situation and its presumed consequences, a cognitive activity that relies heavily on a person's belief system. A person's beliefs determine what reliance the individual will place on environmental resources for mastering difficult situations and how such resources will be utilized.

Parents' Views of Development

Large-scale studies of parental cognition have not been reported in the literature. Those studies that have looked at parental cognition have paid most attention to child-rearing attitudes and values because these have been assumed to be the major factors underlying parental behavior. A number of tools have been developed to assess parental attitudes concerning child rearing, of which the Parental Attitude Research Instrument (PARI), developed by Schaefer and Bell (1958), has been the most widely used for determining dimensions of parental style (e.g., authoritarian versus democratic). In their review of the usefulness of the PARI, Becker and Krug (1965) noted that this measure has not been found to correlate highly with parental behavior or with subsequent developmental outcomes for the child. Schaefer himself (1971) has proposed the need for assessment tools that measure more specific components of parental cognition.

The possibility must be raised that specific parental attitudes are organized into more or less complex theories of development that reflect the parent's ability to cope with child-rearing problems. Sameroff (1975) suggested that the complexity of these theories could be placed at one of four levels—the symbiotic, the categorical, the compensating, and the perspectivistic—which are analogous to Piaget's stages of cognitive development. Within this model parents may differ in the importance for development they give to the characteristics of the child (a constitutional approach), to child-rearing techniques (an environmental approach), or to some combination of the two (an interactive or transactive approach) (Sameroff & Chandler, 1975). However, the degree to which parents can hold complex theories of development will depend on the degree to which they can deal with complexity in general. For example, if parents cannot consider two variables in the same context, like Piaget's preoperational child, they will be unable to have an interactional view of development.

According to Sameroff (1982), the symbiotic parent responds to the here-and-now affective circumstance of his or her relationship to the child. If the child is happy the parent is happy, but if the child feels upset the parent also experiences pain. Parents restricted to the symbiotic level have no theory of development because being tied to the present prevents reflection about antecedents or consequences of their child's behavior.

Parents at the categorical level do have theories of development but they are restricted to single determinants for single outcomes. They can believe that intelligence is either the result of heredity or a good education but not both. Some behaviors can be constitutionally determined (e.g., artistic talent) while others can be determined by child rearing (e.g., good manners).

At the compensating level parents are able to see child behaviors as having multiple determinants. Intelligence is the result of a good genetic endowment and a good education. If a 2-year-old has a tantrum it is because 2-year-olds do that, but if a 10-year-old has a tantrum it must be because the child wasn't raised right. The same behavior can be seen to stem from quite different determinants.

Additional context is available to parents at the perspectivistic level. Whereas at the compensating level factors are seen as constraints that can place limits on development (e.g., it doesn't matter how much children are trained, if they do not have the brain power they can only go so far), at the perspectivistic level growth is seen more dynamically. Even if a child is handicapped, alternative bases can be hypothesized for developmental progress. The parent is included in the model as another dynamic factor that can be altered by experience with the child to become a better or worse partner in the growth process. The case of a particular child in a particular family can be placed in a hypothetical context of any child in any family so that the full range of developmental possibilities can be examined.

Sameroff and Feil (1984) reported several methods of assessing a parent's level of conceptualizing development. A short Concepts of Development Questionnaire (CODQ) was constructed from 10 categorical and 10 compensating–perspectivistic items. Categorical items focused on single explanations of behavior based on either constitution or environment alone (e.g., "an easy baby will grow up to be a good child") or identification of people with single labels (e.g., "fathers cannot raise their children as well as mothers"). Compensating –perspectivistic items implied a coordination of environmental and constitutional determinants (e.g, "children have to be treated differently as they grow older") or an open-ended set of developmental possibilities (e.g., "children's problems never have a single cause"). Each item of the CODQ was scored on a 4-point scale from "strongly agree" to "strongly disagree."

In relation to parents of handicapped children, Sameroff (1975) theorized that parents with simpler understandings of development may be less able to deal effectively with problematic development of a child, whether it be perinatal complications, congenital disabilities, emotional disorders, or retarded development. Parents whose conception of development is more sophisticated should be able to work more effectively with the problems presented by the birth of a handicapped child through consideration of alternatives and mobilization of resources.

If Sameroff's cognitive levels are considered in light of Farber's theory of minimal adaptation, it seems likely that individuals whose understanding of development is more complex would engage in more effective mobilization, resulting in significant adaptation and role change within the family, than would those whose conceptualization of development is less complex. In this light an interesting paradox is seen. While the parent whose conception of development is more sophisticated may work more effectively with the child and achieve better outcomes for the child, the result for the parent may be an increase in internal stress.

The direct effects of concepts of development, an individual variable, were compared with the direct effects of social support, an environmental variable, in a study of stress experienced by parents of handicapped children (Granger, 1983). Three questions were addressed in the study. The first was whether the availability of social support significantly reduced stress for all mothers, the most common view among helping professionals, or whether there were mothers who were either not helped or even made more stressed by increased social support. The second question was whether the level of parental understanding of the developmental process influenced the amount of stress experienced by parents of children with handicapping conditions. The third question was whether a more complex model would be necessary to explain the determinants of stress where neither parental support nor cognition alone were adequate predictors of outcome.

The sample consisted of mothers who had a developmentally disabled child between the ages of birth and 3 years. About half the mothers were recruited from early intervention programs in which maternal involvement was emphasized. The other half of the mothers were recruited from programs in which there was minimal maternal involvement. The mothers were distributed across socioeconomic status (SES) groups as defined by an updated version of Hollingshead's (1957) Index of Social Position. About 21% were in high-SES groups, 19% in middle-SES groups, and 60% in low-SES groups. The children's disabilities included cerebral palsy, Down's syndrome, spina bifida, and a mixture of motor and cognitive delays.

Granger found that the more complex model was needed to understand parental stress. Neither social support nor concepts of development alone significantly affected the stress level of the mothers; only an interactive effect was found. Social support primarily reduced anxiety only for perspectivistic mothers. These mothers' conceptualization of development is such that they may be more aware of the many factors that influence developmental outcomes for their child and may not subscribe to simple definitions of their role in working with their child. Social support offered the assistance needed to help the perspectivistic mothers cope with the demands of their role as they perceived it.

On the other hand, mothers whose understanding of development was more concrete (categorical) experienced more anxiety as they experienced greater social support. To explain this finding, Granger suggested that as the categorical mothers interacted more with others, they were more likely to be confronted with perspectives that they had not considered, raising their level of anxiety. For example, through talking with relatives, friends, or other mothers of handicapped children, the categorical mother may have perceived others' concerns regarding the future development of the child. Her concept of her existing role in relation to her child's development may be challenged. Exposure to alternative views that are not held by the categorical mother may result in greater confusion, pressure, or anxiety. The increased exposure to information and ideas that occurs as a result of the greater breadth of contacts and interpersonal relationships may contribute to the increase in stress level for these mothers.

While this finding is somewhat counterintuitive, similar results have been reported in the literature. For example, Waisbren (1980) found that support from family and friends was positively correlated both with a better relationship with the child and with more symptoms of internal stress for the parents. The concepts of development research also relates to Philipp and Siefert's (1979) finding that while parents improved in child-rearing attitudes in such domains as discipline and training, they also expressed more negative feelings about their child when they were more actively involved with formal support services offered by the community. Granger (1983) suggested that not all parents of handicapped children respond in the same way to social support. A kind of trade-off may exist between the benefits and liabilities of social support systems for at least some mothers who have a handicapped child. The determining factor appears to be parental understanding of the developmental process. While social support may offer needed assistance in providing people to supply information, people to help with child care, and people to talk to and do things with, these same resources may place demands on the mother's emotional and cognitive resources that result in an increase in symptoms of anxiety for some mothers.

Granger also explored the relation between concepts of development and social support separately for mothers whose children were enrolled in two types of early intervention programs: those in which parent involvement was emphasized and those in which parents were less involved. The highest level of anxiety was experienced by perspectivistic mothers with little support in low-involvement intervention programs, while the least anxiety was experienced by perspectivistic mothers with high support who were in high-involvement intervention programs. It seems that the most effective coping for mothers of handicapped children is the result of a combination of maternal attributes and environmental resources. The mothers who appear to be coping most effectively as reflected by their emotional and physical well-being are those who view development as a dynamic process involving reciprocity between parent and child and who receive adequate social and professional support from family, friends, and social service institutions. However, if these more perspectivistic mothers do not have the resources available to them to provide the information and guidance that they need and that they are capable of utilizing, or if they do not perceive themselves as having a network of people to provide support for them in fulfilling the demands of their role, they are likely to experience distress.

The overall findings suggest that neither parental beliefs nor availability of social support can be considered in isolation if a better understanding of parental adjustment to rearing a handicapped child is to be attained. Only by looking at the complex interaction of the characteristics that comprise parental appraisal of their situation can a clearer picture be drawn. The simple notion that support (whether from family, friends, or professionals) has the same positive impact on all mothers needs to be examined more carefully. As has been suggested in previous studies, increased social support does not necessarily lead to a decrease in symptoms of anxiety, but may even be correlated with an increase in stress.

Such studies emphasize that the relationships among child development, intervention programs, and family environment is a complex one. What from the educator's view seem like simple strategies for helping parents to help their children may have quite different meanings from the parent's viewpoint. There is a growing awareness that further progress in designing effective intervention programs depends on further progress in understanding how parents think and feel. A necessary preliminary requirement is that professionals realize that how parent's think and feel plays a very significant role in how their children will fare.

Perspectives on Development

In the 1960s and 1970s major changes occurred in our understanding of the relationship between parents and children. Before this period there was a singular belief that parents unilaterally raised their children. During this period much more attention was paid to the converse, that is, how children raise their parents. At this point these two points of view can be joined into a unified theory about how children grow up. In this new view, it is neither the parental behavior nor child behavior alone that can predict how the child will develop, but rather the two taken in combination.

The earlier conception was based on a strong faith in the educational process and the effects of an improved environment on the development of children. This faith was moderated when it was found that in what appeared to be very good environments children were growing up with many problems. An explanation for this phenomenon was found in the work of Thomas, Chess, and their associates (Thomas & Chess, 1977; Thomas, Chess, & Birch, 1968), who found that children with different behavioral characteristics (e.g., temperaments) elicited different reactions from their parents. The child had an effect on his or her care givers (Lewis & Rosenblum, 1974). A child with an "easy" temperament would be easier to raise than a child with a "difficult" temperament. The blame for why a child did not turn out well could be shifted from the parents to the child. It was not that the family environment or educational system was at fault but rather the child who was unable to elicit loving responses. This simple shift from blaming the parent to blaming the child, however, only characterized simplistic notions of development. More complex views did accept the new emphasis on the importance of individual differences among children but only in combination with an emphasis on the social environment's ability to adapt and cope with different children.

Caretaking Casualty

A number of years ago Sameroff and Chandler (1975) reviewed the role of perinatal factors in later developmental deviancy with the expectation of finding clear indicators from early assessments that would

show straightforward linkages with late disorders. They were quite surprised to find that these indicators were not evident.

Whenever a perinatal risk factor was hypothesized to be related to
later dysfunction, prospective studies found no greater incidence of
disorder in the risk population than in control populations without the
risk factor. Whether the risk was related to preterm birth, low birth
weight, anoxia, or neurological signs, few causal chains were found
when appropriate control populations were studied. The most important
variable that needed to be controlled was socioeconomic status. Where
later deficits were associated with perinatal factors, it was generally in
combination with an economically deprived environment. Where birth
status showed little relation to later outcome, it was generally in combination with a better economic situation. The reason that birth complications are thought to be important is that high percentages of infants
with such problems have poor intellectual outcomes. However, the confounding factor is that most children who have these complications are
from the poorer segments of society (Birch & Gussow, 1970). These findings led Sameroff and Chandler to propose a continuum of caretaking
casualty. At one end of the continuum, the caretaking environment was
sufficiently supportive and adaptive to compensate for almost any
biological risk factor so that it was not transformed into later intellectual
or emotional problems. At the other end of the continuum, the caretaking environment did not have the educational, emotional, or economic
resources to deal with even the slightest perinatal problem. Thus, the
child, if allowed to survive, would maintain deficits into later stages of
intellectual and emotional growth.

Transactional Model

Sameroff and Chandler (1975) identified three models that could be
used to explain the relation between early risk factors and poor developmental outcomes. The simplest version was a single-factor model that
emphasized either constitutional or environmental determinants of
development. A more complex version was an interactional model in
which constitutional risk factors combined additively with environmental supports so that the effects of the risk would be reduced or aug-
mented by better or worse environments. However, the static quality of
these two models, in which neither constitution nor environment were
seen in dynamic terms, pointed to the need for a third, transactional
model in which development was believed to result from a continual interplay between a changing organism and a changing environment.
From this perspective, an early deviancy would be maintained into later
life only if it was perpetuated by a frozen relationship between the child

and his or her environment. Developmental continuities as well as discontinuities were to be sought in the child–environment relationship rather than in either component taken alone.

It has become increasingly clear that what have previously been considered characteristics of the child that are independent of child-rearing context are inextricably tied to the experiential environment. Only the most extreme cases of brain damage still present us with immutable children. For every other category of handicap, there has been clear evidence that variations in experience produce variation in outcome. More importantly, the relation between the child's characteristics and the characteristics of the environment should not be seen as additive. There are many handicaps, especially in the sensory domain, for which the human outcome is no different than for children without those handicaps. A child may remain deaf or blind but reach high levels of intellectual and social achievement.

What we have learned from our intervention efforts in the past is that the limits of human plasticity have not yet been reached. What is also clear, however, is that this individual plasticity is a consequence of contextual placticity, that is, the ability of care givers to adapt to the needs of the developing child. As those needs become better studies, our interventions efforts will also improve. Development is an organized system (Sameroff, 1983). Its complexity is also its virtue. The many paths to happiness in life offer us as many opportunities for education and remediation.

Developmental Model

The understanding of the early educational needs of the handicapped child have moved from a model focusing on the differences in the child and in the caretaking context to a model focusing on the similarities to normal child rearing. In both situations children have special caretaking needs that must be met by their care givers. The care givers must have knowledge about the developmental phases the child will pass through and the different behaviors required of parents during those phases. The parents must accept their parenting role and accept their child as part of the family. Finally, the parents must have the resources in time, energy, and money to be able to rear their child.

In the optimal normal situation a married couple has a child with no special caretaking needs (i.e., eats and sleeps well and regularly), has an easy temperament (i.e., is alert, positive in emotional expression, and undisturbed by environmental variation), and develops normally (i.e., passes through developmental milestones within expected societal norms). The parents are skilled at care giving and have the time to spend with the child; they have a network of relatives, friends, or babysitters whom they can afford to employ as alternative care givers when they are away.

At the opposite extreme is the unmarried, poor teenaged mother who gives birth to a handicapped child who immediately needs special parental skills on the part of the mother as well as a variety of professional interventions to assure the physical survival of the child. The child offers little overt satisfaction to a mother who has not yet found her own identity, much less is able to help a growing child discover his or her identity. The mother has little knowledge of the normal expectations about development and therefore cannot interpret the special needs of her child nor identify the social agencies that could provide assistance. Finally, she has neither the resources nor the support networks to help her understand or care for her child.

The problem for service providers in the area of early intervention is that an increasing proportion of children in need of special education programs are born into the latter family situation instead of into the former. Such families are difficult to get into an adequate service system, and once in they are not equipped to make adequate use of what is available.

The model necessary for understanding the development of the child incorporates the range of factors already described, outlined in Fig. 2.1, and discussed more fully at this point.

Child Competence. The goal of the normal rearing of a normal child as well as of the special education of a handicapped child is to produce a member of society that can participate to the greatest extent possible in the cognitive, emotional, and social spheres of everyday life.

Parent–Child Interaction. It is only within a care-giving environment that acts on children to optimize their behavior that a basis is provided for necessary competencies. In early childhood the primary care givers are usually the parents and, thus, their interactive behavior becomes a major focus for research in early childhood.

Parent Competence. The parent or substitute primary care giver is the mediator of cognitive, emotional, and social influences that facilitate or impede interactions with the child. In addition, feedback from interactions with the child affect the parents' attitudes and feelings about the child as well as attitudes and feelings about themselves.

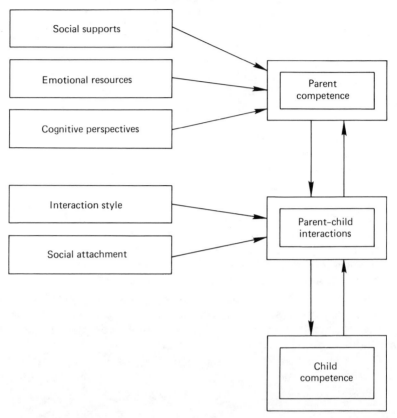

Figure 2.1 Developmental model of family environment characteristics supportive of the handicapped child.

Cognitive Perspectives.   Parents need knowledge about child rearing in order to care for their children. In the case of handicapped children they must also know what is normative behavior and what is behavior that requires special treatment. Parental attitudes toward the child and values about life goals also play an important role in whether they will seek services for the child.

Emotional Resources.   In addition to knowledge and attitudes related to the child, the parents' ability to mobilize their energy becomes an important contributor to child outcomes. To the extent that parents are involved with their own needs, they have little time or energy to devote to those of their child. Anxiety, lack of self-esteem, and lack of belief in their own effectiveness as parents all contribute negatively to the ability of parents to raise a competent child.

Social Supports. While the parents may have appropriate perspectives and emotional stability, they may lack the financial resources and time to interact with the child. Support networks in terms of professional help and social programs, friends and neighbors for discussion and caregiving assistance, and family members for emotional support and stability all impact on the outcome for the child.

From the perspective of the transactional model described earlier, the effect of the child on the parent must also be recognized. The parent's sense of competence and interactive behavior will be profoundly influenced by the nature of the child. This chapter has been primarily concerned with the way parents react to their handicapped children (i.e., the arrows in Fig. 2.1 going upward from the characteristics of the child through parent–child interactions to parent competence. Many of the primary determinants of the parent's reaction are cognitive variables, the ability of the parent to take perspective on the child's behavior within the context of an appropriate model of child rearing and development.

Parental Perspectives

The conclusion to be drawn from research on the care giving of parents of handicapped children and attempts to intervene with their care giving is that the results represent a complicated pattern. While the professional community has a clear feeling about what defines good parenting, it has become increasingly clear that these definitions are not shared by all parents. A new level of analysis would require paying increased attention to the values and beliefs of each parent as an individual.

In this review we have attempted to integrate three levels of analysis. The first level was the definition of the characteristics of the handicapped child that impacted on the parent. The second level was the characterization of the determinants of the parental response to the child. The third level was a description of the different ways in which the social system, through intervention programs, attempts to modify the first two levels. Our conclusion is that any successful program would have to deal with these three levels. There must be an appreciation of the total developmental system. An inseparable part of that appreciation is the individual analysis of the kind of child, the kind of parent, and the kind of program. The role of the family is not an educational extension of the intervention program. Rather, the opposite is true: The intervention program should be an extension of the family, recognizing the primacy of the parent–child relationship in fostering the development of the child.

As the treatment of handicapped children moves further from the institutionalization model, researchers must get closer to recognizing the forces in normal development that apply to the nonhandicapped as well as the handicapped. Further analysis of parents' feelings, thoughts, and values will bring this goal closer.

References

Adamson, W. C. (1972). Helping parents of children with learning disabilities. *Journal of Learning Disabilities, 5,* 326–330.

Akerley, M. (1978). False gods and angry prophets. In A. Turnbull & H. R. Turnbull (Eds.), *Parents speak out.* Columbus, OH: Charles E. Merrill Press.

Bakeman, R., & Brown, J. (1980). Early interaction: Consequences for social and mental development at three years. *Child Development, 51,* 437–447.

Baker, B. L. (1980). Training parents as teachers of their disabled child. In S. Salzinger, J. Antrobus, & J. Glick (Eds.), *The ecosystem of the sick child.* New York: Academic Press.

Barsch, R. (1964). The handicapped ranking scale among parents of handicapped children. *American Journal of Public Health, 54,* 1560–1567.

Barsch, R. (1968). *The parent of the handicapped child.* Springfield, IL: Thomas.

Becker, W., & Krug, R. (1965). The parent attitude research instrument—A research review. *Child Development, 36,* 329–365.

Bell, R. Q. (1964). The effect on the family of a limitation in coping ability in the child: A research approach and finding. *Merrill-Palmer Quarterly, 10,* 129–142.

Birch, H., & Gussow, G. D. (1970). *Disadvantaged children.* New York: Grune & Stratton.

Blacher, J. (in press). Sequential stages of parental adjustment to the birth of a handicapped child: Fact or artifact? *Mental Retardation.*

Block, J. H. (1965). *Childrearing practices report.* Unpublished manuscript, University of California, Berkeley, Institute of Human Development.

Bradshaw, J., & Lawton, D. (1978). Tracing the causes of stress in families with handicapped children. *British Journal of Social Work, 8,* 181–192.

Bricker, D., & Casuso, V. (1979). Family involvement: A critical component of early intervention. *Exceptional Children, 46,* 108–115.

Bricklin, P. M. (1977). Counseling parents of children with learning disabilities. *The Reading Teacher, 23,* 614–619.

Bromwich, R. (1976). Focus on maternal behavior in infant intervention. *American Journal of Orthopsychiatry, 46,* 439–446.

Bromwich, R. (1981). *Working with parents and infants: An interactional approach.* Baltimore: University Park Press.

Bronfenbrenner, U. (1974). *Is early intervention effective? A report on longitudinal evaluations of preschool programs* (Vol. 2) (DHEW No. 76–30025). Department of Health,

Education & Welfare, Offices of Human Development, Office of Child Development & Children's Bureau. Washington, DC: U.S. Government Printing Office.

Bryant, K. N., & Hirschberg, J. C. (1961). Helping the parents of a retarded child. *American Journal of Diseases of Children, 102,* 82–96.

Chilman, C. S. (1973). Programs for disadvantaged parents: Some major trends and related research. In B. M. Caldwell and H. N. Riccuti (Eds.), *Review of child development research* (Vol. 3). Chicago: University of Chicago Press.

Clark, G., & Siefer, R. (1983). Facilitating mother-infant communication: A treatment model for high risk and developmentally delayed infants. *Infant Mental Health Journal, 4,* 67–81.

Clarke-Stewart, K. A. (1973). Interactions between mothers and their young children: Characteristics and consequences. *Monographs of The Society for Research in Child Development, 38,* (6–7, Serial No. 153).

Clark-Stewart, K. A., & Apfel, N. (1978). Evaluating parental effects on child development. In L. Shulmen (Ed.), *Review of research in education* (Vol. 6). Itasca, IL: Peacock.

Cook, J. (1963). Dimensional analysis of child-rearing attitudes of parents of handicapped children. *American Journal of Mental Deficiency, 68,* 354–361.

Cummings, S., Bayley, H., & Rie, H. (1966). Effects of the child's deficiency on the mother. *American Journal of Orthopsychiatry, 36,* 595–608.

Davis, R. E. Family of the disabled child. (1975). *New York State Journal of Medicine, 6,* 1039–1041.

Dingman, H. F., Eyman, A., & Windle, D. R. (1963). An investigation of some child-rearing practices of mothers with retarded children. *American Journal of Mental Deficiency, 67,* 899–908.

Dohrenwend, B. P., & Dohrenwend, B. S. (1969). *Social status and psychological disorder.* New York: Wiley.

Dorner, S. (1975). The relationship of physical handicaps to stress in families with an adolescent with spina bifida. *Developmental Medicine and Child Neurology, 17,* 765–776.

Drotar, D., Baskiewicz, A., Irvin, N., Kennell, J., & Klaus, M. (1975). The adaptation of parents to the birth of an infant with a congenital malformation: A hypothetical model. *Pediatrics, 56,* 710–717.

Eden, G. V. S. (1983). *An instrument to assess parental adjustment to a handicapped child.* Unpublished master's thesis, University of California, Riverside.

Farber, B. (1960). Perceptions of crisis and related variables in the impact of a retarded child on the mother. *Journal of Health and Human Behavior, 1,* 108–118.

Farber, B. (1975). Family adaptations to severely mentally retarded children. In M. J. Begab & S. A. Richardson (Eds.), *The mentally retarded and society: A social science perspective.* Baltimore: University Park Press.

Featherstone, H. (1980). *A difference in the family: Life with a disabled child.* New York: Basic Books, Inc.

Field, T. (1979). Interactions of high-risk infants: Quantitative and qualitative differences. In D. B. Sawin, C. Hawkins, L. Walker, & V. H. Prenticuffs (Eds.), *Current perspectives on psychological risks during pregnancy and early infancy.* New York: Brunner/Mazel.

Fletcher, J. (1974). Attitudes toward defective newborns. *Hastings Center Studies, 2,* 21–32.

Frazier, J. R., & Schneider, H. (1975). Parental management of inappropriate hyperactivity in a young retarded child. *Journal of Behavior Therapy and Experimental Psychiatry, 6,* 246–247.

88   Judith Sewell Wright, Roberta D. Granger, and Arnold J. Sameroff

Fredricks, B. H. D., Baldwin, V. L., & Grove, D. (1975). A home-center based parent training model. In J. Grim (Ed.), *Training parents to teach: Four models*. Chapel Hill, NC: Technical Assistance Development System.

Granger, R. D. (1983). *A study of the effects of concepts of development, social supports, and involvement in community intervention programs upon the stress experienced by mothers of handicapped children*. Unpublished master's thesis, University of Illinois at Chicago.

Grebler, A. M. (1952). Parental attitudes toward mentally retarded children. *American Journal of Mental Deficiency, 56*, 475–483.

Hare, E. H., Lawrence, K. M., Paynes, H., & Rawnsley, K. (1966). Spina bifida, cystica, and family stress. *British Medical Journal, 2*, 757.

Hayden, A. H. (1975). A center based parent training model. In J. Grim (Ed.), *Training parents to teach: Four models*. Chapel Hill, NC: Technical Assistance Development System.

Hollingshead, A. B. (1957). *Two-factor index of social position*. Unpublished manuscript, Yale University, New Haven.

Imamura, S. (1965). *Mother and blind child*. New York: American Foundation for the Blind.

Johns, N. (1971). Family reactions to the birth of a child with a congenital abnormality. *Medical Journal of Australia, 1*, 277–282.

Jones, O. H. (1980). Prelinguistic communication skills in Down syndrome and normal infants. In T. Field, S. Goldberg, D. Stern, & A. Sostek (Eds.), *High risk infants and children: Adult and peer interactions*. New York: Academic Press.

Keenan, V., & Suelzle, M. (1982, June). *Differentials in characteristics between parent group members and non-members*. Paper presented at the joint session of American Academy on Mental Retardation and the Psychology Division of the American Association of Mental Deficiency, Boston, MA.

Kelman, H. R. (1964). The brain-damaged child and his family. In H. G. Birch (Ed.), *Brain damage in children*. New York: Williams & Williams.

Kogan, K. L., Gordon, B. N., & Wimberger, H. C. (1972). Teaching mothers to alter interactions with their children: Implications for those who work with children and parents. *Childhood Education, 49*, 102–110.

Kogan, K. L., & Tyler, N. (1973). Mother-child interaction in young physically handicapped children. *American Journal of Mental Deficiency, 77*, 492–497.

Kogan, K. L., Tyler, N., & Turner, P. (1974). The process of interpersonal adaptation between mothers and their cerebral palsied children. *Developmental Medicine and Child Neurology, 16*, 518–527.

Lazarus, R. S. (1967). Cognitive and personality factors underlying threat and coping. In M. H. Appley & R. Trumbull (Eds.), *Psychological Stress*. New York: Meredith.

Lewis, M., & Rosenblum, L. A. (1974). *The effect of the infant on its caregiver*. New York: Wiley.

Lieberman, M., & Borman, L. (1979). *Self help groups for coping with crisis*. San Francisco: Jossey-Bass.

Mackey, S. K. (1978). *A study of the differences in attitudes and behavior between mothers of disabled and nondisabled children*. Unpublished doctoral dissertation, University of Illinois, Chicago Circle.

MacMillan, D., & Turnbull, A. (1983). Parent involvement with special education: Respecting individual preferences. *Education and Training of the Mentally Retarded, 2*, 4–9.

McWhirter, J. J., & Cabanski, C. (1977). *The learning disabled child: A school and family concern*. Champaign, IL: Research Press.

Mink, I. T., Nihira, K., & Meyers, C. E. (1983). Taxonomy of family life styles: I. Homes with TMR children. *American Journal of Mental Deficiency, 87,* 484–497.

Murray, H. A. (1938). *Explorations in personality.* New York: Oxford University Press.

Nisbet, R. A. (1969). *Social change and history.* New York: Oxford University Press.

Offord, D. R., & Aponte, B. S. (1967). Distortion of disability and effects on family life. *Journal of American Academy of Child Psychiatry, 6,* 499–511.

Olshansky, S. (1962). Chronic sorrow: A response to having a mentally defective child. *Social Casework, 43,* 190–193.

Philipp, C., & Siefert, K. (1979). A study of maternal participation in preschool programs for handicapped children and their families. *Social Work in Health Care, 5,* 165–175.

Poznanski, E. O. (1973). Emotional issues in raising handicapped children. *Rehabilitation Literature, 34,* 322–326.

Roos, P. (1963). Psychological counseling with parents of retarded children. *Mental Retardation, 6,* 345–350.

Roskies, E. (1972). *Abnormality and normality: The mothering of thalidomide children.* Ithaca, NY: Cornell University Press.

Ross, A. O. (1964). *The exceptional child in the family.* New York: Grune & Stratton.

Ro-Trock, L. G., Kostory, J. L., Corrales, R., & Smith, B. (1981). *A study of characteristics of families with a severely handicapped child from a systems perspective.* Unpublished manuscript, Institute for Human Development, Inc., Kansas City, MO.

Rutter, M., Tizard, J., & Whitmore, K. (Eds.). (1970). *Education, health, and behavior.* London: Longmans.

Sameroff, A. J. (1975, July). *The mother's construction of the child.* Paper presented at the meetings of the International Society for the Study of Behavioral Development, Guilford, England.

Sameroff, A. J. (1982). The environmental context of developmental disabilities. In D. Bricker (Ed.), *Handicapped and at risk infants: Research and application.* Baltimore: University Park Press.

Sameroff, A. J. (1983). Developmental systems: Contexts and evolution. In W. Kessen (Ed.), *History, theories, and methods.* Volume I of P. H. Mussen (Ed.), *Handbook of Child Psychology.* New York: Wiley.

Sameroff, A. J., & Chandler, M. J. (1975). Reproductive risk and the continuum of caretaking casualty. In F. D. Horowitz (Ed.), *Review of child development research* (Vol. 4). Chicago: University of Chicago Press.

Sameroff, A. J., & Feil, L. (1984). Parental perspectives on development. In I. E. Sigel (Ed.), *Parental belief systems: The psychological consequences for children.* Hillsdale, NJ: Erlbaum.

Schaefer, E. S. (1971). Development of hierarchical configurational models for parent behavior and child behavior. In J. P. Hill (Ed.), *Minnesota Symposium on Child Psychology* (Vol. 5). Minneapolis: University of Minnesota.

Schaefer, E. S., & Bell, R. Q. (1958). Development of a parental attitude research instrument. *Child Development, 29,* 339–361.

Seitz, S., & Terdal, L. (1972). A modeling approach to changing parent-child interactions. *Mental Retardation, 10,* 39–43.

Sells, S. B. (1963). Dimensions of stimulus situations which account for behavior variance. In S. B. Sells (Ed.), *Stimulus determinants of behavior.* New York: Ronald Press.

Sheimo, S. L. (1951). Problems in helping parents of mentally defective and handicapped children. *American Journal of Mental Deficiency, 56,* 42–47.

Solnit, A. J., & Stark, M. H. (1961). Mourning and the birth of a defective child. *Journal for the Psychoanalytic Study of the Child, 16,* 523–537.

Speer, D. C. (1970). Family systems: Morphostasis and morphogenesis or "Is homeostasis enough?" *Family Process*, 9, 259–278.

Stile, S. W., Cole, J. T., & Garner, A. Y. (1979). Maximizing parental involvement in programs for exceptional children: Strategies for education and related service personnel. *Journal of the Division for Early Childhood*, 1, 68–82.

Stone, N. W. (1975). A plea for early intervention. *Mental Retardation*, 13, 16–18.

Strong, R. (1970). A study of the differences in measures of overprotective attitudes between mothers of high and low functioning mongoloid children (Doctoral dissertation, University of New Mexico, 1969). *Dissertation Abstracts International*, 30, 5290–5291.

Thomas, A., & Chess, S. (1977). *Temperament and development*. New York: Brunner/Mazel.

Thomas, A., Chess, S., & Birch, H. (1968). *Temperament and behavior disorders in children*. New York: New York University Press.

Tronick, E., & Adamson, L. (1980). *Babies as people*. New York: Collier Books.

Tymchuk, A. (1975). Training parent therapists. *Mental Retardation*, 13, 19–22.

Vale, J. R., & Vale, G. R. (1969). Individual differences and general laws in psychology: A reconciliation. *American Psychologist*, 24, 1093–1108.

Vietze, P. M., Abernathy, S. R., Ashe, M. L., & Faulstich, G. (1978). Contingency interaction between mothers and their developmentally delayed infants. In G. P. Sackett (Ed.), *Observing behavior* (Vol. 1). Baltimore: University Park Press.

Wahler, R. (1980). Parent insularity as determinant of generalization success in family treatment. In S. Salzinger, J. Antrobus, & J. Glick (Eds.), *The ecosystem of the sick child*. New York: Academic Press.

Waisbren, E. (1980). Parents' reactions after the birth of a developmentally disabled child. *American Journal of Mental Deficiency*, 84, 345–351.

Watson, L. S., & Bassinger, J. F. (1974). Parent training technology: A potential service delivery system. *Mental Retardation*, 13, 3–10.

Wright, J. (1982). An integrative model of parent involvement. In M. Peters (Ed.), *Building an alliance for children: Parents and professionals*. Seattle: University of Washington, Program Development Assistance System.

CHAPTER 3

A Developmental Perspective on Stress and Coping in Families of Autistic Children*

Marie M. Bristol
Eric Schopler

Introduction

As another child approached her, dark-haired, 5-year-old Elena nimbly maneuvered up the climbing gym, swinging easily, hand over hand across the open spaces, and pulled herself up until she sat at the highest point of the climbing bars. She reached down, carefully pulled a thread from her slacks, and repeatedly stroked the thread, rocking back and forth on her precarious perch. So absorbed was the child in her stroking that she seemed oblivious to the presence of the teacher and the other children. The teacher's words to the child did not intrude on Elena's reverie. She gave so little response that one might wonder if perhaps she were deaf. Elena

* The preparation of this report was supported in part by the Special Education Program, Special Education and Rehabilitative Services, U.S. Department of Education, Contract No. 300–82–0366. The opinions expressed do not necessarily reflect the position or policy of the U.S. Department of Education, and no official endorsement by the U.S. Department of Education should be inferred.

rocked on the climbing gym until the other child climbed up beside her. Without looking at the child, Elena quickly slipped down the gym bars, retrieved the thread from the pocket of her pants, and continued to rock and stroke the thread until an attractive young woman came and brought her her coat. Elena gave no indication that she knew this woman who called her by name. The woman had still not grown accustomed to this lack of recognition even though she was with Elena daily. The woman was Elena's mother.

Elena is autistic, one of approximately 340,000 children and adults in the United States (Warren, 1982) who suffer from the lifelong developmental disability known as autism. This disorder is about as common as deafness or blindness. It occurs throughout the world in otherwise normal families of all ethnic, racial, and social backgrounds. Like many disabilities, it occurs three to four times more frequently in male than in female children.

Although there is no universal agreement on the definition of autism, a growing consensus regarding its essential features is emerging from empirical research (Rutter, 1978). These features, included in the official definition of the National Society for Autistic Children and Adults (National Society for Autistic Children, 1978), include (1) severe impairment in relating to other people, including family members; (2) delayed and deviant language development characterized by inappropriate or nonfunctional use of language and including peculiar patterns of speech such as echoing words or phrases and reversing pronouns; (3) stereotyped behavior ranging from repetitive body movements such as finger flicking to ritualistic behaviors such as lining up toys or furniture in a particular order and becoming excessively upset when this order is changed; and, finally, (4) onset of the disorder by age 3 years.

Before there was a fuller understanding of autism and of the importance of structure in educational programs for autistic children (Schopler, Brehm, Kinsbourne, & Reichler, 1971), children like Elena spent months and even years misplaced in unstructured programs, in mute or singsong rocking and stroking, hand flapping or finger flicking, oblivious not only to other children, but appearing not to recognize their own parents in a room full of strangers. That families of such children should experience stress is not surprising, but an understanding of the type and intensity of such stress requires a knowledge of historical and contemporary factors that have played a particular role in families of autistic children.

In this chapter we will review existing research on stress and coping in families of autistic children. Historically, the majority of studies of families of autistic children have focused on the possible role of parents in causing autism in the child. We will review these psychogenic theories and the empirical evidence for such a parent-causal model and then look at an alternative conceptualization of the parent as part of the solution rather than as the cause of the problem. Earlier findings implying parental pathology will then be reexamined, and will be reinterpreted in light of the child's demand characteristics.

The limited number of studies directly assessing the impact of autistic children on their families will then be reviewed, and evidence of variation in stress as a function of type of handicap and specific characteristics of autistic children will be examined. A developmental progression of stresses in these families will then be presented within the context of "normal" family stress and the overall family life cycle. Issues pertinent to mothers, fathers, and siblings will be included.

Factors related to successful family adaptation to autistic children will be highlighted. This will include discussion of a sociological model for general coping with stress and its applicability to families of autistic children. The contribution of family resources, maternal beliefs, and maternal employment to successful family adaptation will also be noted. The chapter will conclude with implications of this research for interventions with these families and with recommendations for future research.

Information for this chapter is drawn from the research literature on families of autistic children and from our own research and clinical experience at the Frank Porter Graham Child Development Center and in Division TEACCH (Treatment and Education of Autistic and related Communication handicapped CHildren), a statewide network of services to autistic and other severely handicapped children mandated by the North Carolina state legislature in 1972. In addition to its administrative and research functions, TEACCH operates 5 diagnostic and training centers, 37 public school classrooms, and provides consultation services throughout the state of North Carolina.

The Impact of Parents on Autistic Children: Psychogenic Theories and Unidirectional Models

When Kanner defined the syndrome of autism in 1943, he first spoke of autism as an inborn defect of affective contact. This theory was soon overshadowed in his own work as well as in the work of others by the notion of "refrigerator parents" whose rejection of the child was in some way the cause of the child's autism. This was in keeping with the prevailing unidirectional model of child development in which parents, primarily mothers, were responsible for the socialization or failure of socialization of young children. Child deficits were interpreted as evidence of parental, usually maternal, failures. Down's syndrome, for example, was blamed on alcoholism in the family (Hayden, 1976). From this perspective, parental qualities and practices were viewed as primary causes of autism (Bettelheim, 1967), as primary causes of "nonorganic" autism only (Meyers & Goldfarb, 1962), or as necessary but not sufficient conditions for causing autism in biologically vulnerable infants (O'Gorman, 1970). Parents, then, suffered not only the stress of having a severely handicapped child, but the additional stress of being blamed for the child's handicap. Early studies of stress in these families were exclusively focused on how parents may have caused stress in their autistic child.

Psychogenic Theories: Some Hypotheses

Various psychogenic hypotheses were proposed to explain how the parent may have caused the child's autism. These hypotheses generally fell into one of three major theories of causation: (1) severe trauma or stress on the child, particularly during the first 2 years, (2) parental personality or cognitive disorders, and (3) abnormal parent–child interaction, with lack of an integrated, organized family life.

Both physical and emotional separations in the infancy period were implicated in the genesis of autism. Based on intensive psychotherapy with children and their families, some clinicians (Putnam, 1955; Rank, 1949, 1955) stressed the importance of parental absence, parental illness, or the occurrence of sibling births in the onset of infantile autism. Other authors emphasized the emotional separation from the child caused by overintellectualization and maternal rejection or by maternal depression (Ruttenberg, 1971; Sarvis & Garcia, 1967; Szurek & Berlin, 1973). Some authors, such as Szurek (1956), also stressed the role of discord between spouses and the use of the child to resolve marital conflicts.

To counter arguments that it was difficult to explain how these traumas could have affected only the autistic child in an otherwise normal family, Bettelheim (1967) proposed a more specific hypothesis. He maintained that the parent rejected only the particular child who ultimately became autistic. The child perceived the parent's negative feelings toward him or her so withdrew from contact with a world perceived as hostile. Bettleheim used the analogy of the treatment of prisoners in Nazi concentration camps to describe this environment.

The parental personality hypothesis suggested that parents who were themselves abnormal were unable to fulfill their parenting role adequately and were unable to assist their children in forming important object relationships.

The parental thought disorder hypothesis in essence suggested that autistic children either inherited a more severe form of parental psychosis or were affected by parenting practices of parents who were themselves pathological (Goldfarb, Spitzer, & Endicott, 1976).

Proponents of these psychogenic hypotheses postulated a number of different and often contradictory mechanisms through which the parent's deviant interaction with the child could have resulted in the child's autistic behavior. Both lack of parental reinforcement of the child's initial social approaches (Ferster, 1961, 1966) and parental over-response to these same social approaches (Tinbergen & Tinbergen, 1972) were said to cause autistic behavior in children. In a similar vein, lack of parental stimulation of the child (Call, 1963; Ward, 1970), overstimulation (Sarvis & Garcia, 1967), inadequate structuring of the child's environment (Fraknoi & Ruttenberg, 1971), and overstructuring and intrusiveness (Lennard, Beaulieu, & Embrey, 1965) were proposed as causes of autism. Defective maternal language (Goldfarb, Goldfarb, & Scholl, 1966; Goldfarb, Levy, & Meyers, 1966) and inadequate family functioning, including confusion and disorganization (Behrens & Goldfarb, 1958), were also suggested as sources of the child's autistic behavior.

Psychogenic Theories: The Empirical Evidence

Early Trauma Theories. One of the most prevalent of the psychogenic theories, the early stress or trauma hypothesis, has not been substantiated when the family histories of autistic children were examined. Rutter and Lockyer (1967) found that only 9% of autistic children came from single-parent families, compared to 22% of children with other forms of psychiatric disorders. In our own research with young children (age 2–10 years), we found that separations or divorces among families of autistic children recruited from consecutive program referrals were not more common than in general population (Bristol, in press-b). DeMyer and Goldberg (1983) noted a lower-than-average parental rate of divorce among a sample of autistic adolescents and adults (age 12–30 y). Similarly, Bender and Grugett (1956) found that both "broken homes" and "poor emotional climate" were less frequent in the backgrounds of young schizophrenic and autistic children than in the histories of children with other psychiatric disorders. No significant differences were found on any of the measures of early stress when histories of autistic and dysphasic children were compared by Cox, Rutter, Newman, and Bartak (1975). Parents of autistic children did not report more maternal depression during the child's first 2 years, nor were parental deaths, divorces, separations from the child, or financial, housing, or health stresses more common for parents of autistic children than for parents of the comparison group.

Perhaps the most persuasive data challenging the early trauma hypotheses are those found by Folstein and Rutter (1978) in a study of 25 autistic twins. The authors found no evidence of differences in psychosocial factors for autistic or nonautistic twins, but did find a significantly greater occurrence of biological complications at birth for autistic children.

An alternative strategy for challenging the early trauma theory has been to follow up children known to have experienced early deprivation or stress. Although institutionalization, hospital admission, and separation experiences have been shown to be related to substantial increases in psychiatric disorders, cases of autism among these populations are virtually nonexistent (Rutter, 1968). The evidence, regardless of the research strategy used, thus clearly indicates that early trauma is neither a necessary nor a sufficient explanation for the autistic syndrome.

Parental Deviance Theories.   The majority of well-designed studies have also failed to provide empirical support for hypotheses regarding rejecting parental attitudes (DeMyer, Pontius, Norton, Barton, Allen, & Steele, 1972; Pitfield & Oppenheim, 1964); incidence of parental schizophrenia (Creak & Ini, 1960; Kanner, 1954; Kolvin, Ounsted, Richardson, & Garside, 1971; McAdoo & DeMyer, 1977), or personality deviance (Block, 1969; Cantwell, Baker, & Rutter, 1978; Cox et al., 1975; Creak & Ini, 1960; Kolvin, Garside, & Kidd, 1971).

Abnormal Parent–Child Interaction Theories.   The studies reported by Cantwell et al. (1978) address a number of the issues already mentioned and serve to illustrate the more rigorous studies that have failed to find empirical support for psychogenic hypotheses regarding autism. In these studies, parent–child interaction and language patterns in families of autistic boys were compared with those in families of dysphasic boys. Dysphasic children were defined as those who had severe language disorders present from infancy in spite of normal peripheral hearing, but who did not manifest the psychotic behavior and social deficits associated with autism.

Among the measures employed in the study were structured interviews, detailed time-sampled observations in the home, and analysis of audiotaped mother–child conversations. Patterns of verbal and nonverbal interaction were similar for parents of dysphasic and autistic children for the various measures used. Overall, the findings of these studies, which controlled for child IQ, parent's social class, and child's language level, failed to support hypotheses that autism was due to deviant maternal communication or deviant parent–child interactions.

Partial Blame Theories. Like the previously listed findings, the search for differential parental factors in "organic" and "nonorganic" cases of autism has been futile. Attempts to replicate earlier reports of the organic–nonorganic distinction have not been successful, even when undertaken by authors such as Goldfarb (Goldfarb *et al.,* 1976), who originally reported them.

O'Gorman's (1970) hypothesis that parental pathology causes autism only in biologically vulnerable infants is also a plausible one, especially in light of interactional (Bell, 1968) and transactional (Sameroff & Chandler, 1975) models of child socialization and increasing evidence of biological deficits in autistic children (Folstein & Rutter, 1978; Ritvo, 1976; Ritvo, Yuwiler, Geller, Ornitz, Saeger, & Plotkin, 1970). Thus, O'Gorman's hypothesis is in keeping with the notion of a continuum of reproductive causality for handicapping conditions suggested by Pasamanick and Knobloch (1960) and a continuum of caretaking casualty proposed by Sameroff and Chandler (1975). At present, however, there is no evidence that any kind of parenting can prevent the development of autism in an organically impaired child nor that any parental characteristics or practices can cause autism in a normal infant (DeMyer, 1979; Rutter & Schopler, 1978).

Cantwell *et al.* (1978) reviewed over 100 studies of families of autistic children. They concluded that the vast majority of research studies, which used an adequate diagnosis of autism and also controlled for the effects of child characteristics by using a handicapped rather than a normal control group, found no evidence that parents of autistic children were abnormal or engaged in parenting practices that could have caused their child's autism.

Much of this might be of merely historical interest except that many professionals interacting with parents of autistic children received their own training when the "parent-cause," psychoanalytic zeitgeist prevailed. Although there is little evidence linking autism to any deviant parental behaviors or attitudes, and no evidence that psychotherapy or psychoanalysis either for the child or the parents has been effective in improving the child's status (Wing, 1976), many professionals continue to operate on the basis of psychodynamic assumptions regarding the etiology of autism. This approach only increases stress in families they are attempting to help.

The Parent as Part of the Solution

The Case for a Biological Deficit. Additional challenges to the psychogenic parent theories of autism came from research on biological deficits in autistic children. No unique physiologic disorder has been identified in all autistic children, but a variety of biochemical, genetic, and viral agents have been implicated in at least some cases of autism. Rubella during pregnancy (Chess, 1971) and perinatal complications (Folstein & Rutter, 1978) are related to a higher-than-normal incidence of autism in children (Chess, 1971). Other conditions that affect the central nervous system such as encephalitis and meningitis (Paluszny, 1979) and infantile spasms (Taft & Cohen, 1971) may also be associated with autistic patterns of behavior. More recently, chromosomal differences (the fragile X syndrome; Friedman, 1982) have been linked to autism. For most autistic children, however, no single, clear etiological agent is found, although many show evidence of neurological dysfunction and from one-quarter (Rutter, 1970) to one-third (Bartak & Rutter, 1976) of autistic children develop epilepsy at some time during their lives. The majority of researchers believe that autism is the result of some form of biochemical or brain abnormality that is present from birth, and that it is not produced by faulty parenting (Rimland, 1964; Rutter, 1978). As evidence of such biological deficits continued to mount, the case for a psychogenic origin of autism became increasingly untenable.

A New Role for Parents in Autism. Schopler (1971) castigated professionals for making parents the scapegoats for their ignorance about autism and suggested that only by viewing parents as part of the solution, not the problem, would progress be made with autistic children. In fact, it has since been demonstrated that training parents as cotherapists for autistic children results in increases in appropriate child behaviors, decreases in bizarre and inappropriate behaviors (Marcus, Lansing, Andrews, & Schopler, 1978; Short, in press), generalization of treatment gains to other settings, maintenance of gain over time (Koegel, Schreibman, Britten, Burke, & O'Neill, 1981; Lovaas, Koegel, Simmons, & Long, 1973; Short, in press), and a decrease in institutionalization of autistic adolescents (Schopler, Mesibov, DeVellis, & Short, 1981). Such training is necessary, not because these people are poor parents, but because autistic children do not readily respond to the social reinforcement, modeling, and incidental teaching that are effective with most normal children. "Normal" parenting alone is not sufficient to overcome the children's serious cognitive and social deficits.

The Impact of Autistic Children on Parents: Reinterpretation of Direction of Effect

The Child's Contribution

How is it that reputable scholars could conduct research regarding families of autistic children and reach such diametrically opposed views of the parent's role in the causation of autism? Schopler (1978) reviewed the results of over 100 research studies and found a statistically significant effect for time of publication. He found that the majority of research studies that emphasized psychogenic causes of autism in children were published prior to 1965 and were based on clinical impressions and theory rather than on empirical data. Thus they tended to confirm the prevailing psychoanalytic, parent-cause theory of child development.

Bristol (1979) found that most of the "evidence" indicating that parents of autistic children were pathological was based on correlational data and usually compared parents of autistic children with parents of normal children. Differences found between the two groups were attributed to defective parenting without considering differences in the autistic and normal children's behaviors that may, in fact, have made differential parental responses appropriate. In such comparisons, parents of autistic children were said to be "mechanical" and "cold" (Eisenberg & Kanner, 1955; King, 1975), and "overprotective" or "restrictive" (Donnelly, 1960). Parents who gave directions, asked questions, or structured situations were said to be "intrusive" (Lennard et al., 1965). Those who did not were said to be "perplexed" (Meyers & Goldfarb, 1961). In a review of approximately 100 such studies of families of autistic children, Cantwell and associates (1978) cited numerous methodological, definitional, and design problems. Equally important, since the focus was on how the parent might have stressed the child, almost no attention was paid to differences in the autistic and normal children. Only four studies addressed the effects of the child on the family and none directly assessed specific child behaviors that might have accounted for the observed parental differences. Even those studies that involved in-home observations of parental behaviors, some of which were as long as 4 hours, failed to record child behaviors or characteristics that might have affected observed parental responses.

Upper- and Lower-Limit Control:
Restrictiveness–Intrusiveness

When Bell (1968, 1971) proposed his interactional model of child development, he considered both the effect of the parent on the child and the effect of the child on the parent. His model states that the social response and control behaviors of parents are organized in hierarchical caretaking repertoires. Congenital child characteristics, including those involving impaired sensorimotor capacities, differences in responsiveness to parents, and differences in activity level, elicit different levels and intensities of parent caretaking responses. These child behaviors also differentially reinforce parent behaviors that have been evoked. Parental response, then, may reveal as much about the child as about the parent.

There is increasing evidence of neurological, biochemical, and other organic impairment in autistic children (Rimland, 1964; Ritvo, 1976; Rutter, 1968). Much evidence suggests that these children are, in fact, different from birth and suffer deficits in all of the areas Bell has indicated as instrumental in affecting parent caretaking behaviors. As pointed out in Chapter 1 of this volume (Blacher), it is therefore reasonable to expect that such children may affect their parents' responses to them and that parents may need special training to deal with their children's unique needs.

Bell's (1968) discussion of upper- and lower-limit control behaviors in parents may be particularly relevant to previous characterizations of parents of autistic children as "restrictive," "intrusive," or "demanding." Parent upper-limit control behavior is aimed at reducing and redirecting behavior of the child that exceeds parental standards of intensity, frequency, or appropriateness. This parental behavior, according to Bell, is elicited by impulsive, hyperactive, or overly assertive behavior in the infant or child. Without reference to child behavior, however, he points out that parents who are in fact responding to the stimulus provided by the child are likely to be described as "punitive" or "restrictive." Lower-limit control behavior, on the other hand, stimulates child behavior and is a parental response evoked by lethargic, inactive, or incompetent behavior in the infant or child. Once again, although the parent behavior is, in fact, a response to child behavior, Bell noted that the parent may be described as "intrusive" or "demanding" if no reference is made to the child's behavior or characteristics. Without reference to child characteristics or behaviors, in both instances, parents could be considered "controlling."

Epithets of "restrictive" or "intrusive" have also been applied to mothers of retarded children (Buium, Rynders, & Turnure, 1974; Kogan, Wimberger, & Bobbitt, 1969; Mash & Terdal, 1973), mothers of physically handicapped children (Kogan & Tyler, 1973), and of cerebral palsied children (Cook, 1963). It is unlikely, in the context of these handicaps, that the parent's behavior could have caused the child's handicap. A more reasonable explanation in families of handicapped children is that parents respond to the child's needs by providing structure and whatever degree of "intrusiveness" is necessary to elicit a response. Similar findings on depression (Cantwell et al., 1978; Cox et al., 1975; Cummings, Bayley, & Rie, 1966), and maternal language (Rondal, 1978) across handicapping conditions demonstrate that the parental behavior is a response to, not a cause of, their child's disorder.

Since the publication of Bell's original studies, a number of other researchers have published reports on behaviors of normal and handicapped infants that affect maternal caretaking behaviors and attitudes. These include eye contact (Fraiberg, 1974; Stern, 1974), ability to discriminate mothers from strangers (Lewis & Rosenblum, 1974), imitation and reciprocal play (Stern, 1974), responsiveness (Prechtl, 1961), effective prelinguistic communication systems including differential crying and hand gestures (Mahoney, 1975; Trevarthen, 1975), and reinforcement of parental social interactions with the child (Lewis & Rosenblum, 1974).

Autistic children generally manifest deficits in all the critical behaviors cited by Bell and by other researchers. They could thus be expected to elicit very different behavioral and attitudinal responses from parents in comparison with normal children or children with handicaps that do not affect the social behaviors in question.

From this perspective, the most interesting finding in reviewing earlier parent studies in autism is that so few differences were found between parents of autistic and other children. This is not surprising, however, since the vast majority of parent studies in autism have been designed to test the effect of the parent on the child. In poorly designed parent studies, child characteristics were ignored. In well-designed parent studies, child characteristics have generally been controlled as sources of error. In either case, little information was generated regarding specific effects of the autistic child on the parent or family. The few studies that have assessed such effects are discussed in the following section.

Direct Assessment of Child Effects

Effect on Maternal Behaviors

An observational study by Gardner cited in Cantwell *et al.* (1978) directly assessed the impact of autistic and normal children on mother's behaviors. Gardner used a cross-over design in which mothers of autistic and normal children interacted with autistic and normal children. He controlled for familiarity by having each mother interact with someone else's child, either normal or autistic, depending on her own child's diagnostic category.

Gardner found that both groups of mothers spoke more to autistic children, using shorter sentences, more commands, questions, and verbal rewards and punishments. Although no specific child characteristics were included in the report, the results indicate that something about the autistic child evoked these behaviors, not only from their own mothers, but from mothers of normal children as well. Although the author did not use the label, such behaviors could be considered "intrusive" and were clearly a parental response to the autistic child rather than an enduring situation-free personality trait of the mothers.

Effect on Family Stress

Acknowledgment of child effects has led to a limited number of research studies that have directly assessed the effects of autistic children on family stress.

General Impact on the Family

DeMyer and Goldberg (1983) reported on a retrospective account of developmental stresses in 23 families of autistic children and adults aged 12–30. All but three of the families had been followed by one or both authors since the preschool years. It was clear that the stress of the autistic child affected most aspects of family life. Overall the families reported that living with an autistic child impacted most severely on the following aspects of family life (listed in decreasing order of severity): family recreation, finances, emotional and mental health of parents, physical health of the parents, housekeeping, meeting needs of brothers and sisters, relations with friends and neighbors, sibling relationships, marital relationships, the personal development of each family member, and relations with relatives. Formal assessment of the parents (DeMyer,

1979), however, revealed that although these parents were experiencing the stress of having an autistic child, the incidence of psychiatric disturbance was not more common among the sample of families of autistic children than among a matched sample of families of normal children. Although depressive symptoms in response to the child's handicap were more common than in the normal sample (as has been found for most types of handicapping conditions [Burden, 1980; Cummings et al., 1966; McMichael, 1971]) the parent was not incapacitated by such symptoms. She found the parents to have essentially a normal range of personality characteristics and child-rearing attitudes and practices that did not differ from comparison groups of families of normal and intellectually subnormal children.

Comparisons with Other Handicapped Groups

Although there is evidence that parental dysfunctions such as depression are no more common in families of autistic children than in families of children with other types of handicapping conditions (Bristol, in press-b; Cox et al., 1975), it does appear that the particular nature of autism is more stressful than other types of handicapping conditions. For example, in a study of coping problems of stress in families of Down's syndrome, autistic, and psychiatric outpatient children, Holroyd and McArthur (1976) found greater stress reported by families of autistic children than by either of the other two groups. Both mothers of Down's syndrome and autistic children reported problems that appeared to be related to a common retardation factor. These included problems of excessive time demands, poor maternal health, and pessimism about the child's future, as well as limitations in occupational or educational opportunities for their families because of the child.

Comparative scale scores reported by Holroyd and McArthur indicate, however, that mothers of autistic children reported greater stress than mothers of Down's syndrome children in areas such as difficulties in taking their children to public places and more embarrassment and disappointment than the parents of the Down's syndrome children. Reports also indicated that autistic children had fewer activities that occupied them and lower scores on a scale that measured availability of services, and, consequently, poorer prospects for employment and independent living. Autistic children were also reported to be more disruptive of family integration as measured by activities such as family vacations, mealtimes, or outings. The autistic children themselves were reported to have more difficult personality characteristics or management problems than the Down's syndrome children.

A Characteristic Pattern of Stress

Similarities between data reported by Holroyd and McArthur (1976) for families of autistic children in California and data reported by Bristol (1979) for families in North Carolina suggest that there may be a characteristic pattern of stress associated with parenting an autistic child (Bristol & Schopler, 1983). In light of continuing professional confusion regarding the diagnosis of autism, it is noteworthy that mothers' descriptions of characteristics of autistic children in studies by independent investigators a continent apart are strikingly similar and differ considerably from maternal descriptions of characteristics of both Down's syndrome and psychiatric outpatient children (see Table 3.1; Bristol, 1984).

Stresses, then, in families of autistic children are both similar to and different from those experienced by families of children with other types of handicapping conditions. Stress varies depending upon the characteristics of the particular child, the particular family, and the developmental stage of both the child and the family.

Variation in Stress as a Function
of Child Characteristics

Bristol (1979) found that the number of coping problems in families of autistic children varied as a function of the age and sex, but not the birth order, of the autistic child. In this study, 40 mothers of autistic children aged 4–19 were selected from a TEACCH computer list without prior knowledge of the parents' willingness or ability to cope with their autistic children. A median split (9.5 years) was used to divide the fam-

TABLE 3.1

Comparison of Mean Child Problem Scores as Reported by Mothers of Autistic, Down's Syndrome, and Psychiatric Outpatient Children

	Child's diagnostic category							
	Autism[a]		Autism[b]		Down's syndrome[b]		Psychiatric outpatients[b]	
Child problems	$\overline{X}$	SD	$\overline{X}$	SD	$\overline{X}$	SD	$\overline{X}$	SD
Physical incapacitation	3.4	2.2	3.2	2.2	2.1	1.8	1.9	1.7
Lack of activities	2.3	1.6	2.7	1.8	1.2	1.7	1.7	1.7
Occupational limitations	4.0	1.2	3.9	1.0	3.3	0.8	1.9	1.8
Social obtrusiveness	2.6	1.2	2.8	1.1	2.2	1.4	1.8	1.6
Difficult personality	19.2	5.6	18.5	5.9	12.7	4.7	13.0	6.8

[a] North Carolina: Bristol (1979).
[b] California: Holroyd & McArthur (1976).

ilies into younger and older child age groups. Although autistic boys actually outnumber girls 4:1, to test for the effect of sex, an equal number of boys (20) and girls (20) were included in the study, approximately equally represented in both the younger (11 boys, 9 girls) and older (9 boys, 11 girls) age groups. These four groups of children from intact biological families were comparable in terms of social class, racial composition, number of children in the family, birth order of the autistic child (first- or later born), and number of hours of maternal employment.

Younger versus Older Autistic Children. One of the clearest findings was that mothers of older children, both boys and girls ($N = 20$; 9.5–19 years), reported significantly more parental coping problems and more adverse effects on family integration than mothers of younger children ($N = 20$; 4–9 years). This was true even though families in the older and younger groups did not differ in terms of socioeconomic status, number of children in the family, number of firstborn children, the children's mean IQ scores, or severity of the children's autism. The effect for age continued to be significant even when the mother's age, the number of other family stresses, and the degree of child's dependence were statistically corrected.

Two of the major reasons for the greater stress in this older age group were parental realization of the permanency of the child's handicap and a greater lack of activities and services for older autistic children. Parents of older autistic children scored significantly higher on a measure of pessimism regarding child outcome than parents of younger children, and also reported significantly more problems on scales related to lack of activities for the autistic children and general lack of services and prospects for independent living. Additional explanations will be discussed in the section "Adolescence."

Boys versus Girls. In study just described, Bristol (1979) also found that autistic boys had a more adverse effect on family integration than girls, and, when degree of child dependency was statistically controlled, boys had a more adverse effect on parent problems such as parental mood, attitude, and pessimism.

Greater stress for boys is consistent with findings by Farber (1959) for severely retarded children, for behavior-disordered children (Patterson, 1980), and for nonhandicapped children in divorced families (Hetherington, 1981). Unlike Farber's study, no interaction effect was found for age with sex and the measure of stress was not significantly correlated with social class.

The more adverse effect for boys may be related to intrinsic differences in boys such as larger physical size, greater irritability, less social responsiveness, and more difficult caretaking, as suggested by Bell (1968) for nonhandicapped children. An alternative cultural expectations explanation was proposed by Farber (1959) for retarded children. He suggested that, at least in lower socioeconomic class families, parents have higher career expectations for males than for females. Mothers of girls in the Bristol (1979) study, in fact, commented that girls could be taught to cook and do housekeeping and appeared less distressed that their daughters might not find competitive employment. Although there has been an evolution in parental attitudes toward female career roles, among our largely rural, mostly lower-middle or lower socioeconomic status families parents persisted in having higher career expectations for boys than for girls.

Since fixed child characteristics such as age and sex cannot be changed, an attempt was made to see if specific child characteristics amenable to intervention were predictive of stress for the total group. In fact, approximately three-quarters of the variance in reported maternal and family stress problems could be predicted on the basis of characteristics of the children and their environments. These characteristics included difficulty of the children's personality characteristics such as their management problems, their degree of dependency and need for assistance in self-help skills, and the perceived adequacy of the children's activities, services, and prospects for independent living (Bristol, 1979). The stress predicted was independent of socioeconomic status, the mother's age, or birth order of the child and was comparable in black and white families. Similar findings for families of children with a variety of other handicaps (Beckman-Bell, 1980) suggest that stress in families of handicapped children can be better understood as the impact of the child on the parents and not the other way around.

When the highest-stress and lowest-stress mothers in this group were compared (top and bottom quartiles), these same child characteristics discriminated the two groups as did the perceived adequacy of the families' informal social support network, maternal employment status, and child placement. The differentiation of these groups on the basis of these child characteristics was especially significant because the groups were otherwise comparable in terms of socioeconomic status, number of children in the family, mother's age, children's mean IQ, percentage of more severely autistic children, and number of mothers employed outside the home. It is interesting that the more fixed characteristics of the children (IQ, degree of severity of autism) did not differentiate the groups when those more amenable to intervention, such as degree of dependency and self-help skills, did do so.

Ambiguity of Handicap

Many professionals assume the autistic child's normal appearance should be related to lower stress than would be found in families of "obviously" handicapped children such as Down's syndrome or physically handicapped youngsters.

In fact, it appears that the very ambiguity of the autistic child's handicap contributes to increased family stress. In studies of general family stress, McCubbin and associates (McCubbin, Cauble, & Patterson, 1982) pointed out that ambiguity of the stressor increases the risk of family crisis by engendering disagreements both within and outside the family regarding what the proper course of action should be. Because autistic children appear physically normal and are often extremely attractive children, parents as well as professionals often disagree as to the existence, the nature, and the appropriate treatment for the disorder. The earlier discussion of psychogenic theories of autism should highlight this confusion.

In a recent study (Bristol, in press-b), less obviously handicapped autistic children were found to have a more adverse effect on families and especially on marital adjustment, at least before formal diagnosis, than those children whose handicap is more obvious.

In a study of parental estimates of their autistic children's developmental levels (Schopler & Reichler, 1972), parents of mildly autistic children were also much less accurate in their estimates than were parents of severely autistic children whose degree of handicap was clearer. The ambiguity of the less severely affected child's handicap makes it difficult for parents to know what to expect realistically from the child. Such ambiguity causes disagreements not only within the immediate and extended family, but even in the larger community regarding the appropriate response to the child's behavior.

The ambiguity caused by severely disordered behavior in a child who appears to be normal also affects the extent to which neighbors and the larger community either increase stress or provide support to the families of autistic children. Bizarre or disruptive behavior in church or at the local shopping mall by an obviously handicapped child may be greeted with disdain or even unwanted pity. The same behavior exhibited by a child who appears to be normal often engenders outright hostility and unsolicited advice on "proper parenting" that significantly increases stress, particularly in naive families who have not yet realized the biological basis for the child's disorder.

Parents who do not agree between themselves that their child is, in fact, handicapped may also delay bringing their child in for diagnosis and intervention. In in-depth interviews with families of autistic children (Bristol, in press-b), families noted that the mother usually recognized the severity of the child's disability first, but was often dissuaded from seeking services, either by the father who had less contact with the child or by relatives reluctant to acknowledge a handicap in "such a beautiful child." Such delay is also often encouraged by well-meaning professionals who suggest to the parent that the child will either "outgrow the problem" or, sometimes more destructively, may subtly imply that if the parent were more adequate the child's bizarre and deviant behavior would be under control.

Ambiguity of Outcome

Related to the issue of the ambiguity of the child's handicap has been the stress caused in families by the difficulty of forming realistic expectations regarding the child's prognosis. Two prevailing and contradictory myths regarding the child's learning ability have added to parental stress. On the one hand, autistic children were thought to have normal or better intellectual potential and, on the other hand, were excluded from public schools because they were thought to be unable to profit from instruction.

Kanner's early definition of autism was limited to children with certain peak skills in such areas as number manipulation or music. This led many professionals to assume that all autistic children had normal or even above-normal intelligence and caused them to raise such high expectations for all of these youngsters that parents were subsequently disappointed by the very real, although sometimes limited, progress those children made. This led also to the mistaken belief that autistic children were capable of doing whatever was asked of them, and failure to perform was seen as willful opposition. One autistic child known to the first author was a child who could sing the "Star Spangled Banner" but could not say "mama" or use any functional speech. Because of the complexity of the song the child could sing (although did not understand), the child's parents and many professionals who had worked with the child assumed that the child could, in fact, talk but chose not to. It is not difficult to imagine how much more stressful this child's lack of speech was to the parents than that of the obviously retarded or deaf child who clearly attempts but often fails at communication.

Repeated follow-up studies have shown (DeMyer, Barton, Alpern,

Kimberlin, Allen, Yang, & Steele, 1974; Gittelman & Birch, 1967; Lock-yer & Rutter, 1970) that most autistic children also suffer from varying degrees of retardation, although a minority of them (about 15–20%) display the higher intellectual functioning noted by Kanner.

Ironically, at the same time that some autistic children were reputed to have normal intelligence, they were also excluded from school (as were most other severely handicapped children) because it was thought that they were unable to profit from instruction. It is clear, however, that all autistic children, regardless of severity of the child's handicap, can profit from instruction. In a 4-year follow-up comparing autistic children randomly assigned to three classroom types, Rutter and Bartak (1973) found that all of the children increased their social skills and decreased their bizarre and disruptive behaviors. Two-thirds of the children learned to communicate verbally, one-third were reading on a third-grade level or better, and a third of the children learned the four basic arithmetic skills. Greater progress was made in the more highly structured, teacher-directed classrooms, although higher-functioning children required less structure than the more retarded autistic children, a finding previously demonstrated by Schopler and associates (Schopler et al., 1971). In general, children with tested IQs above 50 made progress in academic areas. Children with IQ's below 50 made progress in behavioral and nonacademic areas.

Similar results have been found in the statewide TEACCH program in North Carolina. All autistic children can learn if an individualized education plan keyed to the child's unique pattern of skills and deficits is carried out in a responsive and structured environment (Schopler & Reichler, 1979; Schopler, Reichler, & Lansing, 1980). Children with IQs above 50 have been known to make marked progress, some making dramatic improvements as late as adolescence (Lotter, 1978; Rutter, 1978) or even early adulthood (Park, 1983). In a moving account of her autistic daughter's progress into adulthood, Park points out that because of myths regarding the educability of autistic children her daughter was not able to attend school full time until she was 14 years old (Park, 1983). Surely our estimates of outcomes for autistic children and accounts of stress in these families should be tempered by a realization of how inadequate our knowledge and services were for autistic persons now in adulthood.

Because of these real and imagined characteristics of autistic children, their families experience considerable stress. This stress varies with the age of the child and the developmental stage of the family.

A Developmental Progression of Stresses
in Families of Autistic Children

Stages in the Overall Family Life Cycle

Any discussion of a developmental progression of stresses must take into consideration the developmental stages both of the family and of the child. Sociologists have generally attended more closely to the former and psychologists to the latter. Although particular stages of family development discussed vary somewhat depending on the author cited, there is evidence that family tasks, roles, expectations, and levels of satisfaction vary depending on whether (1) there are no children, (2) the oldest child is under 6, (3) the oldest is 6–12, (4) the oldest child is 13–20, (5) the children have gone off to live independently, (7) the wage earner or earners are retired, or (8) one or more of the family members dies (Burr, 1970; Hill, 1970).

A detailed discussion of life cycles in families of handicapped children is beyond the scope of this chapter (see Turnbull, Brotherson, & Summers, in press, and Chapter 6 of this volume for more complete reviews). However, a few examples of how the stage of family development affects stress in these families of autistic children should suffice to highlight the importance of maintaining a life-span perspective on families in order to design or interpret research on stress in families of both handicapped and normal children.

Normal Family Stress

An important consideration related to family stress is acknowledging that whether or not these families had autistic children they would be experiencing some predictable stresses at different points in the family life cycle. For example, Burr's cross-sectional life-span research (1970) with families of nonhandicapped children suggests that mothers and fathers appeared to have roughly similar patterns of satisfaction with their children over the family life span with greatest satisfaction during the children's preschool years and after the children are grown and living independently, and less satisfaction during the children's school years. The lowest point in satisfaction for fathers was clearly during the children's adolescent years. One of the lowest points in marital happiness also occurred during the children's adolescent periods. During this time, these parents of nonhandicapped also reported their lowest levels of satisfaction with companionship, financial management, sex, and allocation of household tasks. Some of the stress experienced by parents of adolescent autistic children, then, may be a "normal" response to the child's increasing sexuality and attempts at independence as well as to the "normal" midlife issues faced by all families. Parents of nonhandicapped adolescent children, too, are often facing frustration of early career plans or, in the case of homemakers, mourning the loss of opportunities for a career and dealing with their own fears of aging and mortality (Levinson, 1978, Sheehy, 1976). These "normal" problems and swings in satisfaction should also be expected for families of autistic and other handicapped children.

The question in interpreting research on families of autistic children (or any handicapped children) during any stage of the family life cycle is to what extent the normative family stresses are accentuated or exaggerated by having a handicapped child, which stresses are really caused by inadequacy of services rather than the child's age or family stage per se, and which stresses are, in fact, necessary if adolescents or young adults are eventually to achieve some measure of functioning independent of their families. The family that appears at one point to be in crisis might, in fact, be the family dealing with the risk (and the temporary failures and setbacks) associated with helping the child to function without the constant guidance of the parents. Families who maintain the status quo and do not allow or encourage such independence may appear more well adjusted or stress-free in the short run, but may have gained their equilibrium by sacrificing their child's growth toward independence and/or their own development as a family. This is why longitudinal studies are essential. Data collected at a single point in time may be misleading.

Much of the research on stress in families of handicapped children has also relied on instruments for which comparative norms for nonhandicapped children have not been available. In these cases, if a comparison sample of families of nonhandicapped children of similar ages is not included, it is not possible to judge what the "normal" stress in such families may be and we may do a grave injustive to these families by exaggerating apparent dysfunction found.

Arrest in the Life Cycle

Early work by Farber (1959) suggested that the presence of a severely handicapped child in the family may result in an arrest in the life cycle of the family and may affect the entire patterning of family roles. Such effects may only be seen by studying families over time. Generalizing conclusions from one child age or stage of family development to another may be misleading. For example, Silverman and Hill (1967) indicated that during the period when children are preschoolers, most mothers of nonhandicapped children (although a rapidly decreasing majority) traditionally do not work outside the home and generally assume major responsibility for care of the dependent children. Although mothers of autistic or other severely handicapped children during this period face even greater demands than mothers in families of nonhandicapped children, it is likely that their friends who have young normal children are also often "homebound," dependent on babysitters, and either postponing or struggling to juggle career and home obligations. The child's dependency, then, though it is a far more severe for parents of young autistic and other handicapped children than for parents of nonhandicapped children, is at least in synchrony with the normal stage of family development at that time.

Later, however, when families of normal children become increasingly independent and parents of nonhandicapped children are free of expensive and often difficult child care arrangements, families of autistic and other severely handicapped children are still dealing with developmentally young and often very dependent children. This contrast may be especially marked when the nonhandicapped child reaches adulthood and leaves home, and parental satisfaction with life rises to early parenthood levels (Burr, 1970). The prospect of permanent dependency can so overwhelm parents in these later stages of development that they "burn out" in their ability to care for their autistic children and seek institutionalization for autistic children who might have been able to function in a less restrictive environment.

What research evidence is there regarding a developmental progression of stress in families of autistic children? A limited amount of systematic investigation of developmental issues has been attempted by various researchers, much of it (including our own research) cross-sectional or retrospective rather than longitudinal. It is presented, however, to emphasize that there may be developmental changes in stress and to stimulate interest and additional research in this important area.

Although this discussion of stresses is divided into preschool, early school age, and adolescence stages, it is important to remember that coping with stress is a process, not a solution achieved at one point in time. Some stresses, such as the need for appropriate educational services or parental fatigue, are common across all developmental stages, although they may take different forms in one period than in another. Others, such as the need for a clear diagnosis, may be resolved in the early stages, while still others such as embarrassment in public may surface during the preschool stage, abate somewhat during the elementary school years, and then resurface in adolescence. The divisions into time periods, then, are somewhat artificial, but represent an attempt to focus on those stresses that appear to be most salient to parents of children in that particular stage. The majority of the information reported by families in our own studies was gathered from mothers and siblings. An intensive study of fathers has been initiated.

In the course of our interviews with 40 parents in the Bristol (1979) study and with 27 additional mothers of autistic children aged 2–10 (Bristol, in press-b), we identified specific stresses common to both boys and girls in the preschool, elementary, and adolescent periods. Many of these are similar, and some are different from, those suggested by Turnbull et al. (in press) for retarded children and those found by DeMyer (1979) and DeMyer and Goldberg (1983) for autistic children.

Maternal Stress: The Preschool Period. Mothers of preschool children emphasized the stress caused by the ambiguity of the child's handicap and the need for a clear diagnosis on which professionals would agree. Although early diagnosis may be important for all handicapped children (Turnbull et al., in press), the ambiguity of the autistic child's handicap makes it especially critical for these families. Such a clear and early diagnosis helps to make a family "invulnerable" to the stress of self-doubt and self-criticism (Akerley, 1975; DeMyer & Goldberg, 1983). In addition, because autism is a relatively rare condition, some clinicians asked to diagnose these children have never seen an autistic child before and add to the parent's confusion through their own diagnostic inexperience.

The problem of accepting the child's handicap was also one that began in the preschool years, but resurfaced for parents of autistic children of all ages as the reality of the autistic children's limitations gradually became apparent when they failed to achieve normal milestones such as entering "regular school," dating, or obtaining a job. Because of the autistic child's normal physical appearance and the frequent presence of "splinter skills," acceptance of the child's handicap is more difficult than it is for parents of more obviously handicapped children.

Mothers of preschool children also noted the chronic fatigue caused by the constant vigilance required for some of these children who were extremely hyperactive, in a constant blur of motion during the day and frequently up during the nights. Mothers spoke of fears for children who had no concept of danger and could not be left alone in the yard or even in another room for fear they would walk into traffic or turn on stoves in the night. Fear at this point was often for the physical survival of the child because of actual dangers and poor food habits that sometimes consisted of eating only two or three foods. In cases where the child was first born, mothers also spoke of the stress caused by their own lack of confidence before they received training in handling their autistic child.

The problem of not knowing whether the children were sick or hurt because they often failed to register pain and could not communicate their distress was frequently mentioned by parents. Although such communication may also be difficult for retarded or deaf children, these children generally use gestures or facial expressions to try to communicate their needs. The only distress signals used by very young autistic children may be crying or having a tantrum, and it is up to the parent to guess whether the child is ill, irritable, or wants something. Some of these children also did not appear to recognize their parents, and parents reported feeling rejected or rebuffed by the children in spite of the Herculean efforts they were investing in them. Most, however, felt that the child knew them "in his own way" and said that the child would be aware of and would object to their absence (Bristol, 1979; Bristol, in press-b).

The lack of trained babysitters was a source of stress during the preschool period and continued to be reported by parents of children of all ages.

The Early School Years. By the time their children were of school age, most parents who had received training had established a routine for caring for the children and the acute crises of the uncertain preschool period abated somewhat. When the children were 6–12, parents generally established mealtime, bedtime, nighttime patterns that were acceptable to the family, although messy and finicky eating and toileting problems often continued well beyond expected developmental levels.

For some families the child's hyperactive behavior was a significant problem, although in most cases it decreased as the child approached adolescence. Before the hyperactivity decreased, however, parents of these children spoke of being constantly "on red alert," unable to predict what the child would do next, and often felt that there were few places they could visit because of their fear that the child would inadvertently break something or disrupt the whole occasion. One mother noted that she felt "chained like an extension cord" to this dynamo of activity.

Parental fatigue continued to be a problem, although most families during this period were at least getting a regular night's rest through a combination of improved child behavior and, where necessary, child-proofing the home through locks and bolts on bedroom and outside doors. In spite of this, mothers sometimes expressed the feeling that they, not the child, felt fenced in by the elaborate system of safeguards.

In some families, the child's destructive behavior was a problem during this period. Although their behavior is often seen as accidental DeMyer (1979), these children often made more work for their parents by pulling down of drapes or shades, or pulling threads out of furniture.

During this period, parents saw more clearly the extent of the child's social handicaps and were concerned about the child's lack of friendships and ability to relate to other children. Other inappropriate social behaviors such as smelling objects or touching visitors or strangers that were less offensive in tiny children became an increasing matter of concern as the child grew larger. Parents at this time began to have some real sense of the severity of the child's impairment.

Tantrums, however, generally subsided during this period as both parent and child became more adept at communicating, sometimes through the use of signing, communication boards, or other more informal means of nonverbal communication.

One major source of stress reduction during this period was the respite provided by the child's (usually) full day in school. For some mothers, this meant an opportunity to work outside the home or to become more involved in community activities, school, or hobbies. Half of the mothers in the Bristol (1979) study of children aged 4–19, however, still felt that the autistic child did limit the development of some family member, usually themselves. Mothers especially noted that although their children were in school all day, they still could not get suitable employment because they often did not have anyone who could "manage" the autistic child before and after school, on school holidays, or in the summer. This often caused financial worries for families as increasing numbers of mothers of nonhandicapped children in the neighborhood joined the work force and supplemented family incomes. For some families this meant that even though services for their autistic child were provided free of charge by TEACCH or the public schools, they were still strapped financially because of the limitation to one income. In lower-income families, as inflation soared this meant real need in terms of necessities. For higher-income families, the lack of maternal employment meant the sacrifice of trips, children's piano lessons, or other "extras" that their neighbors were increasingly able to afford.

As children grew older, parents increasingly sought short-term overnight respite care. Sometimes this was needed in times of particular crisis, but most families expressed a preference for regular and periodic respite care in order to prevent having stress build to crisis proportions.

Adolescence. Some of the sources of stress in adolescent autistic children have been discussed in the section "Younger versus older autistic children." For a detailed review of the concept of autism in adolescents, the research literature, parental accounts, and interventions for this group, see Schopler and Mesibov, 1983.

Because of the meager research base regarding autistic adolescents and adults, and because few of the autistic children now grown have received early and continued appropriate intervention, knowledge of family functioning in this group is very tentative. Many autistic adolescents and adults did not receive any intervention services until the passage of Public Law (PL) 94–142 (the Education for All Handicapped Children Act of 1975) in 1976, and many are still not receiving services that could be deemed appropriate or effective. For this reason, it is virtually impossible to know whether many of the observed stresses are related to the age of the children studied or whether they represent the cumulative effect of the stress of inadequate or unavailable services. This caveat should be kept in mind in reading the remainder of this chapter and in considering differences across descriptions of this population, especially descriptions of child outcome.

In our earlier study (Bristol, 1979) we did find that parents of autistic children in adolescence were experiencing the stress of dealing with the emerging sexuality and independence of their adolescents, the stress of realizing both the extent and the permanency of the child's handicap, the fatigue of "perpetual parenthood" (DeMyer, 1979) and of endless battles for services, and the fear of what will happen in the future when they are no longer able to care for the child.

Our parents of adolescents also noted many of the improvements in behavior summarized by Mesibov (1983) in his review of the follow-up and outcome literature on autistic children. On the basis of his review, Mesibov concluded that studies have shown there is a general improvement in specific skills during adolescence and adulthood. Hyperactivity generally diminishes, behavior is more manageable, ritualistic and compulsive behaviors decrease, speech, language, and self-help skills improve, and the children become more sociable.

On the negative side, he noted—as did some families in our study—the onset of seizure activity and the relative stability of IQ in spite of improved language and behavior. (However, Park [1983] noted that her autistic daughter gained more than 25 IQ points between the ages of 14 and 24. It may not be coincidental that Park's daughter also began full-time schooling at the age of 14). Mesibov attributed the mixed results of studies of aggressive behavior to the fact that the actual frequency of these behaviors may have decreased but that the dramatic impact of any such occurrences may increase because of the increased size and strength of older autistic people, a fact noted by our parents of aggressive adolescents.

One of the major sources of stress during all developmental periods was finding adequate and appropriate services, especially school services and particularly in remote, rural areas. Inadequate educational programs were an acute source of stress for parents who had received training and had seen from their own direct experience that their child could make progress given adequate structure and proper programs.

Although there was continuing stress during this period, mothers of children in this age group also recounted an awakening sense of themselves as survivors, as capable people who had learned through training and through their own trial-and-error experience that they could handle not only their own "difficult" child, but also "difficult" professionals, school boards, and sometimes even legislatures when services were needed for their children. Both mothers and fathers who were active in groups such as the National Society for Children and Adults with Autism seemed to have a particularly strong sense of their own strength, as they saw the whole service ecology for their autistic children change, largely through parental advocacy that culminated in both state and federal legislation guaranteeing their children's rights.

McCubbin (1979) pointed out, in his studies of families of prisoners of war and men missing in action, that coping with stress is an active, not just a passive, process. Families who did more than just survive or endure, who through collective action actually changed the resources available to them such as college tuition for their children or access to information, were more able to cope with the continuing stress of their father-missing situation. Similar collective action for parents of autistic children not only increases resources for families of autistic children and parents' sense of potency, but also provides parents with a valuable norm reference group on whom they can depend for advice and for affirmation of their efforts on behalf of their autistic child.

Fathers and Stress

Some fathers, especially fathers who had minimal contact with the child, refused to accept the diagnosis of autism as did other relatives and friends, thereby increasing the mother's stress by suggesting that the child's lack of performance was either willful or due to maternal inadequacy. Early diagnosis and parent education helped mothers to have confidence in their own ability and to explain the child's condition to spouses and other relatives.

In the preschool period, before formal diagnosis, mothers also reported that fathers who failed to realize the significance of the child's handicap resented the fact that mothers not only spent all their time with the autistic child, but were so tired and saddened by the child's problems that they had little time or energy to devote to their marital relationship. Once the child was known to be handicapped, most fathers were more sympathetic and supportive.

During the 6–12 age period, it became increasingly difficult for even minimally involved fathers to deny the reality of the autistic child's handicap. As Tallman (1965) pointed out in his study of retarded children, the father's role is often conceived of as a task-oriented or instrumental one and has traditionally focused on achieving and being concerned about his children's achievement in the "outside" world. Tallman suggested that fathers may be more affected than mothers by the social stigma of the child's handicap and be most stressed when the child comes into contact with the outside world and fails to conform to its norms. Autistic children's delayed school entry or exclusion from "regular" education, their bizarre behaviors such as hand flapping in public places and their difficulty in grasping social rules and participation in competitive activities such as sports may be particularly stressful for fathers. One father of a handsome but severely autistic son recounted the stress he experienced when he took his son to a baseball game and sat behind a man with a nonhandicapped son who jabbered away about specific players and particularly good plays on the field. "Not only can't he play ball," the father lamented, "he won't even watch it!" All the boy did was flap his hands and get upset, covering his ears when the huge crowd roared its approval or disapproval of the game.

On the other hand, fathers often had greater distance from the child's immediate problems and sometimes seemed more aware of the impact of the child on the wife and the rest of the family. In such cases fathers played an important role in helping the family avoid an autistic-child-centered home and in attending to the needs of all the family members.

Effects on Siblings

Although older siblings sometimes resented the seemingly inordinate amount of parental attention their preschool autistic brother or sister required, many were proud of their ability to "teach" their siblings. A young autistic child who engages in hand flapping or twirling is still considered "cute" and most siblings appeared to feel no marked embarrassment regarding their young sibling. Younger brothers and sisters close in age to the autistic child were reported not even to be aware of the child's handicap and appeared to accept the fact that "that's just the way Anthony is."

Two TEACCH studies of siblings of autistic children in the school-age group addressed the issue of impact on these other, often neglected family members. McHale, Sloan, and Simeonsson (1982) analyzed maternal ratings of sibling relationships and in-depth interviews with siblings. They found that siblings in families of 30 autistic, 30 retarded, and 30 normal children matched for sex, age, and birth order (older versus younger than the target child) of both target child (ages 6–15) and siblings looked very similar both in the interview and on the maternal ratings. The few statistically significant differences between the groups were minimal and no more than a 1-point mean group difference on these 5- and 6-point scales. The authors noted, however, that these mean differences obscure the fact that there are considerable differences in variability of responses in the handicapped and nonhandicapped groups. Responses of siblings of nonhandicapped children clustered around the mean value on each interview scale item. In contrast, although mean scores for both the siblings of retarded and autistic children resembled those of siblings of nonhandicapped children, in fact about half of the siblings in each of the handicapped groups gave very positive and half fairly negative views about their sibling relationship. (Parental estimates by DeMyer [1979] also indicated that 54% of the parents thought that siblings were positively affected by the presence of the autistic child, 30% negatively affected, and the remainder somewhere in between.)

A subsequent study of siblings (ages 5–13) of autistic children (Mates, 1982) that assessed the effect of sibling age and sex on sibling home adjustment, school adjustment, achievement, and sibling self-esteem did not find predicted age and sex effects, and generally found siblings to score at or above norms for nonhandicapped standardization samples. A related study (Bristol, 1982a) has investigated the extent to which sibling adjustment is related to characteristics of the autistic child and/or family characteristics.

Negative effects on siblings, then, although sometimes present are not universal. In some cases sibling personality attributes such as self-esteem may conceivably be enhanced by the understanding and skills acquired in dealing with an autistic sibling (Mates, 1982). Without a closely matched control sample, however, such statements are suggestive rather than conclusive, but indicate a fruitful area for future research.

Successful Adaptation in Families of Autistic Children

"Invulnerable" Parents

Although researchers have generally focused on the negative effects of autistic children on families, parents themselves—while acknowledging the very real difficulties involved—have written convincingly of their successes in coping with their autistic children (Akerley, 1975; Dewey, 1983; Park, 1983). Akerley (1975), in paraphrasing Anthony's (1974) description of the "invulnerable" child, provided a description of "invulnerable" parents of autistic children who are healthy, resilient, competent persons in spite of an environment that is stressful in the extreme. She described them as having a "stubborn resistance to the process of being engulfed by the illness; a curiosity in studying the etiology, diagnosis, symptoms, and treatment of the illness" (p. 275) reaching a level of knowledge that is equal or greater than many professionals. She noted that they have the capacity to develop an objective, realistic, and yet distinctly compassionate approach to the child's handicap and that they typically have a history of successfully dealing with other stresses before being forced to cope with their child's autism. With support and encouragement from successful parenting experiences with a normal child, they develop an understanding of the handicap as both a personal experience invading their lives and a phenomenon to be investigated and treated. From a clinical point of view, Marcus (1977) has also discussed coping in these families. Having described the enormous stresses these families experience, we will discuss the research evidence regarding specific factors related to either successful or unsuccessful coping in these families.

A Model for General Family Coping

Before discussing successful coping in these families of autistic children, it is helpful to consider some of what researchers have discovered about successful coping with stress in families of nonhandicapped children. (For a more detailed discussion see Burr, 1973; McCubbin et al., 1982). First, it is clear that not every stressor, no matter how severe, causes a family crisis. Hill (1949, 1958) proposed a classic *ABCX* model of coping with family stress. In his review of research on the impact of a variety of stressful events ranging from military separations to natural disasters, Hill noted that whether a particular stressor or stressful event A will result in a family crisis X depended on characteristics of the stressful event itself and on its concomitant hardships A interacting with both the crisis meeting resources B the family has and the subjective definition C the family makes of the event. Family crisis was less likely, for example, when the family saw the source of the stressor as outside the family (e.g., a tornado is stressful but is less apt to cause a crisis because the family does not blame itself for its occurrence).

McCubbin (1979) has extended Hill's model by integrating into it the importance of active coping strategies in dealing with resulting crisis, the pile-up of other hardships (financial, etc.) that often result from a particular stressor, and the importance of studying adaptation, both precrisis and postcrisis, over time.

Hill's Model and Families of Autistic Children

The application of Hill's model to families of autistic children has been discussed in detail elsewhere (Bristol & Schopler, 1983). It was supported empirically in research with families of autistic and developmentally disabled children (Bristol, in press-b) that included 45 mothers recruited from consecutive referrals to the TEACCH program in a study of family adaptation to their disabled children. Of these families, 27 had autistic children and the remaining 18 had nonautistic children with significant communication and/or behavioral problems. The children ranged in age from 2 to 10 with a mean age of 5 years.

Data were collected through structured interviews, interviewer ratings, parental self-assessments, and direct assessments of the child. The study tested Hill's model of family coping with stress and identified factors associated with successful family adaptation to the autistic and nonautistic handicapped children.

The most striking result of this study was that, in spite of the severe and continuing stress to which these parents were exposed because of their autistic child, the vast majority were functioning well both as persons and as families. The divorce or separation rate for this group of young families was not higher than that for the general population in the area. Furthermore, of those mothers who remained married, 80% were reported to be happily married. The number of depressive symptoms reported by mothers of autistic children was comparable to that reported by the mothers of the nonautistic, communication-impaired children and was comparable to or lower than that reported for mothers of children with other types of handicaps (Bradshaw & Lawton, 1978; Burden, 1980; Cox et al., 1975; McMichael, 1971). Over 90% of the mothers were rated as being accepting of the child in spite of the difficulties involved. Single parents (N = 10) reported and were rated as having more difficulty than two-parent families, but differences in socioeconomic status between two-parent and single-parent families make such differences difficult to interpret. Parental and clinical accounts of successful adaptation for the majority of families, then, were corroborated in this research.

A subsequent test of Hill's ABCX model to identify factors associated with more successful adaptation within the group was also positive. Using canonical correlation techniques and adjusting the coefficient to take into account the ratio of variables to subjects, Bristol (in press-b) found that a model including descriptors of child characteristics and other family stresses (A), family resources including specific coping strategies and formal and informal sources of support (B); and maternal definitions of the meaning of the child's handicap (C) significantly predicted marital adjustment, maternal depressive symptoms, and an interviewer rating of family adaptation to the child with a canonical correlation of .80 (p < .001). The model also significantly predicted each of the family outcomes individually (marital adjustment, maternal depression, and family adaptation to the child) yielding adjusted coefficients that accounted for 61, 38, and 53% of the variance in the respective criteria. Knowledge of characteristics of the child, family resources, and maternal beliefs, then, do significantly predict some kinds of successful adaptation in families of autistic children. What specific variables, in addition to the child characteristics already discussed, then, might we expect to be related to either successful or unsuccessful adaptation in these families? The remainder of this section will highlight some of the findings of research studies in this area.

Maternal Beliefs and Successful Adaptation

In the study of 45 mothers of autistic and communication handicapped children, Bristol (in press-b) found that although marital adjustment, number of depressive symptoms, and rating of family adaptation were related to child characteristics, they were also significantly related to maternal beliefs about the child's handicap and to family resources (see following section). Mothers were seen before formal diagnosis of their children and before some of them were aware of the biological basis for their child's handicap. Although the majority of mothers expressed no guilt regarding the child's handicap, those who did endorse statements implying that the child had a handicap because of their inadequacy as parents or as a punishment for something someone in the family had done (approximately one-third of the mothers) reported fewer happy marriages, more depressive symptoms, and were rated by interviewers as having made a less-successful family adaptation to the autistic child. As pointed out earlier, both the ambiguity of the child's handicap and the previous parental-blame theories that fuel such guilt could be expected to have a negative effect on family coping with the autistic child.

Family Resources and Successful Adaptation

A number of resources such as the psychological, educational, material, and interpersonal resources of families and of individual family members have been shown to be related to successful coping with family stress (Gallagher, Beckman-Bell, & Cross, 1983; Gallagher, Cross, & Scharfman, 1981; McCubbin et al., 1982). A detailed discussion of family resources and successful adaptation in families of autistic children is beyond the scope of this chapter (see Bristol, in press-a), but the importance of family environment, informal social support, and specific coping responses in the 45 families described earlier can be summarized briefly.

Family Psychosocial Environment

A number of researchers (Angell, 1936; Hill & Hansen, 1962; McCubbin, Joy, Cauble, Comeau, Patterson, & Needle, 1980) have found that certain family styles or attributes appear to make some families more resistant to family crisis or more able to regenerate themselves after such a crisis. These family characteristics include cohesion, integration, and adaptability. More recently, in a study of families with children with spina bifida, Nevin and McCubbin (1979) found that family cohesion and an active recreational orientation together with selected coping patterns and severity of the child's handicap were related to levels of family stress.

In a study related to that described earlier, the family environments of the 27 families of autistic and 18 families of nonautistic handicapped children were assessed using the Moos Family Environment Scales (Bristol, in press-a). Dimensions of family relationships (cohesion, expressiveness, and conflict), personal growth (independence, achievement orientation, intellectual–cultural orientation, active recreational orientation, and moral–religious emphasis), and system maintenance (organization and control) were reported by mothers of the autistic and nonautistic handicapped children; these were compared with national norms and their relationships to family adaptation were assessed.

Results indicated that successful adaptation to the child for the total group was most closely related to the degree of reported cohesion, expressiveness, and active recreational orientation of the families. Families who supported one another, who were able to express their emotions, and who participated in social and recreational activities outside the home or with persons outside the home fared better than those with lower scores on these scales.

Mean scores for both families of autistic and nonautistic handicapped children were similar to Moos's national norms of well-adjusted families on 8 of the 10 scales. Both of the handicapped groups reported a higher moral–religious emphasis and a lower level of involvement in active recreational pursuits. Although mean scores for the nonautistic sample approached ± 1 SD of the means for the norm group on these scales, only the families of autistic children had mean scores beyond those limits. The moral–religious emphasis will be discussed in the section "Coping Strategies," but the lack of recreational activities outside the family for families of autistic children is of particular concern given the importance of such activities to successful family adaptation just noted. The bizarre, often hyperactive and disruptive behavior of autistic children appears to restrict these families more than that of other handicapped but nonautistic family groups. In their study of autistic adolescents and adults, DeMyer and Goldberg (1983) found that parents felt that having an autistic child had had a more serious effect on family recreation than on any of the other 10 family areas studied. Unless trained babysitters or respite care is available, it is unlikely that parents will be able to participate in these outside activities. Our findings indicate (in only a correlational, not a causal, way) that such a lack of participation may take a toll not only on the parents themselves, but also on their ability to cope with their autistic child.

Informal Social Support

In addition to drawing on their own resources, mothers depend on support, both instrumental (e.g., actual assistance with tasks) and expressive (emotional), from an informal network of immediate and extended family, neighbors, and other parents in similar situations. Such support has been linked to positive family outcomes in situations as diverse as complications of pregnancy (Nuckolls, Cassel, & Kaplan, 1972) and coping with unemployment (Gore, 1978). The importance of such social support was demonstrated in the study of families drawn from consecutive referrals (Bristol, in press-a, in press-b) and in the earlier study (Bristol, 1979) of 40 mothers of autistic children. In the latter study, perceived adequacy of such informal social support was significantly related to parental and family stress for the total group and differentiated the highest and lowest stress families otherwise comparable in terms of demographic factors and severity of the child's handicap. Although both groups reported an almost identical degree of support from their own children, the lowest-stress mothers reported more adequate support from spouses, relatives, and other parents of handicapped children.

In the Bristol (in press-b) study, family adaptation to the child as rated by the interviewer was more closely related to perceived adequacy of informal social support than to severity of the child's handicap. The strongest relationship was noted between successful family adaptation and perceived support from the spouse. Mothers who felt this strong support from the child's father were not only rated as having a more successful adaptation to the child, but also reported happier marriages and fewer depressive symptoms. In this study, support from relatives was again significant, but the majority of these just-referred mothers (62 %) did not know any other parents of handicapped children on whom they could call for help. An important function of intervention should be to help parents establish these contacts, either informally or through membership in organizations such as the National Society for Autistic Children and Adults. Previous work with "experienced" parents suggests that such linkages are related to lower levels of stress.

Coping Strategies

Discussion of support networks often seems to imply a rather passive role for families in dealing with stress. As McCubbin (1979) has pointed out, however, there is much that parents can do to cope actively with stress. These coping responses—which include both actions designed to change the stressful situation and actions or beliefs required to tolerate, ignore, or minimize the stressful situation—are important determinants of a family's ability to endure stress over time. In the Bristol (in press-a) study, mothers indicated which of 45 specific coping responses on a modified Coping Health Inventory for Parents (McCubbin & Patterson, 1981) they used to cope with the stress of their handicapped child and indicated how helpful they perceived each to be. The first pattern of coping responses included those aimed at maintaining family integration, cooperation, and an optimistic definition of the situation. It included items such as "Telling myself I have many things to be thankful for" and "Doing things together as a family." The second pattern or factor included those aimed at maintaining self-esteem and social support outside the family, and included items such as "Engaging in relationships and friendships which help me to feel important and appreciated." The third factor involved seeking services, information, and carrying out prescribed activities. It was adapted from McCubbin's original third factor to be suitable for a nonmedical setting. Coping scores were then related to the more objective interviewer rating of family adaptation to the handicapped child.

All 45 coping strategies were used by at least some of the mothers. Each of the 45 were thought to be "extremely helpful" by at least one of the parents, and 33 of the 45 were thought to be "no help at all" by at least one of the parents. Since parents were seen after referral, but before receipt of any services for their children, professionals did not play a central role in their coping repertoires at this time.

The most helpful coping strategies used by at least two-thirds of the families were (in decreasing order of helpfulness) (1) believing that the program (TEACCH) from which they were seeking help had their family's best interests at heart, (2) learning how to help their children improve, (3) believing in God, (4) talking over personal feelings and concerns with their spouses, (5) building closer relationships with spouses, (6) trying to maintain a stable family life, (7) developing themselves as persons, (8) telling themselves that they had many things to be thankful for, (9) doing things with their children, and (10) believing that their children will get better. Among the least helpful were (1) eating (worry about becoming overweight presumably compounded the original stress) and (2) allowing themselves to get angry. Parents remarked that although it felt good to let off steam they subsequently felt guilty for their impatience or lack of tolerance.

To determine if patterns of coping responses were related to better family adaptation, the relationship of the three factor scores with the interviewer rating of adaptation was then assessed. Higher scores on all three factors (i.e., more coping strategies and/or greater utility of various strategies) were significantly related to more favorable interviewer ratings. Coping scores for mothers of autistic children on these three factors were comparable to those reported by Nevin and McCubbin (1979) for mothers of children with cystic fibrosis. Apparently, coping with a handicapped child may elicit similar levels of coping regardless of type of handicap, at least before any specific training or intervention.

Maternal Employment and Successful Adaptation

In two consecutive studies (Bristol, 1979; in press-a) the number of hours of maternal employment was not significantly related to stress in families. In the comparison of the highest- and lowest-stress families in the earlier study (Bristol, 1979), there was no difference in the number of mothers employed outside the home in either group, but a marked difference in the number of mothers in each group who were satisfied with their present employment status. The majority of mothers in the lowest-stress group were doing what it was they wanted to do, whether staying home with their children or working outside the home. In the highest-stress group, the majority were doing something other than what they would have chosen. Apparently for these groups the difference was not one of working or not working outside the home, but having the option to do what one chose. Since the highest-stress group also had children who were more difficult, employment choices and/or stress in staying home may have been related to characteristics of the child or availability of child care for a hard-to-manage child.

Implications for Intervention

We have reviewed how a unidirectional research emphasis on the impact of parents on their autistic children led to one-sided understanding and treatment. A considerable portion of this chapter was devoted to these early research trends because they played a significant role in blocking or detracting from appropriate treatment. Moreover, there is considerable evidence that this unidirectional, psychodynamic theory increased the stress parents experienced beyond that generated by their child's autism (Schopler & Loftin, 1969). This was partially corrected by the development of a research paradigm that acknowledged reciprocal parent–child interaction, including the effects of the autistic child on his or her parents. Having discussed these research directions, we were able then to review some of the stress and coping factors we studied directly in families with autistic children, using a research approach that studied these children in the larger, ecological context of their families and their communities.

We have traced the path of stresses in these families across the child's developmental stages. The family's needs for services also follow a parallel path across these developmental periods and are related to factors that increase or decrease stress in these families. Factors predictive of stress and coping include such things as the ambiguity of the

child's handicap and unwarranted maternal self-blame, specific characteristics of the autistic children themselves, lack of child activities and
services, the extent to which parents are able to function as a cohesive
group and to participate in recreational activities outside the home, and
the adequacy of the family's formal and informal support network. Each
of these findings suggests needed services, and each may present more of
a problem during one developmental period than another. Some specific
intervention needs implied by these findings include early diagnosis and
parent education, respect for parental priorities in designing intervention programs, a family-focused rather than a child-centered approach
to intervention, responsiveness to developmental needs of both the child
and the family, and a comprehensive service system that provides a supportive environment not only for the child, but also for the family.

Because of the ambiguity of the child's handicap and unwarranted
maternal self-blame, there is a pressing need for early and consistent
diagnosis of the child's handicap and early parent education regarding
the biological nature of the child's disorder. One child whom the first
author knew had received 24 different diagnoses and a number of conflicting intervention programs before he was diagnosed as autistic and
appropriate treatment begun. Although there is at present no medical
test that unequivocally establishes the existence of autism, important
strides have been made in developing objective and reasonably reliable
and valid assessment instruments for the diagnosis of autism even in
young children (Schopler, Reichler, DeVellis, & Daly, 1980).

Since certain child characteristics or behaviors may be particularly
stressful to parents, it is also critical that parents' input is sought and
their priorities respected in designing intervention programs for their
own children. Behavior management problems, lack of self-help skills,
and lack of appropriate services may be particularly stressful for
parents and demand a high priority in programming. Because of the importance of both family cohesion and the involvement of parents in
recreational activities outside of the family, it is also essential for an intervention program to have a family focus rather than simply a child
focus (Bristol & Gallagher, 1982). Such a focus keeps professionals sensitive to the needs of all family members, and prevents programs from
making such excessive demands on parents that the development of the
autistic child is facilitated at the expense of other family members.

Programs and services must also be responsive to the particular developmental needs of both the child and the family. In a retrospective
study of service needs of families of autistic children, DeMyer and Goldberg (1983) noted a consistent developmental pattern of intervention
needs. Table 3.2 summarizes the most frequently cited needs for each

TABLE 3.2
The Five Most Frequently Reported Family Service Needs for Each
Developmental Period in the DeMyer and Goldberg (1983) Study

Age group (years)	N	Service needs
1–5	23	Early and consistent diagnosis
		Respite services
		Parent or sibling counseling
		Good day- and year-long educational program
		Babysitting[a]
		Financial assistance[a]
6–12	23	Curriculum additions to educational programs
		Respite services
		Good day- and year-long educational program
		Financial assistance
		Better teacher and staff attitudes
13–17	11	Good residential treatment
		Sex management and training
		Financial assistance
		Respite services
		Good day- and year-long educational program[b]
		Community acceptance[b]
Adult (18+)	18	Good residential treatment
		Financial assistance
		Sex management and training[c]
		Knowledgeable and concerned professionals[c]
		Contact with other parents[d]
		Community acceptance[d]
		Good day- or year-long educational program[d]
		Curriculum additions to educational program[d]

[a]Tied for fifth rank, 1–5-year age period.
[b]Tied for fifth rank, 13–17-year age period.
[c]Tied for third rank, adult period.
[d]Tied for fifth rank, adult period.

of four child age periods from age 1 to adulthood. The results found
for these parents in Indiana were generally consistent with those found
for our parents in North Carolina, although there was a much higher
percentage of parents in the DeMyer and Goldberg study (1983) who appeared to have burned out and sought institutionalization for their autistic children.

One of the most interesting conclusions to be drawn from our own
work centers on the recognition that autism is a chronic developmental
disability that creates adjustment problems in most such individuals
throughout their life span. Nevertheless, it is our belief that most of the

debilitating stress of the handicap on the autistic persons and their families can be circumvented or prevented by developing programs that reflect the service needs just enumerated. This can be accomplished through the development of strong formal and informal support networks. One example of how such networks can be developed is the North Carolina program for the Treatment and Education of Autistic and related Communication handicapped CHildren (Division TEACCH) (Schopler & Reichler, 1972). This is the first statewide program offering comprehensive services for such children and their families. It focuses on three major needs of autistic persons and their families: home adjustment, schooling, and community advocacy.

Home Adjustment

Each of five regional centers, located at North Carolina sites also housing branches of the state university system, focuses on the home adjustment of autistic children and adults. The centers provide diagnostic evaluations (Schopler et al., 1980a), assessment (Schopler & Reichler, 1979), and individualized education and behavior management programs (Schopler, Lansing, & Waters, 1983; Schopler, Reichler, & Lansing, 1980b). In this process the parent–professional relationship has several different aspects, detailed in Schopler, Mesibov, Shigley, and Bashford (in press). First, the professionals function as trainers and parents as trainees. This is based on the professional's knowledge of the field and its relevant literature. Professionals generally have had experience with a wider range of children than have most parents. In this role, professionals teach both special education procedures and behavior modification techniques that parents carry out and evaluate at home. In the second aspect of the parent–professional relationship, the parents are the trainers and the professionals the trainees. This is based on the assumption that in most ways parents are the foremost experts on their own child. They have lived with him or her the longest and usually have the most incentive for having home adjustment work out well. In this role they provide important assessment information, and also set priorities for home teaching and survival. Two other aspects of parent–professional relationships can best be illustrated in our work with the two other major areas of the child's life, the school and the community.

Schooling

Throughout the five regions of the state, 37 classrooms have been established in the public schools for the purpose of providing special education for autistic and communication handicapped children. Each classroom includes four to six children with a teacher and assistant teacher. Prior to the establishment of such classrooms in 1972, autistic children, under the jurisdiction of departments of mental health, were generally considered emotionally disturbed and excluded from public schools. The operating guidelines for these classrooms in North Carolina preceded PL 94–142 by 5 years, but are quite similar to those of PL 94–142 in most respects (Schopler & Bristol, 1980). Parental collaboration with teachers occurs at different levels depending on the circumstances. At the most intense level, the parent functions as an assistant teacher, participating in the classroom at least 2 days a week. At a second, somewhat less intense level, the parent works in the classroom at irregular intervals or on special occasions. Parents also collaborate with teachers on specific teaching programs. This parent–teacher collaboration plays an important role in overcoming the specific problems characteristic of autistic children and in generalizing learning from one situation to another. The third level of parent involvement in the classroom involves regular parent–teacher conferences; a fourth or minimum level is required, that is, parents meet with the teacher at least once a month to discuss the child's progress and problems. If the parent has transportation difficulties, conference arrangements can be made by phone.

In addition to the two forms of parent–teacher relationships discussed in the preceding section, two forms of parent–professional relationships—mutual emotional support and community advocacy—are used in the TEACCH program. We expect our professional personnel to understand that parents of autistic children are primarily normal people experiencing the considerable stress of having a handicapped child. With this understanding, staff can provide emotional support to parents even when they disagree on some technical aspects of management. Conversely, we expect parents to offer emotional support and understanding to staff who must deal with the frustrations of the autistic child's slow progress and repeated behavior problems. With a supportive administrative structure, most parents and professionals offer each other such emotional support without special training. The fourth type of parent–professional relationship in the TEACCH program involves the collaboration of both parents and professionals in improving community understanding and support. This is best accomplished through parent–professional advocacy groups.

Community Advocacy

Each of the TEACCH regional centers and classrooms has a parent group attached to it. This group in turn is affiliated with the North

Carolina Society for Autistic Adults and Children (NCSAC), which is a chapter of the National Society for Autistic Children and Adults. The object of this collaboration is to provide the community with an understanding of these children's needs, to develop appropriate services, and to facilitate parent-to-parent contact and support.

In recent years the focus of these community advocacy groups has been on services for autistic adolescents and adults. These services include group homes, respite care for exhausted parents, vocational training and placement, vocational advocates to assist in making successful job placements, and social skill training groups. Together, parents and professionals have also provided summer camp facilities, some summer recreation programs, transportation to school, and training programs for new staff. Details of these programs are described in Schopler and Mesibov (1983).

Although not all aspects of this formal support network are equally well developed at this time, its effectiveness has clearly been demonstrated in treatment outcome studies (Marcus et al., 1978; Short, in press). Parent questionnaire studies have also shown a very high degree of satisfaction with the TEACCH program (Schopler, Mesibov, & Baker, 1982; Short, in press). Especially impressive is the reduced rate of institutionalization of these children. In published follow-up studies of autistic children, studies have reported rates of institutionalization ranging from 38% to 76% (Creak, 1963; DeMyer, Barton, DeMyer, Norton, Allen, & Steele, 1973; Lotter, 1978; Mittler, Gillies, & Jukes, 1966; Rutter, Greenfield, & Lockyer, 1967, 1970). Even more recent follow-up studies, such as that by DeMyer and Goldberg (1983), have reported that 33% of the autistic children in their study under 14 years of age and 67% of those over 14 were institutionalized. In contrast, a follow-up of 348 participants served through the TEACCH program revealed that the percentage of TEACCH children in institutions was no greater for children over 17 years of age (N = 115) than for the entire follow-up group (ranging in age from 2 to 26 with a mean age of 6 years). For both groups, the rate of institutionalization was only 7% (Schopler, Mesibov, & Baker, 1982). (For purposes of this study, institutionalization included any out-of-home placement, including residence in a group home.) Clearly, a strong formal support network is conducive to family stress reduction and improved adaptation for autistic children and adults.

Moreover, our clinical observations suggest that the effects of the strengthened formal support system also have a positive and mutually reinforcing effect on the informal support network composed of family and friends. This is especially true if fathers and siblings, and even extended family members, are included in explanations of the child's handicap and in planning and/or carrying out the child's program.

Although at this time it cannot be empirically demonstrated, a reasonable assumption is that if parents are given early training in encouraging their children's learning and independence and if adequate medical, educational, prevocational and vocational services, leisure-time activities, and group homes and other alternative community living arrangements are available, much of the stress associated with the potential arrest in the family life cycle and parental burnout can be avoided.

Implications for Future Research

The studies reviewed suggest needed directions for future research. Especially because our understanding of autism and the provision of services for these children has changed dramatically since the 1960s, there is a pressing need for longitudinal, prospective studies of these families. The available cross-sectional or retrospective studies of these families suggest a developmental pattern of stress and coping, but only longitudinal study of these families can demonstrate such a pattern.

Because of an earlier tendency to interpret any stresses in these families as evidence of pathology, it is important that future research include a handicapped but nonautistic comparison sample to control for stress experienced by all families of handicapped children and to document more clearly the stresses characteristic of parenting an autistic child. When possible, a comparison group of families of nonhandicapped children should also be included so that the normal stresses of child rearing are not mistaken for family dysfunction.

The demonstration of the importance of social support suggests the necessity of studying not only mothers, but fathers, siblings, and extended family members as well. We need to learn more about the mutual effects of both the autistic child on the larger family system and the contribution of other family members and friends to both favorable outcomes for the autistic child and long-term, successful family adaptation to the autistic child. Studies are also needed of alternatives to paternal support in single-parent families. We have recently initiated intensive studies of both fathers' roles and sources of support in single parent families.

Since a large part of successful adaptation to the child depends on the fit between the family's needs and the support of the community, there needs to be more systematic investigation of the beliefs and attitudes of both professionals and the general public (Olley, DeVellis, DeVellis, Wall, & Long, 1981). Studies of the efficacy of interventions designed to change such attitudes or beliefs would be especially useful.

Finally, it is clear that there are "invulnerable" families of autistic children who have persevered and changed the future for themselves and their autistic children. We need to learn more about factors within families of autistic children (child characteristics, social support, etc.) that are related not to stress but to *successful* adaptation to autistic children. An exclusive focus on pathology in these families has for too long limited the opportunity we have to learn from them regarding successful family adaptation to these beautiful, puzzling, and difficult children.

References

Akerley, M. (1975). The invulnerable parent. *Journal of Autism and Childhood Schizophrenia, 5,* 275–281.

Angell, R. C. (1936). *The family encounters the depression.* New York: Scribner's.

Anthony, E. J. (1974). The syndrome of the psychologically vulnerable child. In E. J. Anthony & C. Koupernik (Eds.), *The child in his family: Vol. 3. Children at psychiatric risk.* New York: Wiley.

Bartak, L., & Rutter, M. (1976). Differences between mentally retarded and normally intelligent autistic children. *Journal of Autism and Childhood Schizophrenia, 6,* 109–120.

Beckman-Bell, P. B. (1980). *Characteristics of handicapped infants: A study of the relationship between child characteristics and stress as reported by mothers.* Unpublished doctoral dissertation, University of North Carolina at Chapel Hill.

Behrens, M. C., & Goldfarb, W. (1958). A study of patterns of interaction of families of schizophrenic children in residential treatment. *American Journal of Orthopsychiatry, 28,* 300–312.

Bell, R. Q. (1968). A reinterpretation of the direction of effects in studies of socialization. *Psychological Review, 75,* 81–95.

Bell, R. Q. (1971). Stimulus control of parent or caretaker behavior by offspring. *Developmental Psychology, 4,* 63–72.

Bender, L., & Grugett, A. E. (1956). A study of certain epidemiological problems in a group of children with childhood schizophrenia. *American Journal of Orthopsychiatry, 26,* 131–145.

Bettleheim, B. (1967). *The empty fortress—Infantile autism and the birth of the self.* New York: The Free Press, Collier-Macmillan.

Block, J. (1969). Parents of schizophrenic, neurotic, asthmatic, and congenitally ill children: A comparative study. *Archives of General Psychiatry, 20,* 659–674.

Bradshaw, J., & Lawton, D. (1978). Tracing the causes of stress in families with handicapped children. *British Journal of Social Work, 8(2),* 181–192.

Bristol, M. M. (1979). *Maternal coping with autistic children: The effect of child character-*

istics and interpersonal support. Unpublished doctoral dissertation, University of North Carolina at Chapel Hill.

Bristol, M. M. (1982a, March). The relationship of maternal factors to adjustment of autistic children. A progress report to the Spencer Foundation.

Bristol, M. M. (in press-a). Family resources and successful adaptation to autistic children. In E. Schopler & G. Mesibov (Eds.), The effects of autism on the family. New York: Plenum Press.

Bristol, M. M. (in press-b). The home care of developmentally disabled children: Some empirical support for a conceptual model of successful coping with family stress. In S. Landesman-Dwyer & P. Vietze (Eds.), Environments for developmentally disabled persons. Baltimore: University Park Press.

Bristol, M. M. (1984). A characteristic pattern of stress in families of autistic children. University of North Carolina at Chapel Hill. Manuscript submitted for publication.

Bristol, M. M., & Gallagher, J. J. (1982). A family focus for intervention. In C. Ramey & P. Trohanis (Eds.), Finding and educating the high risk and handicapped infant. Baltimore: University Park Press.

Bristol, M. M., & Schopler, E. (1983). Coping and stress in families of autistic adolescents. In E. Schopler & G. Mesibov (Eds.), Autism in adolescents and adults. New York: Plenum Press.

Buium, N., Rynders, J., & Turnure, J. (1974). Early maternal linguistic environment and normal and Down's syndrome language learning children. American Journal of Mental Deficiency, 79, 52–58.

Burden, R. L. (1980). Measuring the effects of stress on the mothers of handicapped infants: Must depression always follow? Child: Care, Health and Development, 6, 111–125.

Burr, W. R. (1970). Satisfaction with various aspects of marriage over the life cycle: A random middle-class sample. Journal of Marriage and the Family, 31(1), 29–37.

Burr, W. R. (1973). Theory construction and the sociology of the family. New York: Wiley.

Call, J. M. (1963). Interlocking affective freeze between an autistic child and his "as if" mother. Journal of the American Academy of Child Psychology, 2, 319–344.

Cantwell, D. P., Baker, L., & Rutter, M. (1978). Family factors in the syndrome of infantile autism. In M. Rutter and E. Schopler (Eds.), Autism: A reappraisal of concepts and treatments. New York: Plenum Press.

Chess, S. (1971). Genesis of behavior disorder. In J. G. Howells (Ed.), Modern perspectives in international child psychiatry. New York: Bruner/Mazel.

Cook, J. J. (1963). Dimensional analysis of child-rearing attitudes of parents of handicapped children. American Journal of Mental Deficiency, 63, 354–361.

Cox, A., Rutter, M., Newman, S., & Bartak, L. (1975). A comparative study of infantile autism and specific developmental receptive language disorder: Parental characteristics. British Journal of Psychiatry, 126, 146–159.

Creak, E. W. (1963). Childhood psychosis: A review of 100 cases. British Journal of Psychiatry, 109, 84–89.

Creak, M., & Ini, S. (1960). Families of psychotic children. Journal of Child Psychology and Psychiatry, 1, 156–175.

Cummings, S. J., Bayley, H. C., & Rie, H. E. (1966). Effects of the child's deficiency on the mother: A study of mothers of mentally retarded, chronically ill and neurotic children. American Journal of Orthopsychiatry, 36, 595–608.

DeMyer, M. (1979). Parents and children in autism. Washington, DC: Winston.

DeMyer, M., Barton, S., Alpern, G. D., Kimberlin, D., Allen, J., Yang, E., & Steele, R. (1974). The measured intelligence of autistic children. Journal of Autism and Childhood Schizophrenia, 4, 42–60.

DeMyer, M., Barton, S., DeMyer, W. E., Norton, J. A., Allen, J., & Steele, T. (1973). Prog-

nosis in autism: A follow-up study. *Journal of Autism and Childhood Schizophrenia,*
3, 199–246.

DeMyer, M., & Goldberg, P. (1983). Family needs of the autistic adolescent. In E. Schopler
& G. B. Mesibov (Eds.), *Autism in adolescents and adults.* New York: Plenum Press.

DeMyer, M., Pontius, W., Norton, J., Barton, S., Allen, J., & Steele, R. (1972). Parental practices and innate activity in autistic and brain-damaged infants. *Journal of Autism*
and Childhood Schizophrenia, 2, 49–66.

Dewey, M. A. (1983). Parental perspective of needs. In E. Schopler & G. B. Mesibov (Eds.),
Autism in adolescents and adults. New York: Plenum Press.

Donnelly, E. M. (1960). The quantitative analysis of parent behavior toward psychotic
children and their siblings. *Genetic Psychology Monographs, 62,* 331–376.

Eisenberg, L., & Kanner, L. (1955). Child schizophrenia symposium, 1955: Early infantile
autism: 1943–1955. *American Journal of Orthopsychiatry, 26,* 556–566.

Farber, B. (1959). Effects of a severely mentally retarded child on family integration.
Monographs of the Society for Research in Child Development, 24(2, Serial No. 71).

Ferster, C. B. (1961). Positive reinforcement and behavioral deficits of autistic children.
Child Development, 32, 437–456.

Ferster, C. B. (1966). The repertoire of the autistic child in relation to principles of reinforcement. In L. Gottschalk & A. H. Auerback (Eds.), *Methods of research in*
psychotherapy. New York: Appleton-Century-Crofts.

Folstein, S., & Rutter, M. (1978). A twin study of individuals with infantile autism. In M.
Rutter & E. Schopler (Eds.), *Autism: A reappraisal of concepts and treatment.* New
York: Plenum Press.

Fraiberg, S. (1974). Blind infants and their mothers: An examination of the sign system. In
M. Lewis & L. A. Rosenblum (Eds.), *The effect of the infant on its caregiver.* New
York: Wiley.

Fraknoi, J., & Ruttenberg, B. (1971). Formulation of the dynamic economic factors underlying infantile autism. *Journal of the American Academy of Child Psychiatry, 10,*
713–738.

Friedman, E. (1982, July). *The fragile X syndrome and autism.* Paper presented at the
Autism Research Symposium, NSAC Annual Meeting and Conference, Omaha, NE.

Gallagher, J. J., Beckman-Bell, P., & Cross, A. H. (1983). Families of handicapped children:
Sources of stress and its amelioration. *Exceptional Children.*

Gallagher, J. J., Cross, A., & Scharfman, W. (1981). Parental adaptation to a young handicapped child: The father's role. *Journal of the Division for Early Childhood, 3,* 3–14.

Gittelman, M., & Birch, H. (1967). Childhood schizophrenia: :Intellect, neurologic status,
perinatal risk, prognosis, and family pathology. *Archives of General Psychiatry, 17,*
16–25.

Goldfarb, W., Goldfarb, N., & Scholl, M. (1966a). The speech of mothers of schizophrenic
children. *American Journal of Psychiatry, 122,* 1220–1227.

Goldfarb, W., Levy, D., & Meyers, D. (1966b). The verbal encounter between the schizophrenic child and his mother. In G. Goldman & D. Shapiro (Eds.), *Developments in*
psychoanalysis at Columbia University. New York: Hafner.

Goldfarb, W., Spitzer, R. L., & Endicott, J. (1976). A study of psychopathology of parents of
psychotic children by structured interview. *Journal of Autism and Childhood*
Schizophrenia, 6, 327–338.

Gore, S. (1978). Effect of social support in moderating the health consequences of unemployment. *Journal of Health and Social Behavior, 19,* 157–169.

Hayden, A. (1976). Down's syndrome children. In T. D. Tjossem (Ed.), *Intervention*
strategies for high risk infants and young children. Baltimore: University Park Press.

Hetherington, E. M. Children and divorce. (1981). In R. Henderson (Ed.), *Parent-child interaction: Theory, research, and prospects.* New York: Academic Press.

Hill, R. (1949). *Families under stress: Adjustment to the crisis of war separation and reunion.* New York: Harper.

Hill, R. (1958). Sociology of marriage and family behavior, 1945–1956: A trend report and bibliography. *Current Sociology, 7,* 1098.

Hill, R. (1970). *Family development in three generations.* Cambridge, MA: Schenkman.

Hill, R., & Hansen, D. (1962). The family in disaster. In G. Baker & D. Chapman (Eds.), *Man and society in disaster.* New York: Basic Books.

Holroyd, J., & McArthur, D. (1976). Mental retardation and stress on the parents: A contrast between Down's syndrome and childhood autism. *American Journal of Mental Deficiency, 80,* 431–436.

Kanner, L. (1943). Autistic disturbances of affective contact. *Nervous Child, 2,* 217–250.

Kanner, L. (1954). To what extent is early infantile autism determined by constitutional inadequacies? *Proceedings of the Association for Research in Nervous and Mental Diseases, 33,* 378–385.

King, P. D. (1975). Early infantile autism: Relation to schizophrenia. *Journal of the American Academy of Child Psychiatry, 19,* 666–682.

Koegel, R. L., Schreibman, L., Britten, K. R., Burke, J. C., & O'Neill, R. E. (1981). A comparison of parent training to direct child treatment. In R. L. Koegel, A. Rincover, & A. L. Egel (Eds.), *Educating and understanding children.* San Diego, CA: College-Hill.

Kogan, K. L., & Tyler, N. (1973). Mother-child interaction in young physically handicapped children. *American Journal of Mental Deficiency, 77,* 492–497.

Kogan, K. L., Wimberger, H. C., & Bobbitt, R. A. (1969). Analysis of mother-child interaction in young mental retardates. *Child Development, 40,* 799–811.

Kolvin, I., Garside, R., & Kidd, J. (1971). Studies in the childhood psychosis. IV. Parental personality and attitude and childhood psychoses. *British Journal of Psychiatry, 118,* 403–406.

Kolvin, I., Ounsted, C. Richardson, L., & Garside, R. (1971). Studies in the childhood psychoses. III. The family and social background in child psychoses. *British Journal of Psychiatry, 118,* 396–402.

Lennard, H. L., Beaulieu, M. R., & Embrey, M. G. (1965). Interaction in families with a schizophrenic child. *Archives of General Psychiatry, 12,* 166–183.

Levinson, D. J. (1978). *The seasons of a man's life.* New York: Knopf.

Lewis, M., & Rosenblum, L. A. (1974). *The effect of the infant on its caregiver.* New York: Wiley.

Lockyer, L., & Rutter, M. (1970). A five-to-fifteen-year follow-up study of infantile psychosis: IV. Patterns of cognitive ability. *British Journal of Social and Clinical Psychology, 9,* 152–163.

Lotter, V. (1978). Follow-up studies. In M. Rutter and E. Schopler (Eds.), *Autism: A reappraisal of concepts and treatment.* New York: Plenum Press.

Lovaas, O. I., Koegel, R., Simmons, J. L., & Long, J. S. (1973). Some generalization and followup measures on autistic children in behavior therapy. *Journal of Applied Behavior Analysis, 6,* 131–165.

Mahoney, G. J. (1975). Ethological approach to delayed language acquisition. *American Journal of Mental Deficiency, 80*(2), 139–148.

Marcus, L. (1977). Patterns of coping in families of psychotic children. *American Journal of Orthopsychiatry, 47*(3), 383–399.

Marcus, L., Lansing, M., Andrews, C., & Schopler, E. (1978). Improvement of teaching effectiveness in parents of autistic children. *Journal of the American Academy of Child Psychiatry, 17,* 625–639.

Mash, E., & Terdal, L. (1973). Modification of mother-child interactions. *Mental Retardation, 11,* 44–49.

Mates, T. (1982). *Siblings of autistic children: Performance at school and at home.* Unpublished doctoral dissertation, University of North Carolina at Chapel Hill.

McAdoo, W. G., & DeMyer, M. K. (1977). Research related to family factors in autism. *Journal of Pediatric Psychology, 2*(4), 162–166.

McCubbin, H. (1979). Integrating coping behavior in family stress theory. *Journal of Marriage and the Family, 42,* 237–244.

McCubbin, H. I., Cauble, A. E., & Patterson, J. M. (1982). *Family stress, coping, and social support.* Springfield, IL: Thomas.

McCubbin, H. I., Joy, C. B., Cauble, A. E., Comeau, J. K., Patterson, J. M., & Needle, R. H. (1980). Family stress and coping: A decade review. *Journal of Marriage and the Family, 42,* 855–871.

McCubbin, H. I., & Patterson, J. M. (1981). *Systematic assessment of family stress, resources, and coping.* St. Paul, MN: Family Stress Project, University of Minnesota.

McHale, S., Sloane, J., & Simeonsson, R. (1982, July). *Sibling relationships of children with autistic, mentally retarded, and nonhandicapped children: A comparative study.* Paper presented at the Autism Research Symposium, NSAC Annual Meeting and Conference, Omaha, NE.

McMichael, J. K. (1971). *Handicap: A study of physically handicapped children and their families.* London: Staples Press.

Mesibov, G. B. (1983). Current perspectives and issues in autism and adolescence. In E. Schopler & G. B. Mesibov (Eds.), *Austim in adolescents and adults.* New York: Plenum Press.

Meyers, D., & Goldfarb, W. (1961). Childhood schizophrenia: Studies of perplexity in mothers of schizophrenic children. *American Journal of Orthopsychiatry, 31,* 551–564.

Meyers, D. I., & Goldfarb, W. (1962). Psychiatric appraisal of parents and siblings of schizophrenic children. *American Journal of Psychiatry, 118,* 902–915.

Mittler, P., Gillies, S., & Jukes, E. (1966). Prognosis in psychotic children: Report of a follow-up study. *Journal of Mental Deficiency Research, 10,* 73–78.

National Society for Autistic Children. (1978). Definition of the syndrome of autism. *Journal of Autism and Childhood Schizophrenia, 8,* 162–167.

Nevin, R. S., & McCubbin, H. I. (1979, August). *Parental coping with physical handicaps: Social policy implications.* Paper presented at the National Council of Family Relations annual meeting, Boston.

Nuckolls, C., Cassel, J., & Kaplan, B. (1972). Psycho-social assets, life crises and prognosis of pregnancy. *American Journal of Epidemiology, 95,* 431–444.

O'Gorman, G. (1970). *The nature of childhood autism* (2nd ed.). London: Butterworth.

Olley, J. G., DeVellis, R. F., DeVellis, E. M., Wall, A. J., & Long, C. E. (1981). The autism attitude scale for teachers. *Exceptional Children, 47,* 371–372.

Paluszny, M. (1979). *Austism: A practical guide for parents and professionals.* Syracuse, NY: Syracuse University Press.

Park, C. C. (1983). Growing out of autism. In E. Schopler and G. B. Mesibov (Eds.), *Autism in adolescents and adults.* New York: Plenum Press.

Pasamanick, B., & Knobloch, H. (1960). Brain damage and reproductive casualty. *American Journal of Orthopsychiatry, 30,* 248–305.

Patterson, G. R. (1980). Mothers: The unacknowledged victims. *Monograph of the Society for Research in Child Development, 45* (5, Serial No. 186).

Pitfield, M., & Oppenheim, A. (1964). Childrearing attitudes of mothers of psychotic children. *Journal of Child Psychology and Psychiatry, 5,* 51–57.

Prechtl, H. F. R. (1961). Mother-child interaction in babies with minimal brain damage: A follow-up study. In B. Foss (Ed.), *Determinants of infant behavior.* New York: Wiley.

Putnam, M. C. (1955). Some observations on psychoses in early childhood. In G. Caplan (Ed.), *Emotional problems of early childhood.* New York: Basic Books.

Rank, B. (1949). Adaptation of the psychoanalytic techniques for the treatment of young children with atypical development. *American Journal of Orthopsychiatry, 19,* 130–139.

Rank, B. (1955). Intensive study and treatment of preschool children who show marked personality deviations or 'atypical development' and their parents. In G. Caplan (Ed.), *Emotional problems of early childhood.* New York: Basic Books.

Rimland, B. (1964). *Infantile autism.* New York: Appleton-Century-Crofts.

Ritvo, E., Yuwiler, A., Geller, E., Ornitz, E., Saeger, K., & Plotkin, S. (1970). Increased blood serotonin and platelets in early infantile autism. *Archives of General Psychiatry, 23,* 566–572.

Ritvo, E. R. (Ed.) (1976). *Autism: Diagnosis, current research and management.* New York: Spectrum.

Rondal, J. A. (1978). Maternal speech to normal and Down's syndrome children matched for mean length of utterance. *American Association on Mental Deficiency Monographs* (No. 3).

Ruttenberg, B. (1971). A psychoanalytic understanding of infantile autism and its treatment. In D. Churchill, D. Alpern, & M. DeMyer (Eds.), *Infantile autism: Proceedings of the Indiana University Colloquium.* Springfield, IL: Thomas.

Rutter, M. (1968). Concepts of autism: A review of research. *Journal of Child Psychology and Psychiatry, 9,* 1–25.

Rutter, M. (1970). Autistic children: Infancy to adulthood. *Seminars in Psychiatry, 2,* 435–450.

Rutter, M. (1978). Diagnosis and definition. In M. Rutter and E. Schopler (Eds.), *Autism: A reappraisal of concepts and treatment.* New York: Plenum Press.

Rutter, M., & Bartak, L. (1973). Special education treatment of autistic children: A comparative study. II. Follow-up findings and implications for services. *Journal of Child Psychology and Psychiatry, 14,* 241–270.

Rutter, M., Greenfeld, D., & Lockyer, L. (1967). A five to fifteen year follow-up study of infantile psychosis. *British Journal of Psychiatry, 113,* 1183–1199.

Rutter, M., & Lockyer, L. (1967). A five-to-fifteen year follow-up study of infantile psychosis: I. Description of sample. *British Journal of Psychiatry, 113,* 1169–1182.

Rutter, M., & Schopler, E. (Eds.) (1978). *Autism: A reappraisal of concepts and treatment.* New York: Plenum Press.

Sameroff, A. M., & Chandler, M. (1975). Reproductive risks and the continuum of caretaking casualty. In F. D. Horowitz, M. Hetherington, S. Scarr-Salapatek, and I. Siegel (Eds.), *Review of child development research* (Vol. 4). Chicago: University of Chicago Press.

Sarvis, M. A., & Garcia, B. (1967). Etiological variables in autism. *Sourcebook in abnormal psycholocy.* Boston: Houghton Mifflin.

Schopler, E. (1971). Parents of psychotic children as scapegoats. *Journal of Contemporary Psychotherapy, 4,* 17–22.

Schopler, E. (1978). Limits of methodological differences between family studies. In M. Rutter & E. Schopler (Eds.), *Autism: A reappraisal of concepts and treatment*. New York: Plenum Press.

Schopler, E., Brehm, S., Kinsbourne, M., & Reichler, R. J. (1971). Effect of treatment structure on development in autistic children. *Archives of General Psychiatry, 24*, 415–421.

Schopler, E., & Bristol, M. (1980). *Autistic children in public school*. ERIC Exceptional Child Education Report. Reston, VA: Council for Exceptional Children.

Schopler, E., Lansing, M., & Waters, L. (1983). *Individualized assessment and treatment for autistic and developmentally delayed children: Vol. 3. Teaching activities for autistic children*. Baltimore: University Park Press.

Schopler, E., & Loftin, J. M. (1969). Thought disorders in parents of psychotic children: A function of test anxiety. *Archives of General Psychiatry, 20*(2), 174–181.

Schopler, E., & Mesibov, G. (Eds.). (1983). *Autism in adolescents and adults*. New York: Plenum Press.

Schopler, E., Mesibov, G., & Baker, A. (1982). Evaluation of treatment for autistic children and their parents. *Journal of the American Academy of Child Psychiatry, 21*(3), 262–267.

Schopler, E., Mesibov, G., DeVellis, R., & Short, A. (1981). Treatment outcomes for autistic children and their families. In D. Mittler (Ed.), *Frontiers of knowledge in mental retardation* (Vol. 1). Baltimore: University Park Press.

Schopler, E., Mesibov, G., Shigley, R. H., & Bashford, A. (in press). Helping autistic children through their parents: The TEACCH model. In E. Schopler & G. B. Mesibov (Eds.), *The effects of autism on the family*. New York: Plenum Press.

Schopler, E., & Reichler, R. (1971). Developmental therapy by parents with their own autistic child. In M. Rutter (Ed.), *Infantile autism: Concepts, characteristics, and treatment*. London: Churchill Livingstone.

Schopler, E., & Reichler, R. J. (1972). How well do parents understand their own psychotic child? *Journal of Autism and Childhood Schizophrenia, 2*, 387–400.

Schopler, E., & Reichler, R. J. (1979). *Individualized assessment and treatment for autistic and developmentally delayed children: Vol. 1. Psychoeducational profile*. Baltimore, MD: University Park Press.

Schopler, E., Reichler, R., DeVellis, R. F., & Daly, K. (1980a). Toward objective classification of childhood autism: Childhood Autism Rating Scale (CARS). *Journal of Autism and Developmental Disorders, 10*, 91–103.

Schopler, E., Reichler, R. J., & Lansing, M. (1980b). *Individualized assessment and treatment for autistic and developmentally delayed children: Vol. 2. Teaching strategies for parents and professionals*. Baltimore: University Park Press.

Sheehy, G. (1976). *Passages: Predictable crises of adult life*. New York: Dutton.

Short, A. (in press). Short-term treatment outcome using parents as co-therapists for their own autistic children. *Journal of Child Psychology and Psychiatry*.

Silverman, W., & Hill, R. (1967). Task allocation in marriage in the U.S. and Belgium. *Journal of Marriage and the Family, 29*, 353–359.

Stern, D. U. (1974). Mother and infant at play: The dyadic interaction involving facial, vocal, and gaze behaviors. In M. Lewis & L. A. Rosenblum (Eds.), *The effect of the infant on its caregiver*. New York: Wiley.

Sullivan, R. (1976). Autism: Current trends in services. In E. R. Ritvo (Ed.), *Autism: Diagnosis, current research and management*. New York: Holsted Press.

Szurek, S. (1956). Psychotic episodes and psychotic maldevelopment. *American Journal of Orthopsychiatry, 26*, 519–543.

Szurek, S., & Berlin, I. (Eds.). (1973). *Clinical studies in childhood psychosis.* New York: Brunner/Mazel.

Taft, L. T., & Cohen, H. J. (1971). Hypsarrhythmia and infantile autism: A clinical report. *Journal of Autism and Childhood Schizophrenia, 1,* 327–336.

Tallman, I. (1965). Spousal role differentiation and the socialization of severely retarded children. *Journal of Marriage and the Family, 27,* 37–42.

Tinbergen, E. A., & Tinbergen, N. (1972). *Early childhood autism: An ethological approach.* Berlin: Paul Parey.

Trevarthen, C. (1975). Early attempts at speech. In R. Levin (Ed.), *Child alive.* London: Temple Smith.

Turnbull, A. P., Brotherson, M. J., & Summers, J. A. (in press). The impact of deinstitutionalization on families: A family systems approach. In R. H. Bruininks (Ed.), *Living and learning in the least restrictive environment.*

Ward, A. J. (1970). Early infantile autism: Diagnosis, etiology, and treatment. *Psychological Bulletin, 73,* 350–362.

Warren, F. (1982). Autistic population in U.S. expands significantly. *The Advocate, 14*(3), 4.

Wing, L. (1976). The principles of remedial education for autistic children. In L. Wing (Ed), *Early childhood autism* (2nd ed.). Oxford: Pergamon Press.

CHAPTER 4

Placement Alternatives for Mentally Retarded Children and their Families

Marsha Mailick Seltzer
Marty Wyngaarden Krauss

Introduction

This chapter discusses the use of out-of-home residential settings for severely and profoundly retarded children. While the dominant trend in the human services is to maintain the integrity of the family unit (Kadushin, 1980), the challenge to both the family and the human service system presented by a severely or profoundly retarded child is enormous. Many families effectively marshal the stamina, resources, and determination to keep their handicapped child at home. As suggested in several other chapters of this volume (e.g., Blacher, Chapter 1; Kaiser & Hayden, Chapter 8, Baker, Chapter 9), the impact of federal laws requiring educational programs for all handicapped children (Public Law [PL] 94–142, the Education for All Handicapped Children Act of 1975), the growing availability of early intervention programs to assist children and families promptly, and the use of parent support, advocacy, and training groups all help increase the staying power of affected families. Despite these critical forces, there exist, and will continue to exist, a

143

substantial number of families for whom the costs—economic, social, psychological, and physical—of raising a severely or profoundly retarded or otherwise handicapped child will overwhelm their resources. Many of these families will try to secure a decent, caring, and stimulating out-of-home residential placement for their child.

The purpose of this chapter is to review the types of out-of-home placements that have been and are now being used for severely and profoundly retarded children. We also review the literature on the factors leading families to seek out-of-home placements. The primary source for our review is research studies in the published literature, but it should also be noted that parents have been active contributors to our understanding of the impact of a seriously handicapped child on family and personal life (see, e.g., Featherstone, 1980; Greenfeld, 1972; Massie & Massie, 1975). Their portraits often provide startling accounts of the insensitivity of professionals, the public, and society at large to the real concerns and needs of the family raising a handicapped child. Their often eloquently stated concerns are, it is hoped, reflected in the research, policy, and service agenda that concludes this chapter.

While there are four major classification systems used to define levels of mental retardation (Seltzer, 1983), for the purposes of this chapter it is sufficient to describe what is generally meant by the designations of mild, moderate, severe, and profound mental retardation. According to the American Association of Mental Deficiency's definition, mental retardation refers to "significantly subaverage general intellectual functioning existing concurrently with deficits in adaptive behaviors and manifested during the developmental period" (Grossman, 1983, p. 11). The four levels of retardation and their associated IQ ranges are:

Level	IQ score
Mild	56–70
Moderate	41–55
Severe	26–40
Profound	25 and below

This chapter focuses primarily on residential placements for severely and profoundly retarded persons. Like Eyman and Miller (1978), we primarily collapse the four groups into two groups in this chapter. As Eyman and Miller (1978) noted:

> Many have found it useful for certain purposes to identify two subgroups of retarded individuals. In one group, organic pathology is usually demonstrable, retardation is

severe, physical signs of handicaps are frequently present, the parents are normal and have characteristics of the general population in terms of education, social status, etc. The second group is characterized by an incapacity on the part of the individual to meet the demands of the social environment, particularly the school; retardation is generally mild and their parents disproportionately represent the lower occupational and educational strata. (p. lx)

While prevalence rates may vary because of definitional differences, it has been estimated that the prevalence of severe and profound retardation is 0.8 per 1000 and 0.5 per 1000, respectively (Tarjan, Wright, Eyman, & Keeran, 1973). Thus, the absolute number of severely and profoundly retarded persons is not large compared to other levels of retardation or to the general population; however, these individuals are commonly affected by multiple handicapping conditions which, in concert with significant cognitive and adaptive behavior deficits, result in a need for intensive and skilled life-long care.

The primary question with which this chapter contends is this: If a severely or profoundly mentally retarded child cannot live with his or her family, where should the child live? There are no easy answers to this question, as will be made clear. The question, however, has frequently been reduced to arguments about the viability of institutional-based (i.e., physically large, geographically isolated, total care structures) versus community-based (i.e., physically smaller, socially integrated, total care structures) residential placements. The issue has gained significance because the population in traditional institutions for mentally retarded persons is increasingly composed of severely and profoundly retarded persons (Scheerenberger, 1982).

This issue has been further fueled by the heated debate arising from a motion for modification filed by the Partlow Review Committee (Balla, Estes, Hollis, Isaacson, Orlando, Palk, Warren, Siegel, & Ellis, 1978). In the classic *Wyatt v. Stickney* case, Alabama was ordered in 1972 by a U.S. District Court to make major improvements at Partlow, a state institution for mentally retarded persons. Six years later the Review Committee submitted to the court recommendations for amendments to the 1972 standards. One of the three major findings of the Review Committee was that "only a small number of the present Partlow residents can reasonably be expected to adjust to community living" (Balla et al., 1978, Exhibit "A," Memorandum, October 18, 1978). The following statements present their rationale for this conclusion:

To place many of these residents in the community would do them a serious injustice. They require protection from ordinary hazards and close supervision in order to insure both their safety and well being. (p. 4–5)

Most residents now at Partlow will be unable to live adequately outside a highly sheltered environment such as the institution. Implicit in the court order is the assumption that most, if not all, Partlow residents can be appropriately returned to the community to live. This expectation is inappropriate for most residents. Instead, their program should take into account the reality of their plight which surely dictates a more compassionate program. (p. 16)

There is an absence of empirical evidence that severely and profoundly retarded residents are incapable of living anywhere other than in an institution; also, many would challenge the inference that community settings are less compassionate than institutional ones (Blatt & Kaplan, 1966; Dybwad, 1978; Goffman, 1961). While few would argue that institutions are the appropriate out-of-home placement for *all* severely or profoundly retarded persons, the fact that these settings are considered viable for *some* has led to an often acrimonious debate. A statement by the Center for Human Policy at Syracuse University (Center for Human Policy, 1979), for example, cast the issue as follows:

By definition, institutions deny people community living experiences and limit the opportunities of nondisabled people to interact with their disabled peers. This fact exhibits quite clearly that the pivotal issues with respect to deinstitutionalization are moral—the society is richer, the community life more rewarding when all people are valued, when people share in each other's lives—and legal—the Constitution protects liberty—and not merely ones of differing treatment strategies. Thus, we do not make a case for community integration on the grounds that community living will always be more enriching or humane, in a clinical sense, than institutional settings, but rather on the grounds that integration is basic to the constitutional notion of liberty, and that community programs inherently have far greater *potential* for success than do institutions. (p. 5)

In addition to the moral and legal arguments against continued institutionalization of severely and profoundly retarded persons, other arguments have been made in favor of institutional placement. Larsen (1977) presented seven commonly voiced justifications for institutional placement and refuted each one. The arguments for, and his arguments against, institutionalization are shown in Table 4.1.

In our view, it is regrettable that the institution versus community debate assumes such a prominent place in discussions about alternative residential settings for severely and profoundly retarded persons. What clearly requires more attention are the variety of community settings—foster homes, group homes, specialized short-term treatment centers—that may be utilized instead of the institution. Baker, Seltzer, and Seltzer (1977) presented detailed descriptions of 10 types of community residential programs based on a nationwide survey conducted in 1973. They defined a foster home as a residence for between one and six mentally retarded persons who live with a pre-existing family. Group homes, in

TABLE 4.1

Seven Common Arguments for Institutional Placement and Larsen's (1977) Refutations

In favor of institutional placement	In favor of community placement
Placement relieves burden on the family.	With family supportive services, most families prefer not to institutionalize their child.
Placement with "their own kind" leads to better adjustment and greater happiness.	Social integration of handicapped children benefits such children.
The public does not accept people who are so different from society at large.	Social acceptance will result from integration, not segregation.
Not all institutions are bad and those that are can be improved with additional fiscal resources.	Institutions need more than money to reduce their negative impacts.
There is programmatic efficiency of centralized services.	Generic community services are sufficient for all but extreme cases.
There are economic savings from centralized services.	Community services may well be less expensive than the skyrocketing costs of institutions.
It is equally possible for community services to be restrictive, dehumanizing, and segregated.	While community services may not be ideal, they offer more opportunities for freedom, individualization, and integration.

contrast, have paid staff and usually include a larger number of residents than foster homes. Specialized short-term treatment centers are often group homes that are associated with special day programs in which the resident participates on a time-limited basis or until a specified set of goals is achieved. (See Fingado, Kini, Stewart, & Redd, 1970, for example of a specialized short-term treatment center, which at that time was located on the grounds of an institution but has since moved to the community in essentially the same form.)

Severely and profoundly retarded children present an undeniable challenge to the human services system. In the discussion that follows, we review both the impact on families of such children and the utilization of residential services. We hope that the discussion will provide a basis for broadening the analysis of institution versus community settings to include a focus on types of community residences.

A few general comments on the nature of the research reviewed are necessary. First, our review does not include nonresidential out-of-home care (e.g., day care or day treatment programs). Second, we have concentrated almost exclusively on studies in the field of mental retardation because public and professional attention has produced a broad knowledge base in alternative residential placement for this type of handicapping condition. Third, since very little of the published literature provides information about residential placements specifically for children, we have drawn from the literature on adult out-of-home placement patterns. Fourth, there are limitations on the extent to which the literature that we review adequately portrays the total array of existing residential options for severely and profoundly retarded children. The bulk of the published literature focuses on institutional placements. This is expected because until the recent past institutional placements were the only alternative to family care and thus they captured much of the attention of researchers. Further, much of the literature reported describes residential placements of deinstitutionalized severely and profoundly retarded persons, while very little information is available on residential placement options or utilization of such options by children who never were placed in institutions. Therefore, our review covers a more narrow range of the population of severely and profoundly retarded children than would ideally be included in this chapter. Nonetheless, we can begin discussion on a topic deserving far greater research in quantity and scope than is presently available.

This chapter consists of three sections. First, we discuss the problem of family stress and its correlates, and the relationship of such stress to the need for out-of-home placement of severely and profoundly retarded children. Second, data on residential placement patterns are presented, drawing from national and state surveys. Third, a research, policy, and service agenda is presented, which includes the recommendations that emerged from the reviewed research.

Family Stress and the Need for Residential Placement

Although severely and profoundly retarded children constitute less than 5% of the mentally retarded population, they are the majority of those who need full-time and life-long care and services (Landesman-Dwyer & Sulzbacher, 1981). The pressures brought to bear on families who have seriously handicapped children are at times extreme and may result in a high degree of stress, personal tension, and intrafamilial conflict. Farber (1979) described families who have severely and profoundly mentally retarded children as being

> caught in a cross-current of contradictions. . . . They live in a society which advertises freedom and self-realization on the one hand, but which ascribes tremendous responsibilities for them in caring for their disabled children; they are taught that familial relationships should be fulfilling, and then are presented with a reality

which fosters withdrawal and heartache; they are imbued with a concept of childhood that implies development and eventual intellectual maturity, and then are assigned the task of caring for a child who will never attain these aims. (p. 31)

The types of stresses in the lives of families who have severely retarded children have been investigated for several decades (e.g., Cummings, 1976; Cummings, Bayley, & Rie, 1966; Farber, 1959; Fowle, 1968; Holt, 1958; Olshansky, 1962; Waisbren, 1980). In general, these studies have found that the impact on the family is mediated by such characteristics as the type and severity of the child's handicap, the age, sex, and birth order of the handicapped child, the social status of the family, the availability and use of community resources, and the agility of family members in adapting to the changed roles and expectations regarding family life.

A primary problem experienced by families whose severely and profoundly retarded child lives at home is the degree of physical care and supervision required by the child. This was the key problem reported in Holt's (1958) study of 201 families of severely mentally retarded children. He identified three types of children who were particularly stressful in this regard: those who needed nursing care, those who needed constant supervision due to their unpredictable or destructive behavior, and those who needed regular attention at night. Bradshaw and Lawton (1978), in their study of families of handicapped children, also found that the level of family stress was higher when the child needed care at night.

Undoubtedly due in part to the physical burden of caring for some severely and profoundly retarded children, poor parental physical and mental health has been identified as a consequence (as well as a cause) of family stress (Cummings, 1976; Erickson, 1969; Holroyd, Brown, Wikler, & Simmons, 1975; Holt, 1958). Mothers in particular, and fathers to a lesser extent, have been reported in these studies to be fatigued and pessimistic, to have poor self-esteem, to be more anxious and/or depressed, to feel isolated, and to have poor physical health. The psychosocial problems of siblings of severely retarded children have also been noted in the literature (Gath, 1977; Grossman, 1972; Turnbull, Brotherson, & Summers, 1982).

Families of severely and profoundly retarded children have been found to have increased financial problems, which add to the stress they experience. A number of studies have noted the increased everyday costs incurred by families in the care of a seriously handicapped child (Holroyd et al., 1975; Holt, 1958; Maroney, 1981; Turnbull et al., 1982). In addition, families may incur "opportunity costs"—jobs or promotions that parents are unable to accept because of the increased demands made by the child on their time and energy (Boggs, 1979).

There is, of course, great variability in the extent to which families experience, and the ways they cope with, these and other sources of stress. One study that compared the perceptions of parents of severely handicapped children and professionals regarding the impact of the child on the family (Blackard & Barsh, 1982) reported that compared to families, professionals overestimated the negative impact of the child on the family and underestimated the degree of support received by families. The authors cautioned that professionals need to be aware of the variety of ways that families respond to a severely handicapped child and not to assume that the impact is uniformly negative. Grossman (1972), in a study of siblings of mentally retarded children, reported many cases in which the siblings attributed positive aspects of their family life to their handicapped brother or sister. Many of the parental accounts of life with a handicapped child contain numerous examples of greater family cohesion and human understanding that raising a handicapped child may foster (Featherstone, 1980; Turnbull & Turnbull, 1978).

However, it is clear that some families cannot adjust to the additional stresses that a handicapped child may mean for a family. One potential consequence for families is the decision to seek an alternative home for the child. Ellis, Bostick, Moore, and Taylor (1981) found that families reporting higher degrees of stress were more likely to place their children in long-term institutions than those reporting lower levels of stress. Until very recently, and still to some extent, families of severely and profoundly retarded children who considered out-of-home placement had very few placement options other than public institutions. Although placement in community residences, including foster homes, is currently more of an option, the availability of space in these alternatives remains limited.

Hard data about the proportion of severely and profoundly retarded children in the United States who live in settings other than their own homes are not available. However, as will be discussed in detail in the section "Residential Placement Patterns," the best estimates indicate a much higher rate of out-of-home placement among this group than among mildly and moderately retarded persons. Maroney (1979), for example, reported that 25% of severely retarded persons are in institutions at any one point in time. The institutionalization rate among profoundly retarded persons is probably higher still. In addition, according to more recent estimates, the vast majority (over 80%) of persons below the age of 22 who live in institutions are severely or profoundly retarded (Scheerenberger, 1982).

The findings of a number of studies suggest that it is not the severity of the child's retardation alone that causes a family to consider residential placement. Rather, a variety of other factors, such as characteristics of the child, the circumstances of the family, and the available formal and informal supports, in combination with the severity of the child's retardation, contribute to the family's level of stress and subsequently to a decision to place the child out of home. These factors are reviewed in the discussion that follows. (Many of these factors have also been included in the research model presented in Blacher, Chapter 1 of this volume.)

Predictors of Out-of-Home Placement

Child and Family Variables

A number of studies have reported that families whose children exhibit behavior problems or emotional disturbance have a higher level of stress and are more likely to attempt to place their retarded children in institutions. For example, in one study families who had institutionalized their children identified child behavior problems more frequently than the severity of the child's retardation as the primary reason for institutional placement (Fotheringham, 1970). In that study, Fotheringham compared institutionalized retarded children of all levels of retardation with a matched community sample and found that the institutionalized children were also more likely to have behavior problems (especially disruptive behaviors), to have less adequate social relationships, and to have lower social maturity scores than the children who remained home with their families. In addition, the families who placed their children in institutions reported greater difficulty in coping with these behavior problems than did the families who kept their children at home.

Other studies reporting that a higher frequency and/or severity of maladaptive behavior was related to the probability of institutional placement include Eyman, O'Connor, Tarjan, and Justice (1972), Farber (1968), Saenger (1960), and Townsend and Flanagan (1976). In addition, maladaptive behavior has been reported as a major contributing factor in slowing the rate of deinstitutionalization of severely and profoundly retarded persons and/or contributing to their reinstitutionalization (Eyman, Borthwick, & Miller, 1981; Eyman & Call, 1977; Eyman & Miller, 1978; Gollay, Freedman, Wyngaarden, & Kurtz, 1978).

The age of the child has also been found to be related to the likelihood of out-of-home placement. Suelzle and Keenan (1981) found that families of developmentally disabled children between 6 and 12 years and between 19 and 21 years of age reported the highest need for out-of-home placement. The authors attributed the high degree of stress during these periods to the fact that families experience crises when their children enter school and when they complete their schooling. Birenbaum (1971) also found the child's age to be related to parental ability to cope. He reported that mothers of young mentally retarded children coped better than mothers of older retarded children because when the mentally retarded child is younger it is easier for the mother to simulate normal-appearing activities. Holroyd et al. (1975), in their study of stress in families of autistic children, reported that families of older handicapped children reported a greater degree of stress than families of younger handicapped children. (Additional data relating to stress in families of autistic children are reported in Bristol & Schopler, Chapter 3 of this volume.)

Eyman et al. (1972) found age to be a factor related to the likelihood that a mentally retarded child would be institutionalized. However, whereas the Suelzle and Keenan (1981), Birenbaum (1971), and Holroyd et al. (1975) studies suggested that there is a greater degree of family stress and need for out-of-home placement when the child is older, Eyman et al. (1972) found a much higher proportion of young children (under age 7) in the institutionalized group than in the community sample. In accounting for these seemingly contradictory findings, it may be useful to consider the possibility that parents' ability to cope is related in a curvilinear fashion to child age. Early institutional placement is one coping response of families. With respect to those children who remain at home, however, family stress appears generally to increase as the child grows older and to peak at transitional points.

As noted earlier, another constellation of factors found to be related to family stress and out-of-home placement include the child's medical and/or physical problems and the level of physical care and supervision that the child requires. Downey (1965) reported that one of the major reasons identified by parents for their decision to place their child in an institution was that the child needed more care than the family was capable of giving. Eyman et al. (1972) found that families that had placed their children in institutions were three times as likely as those whose children remained at home to have perceived that the supervision and care of the child was a problem for them. Furthermore, this study reported that whereas 83 % of the institutionalized children in the sample had three or more physical disabilities, only 14 % of the children who lived with their families were similarly disabled. Conroy (1982) reported that families who had already placed their child in an institution were more likely to be opposed to their deinstitutionalization if they perceived their son or daughter to have severe medical problems. Similarly, Mercer (1966) reported that a key factor differentiating families who were willing to accept their retarded children back after a period of institutionalization from a matched sample of families who were not willing to do so was the level of physical care and supervision that the child required.

In sum, family stress was higher and/or institutional placement was more common among children who had behavior and physical problems and whose families percieved that they required a greater degree of physical care. The relationships reported in the literature among age of child, parental stress, and the likelihood of out-of-home placement were not as clear and warrant closer examination in future research.

Family characteristics were also found to correlate with degree of family stress and/or with the probability of out-of-home placement. Parental marital stress and/or emotional problems were reported to be higher among families who institutionalized their children than those who did not (Eyman et al., 1972; Ellis et al., 1981; Graliker, Koch, & Henderson, 1965). The family's race or ethnic group was also reported to be a predictor of out-of-home placement by Eyman, Moore, Capes, and Zachofsky (1970), Eyman et al. (1972), and by Eyman and Miller (1978), with Anglo families more likely to place their children than black or Hispanic families. A similar pattern of findings was reported in some studies regarding parental level of education and income. Downey (1965) found that the higher the parents' level of education the earlier they placed the retarded child in an institution. Similarly, Eyman et al. (1972) reported that those families who placed their children in institutions had higher incomes than those who did not. We cannot tell from these studies if race or ethnic group and education or income effects are confounded, nor whether differences are related to the level of stress in families, to differences in access to resources, and/or to cultural differences in childrearing attitudes.

In contrast, Graliker et al. (1965) reported no differences in level of education or socioeconomic status between families who institutionalized their children and those who chose to keep their children at home. Fotheringham (1970) reported that Canadian families who placed their children were at a lower socioeconomic level than those who did not.

Thus, the relationships among parental income, education, and race and the decision to place the child out of the home have not been clearly delineated in the literature; furthermore, because these issues have not been examined in detail since the early 1970s, when the deinstitutionalization movement was just gaining momentum, they warrant study at the present time.

Formal and Informal Supports

A family's level of stress and the decision to place the child out of the home is not only a function of the severity of the child's handicap and other child and family variables. The extent of community resources available to the family may also make placement more or less likely. As Rowitz (1974) noted, "the family must be seen as part of a community network made up of other families, schools, churches, businesses, public and private agencies and so on. Each of these community sources may put pressures on a given family to make certain decisions concerning a deviant family member" (p. 411).

Community resources can be classified as either informal or formal supports. Informal supports include family members and close friends who provide assistance to the parents of a mentally retarded child such as emotional support, time away from the child, or help with other family responsibilities. Formal supports include agency-based professional services and training programs that are utilized by family members and/or by the mentally retarded child. Unfortunately, the published literature includes more studies of the formal support system than of the informal support system, and therefore little empirical knowledge is available about which informal supports are instrumental in preventing or delaying out-of-home placement. Fortunately, this is one of several issues related to out-of-home placement currently under study (Levine, 1981–1983; Meyers & Blacher, 1982).

However, the literature does indicate that a poor or limited informal support system is characteristic of many families who have severely retarded children. Holroyd and colleagues (Holroyd et al., 1975; Holroyd & McArthur, 1976) found that feelings of lack of social support are commonly reported by parents who have children classified as either autistic or having Down's syndrome. Turnbull et al. (1982) reported that for some families there is a risk of social isolation due to the unpredictability or inappropriateness of the retarded child's behavior in public. Farber (1968) found that when the family had close contact with the wife's mother marital integration tended to be high, whereas frequent contact with the husband's mother was associated with a lower degree of marital satisfaction. In explanation, he suggested that the wife's mother may express sympathy for her daughter whereas her mother-in-law may blame her for the retarded child. Suelzle and Keenan (1981) found that among families of seriously developmentally disabled children who live at home the utilization of informal supports by family members declined as the child got older, while the utilization of formal supports increased over time. Although these studies provide useful descriptive data, the cause-and-effect relationship between availability of informal supports and the decision to place the child out of the home has yet to be established.

Formal support services include (1) services provided to families that are intended to assist them psychologically, instrumentally, or

economically in coping with their severely retarded child at home, and
(2) services provided to children to improve their skills and/or reduce
their behavior problems to make them more acceptable to their families.
Larsen (1977) discussed the services that should be made available to
families of severely and profoundly handicapped children in order to
provide them with the maximum degree of support. He identified the
following as essential community services: early intervention, public
education, community residential services (including respite care), in-
home supports (specialized or adaptive equipment and homemaker-type
services), family counseling, and protective services (including advocacy). Larsen (1977) asserted that

> the task of serving all severely and profoundly handicapped individuals in com-
> munity settings is not insurmountable. In fact, community services for this group will
> be neither more expensive nor more difficult to provide than it would be to maintain
> our current fragmented and ineffectual service system for this group. We should
> begin by basing our services and programs on a firm commitment to our consumers,
> and by creating a network of services. (p. 27)

Bjaanes, Butler, and Kelly (1981) conducted a study in California
that examined differences in the extent to which retarded children and
adults and their families utilized the formal support system, depending
on their type of residence and level of retardation. The utilization of four
types of services was studied: social interaction training, independent
living skills training, behavior therapy, and supportive counseling. It
was found that severely retarded persons who lived with their families
were less likely to receive the first three of these services than similar
clients who lived in institutions, large care facilities, or small care
facilities (see Table 4.2). With respect to the fourth type of service—supportive counseling, which included counseling provided to family members—as many families whose severely retarded children lived at home
received counseling as families whose severely retarded children lived
in large and small care facilities. The Bjaanes et al. (1981) findings suggest that with the exception of supportive counseling, the extent of formal support provided to severely retarded persons who live at home—
and thus to their families—is considerably less than the extent of formal
support provided to persons in out-of-home placements. These findings
raise questions about the extent to which the service system has put a
priority on maintaining severely retarded children in their homes.
Maroney (1981) has raised similar concerns.

Another type of formal support that can be provided to families is a
package of services designed specifically to prevent the long-term placement of the child in an institution. One such intervention, described by
Ellis et al. (1981), consisted of the brief (6–12 months) placement of am-

TABLE 4.2
Percentage of Severely Retarded Persons Receiving Services by Placement Type[a,b]

	Type of placement			
Service	State hospitals (n = 103)	Large care facilities (n = 70)	Small care facilities (n = 133)	In-home placement (n = 305)
Social interaction training	77.7	47.1	39.8	22.6
Independent living skills training	68.0	35.7	29.3	8.5
Behavior therapy	63.1	35.7	23.3	19.7
Supportive counseling	13.6	65.7	56.4	60.7

[a] Source: from "Placement type and client functional level as factors in provision of services aimed at increasing adjustment" by A. T. Bjaanes, E. W. Butler, and B. R. Kelley, in Deinstitutionalization and Community Adjustment of Mentally Retarded People (pp. 344–345) by R. H. Bruininks, C. E. Meyers, B. B. Sigford, and K. C. Lakin (Eds.), 1981, Washington, DC: American Association on Mental Deficiency. © 1981 by the American Association on Mental Deficiency. Adapted by permission.

[b] The clients included in this table were categorized as severely retarded, emotionally disturbed, and/or mentally retarded.

bulatory severely and profoundly retarded children in a new building on the grounds of an institution. The goal was to improve the child's skills so that keeping the child at home would be a more acceptable option for the family. In spite of the focus of the intervention, about half of the families who participated in this program noted at the beginning of service that they were inclined to place their children in institutions on a long-term basis anyway. The other half intended to keep their children at home following this short-term placement. A 5-year follow-up revealed that 40% of the children whose families originally intended to place them in institutions and 70% of those whose families had planned to keep them at home still lived at home. While no information was presented on initial differences between children who returned home subsequent to the intervention and those who were placed in the institution on a long-term basis, at the 5-year follow-up the at-home group had significantly higher independent functioning skills.

Townsend and Flanagan (1976) described a somewhat different type of formal support service, which attempted to prevent institutionalization by providing support to families of young (below age 6) severely and profoundly retarded children who had already applied for institutional placement for the child. Families were randomly assigned to either the experimental or the control group. Both groups were given preadmission counseling by a social worker. In addition, the experimental group was given instruction in child rearing, discussion of available community resources, and extra counseling. No differences were found between experimental and control group families with respect to their decision to institutionalize their children. Instead, the strength of the family's initial resolve to place the child was predictive of their ultimate decision regarding placement, as found by the Ellis *et al.* (1981) study. The impact of formal and informal support services is clearly an area in which more research needs to be conducted. Specifically, investigation is needed into the impact of increased availability of community-based support services and programs that emanated from the passage of PL 94–142 (Meyers, Zetlin, & Blacher-Dixon, 1981).

In sum, a number of factors have been identified in the literature as related to family stress and/or the decision to place the child out of home. These factors include

1. child characteristics (level of retardation, behavior problems, age, degree of care needed);
2. family characteristics (socioeconomic status, race, marital satisfaction);
3. informal supports (friends and family); and
4. formal supports (social and psychological services to families and children, respite care, skills training).

According to Horejsi (1979), the family's success in caring for a handicapped child is a function of its motivation and capacity to do so, the environmental opportunities of the home, the available formal services, and the difficulty of the child's problems. When the child's problems are more difficult, family motivation and capacity must be greater, the opportunities of the home must be more enriched, and the support services must be more available in order to maintain the in-home placement.

Although the current philosophy in the field of mental retardation advocates the maintenance of children in the home with their families and the return to the home of children who in the past were placed in institutions, there is considerable variability in the extent to which families can successfully cope with a severely and profoundly retarded child. Turnbull *et al.* (1982) cautioned that

the right to live in the least restrictive environment should apply to family members as well as handicapped individuals. Thus, [the] concept of least restriction should be considered in light of the needs of each family member. Placing many severely handicapped children and youth in the least restrictive environment of their families results in their family being required to live in a highly restricted manner. (p. 63)

As this quote suggests, both the family's and the child's needs must be considered in selecting the optimal residential placement for a severely or profoundly mentally retarded child. The preceding discussion has focused on the factors affecting family decisions regarding out-of-home placement. The next section addresses the consequences of these decisions, namely the types of out-of-home residential settings in which severely and profoundly retarded children have been placed.

Residential Placement Patterns

This section presents the results of national and state studies that have reported on the residential placement of severely and profoundly retarded persons. Two studies are reviewed that provide data on national release patterns from public residential facilities during the 1970s. The results of these studies are compared to illustrate trends in the prevalence of severely and profoundly retarded persons moving from traditional institutional settings. These studies provide a useful contrast to a frequently noted consequence of deinstitutionalization: the increased proportion of residents in institutions who are severely and profoundly retarded. Larsen (1977), for example, noted that in 1968 severely and profoundly retarded persons accounted for 60% of the residents in public residential facilities. By 1972, this percentage had increased to 63% and by 1974 to 71%. More recent national data indicate that 80% of the 128,472 residents in public residential facilities are severely and profoundly retarded (Scheerenberger, 1982).

National Studies on Deinstitutionalization Patterns

Wyngaarden and Gollay (1976) reported the results of a national survey of 252 institutions serving mentally retarded persons, which was conducted in 1974 in order to collect information on the number, age, level of retardation, and placement settings of persons between the ages of 6 and 40 who were released from those institutions between 1972 and 1974. Of the 13,158 persons released, 4161 (31.6%) were children between the ages of 6 and 18 years. Of these children, 919 (22%) were severely retarded and 311 (7%) were profoundly retarded. Thus, less than a third of the children released during this 2-year period were either severely or profoundly retarded.

The most common setting to which children of all levels of retardation were released was the natural or adoptive home. Almost two-thirds

(64%) of the mildly retarded children and over half of the moderately (54%), severely (53%), and profoundly (58%) retarded children were placed in such settings. Foster homes were the next most common setting, receiving 14% of mildly retarded, 29% of moderately retarded, 25% of severely retarded, and 19% of profoundly retarded children. A somewhat greater percentage of profoundly retarded (23%) children were released to group homes than was reported for severely retarded (20%), moderately retarded (14%), or mildly retarded (11%) children.

When comparisons were made with the placement of mildly and moderately retarded children, several patterns were noted. First, natural and adoptive homes received more than half of all deinstitutionalized children and youths, regardless of the level of retardation of the children. Second, foster homes received larger proportions of released moderately and severely retarded persons, regardless of age (children and adults). Third, group homes received an incrementally larger proportion of released children and youths as the level of retardation became more severe. Differences were also found between the types of settings in which severely and profoundly retarded children and adults were placed. Children were more likely to be placed with their natural or adoptive family or in foster homes than were similarly disabled adults. Retarded adults were more likely to be placed in group homes (about a third of the severely and profoundly retarded adult releases) than were children.

There are two major implications for out-of-home placements of severely and profoundly retarded children to be drawn from this study. First, once a severely or profoundly retarded child has been placed in an institution, it is likely that he or she will remain in an out-of-home setting. Of those who were deinstitutionalized, almost half of the severely and profoundly retarded children were released to a setting other than their natural or adoptive family. Second, as previously shown, there were important differences in child and adult placement patterns.

Comparable data (see Table 4.3) based on resident release patterns in 1977 from public residential facilities have been reported (Best-Sigford, Bruininks, Lakin, Hill, & Heal, 1982). Of the total releases, almost a third (31.6%) were children or youth under the age of 22. There were notable differences in the proportion of releases by level of retardation. Almost half (44.6%) of profoundly retarded persons who were released were children or youth. In contrast, about a quarter (27.4%) of severely retarded, almost a third (31.5%) of moderately retarded, and less than a quarter (22.5%) of mildly retarded persons released were under age 22.

Data on the type of residential settings by level of retardation of the

TABLE 4.3
Distribution of Deinstitutionalized Clients by Age and Level of Retardation[a]

Level of mental retardation	Children and youths		Adults		Total	
	n	%	n	%	n	%
Wyngaarden & Gollay						
Mild	1726	31	3898	69	5624	43
Moderate	1205	29	3020	71	4225	32
Severe	919	35	1718	65	2637	20
Profound	311	46	361	54	672	5
Best-Sigford, Bruininks, Lakin, Hill, & Heal						
Mild	23	23	79	77	102	21
Moderate	41	32	89	68	130	26
Severe	37	27	98	73	135	27
Profound	41	45	51	55	92	19

[a] Source: adapted from Wyngaarden & Gollay (1976) and Best-Sigford, Bruininks, Lakin, Hill, & Heal (1982).
[b] The age range in the Wyngaarden & Gollay study was 6–18 for children and 19–40 for adults. The age range in the Best-Sigford, Bruininks, Lakin, Hill, & Heal study was 0–21 for children and 22 and over for adults.

released persons is also provided in the Best-Sigford et al. (1982) study, although it is not tabulated separately for different age groups. Nonetheless, the results indicate that the most common setting to which severely and profoundly retarded persons were released was another public residential facility (26.7 and 38.5%, respectively). This compares to only 11% of mildly retarded and 18% of moderately retarded persons similarly placed. The next most common residential setting for severely retarded persons (24%) was a community residential facility serving 15 or fewer persons, while for profoundly retarded persons (18.7%) it was a nursing home. About a fifth of severely retarded (23%) and profoundly retarded (18%) persons were released to their natural or adoptive homes.

While the study reported by Wyngaarden and Gollay (1976) did not include releases to nursing homes and/or institutional settings, comparisons of their results to the more recent 1977 study just described (Best-Sigford et al., 1982) can be drawn. First, whereas the Wyngaarden and Gollay (1976) study found that about one-half of the released severely and profoundly retarded persons moved to their own homes, less than one-quarter of similarly disabled releases from the Best-Sigford *et al.* study returned home. Two possible reasons for such a dramatic shift are (1) the inclusion of nursing homes and other institutional settings in the Best-Sigford *et al.* study and (2) the increased availability of community residential settings in 1977 compared to 1974. Second, there are striking differences in the percentage of overall releases by level of retardation between the two studies. The percentage of releases for mild, moderate, severe, and profoundly retarded persons in the Wyngaarden and Gollay survey was 43, 32, 20, and 5% respectively. For the Best-Sigford *et al.* survey, it was 21, 26, 27, and 19%, respectively. Thus, assuming that the two studies tapped similar populations, the proportion of released residents who were severely and profoundly retarded was considerably greater in 1977 than during the 1972–1974 period covered by the first study.

Third, the percentage of releases for each level of retardation who were children or youths has remained fairly consistent during the period covered by the two studies. For example, the percentage of profoundly retarded persons released who were children or youths was 46% in the Wyngaarden and Gollay study compared to 45% in the Best-Sigford *et al.* study. Similar results can be observed for the percentage of severely retarded persons released who were children or youths (35% in the Wyngaarden & Gollay study, 27% in the Best-Sigford *et al.* study). Thus, even though a greater proportion of all releases were severely or profoundly retarded in the 1977 survey than in the 1972–1974 survey, the distribution of child and adult releases by level of retardation has remained consistent.

State Studies on Residential Patterns

Studies descriptive of the residential patterns of mentally retarded persons in three states are described below. While two of the studies lack detailed information on the breakdown of residents by level of retardation and age, they are reviewed here to indicate the prevalence of both children and/or severely or profoundly retarded persons in various residential settings.

Landesman-Dwyer and Sulzbacher (1981) surveyed developmentally disabled persons receiving social and health services in Washington State in 1975 and 1976. Data were presented on (1) the distribution of severely and profoundly retarded persons across various residential settings and (2) the percentage of the total population of mentally retarded persons in each type of residence who were severely or profoundly retarded. Their study found that severely or profoundly retarded persons (children and adults) accounted for 40% of the 6487 developmentally disabled persons in public and private residential settings studied. The vast majority (70%) of severely or profoundly retarded persons were living in state institutions. Nursing homes contained 14%, group homes contained 5%, licensed board and care facilities contained 4%, foster homes contained 2%, and natural families had 5% of the severely or profoundly retarded population receiving state social or health services.

Data were also presented on the percentage of the total population of mentally retarded persons in each type of residence who were severely or profoundly mentally retarded. Severely or profoundly mentally retarded persons accounted for 79% of the total institutional population and for nearly a fifth of mentally retarded persons in nursing homes, group homes, and foster homes. They also constituted 14% of those persons living with their natural families who were receiving state services and for 16% of the residents in licensed board and care facilities. It was notable that a substantial proportion of all mentally retarded persons (both children and adults) in all the types of community residences surveyed were so severely disabled.

An analysis of the residential placements of mentally retarded clients served by the Department of Developmental Services in California supported the findings discussed earlier that severely impaired persons are being served in a variety of residential settings. Bjaanes et al. (1981) found that of the 611 persons in the most impaired group in their sample, nearly half were living in in-home placements; a fifth were in small care facilities (serving an average of 3 to 6 clients), slightly less than a fifth (17%) were in institutions, and about 12% were in large care facilities (serving 16 or more residents). However, in comparison to the placement of higher-functioning clients, the most impaired group was least likely to be placed in in-home placements or small care facilities and had the highest rate of placement in large care factilities and state hospitals.

We analyzed the residential settings of severely and profoundly mentally retarded persons receiving services funded by the Massachusetts Department of Mental Health in 1980 (Seltzer & Krauss, in press). The most common residential setting for severely and profoundly retarded persons was state institutions (68.5 and 93.7%, respectively). Only 17.1% of the served severely retarded persons and 2.6% of the served profoundly retarded were living in community residences.

Our analysis also examined the proportion of children and youth (aged 0–21 years) among the severely and profoundly retarded served population. Almost a fifth of severely retarded and profoundly retarded persons (17.7 and 22.2 %, respectively) served were 21 years or younger. Of the 1132 children served, 28.6 % were severely retarded and 34.2 % were profoundly retarded. Thus, over half the total served population of children were either severely or profoundly retarded. Many of these children were in the 19–21-year age range (44 % of the profoundly retarded and 49 % of the severely retarded). Only 11 % of the severely retarded and 12 % of the profoundly retarded children were 12 years or younger. Thus, the vast majority of the severely and profoundly retarded children served were adolescents or young adults (below age 21).

Information on the residential settings of these children was available for 295 severely retarded and 382 profoundly retarded children. Five types of residential settings were analyzed: institutions, congregate care (e.g., nursing homes), community residences (e.g., group homes), family care (including specialized home care), and independent living. Results indicated that 87 % of the profoundly retarded and 53 % of the severely retarded children served were living in institutions. The next most common setting for severely retarded children was a community residence (13 %) and for profoundly retarded children was a family care setting (6 %).

The results of this analysis corroborate the findings of the previously described studies of other state populations. Specifically, the most common out-of-home setting for severely and profoundly retarded persons is an institution. Although information on the out-of-home settings for severely or profoundly retarded children was only available for one state (Massachusetts), the findings suggest that the high rate of institutional placement holds for children as well as adults.

Several other studies have reported the distribution across residential settings of severely and profoundly retarded persons. Miller (1975) found that of those profoundly retarded persons referred for services in several western states in 1973 and 1974, 44 % were placed in convalescent hospitals, 40 % were placed in institutions, 6 % were placed in foster homes, and only 10 % remained in their own family's homes. Among severely retarded children, 32 % were placed in institutions, 25 % in foster homes, and 25 % remained in their own homes. Eyman et al. (1970) reported that two-thirds of the severely retarded Anglo and 95 % of the profoundly retarded Anglo children in their sample lived in out-of-home placements. While the proportions of black and Hispanic families in the Eyman et al. (1970) sample who kept their severely and profoundly retarded children at home were somewhat higher, out-of-home placement was very common in these minority families as well.

Unfortunately, the extent to which these populations are representative of the general population of severely and profoundly retarded children is unknown. While it is possible that these studies have overestimated the prevalence of out-of-home placement among the severely and profoundly retarded, out-of-home placement does appear to be very common in this population. The need for family supports in order to increase the number of severely and profoundly retarded children who remain at home is underscored by these high rates of out-of-home placement.

Studies of Types of Community Residences

Two nationwide studies are available that describe the use of specific types of noninstitutional, community-based residences for mentally retarded persons. Bruininks, Hill, and Thorsheim (1982) reported the findings from a national survey conducted in 1977 of specially licensed foster homes, which collectively served 4999 mentally retarded people. The data indicated that as many as one-third of the foster home residents were reported to be either severely or profoundly retarded. Compared to the level of retardation of residents of public residential facilities, residents of foster homes were found to be less severely handicapped. Also, only 12.8% of the residents served in foster homes were less than 15 years of age.

Several trends in the use of foster homes were noted that may have implications for the use of out-of-home placements for severely and profoundly retarded children. First, only 11.1% of the new admissions to foster homes came directly from the client's natural home. Most came from institutions (42.3%) or from other foster homes (31.8%). Second, Bruininks et al. 1982) noted that while foster care has traditionally been associated with children, their study suggested it has also been and increasingly will be used for adult mentally retarded persons. It is interesting that the percentage of children under age 21 among residents of foster homes, community residential facilities, and public residential facilities is similar (31.3, 38.1, and 27.9%, respectively). The expectation of a greater prevalence of children in foster homes than in other out-of-home placements appears to be incorrect.

Bruininks, Kudla, Hauber, Hill, and Wieck (1981) reported the results of a national survey of community residential facilities (primarily group homes) for mentally retarded persons. These facilities are defined as any community-based living quarter providing 24-hour, 7-day-a-week room, board, and supervision of mentally retarded persons. The 4,427 facilities meeting the study's criteria served 76,250 persons, of whom 62,397 (82%) were classified as mentally retarded. Data on the ages of mentally retarded residents indicated that 2.4% were between 0 to 4 years old, 6.4% were between 5 and 9 years old, 10% were between 10 and 14 years old, and 19.3% were between 15 and 21 years old. Thus, over a third (38%) of the mentally retarded population in community residences were 21 years old or younger.

The study also collected information on the level of retardation of the residents. Over a fifth (21.8%) were severely retarded and another 10.6% were classified as profoundly retarded. Thus, about a third (32.4%) were either severely or profoundly retarded. As is true for many of the studies discussed, breakdowns by age and level of retardation were not reported.

Taken together, the nationwide and state studies and the studies of specific types of community residences suggest a number of trends and issues. First, as noted earlier, there has been an increase over time in the number of severely and profoundly retarded persons among residents who have been released from institutions. Second, the proportion of children among released populations remained constant from the early to the latter part of the 1970s. Third, the studies varied considerably with respect to the percentage of severely and/or profoundly retarded persons who lived in their own homes, from a low of 5% (Landesman-Dwyer & Sulzbacher, 1981) to a high of 58% (Wyngaarden & Gollay, 1976). Even if the highest estimates are used, the rate of out-of-home placement in this population is very high—about 50%.

The Research, Policy, and Service Agenda

The available research on out-of-home placement for severely and profoundly retarded children, although limited in scope, points out a number of issues and problems that warrant professional attention. There are also large gaps in the literature, suggesting areas in need of future research. These issues, problems, and gaps are identified and discussed as five overall recommendations for future research, policy formulation, and service development.

Support Services

First, there is a need to make available services in order to support the efforts of families to maintain their severely or profoundly retarded children in the home. There are at least four specific types of services that should be priorities for development: respite care, financial incentives, counseling for parents and siblings, and parent training.

Respite Care

A number of studies have noted that parents found respite care, or the provision of temporary relief services to the family of a handicapped child, to be a highly valued service (Gollay *et al.*, 1978; Jaslow & Spagna, 1977; Upshur, 1982a, 1982b). Despite its importance, one study found that in many states respite care services are either not available or available only on a limited basis (Bruininks, Morreau, & Williams, 1979). Upshur (1982b), in a survey of respite care in Massachusetts, found that services provided to clients were rarely specialized. Further, clients with severe emotional–behavioral problems or with extensive medical needs were often ineligible. These findings suggest that in addition to the limited availability of respite care services in the community, families with severely or profoundly handicapped children may be denied such services by the exclusionary policies of the providing agencies. Thus, there is a need to increase the availability of respite care services and to extend access to them to families with severely and profoundly retarded children.

Financial Incentives

Several policy analysts have advocated the provision of cash subsidies to families who have severely handicapped children, to maximize the chances that these children can remain at home (Boggs, 1979; Roth, 1979; Tapper, 1979). These authors pointed out that such families are faced with a number of different types of extraordinary costs: extra out-of-pocket expenses, "opportunity" costs with respect to parents' careers, limitations on resources available to siblings of handicapped children, and so on. They have argued that out-of-home placement occurs in part because of the resource drain experienced by families while the child lives at home. Specific recommendations offered by these authors vary, but the basic point made by all is that cash subsidies should be made available to families who keep their seriously handicapped child at home. The two commonly asserted rationales for this policy are (1) cash subsidies will save money for the government because institutional placement is more expensive, and (2) subsidies will improve the quality of life for both the handicapped child and the family. As Roth (1979) argued,

> Added income may spell the difference between being forced to institutionalize the child and taking care of the child at home (coincidentally at a lower cost to the government). Added income can buy time, by substituting services on the market for services provided by the parents. It can buy sanity for parents, providing money for babysitters, movies, and outings once in a while. There are many uses for added income, and society, acting on behalf of the handicapped child and his or her family as

well as on its own behalf, has reason to see that the family of the handicapped child gets such added income. (p. 42)

Counseling

Counseling for parents and siblings of severely and profoundly retarded children is one type of needed service that is somewhat more widely available (Bjaanes et al., 1981). Family members experience a number of specific crises that pose challenges to their ability to function, such as the initial diagnosis of mental retardation or the child's entry into school. Also, family members may need professional support to help them cope with the stresses posed by the child and with the adjustments they have to make in order to maintain the seriously handicapped child at home (Adams, 1971; Dickerson, 1981).

Traditionally, the focus of supportive counseling with families has been on helping them to accept the situation and to progress through various identified stages (Dickerson, 1981; Olshansky, 1962; Solnit & Stark, 1969). While counseling that accomplishes these goals may be very valuable, there is also the need, voiced articulately by some parents, for general supportive counseling to help them cope with the constellation of factors they confront in caring for and rearing a seriously handicapped child (Featherstone, 1980; Parke, 1967; Turnbull & Turnbull, 1978). There are some advantages for families in receiving counseling provided by a professional with expertise specifically in the area of mental retardation. Such professionals can bring specialized knowledge to the counseling relationship. There are also times when family members could benefit as much from counseling provided by generic agencies or by nonspecialized private practitioners; not only are such generic resources more widely available than specialized services, they also may be perceived by families as less stigmatizing.

Thus, there is a compelling reason for mental health professionals to be responsive to the counseling needs posed by family members of severely and profoundly retarded persons. This responsiveness requires the acquisition of specialized knowledge about mental retardation and a willingness to deal with the psychosocial challenges such families present.

Parent Training

Finally, regarding parent training, there are substantial data to suggest that training parents of retarded children does lead to improvement in both child skill acquisition and parental knowledge of teaching and behavior management principles (see Baker, Chapter 9 of this volume for a comprehensive review of parent training and intervention with families of handicapped children). However, studies are lacking that relate parental competence or skills acquired through training to greater acceptance and management of a severely handicapped child at home.

Currently, of the four service types we identified as being central to the support of families who intend to keep their seriously retarded child at home, only counseling is generally available, although this service, too, is somewhat limited in accessibility. In contrast, financial incentives for in-home placement are not available, although some state-level policy analysts have discussed the possibility of their implementation. Respite care and parent training are available in many localities, but not nearly in sufficient quantity or with sufficient accessibility to families of severely and profoundly retarded children. Thus, the true potential for maintaining severely and profoundly retarded children in their own homes will remain unknown until these, and possibly other, needed services are developed and integrated into the community-based service system.

Community Residences

Second, there is a need to develop more community residences for severely and profoundly retarded children. Regardless of the extent of support services provided to families, some will be unable for a variety of reasons to maintain their child at home. Currently, when out-of-home placement is needed, families have a very difficult time securing a residential alternative. Institutional placements are increasingly scarce as a result of the dominant philosophy in the field and the policy of deinstitutionalization. Community residences are not available in sufficient quantity to meet the need. In some states (e.g., Massachusetts), community residence placement priority is given to children (and adults) who previously lived in institutions. The out-of-home placement options for families who have until this point maintained their children at home are thus limited.

In part, the dearth of community residences for severely and profoundly retarded children is due to resource allocation decisions. For example, state budgets for mental retardation services have traditionally been heavily weighted toward institutions rather than community residences. At the same time, resources that have been targeted for community residential services have been spent primarily on programs for mildly and moderately retarded adults. Children's residential services and residences specifically for the severely and profoundly retarded are much more limited in availability. One exception is the Macomb-

Oakland Regional Center in Michigan, which has developed over 60 group homes and 175 specialized foster homes that primarily serve severely and profoundly retarded children (Provencal, 1981).

Community residences for severely and profoundly retarded children should be structured in order to meet two goals. First, they should provide a high quality, habilitation-oriented home for the children. Second, and perhaps equally as important, they should provide a sufficient degree of respite for the families so that parent–child involvement can be maintained to the maximum extent possible. Five-day-a-week residential placement, part-time and/or temporary foster care, and residential schools are examples of alternatives to full-time and long-term community residential placement.

Innovation in Residential Services

Third, innovation in the structure and content of community residential services for severely and profoundly retarded children is needed. The dominant ideology of community residences—informal, familylike, paraprofessional, nonhierarchically structured—is particularly geared to the needs of mildly and moderately retarded adults (Baker et al., 1977). Most community residences have been developed to provide a normal homelike atmosphere and flow of events to persons whose skills and behaviors need less intensive supervision and intervention than is true for more severely handicapped persons. Further, the staff in community residences has traditionally been nonprofessional and relatively inexperienced, and has exhibited high turnover rates (Fiorelli, 1982). It is reasonable to assume that residences serving severely and profoundly retarded children require professional, experienced, and stable staffing patterns. Research is needed to identify the constellation of resources—programmatic, personal, and technological—that are necessary to create a viable, safe, behaviorally challenging, and growth-producing residential environment for severely and profoundly retarded children.

Additional Research

Fourth, there is critical need for more research on the prevalence of out-of-home placement, the appropriateness of different types of residential settings, and the effectiveness of family support services to understand better the factors that lead to out-of-home placement. While it is hardly surprising that there is a need for more research, this conclusion contains a number of challenges to the professional community with respect to the financial and intellectual commitment involved in conducting new research on this population. For example, and least difficult, survey data on the residential placements of mentally retarded persons have not been analyzed by both age and level of retardation jointly (Bruininks et al., 1981). Consequently, we do not know the real prevalence of out-of-home placement for severely and profoundly retarded children or the true proportion of this population among all mentally retarded persons in community residences. Thus, we need additional analyses of existing survey data in order to develop an accurate understanding of the current utilization patterns of out-of-home residential placements for severely and profoundly retarded children.

Further, we need longitudinal studies on the effectiveness of specific types of residential settings for this population. While this can also be said for mildly and moderately retarded children (and adults), longitudinal studies on severely and profoundly retarded children have methodological and analytic requirements that may differ from those for less handicapped persons. In order to observe and measure changes in behavioral, cognitive, and/or emotional status, more refined instruments and powerful statistical analysis methods are needed (Berkson & Landesman-Dwyer, 1977).

Prospective studies are also needed in the analysis of family stress issues. Most of the studies reviewed earlier on family stress and the decision to seek out-of-home placement are retrospective studies. Thus, differences in the coping abilities of families who did and did not place their children have often been documented after the placement was made. Preplacement differences between these types of families have generally not been examined. Additionally, in order to assess the effectiveness of support services to families, we need experimental research on the capability of services—counseling, respite, parent training, and financial support—to prevent or delay out-of-home placement.

Additional Attention to Needs of Children

Fifth, there is a need to elevate and intensify the amount of professional, practitioner, and research attention paid to the needs of severely and profoundly retarded children. These issues must be placed on the public agenda. The services needed by these children are difficult to assess, demand creative approaches, and require substantial investments of financial resources. Yet, as Bjaanes et al. (1981) pointed out, "the general pattern tends to be that those who are the most severely impaired, and hence also in most need of habilitation services, are those for whom services are least likely to be provided. This raises the philosophical and moral dilemma: to whom should service be provided?" (p. 346).

Further, the findings for services provided to natural families are not encouraging. Gollay et al. (1978) reported that "natural families had by far the lowest utilization rate on almost all the services. . . . It appears that many natural families with mentally retarded children are receiving far fewer services than other types of residential placements" (p. 108). These studies suggest that two major obstacles to the receipt of services are level of retardation (the more severe, the fewer services) and living with the natural family. This is clearly at odds with the documented need for services and with the current public policy emphasis on supporting the natural family.

References

Adams, M. (1971). *Mental retardation and its social dimensions.* New York: Columbia University Press.

Baker, B. L., Seltzer, G. B., & Seltzer, M. M. (1977). *As close as possible: Community residences for retarded adults.* Boston: Little, Brown.

Balla, D., Estes, O., Hollis, J., Isaacson, R., Orlando, R. Palk, B. E., Warren, S., Siegel, P. S., & Ellis, N. R. Wyatt v. Hardin, Petitioners' Motion for modification (Oct. 20, 1978).

Berkson, G., & Landesman-Dwyer, S. (1977). Behavioral research on severe and profound mental retardation. *American Journal of Mental Deficiency, 81,* 428–454.

Best-Sigford, B., Bruininks, R. H., Lakin, K. C., Hill, B. K., & Heal, L. W. (1982). Resident release patterns in a national survey of public residential facilities. *American Journal of Mental Deficiency, 87,* 130–140.

Birenbaum, A. (1971). The mentally retarded child in the home and the family cycle. *Journal of Health and Social Behavior, 12,* 55.

Bjaanes, A. T., Butler, E. W., & Kelly, B. R. (1981). Placement type and client functional level as factors in provision of services aimed at increasing adjustment. In R. H. Bruininks, C. E. Meyers, B. B. Sigford, & K. C. Lakin (Eds.), *Deinstitutionalization and community adjustment of mentally retarded people.* Washington, DC: American Association on Mental Deficiency.

Blackard, M. K., & Barsh, E. T. (1982). Parents' and professionals' perceptions of the handicapped child's impact on the family. *The Journal of the Association for the Severely Handicapped, 7,* 62–70.

Blatt, B., & Kaplan, F. (1966). *Christmas in purgatory.* Boston: Allyn & Bacon.

Boggs, E. M. (1979). Allocation of resources for family care. In R. H. Bruininks & G. C. Krantz (Eds.), *Family care of developmentally disabled members: Conference Proceedings.* Minneapolis: University of Minnesota.

Bradshaw, J., & Lawton, D. (1978). Tracing the causes of stress in families with handicapped children. *British Journal of Social Work, 8,* 181–191.

Bruininks, R. H., Hill, B. K., & Thorsheim, M. J. (1982). Deinstitutionalization and foster care for mentally retarded people. *Health and Social Work, 7,* 198–205.

Bruininks, R. H., Kudla, M. J., Hauber, F. A., Hill, B. K., & Weick, C. A. (1981). Recent growth and status of community based alternatives. In R. H. Bruininks, C. E. Meyers, B. B. Sigford, & K. C. Lakin (Eds.), Deinstitutionalization and community adjustment of mentally retarded people. Washington, DC: American Association on Mental Deficiency.

Bruininks, R. H., Morreau, L. E., & Williams, S. M. (1979). Issues and problems of deinstitutionalization in HEW Region V. Minneapolis: University of Minnesota.

Center on Human Policy. (1979). The community imperative: A refutation of all arguments in support of institutionalizing anybody because of mental retardation. Unpublished paper, Syracuse University.

Conroy, J. W. (1982, November). Reactions to deinstitutionalization among parents of retarded adults and children. Paper presented at the Working Conference on Deinstitutionalization and the Education of Handicapped Children, Minneapolis.

Cummings, S. T. (1976). The impact of the child's deficiency on the father: A study of mentally retarded and chronically ill children. American Journal of Orthopsychiatry, 46, 245–55.

Cummings, S. T., Bayley, H. C., & Rie, H. F. (1966). Effects of the child's deficiency on the mother: A study of mothers of mentally retarded, chronically ill, and neurotic children. American Journal of Orthopsychiatry, 36, 595–608.

Dickerson, M. U. (1981). Social work practice with the mentally retarded. New York: The Free Press.

Downey, K. J. (1965). Parents' reasons for institutionalizing severely mentally retarded children. Journal of Health and Human Behavior, 6, 147–155.

Dybwad, G. (1978, December 9). A society without institutions. Unpublished paper presented to the Residential Alternatives Symposium, University of Hartford, Hartford, CT.

Ellis, N. R., Bostick, G. E., Moore, S. A., & Taylor, J. J. (1981). A follow-up of severely and profoundly mentally retarded children after short-term institutionalization. Mental Retardation, 19, 31–35.

Erickson, M. (1969). MMPI profiles of parents of young retarded children. American Journal of Mental Deficiency, 73, 5.

Eyman, R. K., Borthwick, S. A., & Miller, C. (1981). Trends in maladaptive behavior of mentally retarded persons placed in community and institutional settings. American Journal of Mental Deficiency, 85, 473–477.

Eyman, R. K., & Call, T. (1977). Maladaptive behavior and community placement of mentally retarded persons. American Journal of Mental Deficiency, 82, 137–144.

Eyman, R. K., & Miller, C. (1978). A demographic overview of severe and profound mental retardation. In C. E. Meyers (Ed.), Quality of life in severely and profoundly retarded people: Research foundations for improvement. Washington, DC: American Association on Mental Deficiency.

Eyman, R. K., Moore, B. C., Capes, L., & Zachofsky, T. (1970). Maladaptive behavior of institutionalized retardates with seizures. American Journal of Mental Deficiency, 75, 651–659.

Eyman, R. K., O'Connor, G., Tarjan, G., & Justice, R. S. (1972). Factors determining residential placement of mentally retarded children. American Journal of Mental Deficiency, 76, 692–698.

Farber, B. (1959). Effects of a severely mentally retarded child on family integration Monographs of the Society for Research in Child Development, 24(2, Serial No. 71).

Farber, B. (1968). Mental retardation: Its social context and social consequences. Boston: Houghton-Mifflin.

Farber, B. (1979). Sociological ambivalence and family care: The individual proposes and society disposes. In R. H. Bruininks & G. C. Krantz (Eds.), *Family care of developmentally disabled members: Conference proceedings.* Minneapolis: University of Minnesota.

Featherstone, H. (1980). *A difference in the family.* New York: Basic Books.

Fingado, M. L., Kini, J. F., Stewart, K., and Redd, W. H. (1970). A thirty-day residential training program for retarded children. *Mental Retardation, 8,* 42–45.

Fiorelli, J. S. (1982). Community residential services during the 1980s: Challenges and future trends. *The Journal of the Association for the Severely Handicapped, 7,* 14–18.

Fotheringham, J. B. (1970). Retardation, family adequacy, and institutionalization. *Canada's Mental Health, 18,* 15–18.

Fowle, C. (1968). The effect of the severely mentally retarded child on his family. *American Journal of Mental Deficiency, 73,* 468–473.

Gath, A. (1977). The impact of an abnormal child on the parents. *British Journal of Psychiatry, 130,* 405–410.

Goffman, E. Asylums, (1961). Garden City, NJ: Anchor/Doubleday.

Gollay, E., Freedman, R., Wyngaarden, M., & Kurtz, N. (1978). *Coming back: The community experiences of deinstitutionalized mentally retarded people.* Cambridge, MA: Abt Books.

Graliker, B. V., Kock, R., & Henderson, R. A. (1965). A study of factors influencing placement of a retarded child in a state residential institution. *American Journal of Mental Deficiency, 69,* 553–559.

Greenfeld, J. *A place for Noah.* (1972). New York: Holt, Rinehart & Winston.

Grossman, F. K. (1972). *Brothers and sisters of retarded children: An exploratory study.* Syracuse, NY: Syracuse University Press.

Grossman, H. J. (Ed.). (1983). *Classification in mental retardation.* Washington, DC: American Association on Mental Deficiency.

Holroyd, J., Brown, N., Wikler, L., & Simmons, J. Q. (1975). Stress in families of institutionalized and non-institutionalized autistic children. *Journal of Community Psychology, 3,* 26–31.

Holroyd, J., & McArthur, O. (1976). Mental retardation and stress on the parents: A contrast between Down's syndrome and childhood autism. *American Journal of Mental Deficiency, 80,* 4.

Holt, K. S. (1958). The home care of severely retarded children. *Pediatrics, 22,* 744–755.

Horejsi, C. R. (1979). Social and psychological factors in family care. In R. H. Bruininks & G. C. Krantz (Eds.), *Family care of developmentally disabled members: Conference Proceedings.* Minneapolis: University of Minnesota.

Jaslow, R. I., & Spagna, M. B. (1977). Gaps in a comprehensive system of services for the mentally retarded. *Mental Retardation, 15,* 6–9.

Kadushin, A. (1980). *Child Welfare Services* (3rd ed.). New York: Macmillan.

Landesman-Dwyer, S., & Sulzbacher, F. (1981). Residential placement and adaptation of severely and profoundly retarded individuals. In R. H. Bruininks, C. E. Meyers, B. B. Sigford, & K. C. Lakin (Eds.), *Deinstitutionalization and community adjustment of mentally retarded people.* Washington, DC: American Association on Mental Deficiency.

Larsen, L. A. (1977). Community services necessary to program effectively for the severely/profoundly handicapped. In E. Sontag (Ed.), *Educational programming for the severely and profoundly handicapped.* Reston, VA: The Council for Exceptional Children.

Levine, S. (Principal investigator). (1981–1983). *Study of stress, coping, and social supports.* Boston: University Professors Program—Boston University, W. T. Grant Foundation.

Maroney, R. M. (1979). Allocation of resources in family care. In R. H. Bruininks & G. C. Krantz (Eds.), *Family care of developmentally disabled members: Conference proceedings.* Minneapolis: University of Minnesota.

Maroney, R. M. (1981). Public social policy: Impact on families with handicapped children. In J. L. Paul (Ed.), *Understanding and working with parents of children with special needs.* New York: Holt, Rinehart & Winston.

Massie, R., & Massie, S. (1975). *Journey.* New York: Knopf.

Mercer, J. R. (1966). Patterns of family crisis related to reacceptance of the retardate. *American Journal of Mental Deficiency, 71,* 19–32.

Meyers, C. E., & Blacher, J. (1982). *The effect of schooling severely impaired children on the family* (NICHD Grant No. HD14680). UCLA/MRCC Group at Lanterman State Hospital, Pomona, CA.

Meyers, C. E., Zetlin, A., & Blacher-Dixon, J. (1981). The family as affected by schooling for severely retarded children: An invitation to research. *Journal of Community Psychology, 9,* 306–315.

Miller, C. R. (1975). Deinstitutionalization and mortality trends for the profoundly retarded. In C. Cleland & L. Talkington (Eds.), *Research with profoundly retarded.* The Western Research Conference and the Brown Schools.

Olshansky, S. (1962). Chronic sorrow: A response to having a mentally defective child. *Social Casework, 43,* 190–193.

Parke, C. (1967). *The siege.* Boston: Little, Brown.

Provencal, G. (1981). Issues of social policy. In M. U. Dickerson (Ed.), *Social work practice with the mentally retarded.* New York: The Free Press.

Roth, W. (1979). An economic model of social and psychological factors in families with developmentally disabled children. In R. H. Bruininks & G. C. Krantz (Eds.), *Family care of developmentally disabled members: Conference proceedings.* Minneapolis: University of Minnesota.

Rowitz, L. (1974). Social factors in mental retardation. *Social Science and Medicine, 8,* 405–412.

Saenger, G. (1960). *The adjustment of severely retarded adults in the community.* Albany: New York State Interdepartmental Health Resources Board.

Scheerenberger, R. C. (1982). Public residential services, 1981: Status and trends. *Mental Retardation, 20,* 210–215.

Seltzer, G. B. (1983). Systems of classification in mental retardation. In J. L. Matson & J. Mulik (Eds.), *Comprehensive handbook of mental retardation.* London: Pergamon Press.

Seltzer, M. M., & Krauss, M. W. (in press). Family, community residence, and institutional placement of a sample of mentally retarded children. *American Journal of Mental Deficiency.*

Solnit, A. J., & Stark, M. H. (1969). Mourning and the birth of a defective child. In W. Wolfensberger & R. Kurtz (Eds.), *Management of the family of the mentally retarded.* Chicago: Follett Educational Corporation.

Suelzle, M., & Keenan, V. (1981). Changes in family support networks over the life cycle of mentally retarded persons. *American Journal of Mental Deficiency, 86,* 267–274.

Tapper, H. (1979). Barriers to a family subsidy program. In R. H. Bruininks & G. C. Krantz (Eds.), *Family care of developmentally disabled members: Conference proceedings.* Minneapolis: University of Minnesota.

Tarjan, G., Wright, S. W., Eyman, R. K., & Keeran, C. V. (1973). Natural history of mental retardation: Some aspects of epidemiology. *American Journal of Mental Deficiency, 77*, 369–379.

Townsend, P. W., & Flanagan, J. J. (1976). Experimental preadmission program to encourage home care for severely and profoundly retarded children. *American Journal of Mental Deficiency, 80*, 562–569.

Turnbull, A. P., Brotherson, M. J., & Summers, J. A. (1982, November). *The impact of deinstitutionalization on families: A family systems approach.* Paper presented at the Working Conference on Deinstitutionalization and the Education of Handicapped Children, Minneapolis.

Turnbull, A. P., & Turnbull, H. R. (1978). *Parents speak out.* Columbus, OH: Merrill.

Upshur, C. C. (1982a). An evaluation of home-based respite care. *Mental Retardation, 20*, 58–62.

Upshur, C. C. (1982b). Respite care for mentally retarded and other disabled populations: Program models and family needs. *Mental Retardation, 20*, 2–6.

Waisbren, S. E. (1980). Parents' reactions after the birth of a developmentally disabled child. *American Journal of Mental Deficiency, 84*, 345–351.

Wyatt v. Stickney, 344 F. Supp. 387 (M.D. Ala. 1974), *Aff'd sub nom. Wyatt v. Aderholt*, 503 F.2d 1305 (5th Cir. 1974).

Wyngaarden, M., & Gollay, E. (1976). *Profile of national deinstitutionalization patterns 1972–1974.* Cambridge, MA: Abt Associates.

PART II

Child Influences on Family Dynamics

Research with Families of Severely Handicapped Children: Theoretical and Methodological Considerations*

Zolinda Stoneman
Gene H. Brody

Introduction

As the deinstitutionalization movement gains momentum, increasing numbers of severely handicapped persons are living with their family of origin instead of in an institutional setting. Additionally, resources are being committed to prevent the initial institutionalization of handicapped individuals, allowing them instead to remain at home with their families. Advocates of deinstitutionalization have argued persuasively that, in most cases, severely handicapped children will be more likely to

* The preparation of this chapter was supported in part by the National Institute of Child Health and Human Development Grant No. HD16817–01A1, National Foundation for the March of Dimes Grant No. 12–120, and a Faculty Research Grant Award from the University of Georgia Research Foundation. The authors wish to thank Cathy Davis for coordinating the demonstration study included in this chapter.

179

receive the stimulation, guidance, and nurturance necessary to foster development within a family context than they would in an institutional context. Relatively few studies, however, have gathered scientific data on the day-to-day lives of families with severely handicapped children. Before we can effectively facilitate the deinstitutionalization process and help families maintain their severely handicapped family members at home, more information must be obtained about the needs and experiences of these families.

It is fair to say that severely handicapped children are expected to place great demands in terms of time and sheer physical energy on parents and other family members. Such demands affect not only the parent–child relationship but other aspects of family functioning as well, which in turn reciprocally affect the parent–child relationship. More will be said about this subsequently. It is clear that the research community must provide policymakers and families with scientifically sound information if the deinstitutionalization movement is to fulfill the goals intended by its architects. Therefore, the purpose of this chapter is to present conceptual issues and methodological options to the would-be researcher interested in studying families with severely handicapped members.

We begin by examining the family as a system, discussing the role relationships and the reciprocal nature of family interactions. Our focus in later sections shifts to methodological issues in selecting observational and self-report research models. We then examine issues in using observational methodologies with families of severely handicapped children and conclude the chapter by presenting a pilot demonstration study that uses multimethod procedures to study interactions in families with a severely handicapped child.

The Family as a System

Interrelated Subsystems

The study of parent–child or family interactions involving a severely handicapped child should be based on some implicit theory of family functioning. This implicit theory will influence a series of decisions that any would-be researcher will make, including the nature and operationalization of the independent and dependent variables and the direction of influence or causality within families. The implicit theory guiding our efforts is that the family is composed of several different subsystems, which reciprocally influence one another. Thus, the nuclear family can be partitioned into the spouse subsystem, the sibling subsystem, and the parent–child subsystem. Changes in any one subsystem are assumed to have a reciprocal impact on the other family subsystems.

Empirical support for viewing the family in this manner can be found in the clinical literature. First, consider what happens to children when parents (the spouse subsystem) engage in recurrent conflict. The literature has consistently demonstrated that interparental conflict is associated with childhood behavior problems. For example, researchers have found that children from broken but conflict-free homes were less likely to experience behavior problems than were children from unbroken homes marked by conflict (Gibson, 1969; McCord, McCord & Thurber, 1962; Nye, 1957; Power, Ash, Schoenberg, & Sorey, 1974). This line of research is corroborated by a conceptually similar line of research that demonstrates that children of divorced parents who continue to have conflicts beyond the divorce manifest more behavior problems than do children from conflict-free single parent homes (Anthony, 1974; Hetherington, Cox, & Cox, 1978; Kelly & Wallerstein, 1976).

Patterson (1980) and his colleagues at the Oregon Social Learning Center have demonstrated how exchanges within the parent–child subsystem can affect the spouse–spouse subsystem. Mothers with aggressive and acting-out boys were found to be subjected to high rates of noxious behaviors to which they often submit, and therefore negatively reinforce. Such interaction episodes teach the child that he can obtain desired consequences by emitting specific classes of noxious behavior. As this pattern of exchange continues, the father holds the mother responsible for the child's behavior. The net result for the mother is that she reports increased levels of depression and less satisfaction with her marriage. Again, this is another example of how exchanges in one subsystem have implications for other areas of family functioning.

Reciprocity

A second assumption that we make about family socialization and functioning is that it is best characterized by a dual-process, reciprocal influence model; sequential exchanges between spouses, parents and children, or siblings influence the contemporary behavior of family members as well as the form interactions will take in the future. In its simplest form, a sequential exchange is composed of a purposeful behavior directed from one family member to another and a contingent response or nonresponse from the second family member. Research on social interaction has consistently demonstrated that the frequency with which behavior is directed towards persons is a function of their contingent responsiveness. As contingent responsiveness decreases, so does the frequency of interaction between two persons (Bakeman, 1978; Gottman & Parkhurst, 1980; Sackett, 1977).

Our emphasis on the reciprocal nature of family interactions implies that a severely handicapped child will influence his or her parents' behavior as well as vice-versa. In the past, many researchers assumed that influence flowed only from parent to child. Since most studies of parent–child relations are correlational in nature, it is not immediately obvious whether the significant relationships that have been reported reflect the influence of parents on the child or, alternatively, the impact of the child (habits, temperamental characteristics, etc.) on the parent (see Bell, 1968; Martin, 1975). As suggested in Blacher (Chapter 1 of this volume), an array of studies have demonstrated that child-rearing behavior is influenced by child behaviors and characteristics. For example, temperament (Milliones, 1978), coercive behavior (Patterson, 1976), dependency, friendliness, and aggression (Yarrow, Waxler, & Scott, 1971), attractiveness (Dion, 1972, 1974), age (Clifford, 1959), and gender (Korner, 1974) have been found to influence child-rearing behavior.

Family Roles

Our third assumption about family functioning is that family members assume roles that to some extent determine their behavior during the course of family interactions. Family members assume many role relationships with each other. Parents may assume caretaker, teacher, playmate, and manager roles, to name a few (Brody, Stoneman, & Sanders, 1980; Clarke-Stewart, 1978; Stoneman & Brody, 1981). Siblings also assume different roles in interacting with one another. Older siblings have been observed to assume manager and teacher roles while playing with their younger siblings (Brody, Stoneman, & MacKinnon, 1982; Stoneman, Brody, & MacKinnon, 1984). Additionally, the asymmetrical nature of these sibling role relationships do not remain static as children grow older (Brody, Stoneman, & MacKinnon, 1984). A further description of this theoretical perspective can be found elsewhere (Brody & Stoneman, 1983; Stoneman & Brody, 1982; Stoneman & Brody, in press).

Direct and Indirect Influences in the Family

Researchers interested in child development and family relations have been interested primarily in how family members directly influence one another. That is, they have traditionally focused on how family members sanction and discourage one another's behaviors or serve as sources of information and nurturance. There is, however, a whole set of other influences that are best described as indirect influences. They are indirect because they refer to how sets of circumstances affect the interactions that family members have with one another. For example, the presence of a severely handicapped child in a family could have a marked effect on the socialization of a nonhandicapped sibling. The severely handicapped child may cause the parents considerable fatigue which could affect the parents' socialization practices and thus the quality of the relationship with the nonhandicapped child.

Such indirect effects have come to the attention of researchers interested in behavioral genetics (McCall, 1983; Rowe & Plomin, 1981), who have argued that too much emphasis has been placed on environmental differences between families and the contribution of these differences to intellectual and personality development. The hidden assumption in using "between-family environmental factors" to explain differences among children is that such factors are expected to influence all children in the family in the same manner. These authors have suggested that "within-family factors" account for as much or more of the variance among children as do between-family factors. Within-family factors include differential treatment of children by parents, family alliances, and so forth.

Thus, concern with the effects of having a severely handicapped child on family functioning includes as much, if not more, concern with indirect effects as with direct effects. If these effects are ignored, an entire class of environmental factors that may account for a substantial proportion of variation in family functioning within the family subsystems discussed earlier may be overlooked.

Roles Assumed in Families
with a Mentally Retarded Child

Relatively little is known about the form that family interactions in general, or parent–child interactions in particular, take when a family member is mentally retarded. Much of the extant research has focused on parent–child (usually mother–child) interactions. A close look at this literature shows that mothers of mildly and moderately retarded children spend much of their time in what might be termed a "manager" role (Cunningham, Reuler, Blackwell, & Deck, 1981; Kogan, Wimberger, & Bobbitt, 1969; Marshall, Hegrenes, & Goldstein, 1973; Terdal, Jackson, & Garner, 1976). The Kogan et al. (1969) study also found that mothers of retarded children spend much of their time in an active teaching role with their children. Based upon the literature it would be fair to argue that mothers of retarded children spend an appreciable amount of their time during interactions with their children directing and guiding behavior (manager role) while also serving as a promoter of cognitive growth (teacher role), while the retarded child assumes the reciprocal of these roles (learner and managee).

We sought to build on this literature by observing in-home interactions among members of 16 families (mothers, fathers, and their 4–7-year-old children) (Stoneman, Brody, & Abbott, 1983). Observations were obtained during three family groupings: (1) mother and child, (2) father and child, (3) mother, father, and child. Half of the children had Down's syndrome and half were nonhandicapped. Analysis of the roles and behaviors assumed by the parents and children in the three family contexts revealed that parents of Down's syndrome children structured their interactions with their offspring by assuming manager and teacher roles more than parents of nonhandicapped children. Conversely, parents of nonhandicapped children interacted as playmates with their children more frequently. Mothers of Down's syndrome children assumed the teacher role more than fathers. Fathers of both groups of children interacted less with their offspring in the triadic family grouping, and mothers were more consistent, assuming a parenting role across family contexts.

There are, however, no comparable studies focusing on families of severely handicapped children. In particular, there is a dearth of research describing family interactions involving a severely handicapped child. Without careful, detailed descriptions, an important phase of scientific investigation is minimized; skipping this phase results in theorizing about families with a severely handicapped child that is likely to be simplistic and generate controversies rather than produce answers. Therefore, we would like to encourage researchers to conduct studies with observational methodologies that paint a picture of how families with a severely handicapped child function. Efforts should be made to focus on each of the family subsystems with an eye toward examining indirect as well as direct influences. In the following sections we address methodological issues for such studies that affect the building of a solid data-based foundation for social policy and family intervention programs.

Research Models

There is no one best way to study families. All methodologies have their strengths and weaknesses. In this section we point out some of the strengths and weaknesses of self-report and observational methodologies. A word of caution is in order. Often researchers argue either that self-report methodologies are superior to observational methodologies or vice versa. Such arguments have been and will always be futile. One methodology is not superior to another; some *questions* are superior to others. Methodologies are vehicles for answering a research question or hypothesis. A methodology should be selected on the basis of whether or not it best addresses a research question. Thus, for example, researchers interested in a family member's thoughts, feelings, or perceptions should select a self-report methodology. On the other hand, researchers who want to generalize results to how families interact would select an observational methodology. We hope to begin posing questions that require the interplay of both self-report and observational methodologies so that the reciprocal influences of thoughts, feelings, attitudes, and behavior will be captured.

Self-report Methodologies

Much of what is known about families with a handicapped child has been obtained by asking parents or siblings about their feelings, perceptions, attitudes, and behavior, and drawing conclusions from these self-reports. The most prominent example is Farber's research (Farber, 1959, 1960; Farber & Jenne, 1963). During the middle to late 1950s, Farber and colleagues collected self-report information from approximately 240 families residing in Chicago. About half of the families who participated had a retarded child; the other families did not. Farber recognized that the presence of a handicapped child in a household could have a wide-ranging effect on all segments of family functioning. For instance, measures seeking to assess marital satisfaction, relationships with extended family members, community relationships, and perceptions of sibling development were all obtained. Farber appreciated both the direct and indirect effects that the presence of a handicapped child had on all members of the family.

Farber's work posed elegant research questions and hypotheses that can still serve as guides for research efforts. This work has also provided a vehicle for evaluating the strengths and weaknesses of self-report methodologies. Farber's reports are rich in detail and provide insight into how families feel about having a handicapped child living at home. Farber was thus able to capture the thoughts, feelings, and attitudes of families by employing a self-report methodology that was based on a sound conceptual framework (role theory). A close look at Farber's data reveals that generalizations about family interactions were also made on the basis of self-report data. Specifically, maternal reports were used to assess interactions in the spouse–spouse, parent–child, and sibling–sibling subsystems. Most researchers utilize self-report methods at one time or another and it is worth reflecting on the costs of using such information to draw conclusions about actual interpersonal interactions.

If researchers wish to use self-report information, they should stand ready to demonstrate the empirical link between the self-report responses and actual behavior. In other words, before the self-reports can be used as a proxy for family interactions, the predictive validity of these measures should be established. The literature is consistent in demonstrating that adequate information about family interactions cannot be obtained solely through self-report methodologies. Several orthogonal but converging pieces of information support this view. For example, there are data to suggest little convergence between parental reports and actual parental behavior (Becker & Krug, 1965; Lytton, 1971; Yarrow, 1963). There are other data suggesting that married persons display inaccuracies in reporting interactions with their spouses (Douglas & Wind, 1978; Olson & Rabunsky, 1972). Taken together, these data make it clear that family members do not always provide veridical accounts of family interactional behavior.

Why are people poor reporters of their own interactional behavior? A commonly offered reason is that people provide socially desirable responses to create a particular impression to others or to themselves. There is no question that personality and motivational variables influence the memory system (see, e.g., Cantor & Kihlstrom, 1981; Goethals & Reckman, 1973; Kihlstrom, 1980; Markus, 1977; Snyder & Uranowitz, 1978). The ways in which individuals think about themselves affect the organization and subsequent recall of memories. As Kihlstrom wrote, "The self is a cognitive structure which guides the processing of information in memory: New information is examined for self-reference and coded accordingly; and the self-scheme can interact with the encoded attribute of self-reference to guide subsequent retrieval attempts" (Kihlstrom, 1980, p. 23). Simply, our memories are filtered through our self-perceptions. Those memories that are at odds with self-perceptions stand a high probability of distortion.

Another factor that contributes to the distortion in self-report information is its divorce from the feedback processes that are a part of all social behavior. Making a self-report response on a questionnaire is consequence-free. That is, such responses do not occasion any consequences from other people. Behavior, on the other hand, has the potential to elicit a wide array of responses.

In sum, self-report methodologies can make important contributions to understanding families. These methodologies allow outsiders a glimpse into the attitudes, feelings, and perceptions of family members.

There is simply no other way to obtain this kind of information. Again, the only caution we offer is that unless self-report measures have proven predictive validity they should not be used as a proxy for actual family interactions.

One strategy for enhancing the strength of self-report information is to obtain the same information from multiple family members. This approach allows the researcher to examine the convergent (or divergent) views of different members of the same family, thus capturing the views and perceptions of the family as an interactive system, rather than only the views of one individual.

Observational Methodologies

The philosophical underpinning of this research approach is the belief that family processes should be approximated as closely as possible when they are researched. The source of this belief can be traced to an implicit assumption that research participants have to be psychologically involved with the variables under investigation. In other words, research subjects, whether adults or children, must get involved so that the form of their behavior bears some resemblance to their behavior as it might occur on a day-to-day basis (Bronfenbrenner, 1979).

Proponents of observational methodologies often suggest that there is no substitute for obtaining data on actual interactions. Many reasons are often given for this bias; however, we think they can be summarized as having to do with external validity and with method variance. The external validity argument is straightforward. If family interactions are a researcher's concern, why not observe actual interactions instead of asking people what they do in the presence of family members? This eliminates having to establish external validity indirectly as is often the case when self-reports are used.

The second issue has its roots in what Campbell and Fiske (1959) have described as method variance, that is, those sources of error attributable to the measurement process itself. Many self-report instruments are casually constructed with regard to psychometric issues such as temporal reliability or assessments of internal consistency. Some critics have claimed (e.g., Mischel, 1968) that in many cases researchers assume, having decided on an item pool, that a valid measure is likely to be forthcoming. Unless reliability studies are conducted to assess the extent to which the same responses are obtained under similar circumstances on other occasions, no statements are justified about the stability of the sampled self-reported behavior. In sum, many researchers have opted to employ observational methods when studying families to avoid using instruments that lack predictive validity and psychometric precision.

Researchers who employ observational procedures also share some assumptions about the dynamic nature of family interactions. An assumption is made that the behaviors of family members cannot be understood without examining the contexts in which they occur. A context may be a physical setting, the presence or absence of specific persons, or a combination of settings and persons. Families are viewed as both adapting to existing contexts as well as contributing to the creation of new contexts through their thoughts and actions.

A growing number of studies have examined how different family contexts influence interaction patterns among family members. One such study is that of Clarke-Stewart (1978), who found that when fathers were present in the room, mothers talked less, were less responsive, and played with their child less than when the same mothers were alone with their children. We also found differential decreases in interactions within specific family subgroups during triadic interactions in studies of family nonverbal behavior (Brody & Stoneman, 1981), family language patterns (Stoneman & Brody, 1981), and sibling–peer interactions (Brody et al., 1982; Stoneman et al., 1984).

One of the questions posed by our study of families with and without a Down's syndrome child (Stoneman et al., 1983) concerned the effects of the presence of one parent on the interactions of the other parent with their child. As expected, all family members displayed fewer behaviors in the triadic family context relative to their behavior in the dyadic contexts. It was interesting that fathers (with and without a Down's syndrome child) became less interactive with their child and to some extent withdrew from the family interactions during the triadic grouping when the mother was present. Mothers, on the other hand, remained involved with their children in both the dyadic and triadic family contexts. Imagine the conclusions if only dyadic or triadic family interactions were observed: The triadic family context would have suggested that fathers are uninvolved with their children. The dyadic observations, however, revealed few differences in the interaction patterns of mothers and fathers. The dynamic nature of family interactions in general, and the fathers' behavior in particular, would have been distorted had we decided to obtain data on only dyadic or triadic interactions.

There are some other contextual variables that researchers should consider when designing an observational study. Different physical milieus within the home have been found to occasion different interaction patterns. For example, in observations of families interacting while viewing television, the amount of talking and attention directed toward other family members is reduced in contrast to interactions that occur during toy play (Brody et al., 1980). One should also not overlook that different activities or materials occasion different interaction patterns. Toys, for example, vary in the degree to which they involve active participation by more than one person. Thus, when conceptualizing an observational study of family interaction, the researchers must ask *who* will be observed and *what* will they be doing when they are observed. Of course, the answers to these questions are related to the research question that is initially posed.

One theoretical issue related to the study of family members as an interacting system concerns the concept of reciprocity. Reciprocity of exchanges is often implicated as an important index of healthy family functioning. It is important to point out that high frequencies of behaviors are not equivalent to reciprocity. As a hypothetical example, suppose the parent–child interactions of two groups of fathers are being observed. Further, suppose that one group of fathers emits a higher frequency of positive responses than the other. Can the conclusion be drawn that these fathers are more responsive or more likely to reciprocate the overtures of their offspring? The answer is no. Nothing is known about the contingent (or noncontingent) nature of these positive behaviors. Obtaining only frequencies of behavior does not allow any conclusions to be drawn regarding the reciprocal nature of family interactions.

There are two avenues that researchers can take when they want to draw conclusions about the reciprocal nature of family interactions. The first is to ask questions about contingent responsiveness. That is, if a given family member makes a response, what is the probability that another family member will or will not reciprocate the response? The unit of analysis becomes the mean proportion of behaviors that are reciprocated by Group A compared to the same proportion reciprocated by Group B. We used this approach in our own research (Stoneman et al., 1983). We found that mothers and fathers of Down's syndrome children were very responsive to overtures made by their children. In fact, we found that parents of Down's syndrome children were more responsive to the overtures of their children than were parents of nonhandicapped children, as they ignored proportionally fewer of their children's questions and requests. When we examined the children's responses to their parents overtures, our analyses revealed that Down's syndrome children were less responsive than nonhandicapped children, failing to respond to maternal and paternal directions, teaching, and information-seeking attempts proportionally more often than nonhandicapped children. Thus, by coding both frequencies and the contingent responsiveness of family members to those behaviors, we were able to paint a more accurate picture of family interactions.

The second route that researchers can take in examining the reciprocal nature of family interactions is to obtain data on streams of behavior. Detailed sequences of behavior are obtained from family interactions that go beyond first-order sequences that were described in the preceding paragraph. Instead of obtaining observations of the response of one family member to another family member's overtures, all family interactions are continuously recorded in order to examine the sequential patterning of family behavior. Such data are usually analyzed using a method called lag sequential analysis. More information on this approach can be found in a paper by Sackett (1977).

It seems evident to us that observational methodologies can describe the dynamic and fluid nature of family interactions. There are, however, some drawbacks in selecting this research method that must be mentioned. First, it is a labor-intensive endeavor. Persons to observe families must be recruited and trained in the use of the observational system until they demonstrate a high level of proficiency, or reliability. This process is extremely time consuming. Second, families must be found who are willing to allow researchers to come into their homes. Such families are often difficult to locate, and thus the resulting data are subject to selection biases that limit generalization. The researcher must recognize that the obtained findings may be specific to families who allow researchers into their homes. Whether the behavior patterns found in such families are different from families who choose not to participate is an empirical question.

Our remaining comments are specific to families with severely handicapped children. Given the low incidence of severely handicapped children in the general population, observational researchers are faced with the task of making generalizations from small samples of families. When confronted with this problem, our recommendation is to design research that intensively studies a few families, thus increasing the amount of observation time for each family. Still, generalizations can be made only with caution. Children who are termed severely handicapped comprise a heterogeneous group, a factor that has implications for the research process itself, for external validity considerations, and for generalizations that might be drawn. A prudent way to proceed is to describe in detail the characteristics of the children in the sample and to remind readers how these characteristics limit generalizations.

Issues in Using Observational Methodologies

Comparison Groups

An observation made by Baumeister in 1967 still holds true: All too often the choice of a matching comparison group has little to do with a conceptual viewpoint, but rather reflects both the availability of subjects with certain characteristics and the structural limitations in the research task. Although this comment was made about the general field of mental retardation research, it applies to many family studies as well. One important decision in designing observational research with families of severely handicapped children thus concerns the selection and use of comparison groups.

The following section is an attempt to come to grips with the issues surrounding the selection of comparison groups in family observational research, with particular emphasis on the utility of certain strategies with families containing a severely handicapped member. No one approach is appropriate for all research questions. The choice of a comparison group (or the lack thereof) is a straightforward, logical consequence of the theoretical viewpoint of the researcher and the demands of the specific research question.

Groups Matched on Chronological Age

One of the most popular strategies is to match families with and without a handicapped child according to the chronological age (CA) of the children in the family (CA-match design). Thus a family with a severely handicapped child who is 7 years old and a nonhandicapped child who is 10 would be matched with a family with two nonhandicapped children aged 7 and 10. The families without handicapped members act as a baseline against which to examine the relationships in the target families. The question then becomes: What are the differences between families with and without a handicapped child? Since the presence of a handicapped child in the family does not, by itself, "explain" any difference between families that might appear, the researcher is confronted with the subsequent task of identifying the controlling processes or mechanisms through which these group differences occur. This may often necessitate subsequent research, utilizing different research strategies or multiple comparison groups in the original study (which is addressed later in this section).

The CA-match design has been generally linked to Ellis and the difference theory of mental retardation (Ellis, 1969), but this design has been used by observational family researchers of a variety of theoretical perspectives. For example, CA-match designs have been used by ecological psychologists (Schoggen, 1975), researchers interested in family communications and language (Buckhalt, Rutherford, & Goldberg, 1978; Berger & Cunningham, 1981; Kogan et al., 1969; Marshall et al., 1973), behaviorists (Breiner & Forehand, 1982), and researchers taking a family systems and/or role theory approach (O'Connor & Stachowiak, 1971; Stoneman et al., 1983). Such CA-match designs have also been used by researchers interested in the development of attachment (see Blacher & Meyers, 1983, for a review of this literature).

There are several difficulties inherent in adapting the CA-match design to the observational study of families with a severely handicapped member. Particularly for older children, there is an extremely wide gap between the competencies of a severely handicapped child and a nonhandicapped child of the same age. This is especially true for severely mentally retarded children and children with multiple disabilities. This gap in competency level makes it difficult for the researcher to select tasks or play materials that are equally valid for both groups of children. This problem can be addressed in at least three ways: (1) comparable tasks or play materials at different levels of difficulty or complexity can be used with each group, (2) observations can be made of totally naturalistic interactions, occurring during activities in which the family typically engages, with no attempt to equate activities across groups, or (3) specific family activities common to both groups (i.e., mealtime) can be used as the context of observation. Once again, each of these methodologies addresses a different research question. Another difficulty encountered in adapting the CA-match design to observational studies of families with severely handicapped children involves the development of an interaction coding system that is equally reliable and valid for interactions involving children of widely discrepant competency levels. This can only be achieved through extensive piloting with both populations.

All of the aforementioned difficulties are minimal when infants are the subject of study, but intensify as researchers focus on families with older children and adolescents. Thus, much of the family research utilizing this design has focused on families of infants and preschool children.

Groups Matched on Mental Age

Mental age (MA) has been used by many mental retardation researchers as an indicator of overall cognitive level. In the MA-match design, groups of mentally retarded and nonhandicapped children are equated on MA. Information is then obtained on other measures of interest; if the groups differ on these measures, it can be argued that the differences are due to factors other than cognitive ability. Perhaps the most elegant defense of MA as a criterion for matching groups was written by Zigler (1969) in an elaboration of the developmental viewpoint of mental retardation. One of the few family interaction studies to utilize a MA match design is that by Terdal et al., (1976). Taking a behavioral approach, these researchers attempted to identify deficits in feedback provided by mentally retarded children that might affect maternal behavior.

Numerous problems inherent in adapting the MA-match design to family research probably account for its lack of popularity. These difficulties are particularly pronounced for those researchers interested in families with severely handicapped children. Many of the difficulties with the MA design stem from the differences in chronological age created between groups when older severely handicapped children are matched on MA with younger nonhandicapped children. For instance, to match a severely mentally retarded adolescent one must often select a nonhandicapped infant or toddler in order to achieve equivalent MAs. Finding tasks or activities age-appropriate for both of these groups of children or creating behavioral coding systems sensitive to family interactions involving a toddler as well as a handicapped adolescent pose many difficulties.

Implementing an MA-match design in studies that go beyond the parent–child subsystem can change the birth order and age relationships of siblings in families with and without a handicapped child. For example, a match for a family with a nonhandicapped daughter 6 years old and a handicapped daughter with a CA of 9 and an MA of 4, could be a family with two nonhandicapped daughters aged 6 and 4. In the first family (i.e., the one with the handicapped child), the 6-year-old girl is the younger child, whereas in the second family the 6-year-old is the older child. There might be some research questions, such as those focusing on sibling role relationships (e.g., does an older handicapped child take the role of a younger sibling in family interactions?) where this age reversal might be appropriate. In most studies, however, it would confuse the interpretation of findings.

It is also unclear whether the same behavior coming from two children, one handicapped and one nonhandicapped, who are widely discrepant in age, has the same meaning for both children. It is known, for instance, that certain nonverbal behaviors, including proximity between individuals, are age-related, with behavior that is desirable in a young child being unacceptable in a child who is older (Brody & Stoneman, 1977).

The final difficulty in implementing the MA-match design with families of severely handicapped children discussed here concerns the meaning of mental age scores for these children. Numerous authors have cautioned against the use of standardized tests with severely handicapped children (e.g., DuBose, 1981; Simeonsson, Huntington, & Parse, 1980). Many children are untestable with such instruments, and the scores obtained are often neither reliable or valid. The measurement of mental age in severely handicapped children is a formidable obstacle, further limiting the usefulness of the MA-match design with this group of children.

Criterion-Matched Groups

Another strategy for constituting comparison groups matches children on a competency index that is theoretically related to the dependent measures in the study. This strategy has been widely used by researchers studying the family language environment. These researchers usually match handicapped and nonhandicapped children on mean length of utterance (MLU) and then study parameters of maternal language (e.g., Gutman & Rondal, 1979; Peterson & Sherrod, 1982; Rondal, 1978; Wolchik & Harris, 1982). The purpose of these studies is to compare the language stimulation provided by mothers to handicapped and nonhandicapped children with similar competencies in expressive language. A criterion-match design has also been used to operationalize the tenets of symbolic interaction theory (Eheart, 1982). In this study, groups of retarded and nonretarded children were matched according to the complexity level of their play behavior and observations were made of mother–child mutual play.

Criterion-match designs share some of the difficulties encountered with MA-match designs when an attempt is made to adapt these strategies to observational studies of families with severely handicapped children. Namely, when children are matched on such criteria as MLU or level of play skills, there is the possibility that severely handicapped children with minimal expressive language abilities or simplistic play styles will be matched with nonhandicapped children much younger than themselves. The research problems created by such a wide range in CA are addressed in the discussion of MA-match designs.

The flexible nature of the choice of a criterion to use in matching groups allows the criterion-match design to be adaptable to a wide range of research questions, theoretical perspectives, and family characteristics. This adaptability is a major strength of this design. Like the comparison group strategies mentioned earlier, however, it is most easily employed when the target children are infants or young children and becomes increasingly difficult to implement as the ages of the severely handicapped children increase.

Groups Matched on More Than One Index

Occasionally, groups are matched on more than one relevant dimension. For example, Cunningham *et al.* (1981) matched their mentally retarded group and their nonhandicapped group on both mental age and Peabody Picture Vocabulary Test (PPVT) scores, and Cook and Culp (1981) matched their group of Down's syndrome infants with nonhandicapped infants based on a Piagetian measure of cognitive ability and maternal reports of expressive language skill. Both of these studies focused on the observation of mother–child interaction. Matching groups according to more than one index creates groups that are more similar than those matched on only one criterion, particularly if the two indexes are not highly intercorrelated. This design can be difficult to implement, however, since finding matching families can be time consuming. It is also subject to the strengths and weaknesses of the individual criterion measures used.

Comparison Groups with Similar Handicaps
That Differ on a Relevant Dimension

Several studies have grouped children with similar handicapping conditions on a dimension of theoretical interest for a particular research question. Research by Greenberg and colleagues provides an excellent example of this approach (Greenberg, 1980; Greenberg & Marvin, 1979; Meadow, Greenberg, Erting, & Carmichael, 1981). These researchers observed mother–child interactions involving a hearing-impaired child and based their comparison groups on the communication mode used by the children and, in some studies, on the hearing status of the mother.

This strategy, which does not require a nonhandicapped comparison group, allows for the intensive study of family interactions involving children with a particular disability and an examination of specific factors that might influence these interactions. With families of severely handicapped children, this design can be used to explore the impact of such variables as child mobility, level of self-care, use of nonvocal communication systems, or severity of handicap on family interaction patterns.

One caution is in order, however. Equating groups of severely handicapped children on other important variables (gender, socioeconomic status, birth order, etc.), which have been demonstrated to impact on family interactions but may be unrelated to the research question, can be extremely difficult. For example, assume that a researcher is interested in differences in parent–child interactions between children who use wheelchairs or other adaptive equipment and those who do not. If all the children who use adaptive chairs are girls from wealthy families who have no siblings and also use communication boards, and the ambulatory children are all boys from poor, large families, group differences obviously cannot be attributed to adaptive chairs alone.

Studies Using Multiple Comparison Groups

An approach taken by a number of observational studies involves the use of multiple comparison groups. O'Connor and Stachowiak (1971), for instance, used three groups; families of well adjusted children, families of poorly adjusted children, and families of mentally retarded children. Similarly, Breiner and Forehand (1982) observed mother–child interactions with clinic-referred developmentally delayed noncompliant children, clinic-referred noncompliant children, and non-clinic children. A similar strategy involves the comparison of children with different handicapping conditions. Brooks-Gunn and Lewis (1982), for example, observed the mother–child play behavior of children with Down's syndrome, motor impairments, and developmental delays, as well as children without handicaps.

These strategies permit an in-depth examination of the factors influencing family interaction patterns and might prove useful in the study of families with severely handicapped children. It is important to note, however, that the successful use of multiple comparison groups requires a theoretical reason for the inclusion of each group. The "cafeteria approach" to the selection of comparison groups (Ellis, 1969), in which various groups are included in a study without strong theoretical rationale, is to be avoided.

Matching Groups on Family Demographic Characteristics

In addition to the selection of an appropriate comparison group, consideration must be given to family demographic characteristics that have been reliably related to family interactions. These include family socioeconomic status, parent education, family size, gender and age of siblings, race, maternal employment, sibling birth order, and single versus dual-parent families. The researcher can match groups on each of these factors, or statistical controls can be implemented to equate for group differences. When these family demographic characteristics are ignored, which has too often been the case in research with families of atypical children, the findings of even the best-designed studies are open to alternate interpretations.

Family Research Strategies Not Using Comparison Groups

The final set of strategies to be discussed in this section do not involve the use of comparison groups. Studies utilizing these strategies are characterized not only by the absence of a comparison group, but also by research questions for which the inclusion of a comparison group would be superfluous. This point is important, since in some research the absence of a comparison group can be a critical flaw. The difference resides in the researcher's theoretical orientation and in the research question. Studies without comparison groups tend to focus intensely on families containing handicapped members, with no comparisons made between those families and any other group of families.

Perhaps the largest group of observational family studies without comparison groups have been those evaluating change in parent–child interactions following structured interventions (e.g., Filler, 1976; Filler & Kasari, 1981; Sandler, Coren, & Thurman, 1983; Weitz, 1981). Similar studies have evaluated intervention programs focusing on sibling interactions (Cash & Evans, 1975; Powell, in press). Many of these studies have utilized single-subject designs traditionally associated with a behavioral orientation toward family interactions. Another group of studies have utilized correlational designs to detect relationships between observed family interactions and another variable of interest, such as child competency. Many of these studies have utilized the Home Observation for Measurement of the Environment (HOME) inventory developed by Bradley and Caldwell (1977) (e.g., Affleck, Allen, McGrade, & McQueeney, 1982; Mink, Nihira, & Meyers, 1983; Nihira, Meyers, & Mink, 1980; Nihira, Mink, & Meyers, 1981; Piper & Ramsay, 1980). Others have utilized observations of mother–child teaching style to predict the child's acquisition of specific skills (Filler & Bricker, 1976) and to study the development of mother–child attachment (Cicchetti & Serafica, 1981).

Other research strategies that do not use comparison groups have received minimal attention from researchers interested in families with a handicapped member. The first of these strategies involves intrafamily comparisons. Such comparisons might examine the interaction patterns of different family subsystems (e.g., mother–child, father–child, siblings, grandparent–child) as well as the indirect effect on one family subsystem created by the presence of an additional family member (e.g., the changes in sibling interactions that occur when the father joins the interaction). Another strategy focuses on the contextual specificity of family interactions. As described earlier, family interactions patterns differ from setting to setting. Examination of interactions across several typical family contexts would provide needed information on these important family–context interrelationships. Another underutilized strategy involves the longitudinal study of family relationships. Although longitudinal research is costly, it is extremely important to the understanding of families with handicapped members.

All of the aforementioned strategies can be easily adapted to families with severely handicapped children. Such studies, focusing on families with disabled members for their own sake rather than in an attempt to point out differences with other groups, would provide in-depth knowledge about the significant experiences of these families. These designs also minimize problems due to low sample size and population heterogeneity, which are common in research with severely handicapped individuals. Additionally, these strategies permit an examination of the generalization of interaction patterns across family groupings and contexts. This is a particular strength since the generalization of behavior is a continuing concern for those providing service to severely handicapped persons (Stokes & Baer, 1977).

Modifying Observational Methodologies

Numerous considerations come into play when observational methodologies are modified for use with families of severely handicapped children. Because rates of behavior emitted by most severely handicapped children are very low, numerous hours of observation time are necessary to collect a meaningful sample of family interaction. Similarly, operational definitions of behavior codes need to be changed from those used with nonhandicapped children in order to include interactive behaviors such as the use of sign, nonverbal gestures, and communication boards. Obviously, observers must be trained to understand alternate communication systems if they are to code interactions effectively using these systems. The following sections provide a brief discussion of these issues.

Sampling of Interaction

As in any observational research, the primary determinant of the interactive behaviors to be sampled is the researcher's theoretical orientation. Once observational categories are derived from theory, pilot observation sessions must be conducted to ascertain whether or not the coding system satisfactorily captures the pattern of ongoing family interaction. When the families to be observed include severely handicapped children, certain modifications in traditional coding systems are necessary. Often these modifications include the expansion of operational definitions to include nonverbal and physical behaviors that are an important part of the social behavior of many severely handicapped children but have less meaning for nonhandicapped children's interactions. The coding system must be designed so that it does not distort the family interactions of children with atypical communication patterns, such as youngsters with limited body control or those with sensory impairments.

An argument for the sequential coding of behavior was presented earlier in this chapter. In order for sequential coding to add desired information, however, particularly with sequences examining contingent responsiveness, the researcher must ensure that the antecedent behaviors occur with enough frequency to make response proportions meaningful. For example, if the researcher is interested in the parent's responsiveness to children's questions, the proportion of questions answered can only have meaning if question asking occurs with at least moderate frequency. Thus, pilot observations are necessary to determine if specific antecedent–response sequences occur frequently enough to warrant analysis.

Reliability

Obviously, establishing interobserver reliability is an important consideration in the conduct of observational research. Our purpose here is only to discuss special reliability problems in conducting research with families of severely handicapped children. In this regard, two issues need to be addressed. First, it is important in research that includes comparison groups to ensure that reliability is established both with the families with severely handicapped children *and* with the comparison families. It is quite possible for a coding system (and specific observers) to be reliable with one group of families and not the other.

A second issue concerns the acclimation of observers to the presence of children with severe handicaps. Individuals who do not have prior experience with this group of children may become unsettled at certain appearances or behaviors and thus fail to collect reliable data. Two solutions are possible. The researcher can either select observers who are familiar with severely handicapped youngsters or provide observational and hands-on experiences to help observers become comfortable around the children they will be observing.

Demonstration Study

A multimethod demonstration study focusing on severely handicapped children and their families will be described in the following sections. The demonstration study had four purposes: (1) to determine the
activities and settings that naturally occur in a small group of families
with a severely handicapped child, (2) to field-test a coding system focusing on the parent–child and sibling subsystems, (3) to pilot a set of sequence antecedents to determine their frequency of occurrences in a
small sample of families, and (4) to pilot a series of self-report instruments.

Family Characteristics

In order to field-test this multimethod approach, pilot visits were
completed to the homes of four families, each with a child who was severely handicapped. Each family also contained at least one nonhandicapped sibling who was older than the severely handicapped child. The
handicapped children, two males and two females, ranged in age from 8
to 10 years, and their six older typical siblings ranged in age from 9 to 16.
Three of the older siblings were male and three were female. Two of the
families also had siblings who were younger than the handicapped child.
The size of the families ranged from two to five children, and one of the
mothers was a single parent. Two of the fathers were employed at skilled
labor; one father, also a skilled laborer, was temporarily unemployed.
One of the mothers was employed as a housekeeper. All other mothers
were full-time homemakers. Family incomes ranged from $5000 to
$17,000 per year ($M = \$7800$). Three of the families were black and one
was white.

The handicapped children were all severely mentally retarded with
accompanying motor handicaps. One of the children had cerebral palsy,
one had Down's syndrome, one had muscular dystrophy, and one had
sustained brain damage. Three of the children used wheelchairs for
mobility and one was ambulatory. Language skills, as measured by the
Verbal Language Development Scale (Mecham, 1958) with mothers as
informants, ranged from age equivalents of 1.5 to 8 months ($M = 4.7$
months). One of the children used a BLISS language board at school, but
it was not taken home. None of the children used words. The Vineland
Social Maturity Scale (Doll, 1965) was also completed for each child.
Age equivalents ranged from less than 6 months to 20 months ($M = 10.7$
months).

Procedure

Seven pilot home visits were conducted. Three families were visited twice, approximately a week apart, and the fourth family was visited once. Each visit lasted about 2 hours. Naturalistic observations of family interactions were obtained during 1 hour of each visit. During these observations, family members were asked to engage in their ordinary activities and routines, ignoring the observers as much as possible. Observations were made for an additional 15 minutes before the start of actual data collection to allow time for the family to acclimate to the presence of the two observers. Following the observations, interview information was obtained from the mothers and all older siblings. The interview format is described in a subsequent section.

Sampling of Behavior

Interactions among family members were quantified using interval recording procedures. Ten-second intervals were utilized, yielding 360 observation intervals per visit for each target family member. A role or behavior was coded only once during each interval regardless of its frequency. Operational definitions for the roles and behaviors are presented in Table 5.1. These roles and behaviors were adapted from our earlier studies (Brody *et al.,* 1982; Stoneman *et al.,* 1983; Stoneman *et al.,* 1984).

The observers coded the behaviors emitted by the handicapped target child, the family member to whom the behavior was directed, and all behaviors directed toward the target child by other family members. Additionally, the observers recorded the activity in which the target child was engaged during each interval. Observers were trained through the use of videotaped family interactions until interobserver agreement for each role and behavior exceeded .84. These reliabilities were subsequently obtained in live coding as well.

Maternal Interviews

The first maternal interview, a modification of an instrument developed by Schwirian (1977), measured the child-care responsibilities, out-of-school activities, and peer interactions of the older typical siblings. Parents also were asked to compare the older sibling to other children of the same age on three dimensions: time spent in child care, time spent performing household chores, and time spent playing with

TABLE 5.1

Operational Definitions for Roles and Behaviors

	Definition
Roles	
Interactor	One who engages in physical or verbal interaction with another family member that does not center on toys or other play objects
Helper	One who makes any attempt to offer assistance or aid to another
Playmate	A child who engages in parallel or cooperative play involving toys or other play objects
Manager	A family member who commands or requests (verbally or nonverbally) that another perform (or not perform) a certain behavior; an individual who asserts his or her own rights, thus attempting to influence the behavior of another
Teacher	A family member who explains, models, or demonstrates how to perform a certain task or provides new information about labels of objects or events
Observer	One who watches or observes another person without speaking to or interacting with that person
Behavior	
Verbalization	Spoken word or sound emitted by family member
Positive behavior	Family member hugging, kissing, affectionately touching another; laughing, smiling, giggling, praising another, or expressing verbal enthusiasm
Negative behavior	Family member hitting, attacking, pushing, fighting with, threatening, quarreling with, teasing or insulting another; whining, protesting, yelling, name calling, being sarcastic
Solitary activity	Child playing alone or not interacting with another child

friends. A 5-point scale ranging from "a lot less than other children" to "a lot more than other children" was used.

A second interview, which tapped quantitative and qualitative aspects of the relationship between the handicapped child and his or her older sibling, was also administered to the mothers. Questions on this interview focused on (1) the frequency with which the siblings play together, (2) the activities they share, (3) the closeness of their relationship, and (4) satisfaction with the relationship.

Sibling Interviews

Each older sibling was administered a modified Schwirian (1977) interview, similar to that just described, as well as a sibling relationship interview. This interview contained questions concerning the frequency of sibling play, activities shared, enjoyable and disliked aspects of the sibling interaction, good and bad things about having a handicapped sibling, and advice for other children who have handicapped brothers or sisters.

Results

Before presenting the findings of this demonstration study, we caution the reader that these data are only exploratory. Their primary purpose is to assess the applicability of specific research methodologies to families of severely handicapped children and to suggest fruitful questions for future research.

Naturalistic Observations

The first purpose of the demonstration study was to examine the activities and settings experienced by the severely handicapped children. These children engaged in a much more restricted range of activities during the home observations than would have been expected from previous naturalistic research conducted by the authors with mildly to moderately mentally retarded children (Stoneman & Brody, 1984). As for such children, however, the most popular activity for the severely handicapped children was watching television. Most of the children's time (68%) was spent in solitary activity, and during much of this time the children appeared to be unoccupied. It was striking how infrequently the severely handicapped children manipulated any type of play materials. From their adaptive chairs they had little access to toys or other objects; therefore, when not engaged with another family member they tended to be inactive.

The second purpose of the demonstration study was to field test a coding system for family interactions. Mean frequencies for the roles and behaviors coded during the naturalistic observations are presented in Table 5.2. The "other" columns in the table reflect the behavior of friends and relatives visiting during the observations. Interactor was the most frequently assumed role. In general, this occurred when a mother or sibling held the handicapped child on his or her lap or otherwise maintained physical contact. The helper role was also reasonably common for mothers and siblings. Helping situations included lifting a child out of an adaptive chair and carrying him or her outside, pulling a child up to a more comfortable sitting position in a chair, wiping a child's nose, feeding, and helping a child who was coughing to expectorate.

Playmate appears in the table to be a frequently occurring role for

TABLE 5.2

Mean Frequency of Roles and Behaviors Emitted by and Directed toward
Severely Handicapped Children[a]

	Emitted by SH child, directed toward			Directed toward SH child, emitted by		
	Siblings	Mother	Other	Siblings	Mother	Other
Roles						
Interactor	23.00	107.50	0.50	21.75	107.00	0.50
Helper	0.00	0.00	0.00	9.75	11.50	0.00
Playmate	17.00	0.00	0.00	17.00	0.00	0.00
Manager	0.00	0.00	0.00	0.50	1.00	0.00
Teacher	0.00	0.00	0.00	0.00	0.00	0.00
Observer	49.50	2.50	0.50	1.00	3.50	0.00
Behaviors						
Verbal	0.50	0.00	0.25	16.50	39.00	0.00
Positive	13.00	0.00	0.25	3.00	4.75	0.00
Negative	0.00	0.00	0.00	0.00	0.00	0.00

[a] Figures given represent mean frequencies during 2 hours of observation.

siblings, but this mean is artificially inflated by one sibling pair. The
other sibling pairs never played together with toys or other materials.
The low rates of managing and the total absence of teaching were surprising. Our earlier research (Stoneman et al., 1983) as well as the
research of others (Cunningham et al., 1981; Kogan et al., 1969; Marshall
et al., 1973; Terdal et al., 1976) has consistently found increased managing and teaching in family members who interact with handicapped children. If this finding is replicated, it may denote a U-shaped relationship
between the frequency of family teaching and managing behaviors and
the level of severity of the child's handicap, with mildly and moderately
handicapped children receiving more of these behaviors than either
typical children or severely handicapped children of similar ages.

The severely handicapped children frequently took the observer
role, watching their brothers and sisters play. It is interesting that most of
this observation was focused toward siblings, not parents. The severely
handicapped children also emitted frequent positive affects, also
primarily directed toward siblings.

The third purpose of the pilot study was to determine if the roles included in the coding system occurred frequently enough to be used as
antecedents in subsequent sequential recording. We were particularly
interested in helper, manager, and teacher roles, which had been utilized by the authors as antecedents in previous research. Of these three,

only helper roles occurred with enough frequency to be included in a sequential coding system. It is possible that either more general behavior categories than those included in the demonstration study or more subtle nonverbal behaviors need to be included in order to make sequential recording of more roles feasible.

Self-report Findings

The final purpose of the demonstration study was to field test a set of maternal and sibling self-report measures. A brief description of the types of interview information obtained on these measures follows to allow the reader to compare the qualitative aspects of this information with the preceding observational findings. Although there were not a sufficient number of respondents for systematic compilation of the information on all measures, a sampling of individual responses on several measures will depict the richness of information collected in this manner.

Child-Care Responsibilities. An average was obtained between the mother's and older sibling's reports of the older sibling's child-care responsibilities for the handicapped child. Older brothers reportedly babysat for their siblings about once a week, while sisters reportedly babysat several times a week. Older sisters dressed, fed, and bathed their handicapped siblings almost daily, while brothers performed these tasks infrequently. All siblings were frequently responsible for watching the handicapped child while out in the yard, looking after the child while the parents were busy, and picking up his or her toys.

Out-of-School Activities. Older siblings reported spending 1–2 hours per week in sports activities, and an hour a week or less in each of the following: music or band activities, clubs, and church activities. Boys reported spending more time in out-of-school activities than did girls.

Play with Friends. Older siblings reported an average of seven visits with friends per week. For most siblings, these visits were equally divided between the homes of friends and their own homes. Two older brothers in one family reported that they never brought friends over to their house to play. Unfortunately, they were not asked to explain why. An older sister in the same family reported that she freely brought friends home with her.

Social Comparisons. Older siblings and mothers were asked to compare the older sibling with peers his or her same age on the following dimensions: (1) time spent in child care, (2) time spent performing household chores, and (3) time spent playing with friends. Maternal and sibling perceptions on each dimension were averaged. Both male and female older siblings reportedly engaged in more childcare responsibilities than their peers, while female (but not male) siblings reportedly also spent more time in household chores. Time spent playing with friends was not perceived to differ from that spent by other children.

When asked why the older siblings in the pilot study had more childcare responsibilities than other children, both mothers and older siblings explained that the children had to help with the extra care demands of the handicapped child. The perceived increase in household tasks for girls was explained by suggesting that most children do not help out at home and, thus, these children spend more time in chores than their peers. None of the families specifically mentioned the handicapped child in association with increased household responsibilities.

Sibling Play.   When the six older siblings were asked what activities they liked to do with their handicapped brothers and sisters, they listed an array including giving him a ride in his chair (mentioned by several children), stretching his arms and legs, taking him out of his chair, playing in the house with toys, reading him stories, hitting sticks against each other, wrestling, whispering in her ear to make her laugh, bouncing on her stomach, and doing cheers so she can watch. Mothers, when asked the same question, reported very similar types of activities. When asked how frequently the older brothers and sisters played with the severely handicapped child, both the mothers and the older siblings themselves reported that on average the siblings played together 5–10 hours per week.

Sibling Relationship.   All mothers reported that the target older siblings had a "very close relationship" with the severely handicapped child. When asked in what ways, if any, they would like to see the relationship between the siblings change, one mother wished that her son would spend more time with his severely handicapped younger sister and take her along when he plays outside, while another mother wished that her handicapped daughter had more skills so that the children could do more varied things together.

Positive Aspects of Having a Handicapped Sibling.   Both mothers and older siblings were asked about the good and bad aspects of having a brother or sister who is handicapped. When asked for the positive aspects, older siblings reported "being able to take care of her," "the way she smiles and sometimes tries to talk," and "knowing how to care for people like her." Comments made by the mothers included "She really loves him—likes to play with him," "She takes up for him—is very loyal," "She wants to care for him always," "It makes her more aware of the fact that people are different."

Negative Aspects of Having a Handicapped Sibling. Only two older siblings mentioned negative aspects of having a handicapped sibling. One brother said, "I like and love her but wish she didn't have to be handicapped;" an older sister commented, "Although some people make fun of her, it doesn't bother me." A mother reported that when her son "makes new friends, they upset him with their comments," and another mother said, "It interferes to some extent with her participating and doing things with others."

Effects on Handicapped Child of Having a Nonhandicapped Sibling. All mothers noted positive effects of having a sibling on their handicapped children. These included "He enjoys all of them being around," "His brother shows him a lot of love," "She likes to laugh and play with her sister. She seems fascinated by her [sister's] movement," "His sister takes care and loves him."

Questions from Peers. Older siblings were asked whether their friends ever questioned them about their handicapped brothers and sisters, and if they did what questions they asked. Siblings were also asked how they answered those questions. Questions and answers reported by the siblings included "Why does she put her hands in her mouth?" ("She just does"), "Why doesn't she talk and walk?" ("She fell out of a buggy and had brain damage"), "Why do her lips turn blue?" ("Seizures"), "Is she older than you?" ("No"), "Can she talk?" ("No, I hope she will"), "How's he doin?" ("Doin fine").

Advice to Other Siblings. In the final question of the interview, the older siblings were asked what advice they would give to other brothers and sisters of handicapped children. Their replies included "Take good care of him," "If he gets hurt or has a spell, see to him until your mom gets back," "Take care of him 'cause he can't do for himself," "Not to be mean," "Be nice," "Help her learn things," "Play with her a lot" "Teach her right from wrong," "Help out a lot," "Play with them."

Discussion of Pilot Findings

The conduct of empirical research is always a humbling experience. Assuming that field research involves the art of compromise between the perfect research methodology and the realities of the natural setting or ecology, we suggest that research with families of severely handicapped children is an ongoing process of such compromise. It is in that light that we discuss our findings.

These pilot data were collected during totally naturalistic observations of family interactions, without any structure provided by the researchers. Naturalistic studies such as this are designed to determine the nature and frequency of interaction among family members in the home ecology. When interaction rates are low, however, as they were in these families (between the severely handicapped children and other family members), it takes many hours of observation to collect a large enough sample of interaction to examine its qualitative aspects. Thus, in addition to completely naturalistic observations, it may be necessary to ask family members to engage in certain activities that elicit frequent interactions. For instance, in this pilot study an initial attempt was made to observe families during the evening meal, when family exchanges were expected to be frequent. It was determined, however, that in none of the pilot families did the severely handicapped child eat at the same time as the rest of the family. Additionally, several mothers expressed reluctance and some amount of embarrassment at having observers watch them feeding their children. Thus, observations of feeding were not obtained.

Briefly noting the activity engaged in by the target child facilitated modifications of the coding system. For example (H is the handicapped child, M is her mother, and S is her sister), "H is on porch in wheelchair. S plays basketball in yard. S rearranges H in wheelchair. S goes inside. H alone on porch." In addition to providing a context in which to understand the interaction, these notes provide information against which to judge whether the observational coding system is adequately capturing the interaction. In this pilot study, for example, we determined that the interactor role was too broadly defined, and although it could be reliably coded its definition needed to be fine-tuned in order to facilitate interpretation of findings.

Fathers were not at home during the observation sessions. If pilot data are to reflect the complexity of total family interactions, fathers need to be included as well. Our past research has taught us that special effort is required in order to include fathers of handicapped children.

Comparison of self-report responses of mothers and siblings identified discrepancies in the perceptions of these two family members. In the pilot study, these were handled by obtaining a mean of the two responses. There is some amount of controversy in the family literature, however, concerning the proper treatment of discrepant dyadic family responses. Thompson and Walker (1982) have discussed this issue further.

A final issue concerns the observation of very low frequency behaviors that are theoretically important but may not occur even during extensive observations. In this pilot study, a decision was made to use self-report methods to tap some of these dimensions. For instance, naturalistic observation of the frequency with which older children babysit for their handicapped siblings requires being in the home for several weeks to obtain reliable data on this behavior. The self-report methodology utilized in this pilot study, however, is subject to all the weaknesses described earlier in the chapter. Another approach to obtaining this type of information has been described by Zahn-Waxler and Radke-Yarrow (Zahn-Waxler, Radke-Yarrow, & King, 1979; Zahn-Waxler & Radke-Yarrow, 1983). This methodology involves the intensive training of parents to be the observers of their children's behavior. This method of data collection is extremely time-intensive, particularly in the training phase, but would seem to hold great promise for the study of families with severely handicapped children.

Conclusion

Horejsi (1979) has commented that the study of the family cannot be approached as if it were a group home, a special education classroom, or a clinic environment. Families are fluid systems with intense emotional attachments between family members. Only by approaching the study of families who have handicapped members with clear theoretical perspectives and strong research methodologies can the information about the daily interaction patterns of these families needed for devising appropriate interventions be obtained.

References

Affleck, G., Allen, D., McGrade, B. J., & McQueeney, M. (1972). Home environments of developmentally disabled infants as a function of parent and infant characteristics. *American Journal of Mental Deficiency, 86,* 445–452.

Anthony, E. J. (1974). Children at risk from divorce: A review. In E. J. Anthony & C. Koupernik (Eds.), *The child in his family* (Vol. III). New York: Wiley.

Bakeman, R. (1978). Untangling streams of behavior: Sequential analyses of observational data. In G. Sackett (Ed.), *Observing behavior: Vol. II. Data collection and analysis methods.* Baltimore: University Park Press.

Baumeister, A. A. (1967). Problems in comparative studies of mental retardates and normals. *American Journal of Mental Deficiency, 71,* 869–875.

Becker, W. C., & Krug, R. S. (1965). The parent attitude research instrument—A research review. *Child Development, 35,* 329–365.

Bell, R. Q. (1968). A reinterpretation of the direction of effects in studies of socialization. *Psychological Review, 75,* 81–95.

Berger, J., & Cunningham, C. C. (1981). The development of eye contact between mothers and normal vs. Down's syndrome infants. *Developmental Psychology, 17,* 678–689.

Blacher, J., & Meyers, C. E. (1983). A review of attachment formation and disorder of handicapped children. *American Journal of Mental Deficiency, 4,* 359–371.

Bradley, R. H., & Caldwell, B. M. (1977). Home observation for measurement of the environment: A validation study of screening efficiency. *American Journal of Mental Deficiency, 81,* 417–420.

Breiner, J., & Forehand, R. (1982). Mother-child interactions: A comparison of a clinic-refered developmentally delayed group and two nondelayed groups. *Applied Research in Mental Retardation, 3,* 175–183.

Brody, G. H., & Stoneman, Z. (1977). Social competencies in the developmentally disabled: Some suggestions for research and training. *Mental Retardation, 15,* 41–44.

Brody, G. H., & Stoneman, Z. (1981). Parental nonverbal behavior within the family context. *Family Relations, 33,* 187–191.

Brody, G. H., & Stoneman, Z. (1983). Children with atypical siblings: Socialization outcomes and clinical participation. In B. B. Lahey & A. E. Kazdin (Eds.), *Advances in Clinical Child Psychology.* New York: Plenum Press.

Brody, G. H., Stoneman, Z., & MacKinnon, C. (1982). Role asymmetries in interactions among school-aged children, their younger siblings, and their friends. *Child Development, 53,* 1364–1370.

Brody, G. H., Stoneman, Z., & MacKinnon, C. (in press). Role relationships and behavior among preschool-aged and school-aged sibling pairs. *Developmental Psychology.*

Brody, G. H., Stoneman, Z., & Sanders, A. K. (1980). Effects of television viewing on family interactions: An observational study. *Family Relations, 29,* 216–220.

Bronfenbrenner, U. (1979). *The ecology of human development.* Cambridge, MA: Harvard University Press.

Brooks-Gunn, J., & Lewis, M. (1982). Development of play behavior in handicapped and normal infants. *Topics in Early Childhood Special Education, 2,* 14–27.

Buckhalt, J. A., Rutherford, R. B. & Goldberg, K. E. (1978). Verbal and nonverbal interaction of mothers with their Down's syndrome and nonretarded infants. *American Journal of Mental Deficiency, 82,* 337–343.

Campbell, D. T., & Fiske, W. D. (1959). Convergent and discriminant variation by the multitract-multimethod matrix. *Psychological Bulletin, 57,* 81–105.

Cantor, N., & Kihlstrom, J. F. (1981). Cognitive and social processes in personality: Implications for behavior therapy. In C. M. Franks & G. T. Wilson (Eds.), *Handbook of behavior therapy.* New York: Guilford Press.

Cash, W. M., & Evans, I. M. (1975). Training pre-school children to modify their retarded siblings' behavior. *Journal of Behavior Therapy and Experimental Psychiatry, 6,* 13–16.

Cichetti, D., & Serafica, F. C. (1981). Interplay among behavioral systems: Illustrations from the study of attachment, affiliation, and wariness in young children with Down's syndrome. *Developmental Psychology, 17,* 36–49.

Clarke-Stewart, K. A. (1978). And daddy makes three: The father's impact on mother and young child. *Child Development, 49,* 466–478.

Clifford, E. (1959). Discipline in the home: A controlled observational study of parental practices. *Journal of Genetic Psychology*, 95, 45–82.

Cook, A. S., & Culp, R. E. (1981). Mutual play of mothers with their Down's syndrome and normal infants. *International Journal of Rehabilitation Research*, 4, 542–544.

Cunningham, C. E., Reuler, E., Blackwell, J., & Deck, J. (1981). Behavioral and linguistic developments in the interactions of normal and retarded children with their mothers. *Child Development*, 52, 62–70.

Dion, K. (1972). Physical attractiveness and evaluation of children's transgressions. *Journal of Personality and Social Psychology*, 24, 207–213.

Dion, K. (1974). Children's physical attractiveness and sex as determinants of adult punitiveness. *Developmental Psychology*, 10, 772–778.

Doll, E. A. (1965). Vineland Social Maturity scale. Circle Pines, MN: American Guidance Service.

Douglas, S. P., & Wind, Y. (1978). Examining family role and authority patterns. *Journal of Marriage and the Family*, 40, 35–47.

DuBose, R. F. (1981). Assessment of severely impaired young children: Problems and recommendations. *Topics in Early Childhood Special Education*, 1, 9–21.

Eheart, B. K. (1982). Mother-child interactions with nonretarded and mentally retarded preschoolers. *American Journal of Mental Deficiency*, 87, 20–25.

Ellis, N. R. (1969). A behavioral research strategy in mental retardation: Defense and critique. *American Journal of Mental Deficiency*, 73, 557–566.

Farber, B. (1959). Effects of a severely mentally retarded child on family integration. *Monographs of the Society for Research in Child Development*, 24(1, Serial No. 71).

Farber, B. (1960). Family organization and crisis: Maintenance of integration in families with a severely mentally retarded child. *Monographs of the Society for Research in Child Development*, 25(1, Serial No. 75).

Farber, B., & Jenne, W. C. (1963). Family organization and parent-child communication: Parents and siblings of a retarded child. *Monographs of the Society for Research in Child Development*, 28(7, Serial No. 91).

Filler, J. W. (1976). Modifying maternal teaching style: Effects of task arrangement on the match-to-sample performance of retarded preschool-age children. *American Journal of Mental Deficiency*, 80, 602–612.

Filler, J. W., & Bricker, W. A. (1976). Teaching styles of mothers and the match-to-sample performance of their retarded preschool-age children. *American Journal of Mental Deficiency*, 80, 504–511.

Filler, J., & Kasari, C. (1981). Acquisition, maintenance, and generalization of parent-taught skills with two severely handicapped infants. *Journal of the Association for the Severely Handicapped*, 6, 30–38.

Gibson, H. B. (1969). Early delinquency in relation to broken homes. *Journal of Child Psychology and Psychiatry and Allied Disciplines*, 10, 195–204.

Goethals, G. R., & Reckman, R. F. (1973). The perception of consistency in attitudes. *Journal of Experimental Social Psychology*, 9, 491–501.

Gottman, J. M., & Parkhurst, J. T. (1980). A developmental theory of friendship and acquaintanceship process. In A. Collins (Ed.), *Development of cognition, affect, and social relations: The Minnesota Symposium on Child Psychology*. Hillsdale, NJ: Erlbaum.

Greenberg, M. T. (1980). Social interaction between deaf preschoolers and their mothers: The effects of communication method and communication competence. *Developmental Psychology*, 16, 465–474.

Greenberg, M. T., & Marvin, R. S. (1979). Attachment patterns in profoundly deaf preschool children. Merrill-Palmer Quarterly, 25, 265–279.

Gutmann, A. J., & Rondal, J. A. (1979). Verbal operants in mothers' speech to nonretarded and Down's syndrome children matched for linguistics level. American Journal of Mental Deficiency, 83, 446–452.

Hetherington, E. M., Cox, M., & Cox, R. (1978). The aftermath of divorce. In J. H. Stevens & M. Mathews (Eds.), Mother/Child Father/Child Relationships. Washington, DC: National Association for the Education of Young Children.

Horejsi, C. R. (1979). Social and psychological factors in family care. In R. H. Bruininks & G. C. Krantz (Eds.), Family care of developmentally disabled members. Minneapolis: University of Minnesota.

Kelly, J. B., & Wallerstein, J. S. (1976). The effects of parental divorce: Experiences of the child in early latency. American Journal of Orthopsychiatry, 46, 20–32.

Kihlstrom, J. F. (1980). On personality and memory. In N. Cantor and J. F. Kihlstrom (Eds.), Personality, cognition, and social interaction. Hillsdale, NJ: Erlbaum.

Kogan, K. L., Wimberger, H. C., & Bobbitt, R. A. (1969). Analysis of mother-child interaction in young mental retardates. Child Development, 40, 799–812.

Korner, A. F. (1974). The effect of the infants' state, level of arousal, sex, and autogenetic stage of the caregiver. In M. Lewis & L. A. Rosenblum (Eds.), The effect of the infant on its caregiver. New York: Wiley–Interscience.

Lytton, H. (1971). Observational studies of parent-child interaction: A methodological review. Child Development, 43, 651–658.

Markus, H. (1977). Self-schemata and processing information about the self. Journal of Personality and Social Psychology, 35(2), 63–78.

Marshall, N. R., Hegrenes, J. R., & Goldstein, S. (1973). Verbal interaction: Mothers and their retarded children vs. mothers and their nonretarded children. American Journal of Mental Deficiency, 77, 415–419.

Martin, B. (1975). Parent-child relations. In F. D. Horowitz (Ed.), Review of Child Development Research (Vol. 4). Chicago: University of Chicago Press.

McCall, R. B. (1983). Environmental effects on intelligence: The forgotten realm of discontinuous nonshared within-family factors. Child Development, 54, 408–415.

McCord, J., McCord, W., & Thurber, E. (1962). Some effects of paternal absence on male children. Journal of Abnormal and Social Psychology, 64, 361–369.

Meadow, K. P., Greenberg, M. T., Erting, C., & Carmichael, H. (1981). Interactions of deaf mothers and deaf preschool children: Comparisons with three other groups of deaf and hearing dyads. American Annals of the Deaf, 126, 454–468.

Mecham, M. J. (1958). Verbal language development scale. Circle Pines, MN: American Guidance Service.

Milliones, J. (1978). Relationship between perceived child temperament and maternal behavior. Child Development, 49, 1255–1257.

Mink, I. T., Nihira, K., & Meyers, C. E. (1983). Taxonomy of family life styles: 1. Homes with TMR children. American Journal of Mental Deficiency, 87, 484–497.

Mischel, W. (1968). Personality and assessment. New York: Wiley.

Nihira, K., Meyers, C. E., & Mink, I. T. (1980). Home environment, family adjustment, and the development of mentally retarded children. Applied Research in Mental Retardation, 1, 5–24.

Nihira, K., Mink, I. T., & Meyers, C. E. (1981). Relationship between home environment and school adjustment of TMR children. American Journal of Mental Deficiency, 86, 8–15.

Nye, F. I. (1957). Child adjustment in broken and unhappy unbroken homes. *Marriage and Family Living, 19*, 356–361.

O'Connor, W., & Stachowiak, J. (1971). Patterns of interaction in families with high adjusted, low adjusted, and mentally retarded members. *Family Process, 10*, 229–241.

Olson, D. H., & Rabunsky, C. (1972). Validity of four measures of family power. *Journal of Marriage and the Family, 34*, 224–234.

Patterson, G. R. (1976). The aggressive child: Victim and architect of a coercive system. In E. J. Mash, L. A. Hamerlynck, & L. C. Hardy (Eds.), *Behavior Modification and Families.* New York: Brunner/Mazel.

Patterson, G. R. (1980). Mothers: The unacknowledged victims. *Monographs of the Society for Research in Child Development, 45*(5, Serial No. 186).

Peterson, G. A., & Sherrod, K. B. (1982). Relationship of maternal language to language development and language delay of children. *American Journal of Mental Deficiency, 86*, 391–398.

Piper, M., & Ramsay, M. (1980). Effects of early home environment on the mental development of Down syndrome infants. *Americal Journal of Mental Deficiency, 85*, 39–44.

Powell, T. H. (in press). Teaching mentally retarded children to play with their siblings using parents as trainers. *Education and Training of the Mentally Retarded.*

Power, M. J., Ash, P. M., Schoenberg, E., & Sorey, E. C. (1974). Delinquency and the family. *British Journal of Social Work, 4*, 17–38.

Rondal, J. A. (1978). Maternal speech to normal and Down's syndrome children matched for mean length of utterance. In C. E. Meyers (Ed.), *Quality of life in severely and profoundly retarded people.* Washington, DC: American Association on Mental Deficiency.

Rowe, D. C., & Plomin, R. (1981). The importance of nonshared (E_1) environmental influences in behavioral developments. *Developmental Psychology, 17*, 517–531.

Sackett, G. P. (1977). The lag sequential analysis of contingency and cyclicity in behavioral interaction research. In J. Osofsky (Ed.), *Handbook of infant development.* New York: Wiley.

Sandler, A., Coren, A., & Thurman, S. K. (1983). A training program for parents of handicapped preschool children: Effects upon mother, father, and child. *Exceptional Children, 49*, 355–357.

Schoggen, P. (1975). An ecological study of children with physical disabilities in school and at home. In R. A. Weinberg & F. H. Wood (Eds.), *Observation of pupils and teachers in mainstream and special education settings: Alternative strategies.* Minneapolis: University of Minnesota.

Schwirian, P. M. (1977). Effects of the presence of a hearing-impaired preschool child in the family on behavior patterns of older "normal" siblings. *American Annals of the Deaf, 121*(4), 373–380.

Simeonsson, K. J., Huntington, G. S., & Parse, S. A. (1980). Assessment of children with severe handicaps: Multiple problems—Multivariate goals. *Journal of the Association for the Severely Handicapped, 5*(1), 55–72.

Snyder, M., & Uranowitz, S. W. (1978). Reconstructing the past: Some cognitive consequences of person perception. *Journal of Personality and Social Psychology, 36*, 941–951.

Stokes, T. F., & Baer, D. M. (1977). An implicit technology of generalization. *Journal of Applied Behavior Analysis, 10*, 349–368.

Stoneman, Z., & Brody, G. H. (1981). Two's company, three makes a difference: An examination of mothers' and fathers' speech to their young children. *Child Develop-ment, 52*, 705–707.

Stoneman, Z., & Brody, G. H. (1982). Strengths inherent in sibling interactions involving a retarded child: A functional role theory approach. In N. Stinnet, B. Chesser, J. DeFrain, & P. Knaub (Eds.), *Family strengths: Positive models for family life.* Lincoln: University of Nebraska.

Stoneman, Z., & Brody, G. H. (in press). Observations of retarded children, their parents, and their siblings. In S. Landesman-Dwyer & P. M. Vietze (Eds.), *The impact of residential environments on retarded persons and their caregivers.* Baltimore: University Park Press.

Stoneman, Z., Brody, G. H., & Abbott, D. (1983). In-home observations of young Down syndrome children with their mothers and fathers. *American Journal of Mental Defi-ciency, 6*, 591–600.

Stoneman, Z., Brody, G. H., & MacKinnon, C. E. (1984). Naturalistic observations of chil-dren's roles and activities while playing with their siblings and friends. *Child Development, 55*, 57–72.

Terdal, L. E., Jackson, R. H., & Garner, A. M. (1976). Mother-child interactions: A compari-son between normal and developmentally delayed groups. In E. J. Mash, L. A. Hammerlynck, & L. C. Hardy (Eds.), *Behavior modification and families.* New York: Brunner/Mazel.

Thompson, L., & Walker, A. J. (1982). The dyad as the unit of analysis: Conceptual and methodological issues. *Journal of Marriage and the Family, 44*, 889–900.

Weitz, S. (1981). A code for assessing teaching skills of parents of developmentally dis-abled children. *Journal of Autism and Developmental Disorders, 12*, 13–24.

Wolchik, S. A., & Harris, S. L. (1982). Language environments of autistic and normal children matched for language age: A preliminary investigation. *Journal of Autism and Developmental Disorders, 12*, 43–55.

Yarrow, M. R. (1963). Problems of methods in parent-child research. *Child Development, 34*, 215–226.

Yarrow, M. R., Waxler, C. Z., & Scott, P. M. (1971). Child effects on behavior. *Develop-mental Psychology, 5*, 300–311.

Zahn-Waxler, C., & Radke-Yarrow, M. (1983). The development of altruism: Alternate research strategies. In N. Eisenberg-Berg (Ed.), *The development of prosocial behavior.* New York: Academic Press.

Zahn-Waxler, C., Radke-Yarrow, M., & King, R. A. (1979). Child rearing and children's prosocial initiations toward victims of distress. *Child Development, 50*, 319–330.

Zigler, E. (1969). Developmental versus difference theories of mental retardation and the problem of motivation. *American Journal of Mental Deficiency, 73*, 536–555.

CHAPTER 6

Severely Handicapped Children and Their Brothers and Sisters

Thomas M. Skrtic
Jean Ann Summers
Mary Jane Brotherson
Ann P. Turnbull

I am not so sure that things worked out very well in terms of my own feelings, in terms of where I am at in my own head about it. I have fears, I have doubts, I have guilt feelings about certain things I did. . . . I know when I see Cathy now it is always terribly upsetting for me. I usually come home in tears. *(Klein, 1972c, p. 27)*

Lucy has taught me not to take life so seriously. She is a real nice reminder that life is OK. The eggs can be burning, the baby could be crying, and I'll be in the worst mood, and she'll say, "Isn't it such a nice day?"[1]

Introduction

What is the impact of a handicapped brother or sister on nonhandicapped siblings? The remarks above illustrate that the process is not a simple one to trace. No formulas exist; it cannot categorically be said that a given sibling will react in a given way to a set of given circumstances. Indeed, some people seem to benefit from their association with a severely handicapped brother or sister, while others are harmed. The

---

[1] Taken from data files of a 12-family case study conducted by the authors at the University of Kansas Research and Training Center on Independent Living, 1982. For further information on this research, contact Dr. A. P. Turnbull, Bureau of Child Research, University of Kansas, Lawrence, Kansas 66045. Unless otherwise cited, all quotations from siblings used in this chapter are taken from these data.

215

search for an understanding of impact thus becomes more complex: What are the impacts, and what are the factors leading to the differential responses siblings make to their handicapped brother or sister? Further, since this volume focuses on families with severely handicapped children, there is an additional complexity to the original question: What are the impact , and the factors leading to those impacts, experienced by people witl *severely* handicapped siblings?

On the face of it, this might seem to be a quantitative problem: Whatever the impact is, it increases along with the severity of the handicap. However, there is some evidence that this is an unwarranted assumption. Families in general, and siblings in particular, face significant problems in their interactions with a mildly handicapped family member. For example, siblings may have a tendency to overidentify with a mildly handicapped brother or sister, especially if the handicap is not a visible one (Grossman, 1972). Furthermore, a mildly handicapped child will more often be in situations (e.g., a mainstream class placement) where the nonhandicapped sibling must face problems of embarrassment, the need to protect the handicapped sibling from teasing or other harm, and the necessity of explaining the handicap to peers. Finally, in contrast to severely handicapped children whose future inability to perform "normally" is fairly well settled, mildly handicapped children tend to produce a roller coaster of emotions in their families, as hopes are continually raised only to be dashed (Wadsworth & Wadsworth, 1971).

Thus the factors contributing to the impacts on siblings of severely handicapped children cannot be documented simply as quantitatively greater than the impact on siblings of mildly handicapped children. The impacts may or may not be different, but they are certainly not greater.

The point of this discussion is that the determination of patterns of impact of severely handicapped siblings is extremely complex, as are all qualitative issues. Nor is the task simply a matter of teasing out patterns related to severe handicap from the accumulated body of literature concerned with siblings of handicapped children in general. There are few studies related specifically to severely or profoundly handicapped siblings, and research on siblings in general is sparse and conflicting. Problems with the literature are numerous, as discussed later in the chapter. At this point, however, two important problems should be noted. First, literature concerned with siblings of handicapped children too often is divorced from a consideration of sibling relationships in general. Handicapped people, after all, are "people" first and only secondarily "handicapped." A reviewer of this literature is frequently left with the difficult problem of determining which parts of the observed phenomena are a result of factors related to sibships in general and which can be attributed to the factor of handicap. The second, and perhaps most glaring, difficulty is the narrow focus of most of the studies. The issue, as we have noted, is very complex. Focusing on the sibling dyad without consideration of the broader context in which the interaction operates is analogous to removing the heart from a laboratory animal and then trying to determine how it functions in the animal's body. While numerous inferences can be made, the heart must be observed as it functions within the body in order to draw any definitive conclusions. Studies of human interaction, like studies in physiology, cannot be removed from the context in which the interaction exists.

The "body" in which the sibling interaction functions is the family. The family is a matrix shaping the personalities of its members. It engrains and habituates the responses that lead its individual members to success or failure, happiness or distress. An understanding of a severely disabled individual, a nonhandicapped sibling, and the relationship between the two involves an understanding of the entire family (Montalvo & Haley, 1973).

This chapter analyzes existing research on siblings of severely handicapped children, and sibships in general, from the perspective of the family as a whole. To accomplish this task, it is necessary to use an organizing framework from which this complex entity—the family—can be understood. Such a framework must be designed with care. As Freeman (1976) has emphasized, "the framework that we bring to understand how families behave can facilitate or retard our work. If we have too narrow a view of family functioning, the types of questions, goals, and strategies we can use become more of a disservice than help to families" (p. 746). The first step in developing a sufficiently broad framework is an appreciation of the fact that there is no such thing as *the* family. Families differ widely in their makeup or structure, and these differences lead to endless variations in the ways in which they function to meet the needs of their individual members. Further, even the same family will differ in the ways in which it approaches its functional tasks at different stages in its life span.

One framework for understanding families has been developed at the University of Kansas Research and Training Center on Independent Living (see footnote 1). The framework first considers the family system to be composed of three major subsystems (Minuchin, 1974): the spouse subsystem (husband and wife interactions), the parental subsystem (child–parent interactions), and the sibling subsystem (child–child interactions). Again, while the focus of this chapter is on the sibling subsystem, it is important to remember that siblings affect, and are affected

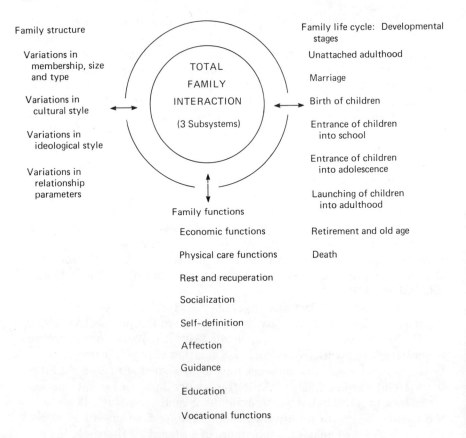

Family structure

Variations in
  membership, size
  and type

Variations in
  cultural style

Variations in
  ideological style

Variations in
  relationship
  parameters

TOTAL
FAMILY
INTERACTION

(3 Subsystems)

Family life cycle: Developmental
  stages

Unattached adulthood

Marriage

Birth of children

Entrance of children
  into school

Entrance of children
  into adolescence

Launching of children
  into adulthood

Family functions

Economic functions

Physical care functions

Rest and recuperation

Socialization

Self-definition

Affection

Guidance

Education

Vocational functions

Retirement and old age

Death

Figure 6.1 Multidimensional framework of the family system.

by, the other two systems. Second, the model views these family sub-systems from three general perspectives: family function, family structure, and family life cycle. Each perspective has been employed by family theorists as a single avenue for inquiry or intervention. Combining them, however, creates a multidimensional framework for understanding the total family system. Figure 6.1 is a representation of this framework, depicting the three subsystems and the interrelationship of family function, structure, and life cycle.

Figure 6.1 serves as an outline for this chapter. We focus in turn on family function, structure, and life cycle. Within each area we examine the meaning of the various components for families in general, for siblings in general, and for siblings of handicapped children in particular. In this way we hope to provide a context for understanding the existing body of research and to develop guideposts for intervention and further study.

Family Functions

Families perform essential functions for individual family members as well as for society at large. The nuclear family, consisting of the subsystems discussed earlier, is characterized by the basic functions it performs. Outside groups and agencies (such as churches and schools) and other extended family members often share in the fulfillment of functions, but the nuclear family remains the orchestrator of those tasks.

Families vary in the number of functions on which they focus as well as in the degree to which they perform any particular function. Also, families differ in terms of how and whether they seek and obtain help from service agencies, friends, and extended family members in performing family functions and meeting the needs of individual family members. Traditionally, professionals serving families with severely handicapped members have focused narrowly on one or two functions (e.g., physical, educational) to the exclusion of others. However, a broader view of family functions includes nine major categories, as shown in Table 6.1.

As the family moves through the various stages of its life cycle, the responsibility for performing these functions shifts among the three subsystems. Many of the functions that initially are performed by parents are eventually assumed by siblings and/or individual family members. This point will become evident as each of the nine family functions is discussed.

Economic Functions

The family can be considered a unit of economic consumption and production. Not only can a handicapped child increase family consumption (e.g., medical care, educational and/or residential services, adaptive equipment), but also the time required to provide care may absorb family time that might have been spent on economically productive pursuits. Thus, a severely handicapped child potentially increases the consumptive demands of the family at the same time he or she decreases its productive power. Naturally, families cope with economic problems in various ways. In general family members are assigned the tasks necessary for survival, including wage earning, maintaining the household, and child rearing. Siblings may be assigned any one or all of these tasks.

TABLE 6.1
Family Functions in Serving Individual Needs

Function	Need served
Economic functions	Income Division of labor
Physical care functions	Food, clothing, and shelter Health care and maintenance Safety and protection Mobility
Rest and recuperation	Recreation Setting aside demands—being oneself
Socialization	Basic beliefs and values Religion Interpersonal relationships Social skills
Self-definition	Establishing self-identity and self-image Place in the community
Affection	Emotional mastery Nuturing love Companionship Sense of belonging
Guidance	Problem-solving Control group feedback
Education	Information and knowledge Information sharing among members
Vocational functions	Career choice Development of work ethic

As the children grow older, the responsibility for financial support of a disabled family member may be transferred to the nonhandicapped siblings. The family may have an unspoken (Klein, 1972b) or explicit agreement that the responsibility for care will pass to the younger generation. In some families, siblings may resent or resist the responsibility of caring for an adult disabled brother or sister (Parfit, 1975). One sibling in the 12-family case study expressed her resentment graphically:

> Very early my role was to take care of George. I was to be responsible for George for the rest of my life. . . . Mother told me I would be responsible when I was about in the sixth grade. She was fearful he would have to be institutionalized and she didn't want that. Then it was fine. I chose my career with George in mind. I

didn't think I would get married, partly because of George. Now I think it is unfair for Mom to expect me to take most of the burden when there are six children in the family.

However, an explicit understanding, even when it is resented, seems to be less stressful than a lack of plans for the future. Fish and Fitzgerald (1980) conducted a group discussion with nine adolescents who had retarded siblings. They reported that all of the nine siblings lacked understanding and awareness of future plans regarding their handicapped brothers or sisters. The absence of future plans caused varying degrees of anxiety among the group regarding how their siblings would be cared for and their prospective roles in that care.

Physical Care Functions

The economic and physical care functions of families are closely related in that food, clothing, shelter, and other physical needs are dependent on the economic productivity of the family. But the physical well-being of family members goes beyond economics and includes such functions as health care and maintenance, safety and protection, and mobility. Siblings may take a large role in providing for all these physical needs. They may help each other with chores, they may teach each other skills, lend each other money, and so forth. They also may provide each other with protection; for example, an older brother may guard against bullies on the way to school, or a younger sister may cover up some transgression to protect a sibling from parental wrath (Bank & Kahn, 1975). As they grow older, they may assist each other in providing transportation.

Older siblings often assist in fulfilling child-rearing functions, especially in large families, in families where both parents work, in families where one or both parents is missing or in some way incapacitated (e.g., alcoholic), and—more relevant to this discussion—in families with a disabled child. There is evidence that the younger members of the sibling subsystem accept their older brothers and sisters as parent substitutes with equinamity. For example, Bossard and Boll (1956), in a study of 100 large families (i.e., 6 or more children), found that 44% of the siblings resented parental discipline, but only 11% resented discipline by siblings.

In families with a severely disabled member, nonhandicapped siblings frequently serve the physical function, for example, by carrying medications at school. Siblings also typically feel compelled to guard their handicapped brother or sister against discrimination. Siblings may explain, scold, or stare back pointedly at starers, fight with peers, or remove their handicapped brother or sister from the situation (Klein, 1972a).

Several authors (Gath, 1974; Grossman, 1972) have reported that older daughters typically share responsibility with their mothers for care of a handicapped brother or sister, especially in lower socioeconomic status families. Some siblings have reported resenting this responsibility as an intrusion on their time (Klein, 1972a); others have found it to be an enriching experience (Grossman, 1972). One sibling in our study described how she and her nonhandicapped sister had developed close bonds through sharing chores and caring for their severely disabled sister: "We worked as a team. Mom would go to town on Saturday, and Donna and I made a game of housework and getting Alice's bath and hair done before she got home. Mom came to expect it but she always acted surprised."

Resentment of added child-care responsibility has been cited as a cause of tension between mothers and nonhandicapped daughters (Fowle, 1968). However, this may not always be the case; Schrieber and Feely (1965) found that daughters sometimes believed they managed the retarded child much better than their mothers and resented what they saw as maternal interference. Whether the experience is rewarding or restrictive, however, as more families make the decision to keep severely disabled children at home, siblings will be more likely to be recruited as participants in the task of caring for their severely handicapped brother or sister.

Rest and Recuperation

In a successfully functioning family, home is a place where family members can let their hair down and set aside pressures of job or school. One sibling described playing this role for her moderately retarded adult sister: "Her coming over to my house is her chance to check out of her everyday life—she lies on the couch and watches TV and I think it's her chance to escape." Family members are allowed and even expected to be themselves, to rest and relax (Caplan, 1976). Recreation is an important aspect of this function.

Family vacations are more difficult for some families with severely handicapped children because of the necessity of special arrangements or potential behavior problems (McAndrew, 1976). Families with a severely disabled member are often restricted in their choice of recreational activities in the community due to a lack of accessibility and/or opportunity. One father of a severely handicapped daughter noted, "We don't go places that don't take wheelchairs. We have gotten to the point where I refuse to fight where they just don't want you." Thus, recreation involving the whole family may be an infrequent event. For nonhandicapped siblings these restrictions may take several forms. Parents may lack time or money to take their nonhandicapped children to activities (e.g., scouting and dance lessons) or may not be able to get away from home to watch their children in school plays, athletics, or other interests. For handicapped children, their nonhandicapped brothers and sisters may be their only playmates. With this lack of available peers, nonhandicapped siblings play an even greater role in the recreation of handicapped children.

Socialization

Socialization involves learning the values, attitudes, and beliefs a society possesses—its culture (Leslie, 1976). The family is a key vehicle in achieving socialization, not only for the children but also for continued growth and socialization throughout the lives of all its members. Religion is deeply involved in this function; for many people religion acts to define and strengthen ultimate values and beliefs. Siblings play an important role in this function by providing continual examples. Bossard and Boll (1956) found that 97 of 100 informants describing their experiences agreed that in large families siblings play an important role in learning fair play, self-control, sharing, and being able to listen as well as talk.

A severely disabled brother or sister can affect the socialization process of nonhandicapped siblings in both positive and negative ways. Simeonsson and McHale (1981) noted in a review of the literature that siblings of handicapped children are often well adjusted and characterized by maturity and a responsible attitude that goes beyond their age. Several authors have found that nonhandicapped siblings learn to accept differences, to be more tolerant of others, and to be more helpful as a result of interacting with a handicapped brother or sister (Cleveland & Miller, 1977; DeMeyer, 1979; Grossman, 1972). Miller (1974) found that nonhandicapped siblings tended to treat their handicapped brother or sister in a more helpful and instrumental way, in contrast to engaging in more horseplay, teasing, and argument as with other nonhandicapped siblings. In fact, siblings may feel guilty about teasing a handicapped brother or sister, even though such teasing may serve as a good training ground for teaching the handicapped child to deal with stigma and discrimination (Klein, 1972a). Parfit (1975) indicated that siblings may be reluctant to bring home friends when there is a severely handicapped child in the home. On the other hand, Klein (1972b) found in an interview with college-aged nonhandicapped siblings that they often judged the worth of potential friends by the reactions of individuals to their handicapped brother or sister. As one respondent said: "The thing is, nobody is going to be your friend who makes fun of your sibling.... If they react poorly, you know that they are not worth it" (Klein, 1972b, p. 27).

Self-definition

Caplan (1976) described the successfully functioning family as a support system, a system that provides individuals with opportunities or feedback about themselves and validation of their expectations about others. It is a social aggregate in which persons are recognized as unique individuals and thereby gain their sense of identity. Membership in a family helps to define a person by establishing a self-identity and identifying his or her place in the community. Leslie (1976) believed there is much less direct participation of the family in defining each member's role in the community than there was in the past; however, families still perform this function to a degree. It is through many of the family's activities and contacts in a community that the individual members develop a sense of their place in the community and a feeling of self-worth and self-identity.

Siblings have a strong impetus to mold their self-images reciprocally through the process of identification. Siblings may identify with each other to a greater extent than with parents, not only because they are members of the same family but also because they are peers within that family (Bank & Kahn, 1975). One father of a congenital quadriplegic amputee suggested that the development of his son's identity could largely be attributed to the boy's sister, who was only a year younger. The handicapped son agreed: "We did everything together. And she looked up to me, thought I could do anything. I had to live up to that." However, the identification process can cause problems for siblings of handicapped children, especially younger siblings. The strong impulse to identify may lead nonhandicapped siblings to question whether they are in some way also handicapped. Identification can lead to anxiety about the characteristics they may share with their handicapped brother or sister (Simeonsson & McHale, 1981). According to Grossman (1972), a critical problem of adolescent siblings is overidentification with their retarded brothers or sisters. Grossman also pointed out that overidentification seems to be more prevalent when the handicap is less visible. As the level of severity increases, Grossman found that nonhandicapped siblings are not only less likely to identify with a handicapped brother or sister, but also are less likely to view the sibling as a person.

Self-identity also is shaped by parental expectations. In the case of families where one of the children is disabled, parents may expect their nonhandicapped children to assume responsibility for achieving and making up for the limitations of the handicapped child. One sibling felt that her parents had perhaps centered too much of their ambitions on her. "I felt pressure to achieve. They pressured me to get into the band, to get into dramatics, to get into this or that. I finally just had to rebel." Cleveland and Miller (1977) found that adult siblings frequently reported pressure to overachieve in academics or athletics. This pressure seems to be especially strong in families where there are one or two nonhandicapped siblings, as opposed to a larger family (Trevino, 1979).

Affection

Caplan (1976) emphasized the function of families in helping individual members achieve emotional mastery. He defined this as the assistance the family gives in helping a member work through feelings of guilt, anger, worry, or pain, and in learning to express love and joy. The family provides a sense of belonging, companionship, and an environment that fosters nurturance and support.

Siblings naturally participate in all of these functions. In families with a severely disabled child, nonhandicapped siblings may need to learn to deal with feelings of guilt and jealousy. Guilt may arise through remorse over teasing or anger at the handicapped sibling. Even though teasing is a common behavior among siblings, teasing a handicapped brother or sister seems to trigger feelings of guilt in nonhandicapped children. As one sibling put it, "In some way they are at a disadvantage to you. It is like picking on somebody who is smaller" (Klein, 1972a, p. 15). Also, nonhandicapped children may need to master irrational guilt feelings, which younger siblings especially may experience about being "normal" (Trevino, 1979). Additional guilt feelings may arise as the sibling grows older and surpasses an older handicapped brother or sister in capability (Farber & Ryckman, 1965). These feelings may lead the nondisabled sibling to drop behind in achievement in order to ease an overburdened conscience (Trevino, 1979).

Jealousy can arise when the nonhandicapped child perceives that the severely disabled brother or sister is receiving more attention. Parfit (1975) pointed out that resentment of parental attention is a common phenomenon. Handicapped children might be indulged, overprotected, or permitted to engage in behavior not allowed in the other children.

Indulgence and overprotection can be considered extreme manifestations of nurturance and love. Guilt feelings of parents may cause them to overprotect handicapped children to the detriment of their development (Hewett, 1976). Parfit (1975) suggested in this regard that siblings are often more sensible and sensitive than their parents and are capable of serving as a balance and/or as advisors in providing nurturing support without overprotection or overindulgence.

Finally, an important aspect of the affectional function of families is the development of a sense of belonging. There is evidence that the pressure of a handicapped child can disrupt family cohesiveness (Simeonsson & McHale, 1981), or draw the family too close to allow healthy functioning (this point is elaborated on in our discussion of family structure). On the positive side, the presence of a severely handicapped child in the family may improve the family's ability to foster a sense of belonging and cohesiveness (Klein, 1972b). As the family marshals its resources to cope with the handicap it often forms cohesive affectional bonds and a strong feeling of "specialness." One sibling described this feeling thus:

> I always felt there was something very special about our family. Of course, you know, Cathy being that difference. Because of her difference there was a degree of specialness or closeness that made us all very, very close. We all pitched in and helped each other out and Cathy was the one thing in difficult times that we could focus on. (Klein, 1972b, p. 25)

Guidance

In the function of guidance the family serves as a control group for its members, providing feedback and assisting each member in solving day-to-day problems (Caplan, 1976). As a control group, the family renders its judgments of individual behavior and thereby controls and molds the behaviors of its members through reward and punishment. Because family members are likely to be quite sensitive to the opinions and attitudes of the rest of the family they are thereby more likely to adhere to the family code (Caplan, 1976). As opposed to interaction with the outside world, feedback from family members is generally direct and obtrusive. The family can also help each member understand and interpret his or her actions and interactions with outsiders. This function often leads to active guidance in solving specific problems of a routine or a crisis nature.

Bank and Kahn (1975) emphasized the role of siblings in providing these guidance functions. They noted that "siblings provide a self laboratory for experimenting with new behaviors where new roles are tried on, criticized, encouraged, or benevolently acknowledged before being used either with parents or non-family members" (Bank & Kahn, 1975, p. 321). Bossard and Boll (1956) also commented on the guidance role of siblings: "Life among siblings is like living in the nude psychologically speaking. Siblings serve as a constant crude awakening" (p. 92). In families with a disabled child, nonhandicapped siblings can and often do serve a guidance function for their disabled brother or sister or, as pointed out earlier, they may serve as a valuable sounding board for parents in their decisions concerning care and protection of the handicapped family member. The severely handicapped person can him- or herself provide a form of guidance to nonhandicapped siblings. This guidance is often in the form of gaining perspective on life or their own personal qualities. For example, one person in our study with a severely disabled sister noted: "Lucy is constantly teaching me stuff. . . . She has taught me to be more patient in accepting people where they are and not putting my expectations on them."

Education

The education function of families can be viewed from two perspectives. First, the family as a whole has a need for information from the outside world in order to assist it in better fulfilling its many functions. Such informational needs include knowledge and skills in child rearing, time and money management, and so forth. Second, families perform an education function for individual members by teaching and sharing information with each other. For example, children learn cooking, housekeeping, carpentry, rules of etiquette, and many other facts and skills from their parents. As Caplan (1976) pointed out, "It is important that parents share their store of information about the outside world with their children so that the latter are not forced to collect all this information themselves, even though there is a limit to what a person can learn vicariously from the experience of others" (p. 22). But this flow of information is not necessarily a one-way affair; in this time of rapid social and technological change, the younger members of a family are often in a position to provide information and insights to older family members. Of course siblings, especially older siblings, serve this function for each other regularly.

In a family with a severely disabled member, nonhandicapped siblings have a need for education in a variety of areas. Schreiber and Feeley (1965) found in an adolescent guided-group experience that the real need of the group was for accurate and up-to-date information. They also found that it was highly important for parents to communicate with their nondisabled children, and that the group sessions seemed valuable to these adolescents, in providing them with a sense that "somebody cares" and that there are others facing the same problems. Parfit (1975) emphasized the needs for information on a variety of issues, including genetic implications, future plans for support of the handicapped sibling, and more immediate explanations of the nature and cause of the handicap in order to deal with questions from friends and teachers.

Aside from their own needs for education, siblings are an important resource for providing education to their handicapped brothers and sisters. This potential resource has received attention from professionals. Several investigations have shown that nonhandicapped siblings can successfully teach cognitive tasks to handicapped brothers and sisters (Cicirelli, 1976) and can participate in the modification of behaviors (Weinrott, 1974). Simeonsson and McHale (1981) reviewed reports of these interventions and concluded that, while many of the investigations were not rigorously controlled and therefore inconclusive, there seems to be a growing body of evidence that siblings can successfully serve this role. In a series of interviews with parents of autistic children, the parents reported that siblings were often more effective in working with their handicapped brothers and sisters at home than were the parents themselves (DeMeyer, 1979). In short, siblings play important roles within the education function of families, both in terms of their need for education and their ability to provide it.

Vocational Functions

Another important function of families is development of a work ethic and assistance in career choice. For families with a severely disabled member reaching young adulthood, one of the critical issues is finding vocational training or employment. Often the opportunities within communities are limited.

The feeling of identification with a handicapped brother or sister and a desire to understand his or her problems better have often led nonhandicapped siblings to choose careers in education and human services (Crocker, 1981). Farber (1963) found that siblings who interacted frequently with a retarded brother or sister considered devoting their lives to social causes and making a contribution to mankind to be more important life goals than did those who had less contact with their handicapped sibling. Finally, Cleveland and Miller (1977) found that oldest female siblings who shared in caretaking responsibilities were particularly likely to enter the helping professions.

Family Structure

In moving from the description of various family functions to that of family structures, it is important to realize that functions play a primary role in defining the actual presence or absence of a "family." In contrast to the stereotypical image of a family as a specific type of kinship relation consisting of a specific group of people (i.e., mother, father, children), our society has evolved a number of possible social arrangements, each of which serve most of the functions described earlier and all of which must therefore be considered families.

Considerations of family structure are generally descriptive in nature. They recognize the pluralism of families: that families in this country differ greatly in cultural, racial, ethnic, religious, and socioeconomic profiles. Family structure also includes a description of the family's membership in terms of size and type as well as a description of the ideological style of the family regarding its basic philosophies and attitudes. Family structure also includes the family's relationship parameters. This encompasses the internal structure of the family and includes internal hierarchies, roles and responsibilities of each member, and the boundaries between subsystems. Siblings both affect and are affected by all these structural attributes.

It is important to realize the interrelatedness of structure, function, and life cycle. Family structure plays a critical role in defining how ideologies are actualized through the functions families perform as well as determining the family's responses to life-cycle transitions. There are four dimensions to consider under pluralistic family structures. Table 6.2 outlines each dimension.

Variations in Membership, Size, and Type

There are many variations in family membership, size, and type. At any one time families may fit into several of the following descriptive categories: (1) number of parents: single parent, two parents, multiple

TABLE 6.2
Pluralistic Family Structures

Variations in membership, size, and type
  Number of parents
  Nature of kinship relationships
  Family size
  Primary versus reconstituted relationships
  Relationships of members to the labor force

Variations in cultural style
  Ethnic
  Racial
  Religious
  Socioeconomic status
  Location (urban, rural, or suburban)

Variations in ideological style
  Child-rearing philosophy
  Attitude toward disability
  Attitude toward education
  Work ethic
  Attitude toward independence
  Communication style

Variations in relationship parameters
  Enmeshment–disengagement continuum
  Conflict–harmony continuum
  Hierarchy
  Role assignment

---

parents; (2) nature of kinship relations: nuclear, extended, expanded; (3) family size: number of children and extended or expanded family members in the household; (4) primary or reconstituted relationships: whether members consist of an original nuclear structure or whether they have been fragmented and subsequently reconstituted through processes such as death, divorce or adoption, and remarriage; and (5) relationship of the family members to the labor force; unemployed or one, two, or more wage earners (Hubbell, 1981a, 1981b). Taken together these categories comprise the structural elements necessary to describe any given family. It goes without saying that families with different structural elements have different needs and strengths. Even more, the existence of five categories, each with two or more possible elements, graphically illustrates the considerable array of possible family types.

Many aspects of family structure affect the sibling subsystem. The presence of only one parent, or the fact that both parents work, or a large number of children may mean that a larger share of responsibility for fulfilling the family functions devolves on the siblings. Variation in family size is often cited as an important element in determining the effects on nonhandicapped siblings. Trevino (1979) asserted that a larger number of siblings fosters a greater "atmosphere of normalcy" (p. 489) and therefore mitigates adverse effects of the presence of a handicapped child. On the other hand, Gath (1974) found that eldest daughters from larger families with a handicapped child were significantly more likely to exhibit some type of emotional disturbance or deviance. Gath went on to point out, however, that it was difficult if not impossible to distinguish family size effects from the effects of socioeconomic status, since family size often reflects social class. Gath's results do not shed any light on the question of the extent to which the greater risk for disturbance is a function of the presence of a handicapped sibling or is a function of the more general role as eldest daughter in a large family. This is an example of the way in which research in the two areas—general sibling relationships and siblings of handicapped children—have not been correlated.

Another implication for family membership and size is the fear often expressed by siblings of severely handicapped people who are confronted with the possible genetic ramifications of the disability. Murphy (1979) pointed out that the questions of whether to marry and whether to have children illustrate two of the key concerns of siblings. Parfit (1975) noted that even when fears of hereditary causes of handicap are unfounded they may be nonetheless real and anxiety producing for the sibling.

Variations in Cultural Style

A second dimension of pluralism and structure is the variety of cultural styles within families. It is important to realize that by family culture we mean more than the family's ethnic or racial background. The family culture consists of the customs, traditions, and beliefs of the family based upon their unique background, including ethnic, racial, religious, socioeconomic status, and location (i.e., rural, urban or suburban) factors (Hubbell, 1981, 1981b; Rice, 1977). The possibilities for variation are endless.

Simeonsson and McHale (1981) reported that the religious belief of the family is a major factor that may influence parental and sibling acceptance of a handicapped child. Families with some religious affiliations seem to be more accepting of their handicapped child than others. Early studies (Farber, 1959; Zuk, Miller, Bartram, & Kling, 1961) suggested that Catholic families tend to be more accepting of a retarded child than either Protestant or Jewish families. Stubblefield (1965) speculated that these differences may be due to the fact that Catholic doctrine teaches parents to accept a retarded child as a gift from God rather than as a punishment for guilt.

Another cultural factor affecting siblings in families with a severely handicapped member is socioeconomic status. Grossman (1972) found in an extensive survey of young adults that there was a significant difference between the responses of siblings from higher and lower socioeconomic classes to their retarded brothers or sisters. Farber and Ryckman (1965) found that families responded differently to the birth of a handicapped child according to social class. According to these authors, higher socioeconomic status families tend to regard the birth of a handicapped child as a frustration of their future ambitions for the child's achievement and therefore look at the event as a tragedy. Siblings in this group, especially boys, may therefore be pressured to overachieve to compensate for that frustration. On the other hand, in lower socioeconomic status families where aspirations for achievement are more modest the birth of a handicapped child is not so much a tragedy as it is an additional financial and caretaking burden. Therefore, siblings in the lower socioeconomic status families, especially daughters, are under pressure to shoulder some or all of the responsibility for caring for the severely handicapped child.

Variations in Ideological Style

Closely related to cultural style is the ideological style of families. Ideological style stems from cultural style but is concerned mainly with the family's present perspective of the world and how that perspective is actualized. Ideological style includes the family's child-rearing philosophy, attitude toward disability, attitude toward education, attitude toward independence, work ethic, and communications style. Each family is unique in how these beliefs or ideologies are reflected in its members' everyday behavior.

Grossman (1972) and Simeonsson and McHale (1981) both reported that the attitudes that parents demonstrate toward their severely disabled child greatly influence the sibling acceptance of the child into the family. As stated by the brother of a multihandicapped young woman in our study: "The whole thing is your parents' attitude. Kids will take the same attitude as their parents. The attitude always was—'Rachel was our sister.' The fact she was handicapped was on the back burner. In general, our family has gotten a lot of good out of our experiences with

Rachel. It all goes back to attitude because that's what our parents wanted to happen." Also, parental communication style is extremely important for sibling understanding. As emphasized earlier in the discussion of the educational family function, siblings have a need for open communication and information on a variety of fronts.

Finally, the ideological style of a family produces a parental attitude toward the birth of a handicapped child (e.g., level of acceptance, presence of guilt, tendency to overprotect), which seems to be an extremely strong predictor of the attitude of nonhandicapped siblings (Grossman, 1972). As noted earlier, however, more recent anecdotal reports have indicated that siblings may be more objective and freer of constraints that shape parental attitudes (Fish & Fitzgerald, 1980; Parfit, 1975). In fact, the attitude of siblings can exert a considerable influence on parental acceptance or rejection of the handicapped child.

Variations in Relationship Parameters

As discussed earlier, families can be divided into subsystems, including the spouse subsystem, the parent–child subsystem, and the sibling subsystem. Each subsystem makes a particular contribution to the fulfillment of various family functions. The boundaries between these subsystems are rules defining who participates and how they participate in carrying out family functions (Minuchin, 1974). Boundaries delineate the relationship of individuals and subsystems to one another. Boundaries may be rigid, allowing for very little crossing over among the subsystems for communication or for fulfillment of functions, or they may be diffuse, in which case the subsystem boundaries are not clearly defined. Minuchin (1974) referred to the rigidity of boundaries as disengagement and to the blurring of boundaries as enmeshment. Boundaries should be clearly drawn yet flexible. An example of enmeshment is a situation in which a nonhandicapped sibling is given an excessive amount of responsibility for the care of the severely handicapped brother or sister so that the sibling is curtailed in the development of relationships with friends or in extracurricular school activities. Disengagement occurs when the sibling's needs are neglected by parents or other siblings and is thereby left without family support in filling developmental needs. Minuchin placed enmeshment and disengagement on opposite poles of a continuum, and considered both of these conditions in their extreme form to be dysfunctional.

Similar to the enmeshment–disengagement continuum is a conflict–harmony continuum in a family. This continuum examines the amount of support versus the amount of conflict in which a family engages. In a family with a severely disabled child, both parents may or may not agree on the goals for their child, or there may be conflict among siblings over who will care for the severely disabled sibling (in the present or in the future) or how involved the disabled sibling will be in family activities.

Two other areas of variation in relationship parameters are hierarchies (or power relationships) and role assignment. A family hierarchy is defined by the relative powers and authorities assigned to various family members. These are usually, but not always, age-graded, with the greatest power resting with the parents (Foster, Berger, & McLean, 1981). Roles are the mechanism through which responsibility for fulfilling the family functions are assigned. An individual may serve a number of roles depending on the particular family subsystem with which he or she is interacting at the moment. In fact, both roles and hierarchy vary within subsystems and across subsystems. For example, a child may enjoy considerable power within the parent–child system due to status as a favorite, but at the same time have a very low power position in the hierarchy of the sibling subsystem. Similarly, children whose roles call for them to assume responsibility for education and protection functions for other siblings within the sibling subsystem may switch roles and become the recipients of education and protection when interacting within the parent–child subsystem.

As we have emphasized at several points, siblings can be called upon to fill any or all of the roles required to carry out family functions. But the assignment of these roles to specific siblings depends on the sibling hierarchy, which is governed by several components. Besides the obvious differences in personality among individuals, hierarchy is determined to a great extent by birth order. The effect of a child's ordinal position in the family has been the focus of a considerable amount of research. Significant differences in personality variables have been correlated with birth order. Firstborn children have been found to have more verbal ability, to be more likely to attend college (Forer, 1969), and to be more likely to be considered gifted (Terman, 1925). Youngest children, on the other hand, have been found to be more spontaneous and creative (Forer, 1969). Firstborn children are more strongly achievement oriented, while later-born children tend to be more interested in relationships with others (Sinha, 1967). Sutton-Smith and Rosenberg (1970) reported a series of studies on the effects of both birth order and sex on the use of power tactics in the development of the sibling hierarchy. The results showed that both firstborn boys and girls were more likely to use more aggressive power tactics (such as hitting, bossing, or threatening), while later-born boys and girls tended to use less direct tactics (such as calling in parents, crying, sulking, or bribing).

It is hardly surprising that research shows older siblings to exhibit more independence and later borns to be more dependent. Bossard and Boll (1956) found that 82 of 100 large families (6 or more children) employed the older children to some extent in managing the other children, and in a significant number of cases these youths took over much or all of the responsibility for their siblings. At the other extreme, youngest children, because of their status as the baby in the family, have been found to exhibit relatively dependent behaviors longer than their older siblings, including retention of immature speech forms (Forer, 1969).

Another important determinant of hierarchy and roles among siblings is the presence or absence of a handicap. Handicap affects a child's ability to step into the hierarchical position and to take the roles that would otherwise flow from his or her birth order position. Farber and Ryckman (1965) stated that for siblings there is a revision of age roles in coping with a severely retarded brother or sister in the family. Regardless of birth order the severely handicapped child eventually becomes the "youngest" child in the family's social hierarchy. Lavine (1977) observed blind preschoolers who were either firstborns or later borns and found that while firstborn blind children attempted to claim their leadership role in the sibling group, they were often not followed by younger siblings. Conversely, blind preschoolers who were later borns found their role as the youngest child enhanced by their handicap.

In the case of nonhandicapped siblings, birth order affects the way in which they are affected by the handicapped brother or sister. Simeonsson and McHale (1981) reported that younger children adjust more poorly to the presence of a handicapped sibling, while older siblings, with the exception of the eldest daughter, experience better adjustment.

One of the ways in which family functions and responsibilities are assigned depends upon sex roles. Siblings have a strong effect on each other in the development of sex roles (Sutton-Smith & Rosenberg, 1970). While many of the sibling investigations into the development of male or female roles must be considered outdated due to the current state of flux in this area in our culture, it seems clear that siblings do exert influence in the development of sex-role expectations. In the case of families with a handicapped child, these sex roles, again, affect the way in which the nondisabled siblings are affected by a handicapped brother or sister. Grossman (1972), in an investigation of college students, found that individuals seemed to be more affected by handicapped siblings of their own gender, due perhaps to closer identification. Depending on the family culture, sex-role differentiation may mean that nonhandicapped boys will be called upon to overachieve to compensate for the presence of the handicapped child in the family, while girls will be expected to share in the responsibility for caring for the disabled child. Fowle (1968) measured sibling role tension among siblings whose handicapped brothers or sisters had either been institutionalized or remained at home. She found that boys felt more pressure after the sibling was institutionalized, while girls were generally relieved of pressure. Cleveland and Miller (1977) found that in two-child families where the only nonhandicapped child is a girl, the daughter's risk for adverse effects seems to go up dramatically. Cleveland and Miller noted that

> It appears that she experiences the push of the parents' wishes to fulfill vicarious desires through their only normal child, yet also experiences the pull of parent surrogate responsibilities attached to her sex role. The conflict of these role demands may be manifested in tension between the normal child and her parents. It is this sibling that much more frequently reported the feeling that she did not receive enough attention from her parents as a child; and as an adult reported that this influenced career and family decisions. (p. 40)

Family Life Cyle

There has been growing popularity of the notion of a life cycle that extends beyond childhood into stages of development for adults. Carter and McGoldrick (1980) traced the relationship of this concept to the corollary notion of a family life cycle. The family itself might be said to go through its own life cycle as a context and determinant for the development of individual family members. The idea of a family life cycle is more than a simple aggregation of individual life cycles of each member; it is the interaction of these life cycles to produce a family cycle of development. Hill (1970) emphasized the three-generational aspects of a family life cycle. The multigenerational interaction is part of the richness of the family context as generations move through the family life cycle. Hoffman (1980) characterized families as "waterfalls or cascades, where the many-tiered patterns of the generations persist as an overall structure, even though the members pass through it as they are born, grow old, and die" (p. 55). The model of the family life cycle is useful to service providers and researchers in two major ways.

First, stage transitions through the life cycle are characterized by stress, catalysts for change, and coping mechanisms. The family life cycle is not a process of gradual evolution; rather, entry into each stage is usually marked by a distinctive event or series of events and sometimes even ceremonialized, as in marriage. The family life cycle can be visualized as a series of relatively level plateaus separated by transitional events that move the family into a new stage. Neugarten (1976) pointed out that the turning points in life, such as the end of formal schooling, marriage, and birth of children are "punctuation marks along the life cycle" (p. 18). They are brought about by catalysts for change in self-concept and sense of identity, and signal passage into new emotional and social roles for each individual in the family. Periods of relative stability and low stress characterize the plateau periods between stages (Terkelsen, 1980). Stress occurs at the change points, at the time of transition from stage to stage. Again, families respond differently and with different levels of stress to each transition according to their structural makeup (Carter & McGoldrick, 1980). However, this does not negate the fact that some level of stress is inevitably present whenever major life transitions occur. For many families with a disabled child, stage transition may be even more stressful. The future may appear so uncertain that external catalysts for change may be necessary to help the family move to a new stage. Catalysts for change may stem, for example, from membership in a parent support group or from recommendations of service providers.

The second major implication of family life cycle theory is that families at different stages of development exhibit strikingly different characteristics and have widely divergent needs. All of the stages address significant events related to family members, entry into and departure from the system. No consensus has been reached as to the precise number of stages through which a family passes. The eight stages originally suggested by Duvall (1957) have been expanded to as many as 24 separate time frames (Rodgers, 1960). But most often the sociological literature lists the eight stages shown in Fig. 6.1: unattached adulthood, marriage, birth of children, entrance of children into school, entrance of children into adolescence, launching of children into adulthood, retirement and old age, and death. As discussed in the description of variations in family structure, it should be obvious that the wide differences in family types and culture will produce different responses at each stage and even may produce a different profile or breakdown of the actual stages through which the family passes (Colon, 1980; Falicov & Karrer, 1980). Family life cycle stages often overlap, and families may dissolve before some stages occur (Hubbell, 1981a, 1981b). Nevertheless, most families in our culture seem to move through these eight stages at one time or another and in one way or another.

Perhaps the most significant aspect of the life cycle literature is that it is most often ignored by clinicians and researchers. Hill (1964) cautioned that "any research which seeks to generalize about families without taking into account the variation due to the stages of family development ... will have tremendous variance unaccounted for" (p. 190). The importance lies in the fact that each stage involves particular emotional responses and implies distinct sets of adjustment needs. This is especially relevant to research and intervention with siblings of severely handicapped children. Many of the adjustments and problems discussed in the previous sections will be more likely to surface at one stage than another. The following sections summarize the expected effects on nonhandicapped siblings at developmental stages impinging on them.

Birth and Preschool Years

If the nonhandicapped child is a preschooler at the birth of a handicapped sibling, many of the problems experienced will be a result of family turmoil in adjusting to the handicap. The preschooler may find that his or her parents have less time to meet his or her needs for attention, recreation, care, and guidance as they cope with the stress of additional time demands and emotional trauma created by the birth and diagnosis of a handicapped child. The stages of grief, denial, and adjustment faced by parents at this point have been documented extensively. But what is often ignored by both the literature and by parents going through the process is the effect on the nonhandicapped sibling. Preschoolers are often expected to play with their handicapped sibling. One sister in our study remembers this expectation:

> At the very beginning when we didn't know any better and before Alice ever went to school ... I remember Grandma getting on to us because we weren't including Alice in our play ... but we didn't really do it then. ... If I could do anything differently now, it would be only before she went to school, to try to include her more.

School Years

For nonhandicapped children who are younger than their severely handicapped siblings, entry into school may well mark the point at which they have caught up to and passed their brother or sister developmentally (Farber & Ryckman, 1965). Thus, in addition to the changes brought about by a broadened horizon, nonhandicapped siblings may also face a role realignment at home. For nonhandicapped siblings who are older than their severely handicapped brother or sister, the handicapped child's entry into the school system brings new problems, such as explaining the handicap to peers or being responsible for the sibling at school (e.g., carrying medications).

Adolescence

The stormy years of adolescence can be further complicated by the presence of a severely handicapped sibling. Teenagers frequently report an increased sense of embarrassment as a result of stares from strangers or questions from peers (Klein, 1972a). There may be a heightened awareness of the "differentness" of the handicapped sibling. For one sister, in our study, this involved dating: "When I started dating, I used to worry about whether she was wondering why she couldn't go out, too." And for another sibling, this awareness took the form of a sense of loss: "I realized that I would never have a sister like other girls, to share secrets with and do things with." Finally, adolescents are frequently asked to share responsibility for care of the handicapped sibling, and may also be pressured to achieve in school or in sports to compensate for the lack of achievement by the handicapped child.

Launching into Adulthood

Young adults are faced with the implications of their sibling's handicap for their personal lives. Some siblings report feeling guilty about moving away and leaving parents with the burden of care; others feel relief (Grossman, 1972). Career decisions are frequently shaped by experiences with a handicapped sibling (Cleveland & Miller, 1977). Also, siblings must face their fears of marriage and having children of their own. Even when the handicap is not of genetic origin, the fear of having a handicapped child may be very real (Murphy, 1979). Alternatively, the sibling may fear marriage because the expected future responsibilities of care for a handicapped brother or sister may be too expensive in terms of time or money.

Retirement and Old Age

As parents approach retirement and old age, the responsibility for care of a handicapped family member shifts increasingly to the non-handicapped siblings. Promises made or commitments assumed in young adulthood may be increasingly difficult to meet as reality looms. One sibling with an elderly mother expressed her dilemma:

> I had always just assumed that I would take Faye into my home when Mother died. But when I had her for those three months [while her elderly mother was ill] I realized I just couldn't do it. . . . I'm not temperamentally suited for it. . . . But I can't put her in a nursing home, I will not do that. . . . I don't know what I'm going to do.

Implications for Interventions

The conceptual framework and empirical literature reviewed in this chapter have clear implications for sibling-related interventions. Some of these implications are as follows:

1. A conceptual analysis and critique is needed of interventions with siblings of handicapped persons and interventions that use nonhandicapped siblings as intervention agents. The framework of functions, structure, and life cycle described in this chapter can be used to explore the state of the art of sibling interventions further.

2. Sibling interventions should consider the interrelatedness of the three subsystems—spouse, parent, and sibling. Thus, it may be just as important to focus interventions on the relationships between the nonhandicapped sibling and the parental subsystem as it is to concentrate efforts on the relationship between nonhandicapped and handicapped siblings.

3. In considering the nine different functions of families, it becomes clear that numerous possibilities exist for nonhandicapped siblings to assume shared responsibility for the healthy development of their handicapped brother or sister. Rather than prescribing ways that nonhandicapped siblings ought to provide assistance, particular types of interventions need to be tailored to the dynamics of a particular family and to the needs, interests, and resources of the family members. The major consideration should be how the family unit can coordinate the efforts of each member to assist the handicapped child. Thus, the heterogeneity of family structure and individual characteristics should be identified and respected as they relate to interventions.

4. In families with severely handicapped members, communication among all family members should focus on the appropriateness of siblings assuming responsibility at a given point in the life cycle for functions previously performed by parents. It should be recognized that it is not always appropriate for siblings to assume such responsibility.

Although the role of siblings as intervention agents is receiving increasing emphasis in the literature, it does not follow that all siblings should be intervention agents. If it is determined that siblings will assume responsibility, the process and timing of transitions from parental to sibling responsibility needs to be discussed.

5. Interventions should focus on helping handicapped and nonhandicapped siblings develop relationships that have healthy boundaries, avoiding the extreme positions of enmeshment and disengagement.

6. Some elements of family structure (e.g., ideological style and relationship parameters) are more open to change than other structural elements (e.g., membership size and cultural style). Sibling interventions should focus on those variables that are to a greater degree under the sibling's control.

7. Interventions need to be developed for siblings at all stages of the life cycle in accordance with the priority concerns and stresses at each stage.

8. Alternative strategies (e.g., workshops, printed materials, counseling) for preparing nonhandicapped siblings to be intervention agents need to be developed, evaluated, and disseminated. In addition to direct intervention with siblings, parents need information on the implications of having a handicapped member in the family for nonhandicapped siblings and on strategies for enhancing positive relationships.

9. Handicapped and nonhandicapped individuals who are themselves siblings have tremendous insights to share that can substantially increase the relevance and functionality of interventions. Professionals who provide such interventions are encouraged to seek the advice and assistance of the true experts on the subject—the siblings themselves.

Research Recommendations

This chapter represents an attempt to integrate the research literature on the relationships of severely handicapped children and their siblings within an overall conceptual framework that recognizes the family as a system, inclusive of the sibling subsystem. Our approach to integration acknowledges siblings as an integral part of the family system. In turn, the conceptual framework views the family in terms of the functions it performs, its structural characteristics, and its stage or cycle of development. We believe that isolating the sibling subsystem from family function, structure, and life cycle is artificial and may lead to faulty generalizations of research findings.

Using this conceptualization of the family system as a tool, we address the utility of current research on sibling relationships and suggest an agenda for future research.

Utility of Current Research

Although the existing body of literature has some utility for practitioners and researchers, it is seriously lacking in several respects. The most obvious weakness of the total set of literature is the limited number of studies dealing specifically with severely and profoundly handicapped children. This is understandable given the historical tendency to remove these children from the family. Although information from current research has some application to the severely handicapped population, much of it was conducted with other populations. Considering the differential effects level of severity alone can have on reactions to a handicapped sibling (Grossman, 1972), researchers and practitioners should not generalize findings from one population to another.

An area in which research is nearly totally lacking is the family function of rest and recuperation. This function has become more important in society since the 1960s for all families. For families with severely handicapped members, however, the importance of the rest and recuperation function may be even greater. How this family function is affected by the presence of a severely disabled child and how aspects of rest and recuperation might be used to relieve stress in such families are important questions which have not been addressed in the current body of literature.

The effects of a handicapped sibling on the oldest daughter has received relatively more attention in the literature than effects on other family members and on the entire family. Because of the potentially damaging impact on "big sisters," this special relationship needs additional attention, particularly with respect to the effects of a severely handicapped sibling on it.

The changing nature of the family in society is having an impact on the relevance of the literature on sibling relationships. As single- and working-parent families become more prevalent, additional gaps are created in the existing knowledge base. Rarely do current studies address sibling relationships and their impact on handicapped and nonhandicapped children in these family structural types. Another artifact of changing society is the impact of sex roles on both handicapped and nonhandicapped siblings. Much of the research considering sex as a variable dates from the early 1960s, and therefore must be viewed with caution after years of sweeping change in social attitudes towards sex roles. New research in both normative sibling relations and handicapped siblings on the development and impact of sex roles is urgently needed.

The vast majority of the literature is concerned with the effects of a handicapped child on normal siblings. With respect to effects of non-handicapped siblings on handicapped children, only one study (Lavine, 1977) has investigated any aspect of impact other than the efficacy of nonhandicapped siblings as trainers of their handicapped brothers and sisters. Questions such as the role of birth order on the development of dependence or independence in the handicapped child need to be addressed. Other effects of siblings on the handicapped child such as role development and other personality factors should similarly be investigated.

Finally, the most significant weakness in the literature is its lack of attention to the family as a system, including family function, structure, and life cycle. If the conceptualization of the family system proposed herein has merit, the current body of research represents little more than a collection of subject-specific information. Not only is the utility of the current knowledge base minimized, but it may be counter-productive if researchers and practitioners attempt to generalize findings too broadly. Under the proposed conceptualization, family structure and life cycle, in particular, are sources of variance not accounted for in most of the existing research. At a minimum, consumers of this research should interpret it carefully with an awareness of its questionable generalizability.

An Agenda for Future Research

Prior to or concurrent with the generation of new research, a practical approach would include a synthesis of current research (see, e.g., Cooper, 1982) with the aim of identifying the family structural type and/or life cycle for which specific results are applicable. This chapter might serve as a useful first stage in organizing the literature within a framework of family types, functions, and stages of development. A second step for increasing the utility of the current body of research would be to replicate studies that were based on specific family structural types and life cycles with other family structures and life cycles, to determine whether interventions designed for certain types of family contexts have broader utility with other types.

When family structure and life cycle are considered in interaction, a

{ Thomas M. Skrtic et al.

potentially endless array of family contexts emerges. Because of this diversity and the relative ignorance in this field, use of the naturalistic research paradigm with its emphasis on discovery would appear to be most productive. A series of naturalistic inquiries (e.g., Guba, 1978; Guba & Lincoln, 1981; Skrtic, in press) resulting in case studies can potentially provide rich descriptions of these contexts, the values and needs of the various individuals within them, the resultant effects of severely disabled children on them and the family as a whole, and, in turn, the potential effects siblings could have on the development of their severely disabled brothers or sisters. These studies, with their inherent recognition of contextual factors, could then serve to generate hypotheses for an extended research agenda to validate sibling interventions for both handicapped and nonhandicapped siblings. Such interventions may then be tailored to the specific structural and life-cycle features of families.

References

Bank, S., & Kahn, M. D. (1975). Sisterhood-brotherhood is powerful: Sibling sub-systems and family therapy. *Family Process, 14*, 311–337.

Bossard, J. H. S., & Boll, E. S. (1956). *The large family system*. Philadelphia: University of Pennsylvania Press.

Caplan, G. (1976). The family as a support system. In G. Caplan & M. Killilia (Eds.), *Support systems and mutual help: Multidisciplinary explorations*. New York: Grune & Stratton.

Carter, E., & McGoldrick, M. (1980). The family life cycle and family therapy: An overview. In E. Carter and M. McGoldrick (Eds.), *The family life cycle: A framework for family therapy*. New York: Gardner Press.

Cicirelli, V. G. (1976). Siblings teaching siblings. In V. L. Allen (Ed.), *Children as teachers*. New York: Academic Press.

Cleveland, D. W., & Miller, N. (1977). Attitudes and life commitments of older siblings of mentally retarded adults: An exploratory study. *Mental Retardation, 15*(3), 38–41.

Colon, F. (1980). The family life cycle of the multiproblem poor family. In E. Carter & M. McGoldrick (Eds.), *The family life cycle: A framework for family therapy*. New York: Gardner Press.

Cooper, H. M. (1982). Scientific guidelines for conducting integrative research reviews. *Review of Educational Research, 52*, 291–302.

Crocker, A. C. (1981). The involvement of siblings of children with handicaps. In A. Mjiunsky (Ed.), *Coping with crisis and handicaps*. New York: Plenum.

DeMeyer, M. K. (1979). *Parents and children in autism*. New York: Wiley.

Duvall, E. (1957). *Family development*. Philadelphia: Lippincott.

Falicov, C. J., & Karrer, B. M. (1980). Cultural variations in the family life cycle: The Mexican-American family. In E. Carter & M. Goldrick (Eds.), *The family life cycle: A framework for family therapy*. New York: Gardner Press.

Farber, B. (1959). Effects of a severely mentally retarded child on family integration. *Monographs of the Society for Research in Child Development, 24*(2, Serial No. 71).

Farber, B. (1963). Interaction with retarded siblings and life goals of children. *Marriage and Family Living, 25,* 96–98.

Farber, B., & Ryckman, D. B. (1965). Effects of severely mentally retarded children on family relationships. *Mental Retardation Abstracts, 2,* 1–17.

Fish, T., & Fitzgerald, E. M. (1980, November). *A transdisciplinary approach to working with adolescent siblings of the mentally retarded: A group experience.* Paper presented to the Social Work with Groups Symposium, Arlington, TX. (Available from T. Fish, The Nisonger Center, The Ohio State University, 1580 Cannon Drive, Columbus, Ohio 43210.)

Forer, L. K. (1969). *Birth order and life roles.* Springfield, IL: Thomas.

Foster, M., Berger, M., & McLean, M. (1981). Rethinking a good idea: A reassessment of parent involvement. *Topics in Early Childhood Special Education, 3,* 55–65.

Fowle, C. M. (1968). The effect of the severely mentally retarded child on his family. *American Journal of Mental Deficiency, 73,* 468–473.

Freeman, D. S. (1976). The family as a system: Fact or fancy. *Comprehensive Psychiatry, 17,* 735–749.

Gath, A. (1974). Sibling reactions to mental handicap: A comparison of the brothers and sisters of mongol children. *Journal of Child Psychology and Psychiatry and Allied Disciplines, 15*(3), 838–843.

Grossman, F. K. (1972). *Brothers and sisters of retarded children: An exploratory study.* Syracuse, NY: Syracuse University Press.

Guba, F. G. (1978). *Toward a methodology of naturalistic inquiry in educational evaluation* (CSE Monograph Series in Evaluation No. 8). Los Angeles: Center for the Study of Evaluation, University of California at Los Angeles.

Guba, E. G., & Lincoln, Y. S. (1981). *Effective evaluation.* San Francisco: Jossey-Bass.

Hewett, S. (1976). Research on families with handicapped children—An aid or impediment to understanding? In D. Bergsma & A. E. Pulver (Eds.), *Developmental disabilities: Psychologic and social implications.* The National Foundation—March of Dimes, Birth Defects: Original Article Series.

Hill, R. (1964). Methodological issues in family development research. *Family Process, 3,* 186–204.

Hill, R. (1970). *Family development in three generations.* Cambridge, MA: Schenkman.

Hoffman, L. (1980). The family life cycle and discontinous change. In E. Carter & M. McGoldrick (Eds.), *The family life cycle: A framework for family therapy.* New York: Gardner Press.

Hubbell, R. (1981a). The family impact seminar: A new approach to policy analysis. In H. C. Wallach (Ed.), *Approaches to child and family policy.* Boulder, CO: AAAS, Westview Press.

Hubbell, R. (1981b). *Field coordinator's guide: Theoretical framework.* Washington, DC: Family Impact Seminar.

Klein, S. D. (1972a). Brother to sister/Sister to brother. *Exceptional Parent, 3*(1), 10–16.

Klein, S. D. (1972b). Brother to sister/Sister to brother. *Exceptional Parent, 3*(2), 24–27.

Klein, S. D. (1972c). Brother to sister/Sister to brother. *Exceptional Parent 3*(3), 24–28.

Lavine, M. B. (1977). An exploratory study of the sibships of blind children. *Journal of Visual Impairment and Blindness, 71*(3), 102–107.

Leslie, G. R. (1976). *The family in social context* (4th ed.). New York: Oxford University Press.

McAndrew, I. (1976). Children with a handicap and their families. *Child Care, Health and Development, 2,* 213–237.

Miller, S. G. (1974). An exploratory study of sibling relationships in families with retarded children (Doctoral dissertation, Columbia University). *Dissertation Abstracts International*, 35(6-B), 2994–2995.

Minuchin, S. (1974). *Families and family therapy*. Cambridge, MA: Harvard University Press.

Montalvo, B., & Haley, J. (1973). In defense of child therapy. *Family Process, 12*, 227–244.

Murphy, A. T. (1979). Members of the family: Sisters and brothers of handicapped children. *Volta Review, 81*, 352–362.

Neugarten, B. (1976). Adaptations and the life cycle. *The Counseling Psychologist, 6*, 16–20.

Parfit, J. (1975). Siblings of handicapped children. *Special Education: Forward Trends. 2*, 19–21.

Rice, R. M. (1977). *American family policy: Content and context*. New York: Family Service Association of America.

Rodgers, R. (1960, August). *Proposed modifications of Duvall's family life cycle stages*. Paper presented at the American Sociological Association Meeting, New York.

Schreiber, M., & Feeley, M. (1965). Siblings of the retardate: A guided group experience. *Children, 12*, 221–255.

Simeonsson, R. J., & McHale, S. (1981). Review: Research on handicapped children: Sibling relationships. *Child Care, Health, and Development, 7*, 153–171.

Sinha, J. B. (1967). Birth order and sex difference in need-achievement and need-affiliation. *Journal of Psychological Research, 11*, 22–27.

Skrtic, T. M. (in press). The doing of emergent paradigm research into educational organizations. In Y. S. Lincoln (Ed.), *Linking new concepts of organizations with new paradigms for inquiry: A companionate marriage*. Beverly Hills, CA: Sage Publications.

Stubblefield, H. (1965). Religion, parents and mental retardation. *Mental Retardation, 3*(4), 8–11.

Sutton-Smith, B., & Rosenberg, B. G. (1970). *The sibling*. New York: Holt, Rinehart & Winston.

Terkelsen, K. G. (1980). Toward a theory of the family life cycle. In E. Carter & M. McGoldrick (Eds.), *The family life cycle: A framework of family therapy*. New York: Gardner Press.

Terman, L. M. (1925). *Genetic studies of genius*. Palo Alto, CA: Stanford University Press.

Trevino, F. (1979). Siblings of handicapped children: Identifying those at risk. *Social Casework: The Journal of Contemporary Social Work, 60*, 488–492.

Wadsworth, H. G., & Wadsworth, J. B. (1979). A problem of involvement with parents of mildly retarded children. *The Family Coordinator, 28*, 141–147.

Weinrott, M. R. (1974). A training program in behavior modification for siblings of the retarded. *American Journal of Orthopsychiatry, 44*, 362–375.

Zuk, G. H., Miller, R. I., Bartram, J. B., & Kling, F. (1961). Maternal acceptance of retarded children: A questionnaire study of attitudes and religious background. *Child Development, 32*, 515–540.

====== CHAPTER 7 ======

The Severely Handicapped
and Child Abuse

John H. Meier
Michael P. Sloan

Introduction

This chapter addresses several of the critical factors found in family function and dysfunction that precipitate or exacerbate child abuse. Although Part II of this volume is concerned with child influences on family dynamics, we suggest that the subject families themselves also may be severely handicapped and strongly influence the developmental abilities and disabilities of their children. Prosecutable child abuse usually causes moderate to severe physical and psychic handicaps and typically occurs in seriously dysfunctional families. Consequently, a kind of chicken-or-egg question arises: is a child's pre-existing developmental disability sufficiently exasperating to elicit child abuse or is a family's dysfunction so severe as to result in child abuse, which in turn may result in increasingly severe handicaps?

To elaborate on the title of this chapter, most certifiably abused children have been identified as suffering from various developmental handicaps (Scholz & Meier, 1983). It is seldom clear whether or not the handicapping conditions are a result of inflicted trauma or, because of a misreading of the child's abilities by parents, such disappointing delays precipitate further abuse. When the former is true, then abuse itself should be considered to be a handicapping condition and added to the more traditional laundry list of such conditions. When the latter is true, the handicapped child is at greater risk for abuse and its concomitant additional handicaps. A review of the child protection and mental retardation literature (Schilling, Schinke, Blythe, & Barth, 1982) suggested that children of mentally retarded parents are also at a greater risk for abuse and neglect. Parental intellectual deficits, in addition to child developmental delays, often are significant factors in child maltreatment, as discussed subsequently in this chapter. Chapter 1 in this volume (Blacher) elaborates on the relationships between severely handicapping conditions and child abuse; Meier and Sloan (1983) have argued for the simultaneous, mutual interaction among several contributing factors to account for most child abuse.

Handicapping conditions are caused by acts of God or nature and/or acts of humans or nurture. The former elicit support and compassion for the families and active assistance for the children. The latter, until relatively recently, typically resulted in rejection and even rage toward the parents and/or perpetrators and death or a nightmarish series of separations and displacements for the children who survived the abuse episodes that caused their handicaps. However, it has become clearer that not all handicapping conditions have their origins in only nature or only nurture; they are the product of the reciprocal interaction between the two. This chapter addresses some of the similarities, differences, and overlaps among the complex hereditary–environmental causes of handicaps in children, with some specific reference to analogous phenomena in nonhuman animal species.

Abuse and neglect, that is, deliberate acts of commission and/or omission that endanger the lives and well-being of offspring, are not a rarity among nonhuman animals, especially when directed toward the weak or unfit offspring. Moreover, such abuse or neglect seems to have some reproductive payoff from the perspective of individuals striving to maximize their own fitness and survivability. Whether these payoffs hold in human cases of abuse and neglect is questionable and warrants further investigation and discussion. For example, the documented inadvertent or deliberate neglect of handicapped children places them at greater risk for reportable child abuse and helps to substantiate this sociobiological interpretation.

Furthermore, the theory that parents seek to maximize their fitness by discriminately investing their reproductive and nurturing efforts (Trivers, 1974) suggests that removing a child from the parent's care may prompt either a new pregnancy or result in the dissolution of the marital bond. Numerous families served by the Village of Childhelp, USA (The

Village) had a history of marital discord, and, when children were removed because of child assault, the families often dissolved. The mothers then found new mates and became pregnant again to replace their lost families. In this regard, the effects of removing children from their parents may be functionally analogous to the death of the child in some parents' perception, and include confusion and separation trauma experienced by the child. These considerations suggest in turn that, although the removal of abused and handicapped children from their families of origin is a necessary safeguard in some cases, long-term plans for their optimum remediation and continued nurturing in their own culture should include treatment in a family setting with some semblance of stability and permanence.

This chapter presents a generic model of child abuse and neglect dynamics, briefly presents an exemplary case, discusses the nature-nurture causation dilemma and interaction with human and nonhuman referents, and finally proceeds to derive several treatment and prevention considerations. The deliberations are guided by both a review of relevant literature and an analysis of empirical findings, some of which are derived from research on a population of severely abused children at The Village, a large residential treatment center for abused children and their dysfunctional families (many of whom are also under treatment on an outpatient basis).

The Continuing Nature-Nurture Controversy

The relative influences of heredity and environment in shaping the growth and development of organisms remain an unsettled argument throughout studies of the plant and animal kingdoms. Ancient controversies regarding the sequence and potency of hereditary versus environmental forces are recurrent themes in the history of Western philosophy and psychology (Warden, 1927). Attempts (Barash, 1980; Hernstein, 1973; Tinbergen, 1951; Wilson, 1975) to provide an evolutionary framework for studies of the organization of animal and human behavior have again brought the nature–nurture dichotomy before the public eye ("Sociobiology," 1977).

Somewhat akin to the centuries-old nature–nurture controversy is a new debate regarding the relationship between accidental versus inflicted developmental disabilities. The question boils down to the relationship between various handicapping conditions and whether child abuse and neglect contribute to or result from them (Daly & Wilson, 1981; Frodi, 1981). Blacher and Meyers (1983) and Daly and Wilson

(1981) have reported that children suffering such congenital handicaps as spina bifida, fibrocystic disease, clubfootedness, cleft palate, and Down's syndrome are at a relatively higher risk for abuse or neglect than the nonhandicapped child population. They have interpreted these findings to be the result of discriminant parental solicitude or a selective noninvestment by parents in less viable and/or less attractive offspring. It has been clearly demonstrated by Emde and Brown (1976) that Down's syndrome infants display much less ingratiating and less frequent smiling behavior than do their normally developing peers, typically resulting in weaker or defective bonding between infants and mothers or other primary care givers. Do handicapped children have a higher probability of being abused? Alternatively, are abused children more likely to be handicapped? Are those disabling phenomena in some sort of simultaneous reciprocal interaction wherein a handicapped child provokes abuse that worsens the handicap and family dysfunction, thus giving rise to further abuse, and so on?

Intelligence testing at The Village revealed that severely abused children score lower on standardized tests of intellectual functioning (Scholz & Meier, 1983). Applebaum's (1980) report substantiated this finding. Infants abandoned and neglected in traditional orphan settings tend to have a higher probability of becoming developmentally disabled or handicapped (Hunt, 1961). Some children may be abandoned and others rejected as the result of displaying some developmental deviation that prompts parents and families to reject them. Klein and Stern (1981) reported that nearly one-fourth (23%) of 51 battered children in Montreal were low birth weight infants. This figure was three times the expected incidence of battering in newborns of Quebec.

On the neglect or omission side of child abuse, there is a substantial probability (22%) that after defective children are institutionalized they will be abandoned (i.e., visited less than once per year) by their natural parents (Daly & Wilson, 1981). Moreover, it could be that because these parents themselves experienced physical or emotional rejection as children, they are more prone to reject their own offspring. Others have argued that currently desirable mothering behavior does not come naturally and was scarcely evident as recently as 2 centuries ago (Babinter, 1981). At another level of adaptation, parents in various nonhuman species seem to have been selected or programmed over the course of many generations to take stock of available resources and either reduce the number of offspring conceived or dispose of excess offspring by the elimination or abandonment of the less-viable ones (O'Connor, 1978).

In a review of the rapidly growing body of literature regarding abused children and their families, many plausible and some highly controversial explanations emerge of how and why parents might not only abandon or neglect their own offspring, but may even become violent toward them, thereby destroying them or inflicting nearly irremediable psychological and physical trauma on them. The legal dispositions, social histories, medical files, and psychological charts of abused children at The Village and their families provide an alarming array of the many ways in which humankind's child-rearing behavior is neither humane nor kind. In fact, the possible variations on this theme are so numerous and complex that they defy any simplistic description, let alone explanation. The intricate dynamics of each case, while having some common facets, present a kaleidoscopic view of humanity and more particularly of human families in action and transition.

A Multifactorial Model for Child Abuse Dynamics

A multifactorial model (Meier, 1978b) is presented here (Fig. 7.1) to depict a representative but by no means exhaustive set of factors involved in child abuse.

Even the definition of child abuse itself varies, contributing to confusing incidence and prevalence statistics, contradictory estimates of the efficacy of various treatment and prevention programs, and inconclusive research findings in general (Besharov, 1982; Giovannoni & Becerra, 1977; Zigler, 1980). For this chapter child abuse is broadly defined as "the physical or mental injury, sexual abuse or exploitation, negligent treatment, or maltreatment of a child under the age of eighteen by a person who is responsible for the child's welfare under circumstances which indicate that the child's health or welfare is harmed or threatened thereby" (U.S. Department of Health, Education and Welfare, Child Abuse Prevention and Treatment Act of 1973, p. 3), Gelles (1979) called child abuse a political concept and stated, "There is presently no useful legal or scientific definition of child abuse and neglect" (p. 24). He went on to say that malnourishment, sexual abuse, failure to feed and clothe a child, allowing a child to live in a deprived or depraved environment, and helping a child stay out of school have all been defined at various times and in various laws as child abuse. Moreover, the definition of child abuse varies over time, across cultures, and between different social and cultural groups. Regardless of the lack of definitional precision, rigor, or simplicity, the phenomenon of maltreated children is occurring and being reported throughout the world in dramatically rising numbers as the public consciousness is

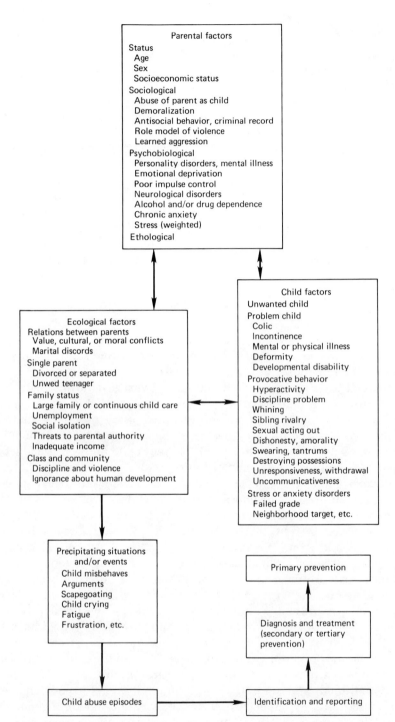

Figure 7.1 Model of child abuse dynamics. Developed by Meier (1978b).

raised and as reporting legislation and criteria are clarified and promulgated (Meier, in press).

It is crucial to understand the dynamics underlying child abuse, however, defined, in order to treat and prevent it. As one seeks common threads in this fabric of child abuse it is important to move beyond the small, select swatch of one culture in order to see the blanket of the entire human population. Ironically, the acceptable child-rearing practices of the world are so varied (Korbin, 1980) that they defy attempts to place them all under a single rubric; thus it is practically impossible to derive a single all-encompassing definition of child abuse (Besharov, 1982; Giovannoni & Becerra, 1979). In addition, there is a conspicuous absence of universally acceptable and effective child abuse evaluation and prevention procedures. Flattening heads with attached boards, piercing ears, extending lips with plates, stretching necks, binding feet, burning brands, scarification marking, tatooing, and even circumcising represent only a sample of the various practices that are presently considered acceptable and normal within certain human cultures. Humiliating, ridiculous, and sometimes hazardous rites, such as fraternity or sorority hazing, are potentially abusive practices that are commonly accepted in U.S. culture. Cosmetic orthodontal correction and plastic surgery, normally painful experiences, are not only accepted but believed by some to be a necessary means for acceptance in our culture. Anthropologist Korbin (1980) has strongly advocated an appropriate cultural perspective, that is, knowing what is culturally acceptable and nonacceptable, in the evaluation of child-rearing practices and the prevention of abuse. In considering abuse with regard to handicapping conditions, a knowledge of different cultural expectations and treatment of handicapped individuals is also important.

Nevertheless, it is apparent that a large segment of the North American population is horror-stricken by the numerous reported episodes of parents' deliberately damaging their children, for whatever reasons and by whatever means. The following case vignette from the authors' files and critical path analysis (Fig. 7.2) exemplify some of the factors enumerated in Fig. 7.1 by illustrating a typical case of child abuse (names and places are ficticious).

Illustrative Case Vignette

Melissa, a 35-month-old caucasian female, was ordered by the court to be removed from her mother's custody and placed in foster care in June, 1980. She was brought to the attention of her local

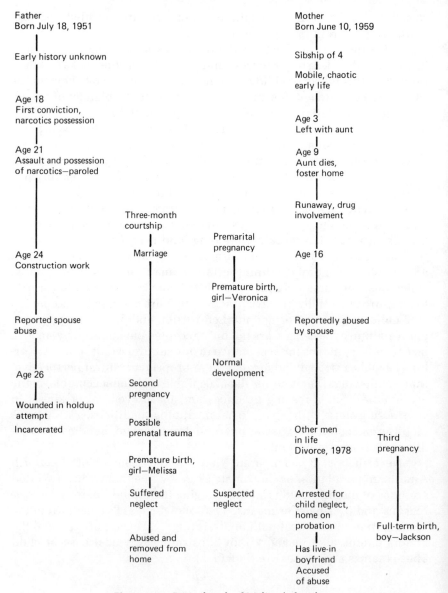

Figure 7.2   Critical path of Melissa's family.

police department's child abuse unit after her babysitter noted numerous welts on her legs, buttocks, and back. The unit's investigation determined that these injuries were the result of belt beatings by her mother's live-in boyfriend. Comprehensive medical and psychological examinations revealed that Melissa had three fractures—on her left forearm, on her left temporal skull, and on her right leg—in various stages of healing and that her intellectual functioning was well below age-appropriate levels, particularly in verbal skills. Neurological examination revealed soft signs of brain damage or dysfunction, but no evidence of seizures was noted. Audiological examination revealed high frequency hearing losses in both ears, severe in her left ear.

Melissa was the second of three living children, she had a full sister, Veronica, aged 5 years, and a younger half-brother, Jackson, aged 11 months at the time of her placement. Melissa's mother, Ellen Taylor (married name Richards), was married at age 16 to Melissa's father. Ellen Taylor's history revealed that she was born in 1959 in Springfield, Arkansas, and lived her early years in Oklahoma, Arkansas, and Nevada. She was living in a car with her mother and three siblings during most of this time. At the age of 4, Ellen was left with a maternal aunt. She was placed in a foster home at the age of 9 after her aunt died and has had no contact with her parents since she was 5. Her adolescence was characterized by frequent running away and drug abuse.

Ellen met Melissa's father, Jerry Taylor, while living in a foster home in Downey, California. He was 24 years old when they were married in 1975 after Ellen became pregnant. Mr. Taylor was marginally employed as a part-time construction worker. He reportedly physically abused his wife regularly throughout both pregnancies. His history revealed numerous arrests for assault and narcotics possession. He was involved in an armed robbery attempt, wounded, and sentenced to a lengthy prison term in August, 1977. Shortly after this, Ellen delivered Melissa. Ellen later divorced Mr. Taylor while he was in prison. He is currently incarcerated.

Melissa's first 3 years of life were somewhat chaotic as her mother frequently changed their place of residence. She was first brought to the court's attention at the age of 19 months, due to neglect; however, she was allowed to remain at her home on probation. Her mother reportedly has had a series of boyfriends living with her who regularly abuse her and Melissa. There is no evidence that Melissa's older sister was ever abused. Likewise, her younger brother's development was unremarkable at the time of Melissa's removal.

Figure 7.2 is a graphic description of Melissa's family as depicted in a critical pathway of events, a technique suggested by Lynch (1976).

Thus, we see in this example the interplay of a variety of ecological, parental, child, and situational factors preceding the abusive incidents. Marital disorder, financial insecurity, and a violent household seem to characterize Melissa's home environment. Additional factors include a single mother whose early life was chaotic and probably quite abusive. Personality factors suggest antisocial behavior, poor impulse control, and strong dependence on violent, aggressive male partners.

Melissa's problems include below-average intellectual functioning, brain dysfunction, and hearing loss. All of these may be the result of traumatic abuse causing various insults to her developing and highly vulnerable brain. Additionally, these handicapping conditions may serve as precipitants of further abuse, since a child with a hearing loss who is slow to learn or to respond correctly to parental instruction may be at risk of additional assaults, particularly if the child's parent or primary caretaker lacks impulse control.

The chaotic and perilous early life histories of such children as Melissa make definitive statements about the origin of brain dysfunction and other handicapping conditions nearly impossible. For example, most of the children in placement at The Village have accurate histories that begin only when the case is brought to the attention of the police or other investigative agencies. Medical and psychological information about the child's life prior to this point is conspicuously absent. Given the sketchy quality and sparse quantity of this information and because the model attempts to account for a variety of causal factors, it is helpful to move on to a more detailed account of acts of God and the rites of the family as they pertain to child abuse and handicapping conditions.

Acts of God and Nature

The history of the human race, whether carefully chronicled by scientific historians or more simply passed down through the generations in folklore and mythology, reveals people's inclination to attribute any significant phenomenon they do not fully understand or cannot control to superhuman forces or gods. Thus, various natural disasters such as earthquakes and floods that destroyed many human lives and crippled many more were difficult to understand without the rationalization that some superior being or God had caused these tragedies. In the minds of some, these events were punishment for perceived transgressions against the laws and commandments of God, revealed to and passed down through certain favored and enlightened humans.

The birth of a handicapped child who appeared disfigured and developed in an abnormal fashion was interpreted throughout much of history by some as the will of God and by others as the interference of the Devil, either of which may have been inflicted on the parents as punishment for their previous misdeeds however defined in their particular cultural mores (Freud, 1927). However, since the parents obviously did not deliberately seek to conceive a handicapped child, they would eventually accept their special offspring and draw some support from their fellow parents and humans who might say, "There but for the grace of God go I." In some more primitive cultures, the grotesquely disfigured child might take on a kind of special mystique and be given a great deal of additional consideration or even be worshiped for the God-given idiosyncracies. Ironically, some of these same uncivilized persons are known to have sacrificed their more perfect children to appease their imagined punitive gods in the hope of preventing future punishments (deMause, 1975; Mead, 1977).

In contemporary times a "more realistic" reaction on the part of parents of a handicapped child requires several stages of adjustment to the death of their idealized child (Kubler-Ross, 1969) in order for them to accept their less-than-idealized or imperfect child. Many of the enlightened clinics dealing with the families of handicapped infants enable the parents to go through the emotion-laden stages of (1) denial that such a child could be the product of their relationship, (2) anger at whatever perceived causes, including God, (3) open grieving, almost to the extent of burying the idealized child, (4) a more constructive acceptance of the handicapped child, and (5) preparation of the family to accept and collaborate in providing for the handicapped child's habilitation and normalization as far as possible (Klaus & Kennell, 1976; Meier, 1976).

A generation or more ago, the unknown or poorly understood causes of numerous handicapping conditions led to the growth and development of children for whom it was very difficult to generate an accurate diagnosis or prognosis of ultimate development and growth. Clinicians may well remember the "Gork syndrome," an acronym for "God only really knows." Whether the developmental delays and deviations were due to genetic anomalies, intrauterine insults, birth trauma, and/or the young child's eating chocolatey-tasting lead-based paint off the woodwork and radiators did not really seem to matter, since these were all phenomena not understood by scientists, let alone by theologians and philosophers. Such events were simply acts of God or mistakes of nature that could not have been prevented except, in some cases, by getting the lead out of the paint.

In those cases requiring maximum life-support provisions and intensive and extensive professional care, centralized institutions were developed where severely handicapped children were placed for extensive diagnostic studies, intensive treatment efforts, and often for specialized custodial care for the rest of their lives. Some of the more grotesque were even depicted and paraded as examples of what God does to sinners or to the most prized possessions of sinners, their children. This certainly evoked a great deal of guilt on the part of parents who would begin an obsessive soul searching of their histories and behaviors to discover what may have provoked the "wrath of God" as expressed in their disfigured offspring.

Of course, as the state of the art has improved regarding embryological growth and development, genetic intricacies, optimal birthing procedures, and potential environmental hazards to young children, many of the aforementioned developmental enigmas became less frequently referred to as natural and unpreventable and increasingly were defined as unnatural and preventable. People became unwilling even to suggest that an omniscient and omnipotent God could be deliberately causing these peculiar anomalies. Instead, they marveled at and sought to understand more fully the mechanisms established for reproduction of each species, the infinite possibilities for random error, and the evolutionary adjustments species make to a changing environment, including the complex demands placed on those who would have to change in order to survive in it.

Some Treatment Considerations
for Accidentally Handicapped Children

For all of the reasons just discussed, parents of children whose handicaps are diagnosed as not being deliberately caused by the parents find it far more socially acceptable to acknowledge their child's handicap publicly and privately and to seek unashamedly assistance in coping with the handicapping conditions. They know that professionals and lay people alike will generally accept them as unfortunate parents and extend not only sympathy but also a variety of real goods and services to help them to compensate for their sense of loss and disappointment as well as to help the child cope with the inevitable additional difficulties in growing and developing into an adult. There are numerous organizations, agencies, and self-help groups to which parents can turn for help in managing their retarded, epileptic, cerebral palsied, emotionally disturbed, speech handicapped, dyslexic, or otherwise special-needs child—if and when it is understood that these conditions are the results of acts of God or quirks of nature.

The work of Hunt (1961), corroborated by Heber, Garber, Harrington, and Fulender (1972), demonstrated that the environment, including significant adults in it, was the culprit for much of the functional retardation found in mildly delayed children; it marked a major shift in the focus from the statistical inevitability of retarded mothers producing retarded infants. In fact, the challenge to the theory of intergenerational genetic transmission of nearly 80% of the cases of retardation leads right back to the difficult dilemmas posed by attempting to determine whether children's developmental delays caused their being abused or whether their abuse or neglect causes their developmental delays and how these factors, regardless of cause and effect, interact and potentiate each other.

Rites of the Family

A ritual celebrated in many North American families and schools is the solemn ceremony of corporal punishment. Although there is substantial evidence that this practice is generally ineffective, if not ultimately counterproductive (Feshbach & Feshbach, 1976; Hyman, 1980; Meier, 1982b), children and youths are routinely spanked by bigger and stronger parents and authorized school personnel. There may be other debilitating rituals performed daily whereby children are handicapped physically, socially, emotionally, and/or intellectually, often relentlessly and with impunity to the perpetrators.

There appears to be a growing conviction that the rituals or rites of punishment and maltreatment of children inflicted by some families are inhumane and criminal acts against innocent victims. The compassion and empathy shared with parents whose children are accidentally handicapped through acts of God, such as genetically caused mental retardation or congenital deafness and blindness, may be contrasted with the rage expressed toward parents who have been legally determined to have deliberately injured and caused brain damage or loss of hearing and vision in their children.

This differential attitude toward the two groups of parents is a remarkable commentary on the gradual evolution of our civilization. Being civilized goes far beyond the trite notions of common courtesy and politeness represented by an emergence from a more primitive and savage state. Being civilized connotes the refinement and enlightenment alluded to by the late President John F. Kennedy, who stated that a society's degree of civilization is measured not so much by its collective strength but rather by its collective commitment to its weakest citizens. Having a handicapped sister undoubtedly made President Kennedy more sensitive to the needs of the severely handicapped and more supportive of various political moves to bring more of the nation's human and material resources to their aid.

Other Theoretical Considerations

Most of the explanations of child abuse have relied on developmental, psychodynamic, cultural, and socioeconomic explanations. We suggest that another means for understanding abuse, in particular abuse of handicapped children, should include the ethological, phylogenetic, and adaptive significance or function of abuse and neglect. Phylogenetic explanations are nearly all speculation, since current investigators are locked into the current time frame and are unable to examine the behaviors of human ancestors in real time; they must rely upon retrospective analyses and syntheses. Scientists are, however, able to examine the behaviors of other social species with which they share the planet. Whether one is an evolutionist or a creationist by religiophilosophical persuasion, the analogies drawn between human and nonhuman animal behavior are quite instructive and have given birth to the extensive fields of comparative psychology and sociobiology (Leak & Christopher, 1982). Such analogous thinking also informs much folk wisdom regarding human animals (*Homo sapiens*) who, like nonhumans, sometimes act and react in stressful situations with little conscious intent. They are referred to as losing their cool or their heads, referring to a temporary loss of that peculiar reflective or cerebral quality enabling humans to project, consider, and thus be held responsible for the consequences of their commissions or omissions. Can it be that many acts of child abuse and neglect are the results of a temporary loss of humanness and a reversion to the more primitive unthinking reflex centers of the brain whose higher, more civilized inhibiting capacities have been temporarily or perhaps chronically dulled by substance abuse, stress (Holmes & Rahe, 1967), or clinical dysfunctions?

Infanticide, abuse, and neglect of offspring do occur regularly in the nonhuman animal world (Bertram, 1975). Among the hanuman langurs, a primate species of monkey of Southeast Asia, infanticide is a frequent occurrence. Their social system includes females and young associated in groups, usually with a resident male. Resident males are sometimes challenged by other individual males or groups of males and occasionally replaced. The new male has been observed to kill all the new offspring of the old male and their lactating mothers (Hrdy, 1974). This pays off for the new male by terminating lactation in the mothers and reinitiating their estrous cycles, which allows him to invest in and protect his own offspring rather than those fathered by his predecessor. Bertram (1975) reported a similar process in the social system of lions.

Noting that infanticide does occur in nonhuman mammals is not a justification for its occurrence in humans. Nor does it argue that infanticide should be allowed to occur in humans with impunity even if one believes that it is predetermined in the human genes. Nevertheless, the realization that individuals of other social species occasionally attack and kill their own or others' offspring may provide us with a better understanding of the environmental factors and selection pressures thought to contribute to abuse and neglect of human offspring.

An understanding of these factors requires definitions of the terms *individual fitness, inclusive fitness,* and *parental investment.* Fitness is described as differential reproduction of like copies in subsequent generations (Williams, 1966). Evolution occurs by means of genetic processes, the production of phenotypic variation in the population, and the selective reproduction of particular parts from that population (Mayr, 1970). The differential reproduction results in competition among the constituent members of the population. This competition may occur at a variety of levels, including between individuals, between related individuals or kins, between groups, or between species. Since genes pass from generation to generation, they are the currency of evolution. Fitness and competition explanations are most parsimoniously applied at an individual level (Williams, 1966). Hence, most adaptive arguments concern individuals competing with other individuals.

Inclusive fitness provides the genetic link between individual fitness and kin selection. Inclusive fitness states that an individual will strive not only to reproduce parts of itself (i.e., its own genes), but also to invest effort to ensuring that its relatives (i.e., individuals who partially share genes) will survive and reproduce. Thus, adults strive to increase the fitness of their own offspring and the fitness of the offspring of their children (grandchildren). After all, a child shares 50% of each parent's genes. The degree of relatedness between a parent and child is one-half (in diploid species), among siblings is one half, among half-siblings is one-fourth, and among full cousins is one-eighth. Dawkins (1976) presented a clear explanation of the formulation of the degree or coefficient of relatedness. An individual's inclusive fitness consists of the sum of his or her own personal reproductive success and that of all his or her relatives or kin, each weighted by their degree of relatedness to the individual (Daly & Wilson, 1981).

Trivers (1974) suggested that a parent is willing to gamble effort and possible future chances to reproduce (parental investment) toward offspring survival and reproduction of a subsequent generation one step removed from the parent (i.e., grandchildren). Parental investment can be defined as an investment by a parent in an offspring that increases the recipient's fitness at the cost of parental capacity to invest elsewhere (Trivers, 1974). In other words, the effort parents invest in their offspring has an upper limit because parents have only so much reproductive capacity in their lifetime. Theoretically, to achieve the greatest fitness a parent must spread this effort in such a manner as to produce the most offspring possible.

Because parents strive to maximize their fitness by investing effort in their young, it is expected that there is a strong selection factor favoring the ability of parents to distinguish their own young from others. A study of the American Humane Society's data on abuse and neglect (Wilson, Daly, & Weghorst, 1980) has suggested that the probability of a child's being abused is somewhat dependent on whether he or she lives in a stepfamily or in a family with natural parents. Depending on the age of the child, a stepchild is two to six times more likely to be abused or neglected than a child living in a home with both of his or her natural parents. An analysis of the histories of The Village population has indicated that children living in a household with an adult care giver who is not blood-related to them are three times more likely to be sexually abused than children living with both natural parents. Although other factors help to explain sexual abuse episodes, this finding is alarming, particularly in light of the high rate of divorce and remarriage in our culture.

While the degree of relatedness may be an important consideration, especially the nonrelatedness between parent and offspring in the case of step-parenting, there is still a great deal of evidence that natural parents also abuse their own children (Meier, in press). Trivers (1974) has suggested a possible theoretical explanation for what he calls parents versus offspring conflict. His model is based upon the assumption that individuals strive to maximize their reproductive success. Parental objectives and strategies for reaching them may differ from those of their offspring. The basis of the conflict involves parents being selected who accurately assess the needs of their children, limit the resources invested in each child, and thereby free themselves to invest in other offspring. Offspring would tend to strive toward gaining more investment than a parent is willing to provide. This leads to conflict.

Parents may also be willing to withhold their investment or solicitude from those offspring with poor prospects for survival or reproduction. Although there is a great deal of evidence indicating the high incidence of abuse of mentally retarded and emotionally disturbed children, Daly and Wilson (1981) pointed out that these symptoms may be consequences rather than causes of parental abuse. Children suffering congenital defects such as fibrocystic disease, cleft palate, and Down's syndrome also tend to have a high risk for abuse (see Blacher & Meyers, 1983, which explores this in detail). In addition, parents of institutionalized handicapped children tend to abandon them and prefer the large institution over a group home or supervised apartment as a living situation for their own children, while simultaneously preferring more normalized living situations for retarded children in general, that is, for other people's children (Meyers, 1980). Even parents who actively maintain contact with their institutionalized, retarded children by taking them for off-ground visits tend to limit and gradually reduce the duration of their visits as a function of the years of prior institutionalization and the presence of convulsive or psychological disorders (D'Onofrio, Robinson, Isett, Roszkowski, & Spreat, 1980). Parents prefer the large institutional setting rather than a more normalized one in hopes that their own children will have better supervision, care, and available resources. While this rationale may indicate concern on the part of the parents, the net effect of their expressed preference, if carried out, would be to reduce rather than to increase or improve the contact between parent and offspring and the overall amount of investment directly provided by the parents. As pointed out earlier in this chapter and in Chapter 1 of this volume (by Blacher), evidence of attachment in institutionalized individuals exists, but the relationship between institutionalization and the development of attachment has not been fully explored.

Parent-Child Attachment

Parental abuse and neglect of handicapped children may be the result of interference in the normal bonding between mother and infant, which is thought to occur after childbirth (Kennell *et al.*, 1974). Studies have suggested that children separated from their mother at birth or soon after birth are at a higher risk for abuse and neglect, because the separation may disrupt the formation of a critical attachment or bonding between mother and child (Ainsworth, 1980). The adverse effects of this disruption seem to be long term, lasting for at least 2.5 years, although there is some question as to the critical length of the time period between birth and the initial exposure of mother and child for the separation to have such deleterious effects (Svejda, Campos, & Emde, 1980).

While the immediate postnatal period may be a sensitive time in the bonding process, bonding between parent and child has at least the potential to occur at any time. Certainly, some adoptions achieve adequate bonding regardless of the many factors involved when a child joins a new family, either at birth or through a later adoption (Ward, 1981). A thorough analysis of various bonding factors that are operative in normal family relationships and are evidently dysfunctional in some abusive families has been presented by DeLozier (1979), who applied attachment theory to design her doctoral research on child abuse. Many of the abusing mothers in her study revealed difficulties in their own attachments as children, which apparently resulted in subsequent difficulties as adults in attaching or bonding with their own offspring; this difficulty may also severely impair their ability to perform appropriate care-giving behavior. The awareness of what is appropriate care-giving behavior may be in part a function of the adult's levels of moral development, a hypothesis given considerable support by Newberger's dissertation (1978), in which she explored the moral reasoning ability of abusing and nonabusing mothers in accordance with the Kohlberg (1976) paradigm. Kohlberg's proposed scheme of moral development, simply stated, includes a premoral or preconventional stage characterized by the "might is right" attitude, a conventional or social conformity stage, and a principled stage characterized by the formulation of and adherence to universal principles of morality. There are several other stages and substages in Kohlberg's model as well as numerous derivations and refinements that cannot be delved into here. Related theoretical and heuristic leads have encouraged the Research Division of Childhelp, U.S.A. to sponsor extensive further research studies at several major universities into the moral development of abusing adults and their child victims (Jensen & Meier, 1983).

When examined cross-culturally, adoptive parents are usually found to be close biological relatives of the adoptee and lack children of their own (Daly & Wilson, 1981). In addition, the relinquishers tend to be young, unmarried, and/or unable to provide adequate care. In the experience of placing abused children from The Village into adoptive homes, the parents are not related and typically have children of their own or have a history of successfully caring for adopted children (Meier, 1983).

Some Treatment Considerations

In considering the treatment of the abusive family, the treatment of abusive parents must be the priority. Many disturbed parents cannot cope with their child's receiving help while they do not. They will be jealous—reminded of the neglect and rejection in their own childhood, and may possibly sabotage the child's treatment. (Kempe and Kempe, 1978, p. 71)

This statement suggests that any program treating institutionalized children who are in contact with their parents should offer treatment to the parents. This treatment may be aimed at reunifying the family or simply toward aiding the treatment of the child by means of treating the parent (Beezley, Martin, & Alexander, 1976).

There is a major paradox in treatment of abusive families. If reunification is the goal, then parents feel forced to commit themselves to programs they would not necessarily choose of their own volition. This sense of being entrapped often seems to undermine treatment efforts, regardless of how well-intentioned or convenient they are. If reunification is not the goal, then parents feel coerced toward what they perceive to be the unacceptable goal of relinquishment; consequently, they tend to see treatment as either contributing to the separation or as a tantalizing message that reunification may eventually become the goal if they change their behavior sufficiently. The usual situation involves court-ordered treatment in an effort to gain reunification and/or avoid prosecution on charges of child abuse. The most workable treatment strategy is to teach parents how to apply what they have learned in their treatment to their parenting.

Experts vary in their estimates of the portion of abusive parents who are responsive to treatment. Kempe and Kempe (1978) suggested that 90% of all abusive parents are treatable. However, experience at The Village, where extremely severe cases are concentrated, suggests that less than 50% of these severely abusive parents are able to make the requisite life changes to become adequate parents, especially within a short enough time frame for children whose developmental clocks keep relentlessly ticking away the critical time periods for normalizing experiences. Of course, the population of children and families at The Village represents a concentration of the most severely abused cases, that is those whose abuse was severe enough for legal intervention and court removal instead of allowing the child to remain in the home during family intervention. Nearly all reports recognize that there are certain groups of abusive parents who are too disturbed to benefit quickly and completely enough, for a variety of reasons, such as overt psychosis, serious substance abuse, intractable tendencies to batter physically as a means of communication, or developmental disabilities that preclude self-sufficiency let alone caring for dependent children.

Abusive parents cover a wide spectrum of pathology, as suggested by Fig. 7.1. Some parents show no other pathology outside of committing child abuse. The most recent *Diagnostic and Statistical Manual of Mental Disorders* (DSM-III; American Psychiatric Association, 1980) includes a classification indicating that in some clients child abuse may be a focus for attention or treatment not attributable to any other classifiable mental disorder (p. 333). Other diagnoses frequently determined for abusive adults include personality disorders, neurotic disorders, and chronic depression (Sloan & Meier, 1983).

In treatment aimed at reunifying separated families as quickly and economically as possible, the major criterion and aim is for parents to relinquish their abusive, neglectful patterns of child rearing and to replace them with a parenting pattern that is mutually rewarding and healthy for the parents and the children (Beezley et al., 1976). Galdston (1979) viewed the abusive pattern as a static form of interaction, rewarding to neither parents nor children. Similarly, Starr (1979) concluded his research into the causes of child abuse with the summary statement that it is usually accompanied by a serious problem in parent–child interaction.

In order to achieve satisfactory parenting skills, a variety of therapeutic modalities may be employed by an interdisciplinary treatment team. A number of more specific treatment goals subsumed under this overall objective are indicated by the individual case (Beezley et al., 1976). These goals include (1) reduction in the potential for neglect, (2) reduction in the potential for emotional abuse, including verbal abuse, (3) reduction in the potential for physical or sexual abuse, (4) identification of the child's needs as independent from the parent's needs, (5) appropriate parenting, that is, effective nonviolent disciplinary and other child-rearing procedures with the child, (6) consistency of parent–child interactions, and (7) decreased family isolation and disintegration. These specific goals may be conceptualized as a system of levels, consisting of a series of successive approximations directed toward the concept of an idealized, engaged, and flexible family (Tomlinson & Peters, 1981).

These goals indicate the direction of treatment for reunification. Treatment of an abusive family involves accomplishing all or any combination of them, depending on the individual case. The methods of treatment should also be shaped to fit the individual needs of the family, relying on residential, private, and/or community resources. These goals and methods may be formulated into an individualized family treatment plan that provides a map for the course of treatment. Treatment may be offered in a variety of modes including individual and group psychotherapy, marital counseling, family counseling, parenting workshops, home visits, or even regular informal social interactions. Jones, Magura, and Shyne (1981) suggested that the most effective programs contain a variety of services including counseling, outreach, and advocacy services.

The court-ordered treatment of abusive families differs from other forms of family therapy in a number of significant respects. The treatment of handicapped families may share some of these differences. Treatment of abusive families requires an interdisciplinary approach that meets the child's and the parent's various needs (Beezley et al., 1976; Steele, 1976). The treatment team ideally includes representatives from the medical, psychological, social, and legal professions as well as paraprofessional individuals trained to aid in the treatment of abusive families. These paraprofessionals may include social service homemakers, health visitors, lay therapists, and child-care workers. Supplemental therapeutic opportunities may include crisis nurseries, therapeutic day care centers or schools, neighborhood family development centers (Meier, 1978a), and parents' groups, including self-help groups such as Parents Anonymous or Parents United.

Nearly all treatment of abusing families, whether short or long term, must address the parent's enormous needs for acceptance and approval. Parents in need of treatment are sensitive to rejection and in need of real long-term relationships with at least one accepting adult, such as a parent aide (Meier, in press). This is the basis for treatment whether it is provided in the home, in an outpatient setting, or in a residential facility.

Other special problem areas for treating abusive families include the need to differentiate court-related services from the therapeutic services; many parents have suffered ongoing investigative and punitive procedures that inhibit the establishment of therapeutic rapport and treatment efficacy. In addition, abusive parents are often suspicious and mistrusting of authority figures, since many have suffered a life-long experience of humiliation, criticism, and probably reportable levels of abuse as children from their own parents and other authority figures (Green, 1978).

Abusive parents often have very fragile self-concepts requiring continual reassurance and support, especially during the initial phases of treatment. Dependent parents must have their own needs gratified before they begin to assess the needs of their children. This phase has been called restitution by Beezley *et al.*, (1976) and includes not only the learning and practice of parenting skills (e.g., Ambrose, Hazzard, & Haworth, 1980; Dinkmeyer & McKay, 1976) but also the receiving of some additional parenting (reparenting) they may have missed while they were children.

A second phase of parent treatment is the resolution period, consisting of a parent's resolving the current, static conflict that has tainted and limited the parent–child relationship by means of emotional insight and understanding from his or her own childhood, which so frequently is discovered to have been abusive. Framo (1979) has demonstrated that bringing in the families of origin is a very effective therapeutic technique in marital counseling. It has proved useful in the treatment of some abusive families because it helps to break down the intergenerational transmission of various abusive rites of families and to substitute more humane and gentle child-rearing practices congruent with the rights of children.

More specialized parent training may be required in the treatment of the abused handicapped child. In addition to the training provided to parents of nonhandicapped abused children, this specialized parent training may focus on the particular limitations and strengths noted in their child's various handicapping conditions so that parent expectations are more closely aligned with their children's abilities and potential.

Clinical experience with abused children reveals that they all suffer considerable and often massive emotional disturbance from the traumatic abusive experience itself and from the multiple subsequent actions taken to rectify the situation and to prevent its recurrence. The developmentally paralyzing impact of this emotional confusion and disturbance must be taken into account in treatment planning and parental counseling regarding realistic expectations for such emotionally handicapped children.

As a further elaboration, Table 7.1 presents some proposed treatment strategies for several different types of handicapped abused children.

To summarize, regardless of whether a child's handicap has its origin in an act of God or nature or in some primitive family rite, the child and family have several common treatment requirements: (1) a need for interdisciplinary services, (2) a need for outreach community services, including trained in-home workers, (3) a need to assess and meet the child's and family's needs, special or otherwise, and (4) a need for parents to gain acceptance of themselves and their children.

TABLE 7.1

Some Proposed Treatment Strategies for Various Handicapped Abused Children

Child characteristics	Parent characteristics	Recommended interventions
Severe retardation No eye contact Hypotonic; lack of cuddleability	Frustration Grief Guilt	General parent education (i.e., use of natural and logical consequences for child behaviors) Restructuring of expectations Group support Specialized parent training
Moderate retardation Evidence of brain injury Impulsiveness	Impulsiveness Possible retardation No social skills	Increase family's coping skills with concrete practice exercises Regular home visits Individual therapy
Cleft palate Low self-esteem Unwanted child Confused sexual identity	Single parent Cleft palate Role reversal	Reconstructive surgery Individual therapy Child: boost self-esteem and find appropriate role model Parent: identify and separate own needs from child's
Identified childhood neurological syndrome (e.g., Refsum's, Tourette's, or Rud's syndrome)	Lack of information, guilt, grief, denial Possible victim of syndrome	Parent education (specialized) Group and individual support Possible foster placement near home if reunification not feasible

References

Achenbach, T. M. (1978). *Research in developmental psychology: Concepts, strategies, methods.* New York: The Free Press.

Ainsworth, M. D. (1980). Attachment and child abuse. In G. Gerber, C. Ross, & E. Zigler (Eds.), *Child abuse; An agenda for action.* New York: Oxford University Press.

Ambrose, S. A., Hazzard, A., & Haworth, J. (1980). Cognitive-behavioral parenting groups for abusive families. *Child Abuse and Neglect, 4,* 119–125.

American Humane Association. (1978). *National Analysis of Official Child Neglect and Abuse Reporting.* Englewood, CO: Author.

American Psychiatric Association. (1980). *Diagnostic and statistical manual of mental disorders* (3rd ed.). Washington, DC: Author.

Applebaum, A. S. (1980). Developmental retardation in infants as a concomitant of physical child abuse. In G. J. Williams & J. Money (Eds.), *Traumatic abuse and neglect of children at home.* Baltimore: The Johns Hopkins University Press.

Babinter, E. (1981). *Mother love: Myth and reality—Motherhood in modern history.* New York: Macmillan.

Barash, D. P. (1980). Evolutionary aspects of the family. In C. Hofling & J. Lewis (Eds.), *The family: Evaluation and treatment.* New York: Brunner/Mazel.

Besharov, D. J. (1982). Toward better research on child abuse and neglect. *Child Abuse and Neglect, 5*(4), 383–390.

Beezley, P., Martin, H., & Alexander, H. (1976). Comprehensive family oriented therapy in child abuse and neglect. In R. Helfer & C. H. Kempe (Eds.), *The family and the community.* Cambridge, MA: Ballinger.

Bertram, B. C. (1975). Social factors influencing reproduction in wild lions. *Journal of Zoology, 177,* 463–482.

Blacher, J., & Meyers, C. E. (1983). A review of attachment formation and disorder of handicapped children. *American Journal of Mental Deficiency, 87*(4), 359–371.

Daly, M., & Wilson, M. (1981). Abuse and neglect of children in evolutionary perspective. In D. Tinkle and R. Alexander (Eds.), *Natural selection and social behavior: Recent research and new theory.* Concord, MA: Chiron Press.

Dawkins, R. (1976). *The selfish gene.* New York: Oxford University Press.

DeLozier, P. (1979). *An application of attachment theory to the study of child abuse.* Unpublished doctoral dissertation, California School of Professional Psychology, Los Angeles. Available from University Microfilms, Inc.: Ann Arbor, MI.

deMause, L. (1975, September). Our forebears made childhood a nightmare. *Psychology Today,* pp. 85–88.

Dinkmeyer, D., & McKay, G. (1976). *Systematic training for effective parenting.* Circle Pine, MN: American Guidance Service.

D'Onofrio, A., Robinson, R., Isett, M., Roszkowski, E. & Spreat, S. (1980). Factors related to contact between mentally retarded persons and their parents during residential treatment. *Mental Retardation, 18,* 293–294.

Emde, R. N., & Brown, C. (1976). Adaptation after birth of a Down's syndrome infant: Grieving and maternal attachment. *Journal American Academy of Child Psychiatry, 17,* 299–323.

Feshbach, N. D., & Feshbach, S. (1976). Punishment: Parent rites vs. children's rights. In G. P. Koocher (Ed.), *Children's rights and the mental health professions.* New York: Wiley.

Framo, J. L. (1979). Personal reflections of a family therapist. In J. Howells (Ed.), *Advances in family psychiatry* (Vol. I). New York: International Universities Press.

Freud, S. (1927). *The future of an illusion.* New York: Doubleday.

Frodi, A. M. (1981). Contribution of infant characteristics to child abuse. *American Journal of Mental Deficiency. 85,* 341–349.

Galdston, R. (1979). Disorders of early parenthood: Neglect, deprivation, exploitation, and abuse of little children. In J. D. Noshpitz (Ed.), *Basic handbook of child psychiatry.* New York: Basic Books.

Gelles, R. J. (1979). *Family violence.* Beverly Hills, CA: Sage Publications.

Giovannoni, M., & Becerra, R. (1979). *Defining child abuse.* New York: The Free Press.

Green, A. (1978). Child abuse. In B. Wolman, J. Egan, & A. Ross (Eds.), *Handbook of treatment of mental disorders in childhood and adolescence.* Englewood Cliffs, NJ: Prentice Hall.

Heber, R., Garber, H., Harrington, C., & Fulender, C. (1972). *Rehabilitation of families at risk for mental retardation.* Madison: University of Wisconsin Press.

Hernstein, R. J. (1973). Nature as nurture: Behaviorism and the instinct doctrine. *Behaviorism, 1,* 23–52.

Holmes, T., & Rahe, R. (1967). The Social Readjustment Rating Scale. *Journal of Psychosomatic Research, 11,* 212–218.

Hrdy, S. B. (1974). Male-male competition and infanticide among the langurs *(Preabytis intellus)* of Abus, Rajaasthan. *Folio Primotologica, 22,* 19–58.

Hunt, J. M., (1961). *Intelligence and experience.* New York: Ronald Press.

Hyman, I. A. (1980). Corporal punishment in the schools: America's officially sanctioned brand of child abuse. In G. Williams & J. Money (Eds.), *Traumatic abuse and neglect of children at home.* Baltimore: Johns Hopkins University Press.

Jensen, M., & Meier, J. H. (1983). *Moral development: Implications for research and intervention in child abuse* (Monograph No. 9:8/83). Beaumont, CA: Research Division, CHILDHELP U.S.A./INTERNATIONAL.

Jones, M. A., Magura, S., & Shyne, A. W. (1981). Effective practice with families in protective services: What works? *Child Welfare, 60,* 60–67.

Kempe, R. S., & Kempe, H. C. (1978). *Child abuse.* Cambridge, MA: Harvard University Press.

Kennell, J., Jerauld, R., Wolfe, H., Chesler, D., Kreger, N., McAlpine, W., Steffa, M., & Klaus, M. (1974). Maternal behavior one year after early and extended post-partum contact. *Developmental Medicine and Child Neurology, 16,* 172–179.

Klaus, M. H., & Kennell, J. H. (1976). *Maternal infant bonding.* St. Louis: Mosby.

Klein, M., & Stern, L. (1980). Low birth weight and the battered child syndrome. In G. Williams & J. Money (Eds.), *Traumatic abuse and neglect of children at home.* Baltimore: Johns Hopkins University Press.

Kohlberg, L. (1976). Moral stages and moralization: The cognitive-developmental approach. In T. Lickona (Ed.), *Moral development and moral behavior.* New York: Holt, Rinehart & Winston.

Korbin, J. E. (1980). The cultural context of child abuse and neglect. *Child Abuse and Neglect, 4,* 3–13.

Kubler-Ross, E. (1969). *Death and dying.* New York: Macmillan.

Leak, G. K., & Christopher, S. B. (1982). Freudian psychoanalysis and sociobiology: A synthesis. *American Psychologist, 37*(3), 313–322.

Lynch, M. (1976). Risk factors in the child: A study of abused children and their siblings. In H. P. Martin (Ed.), *The abused child: A multidisciplinary approach to developmental issues and treatment.* Cambridge, MA: Ballinger.

Mayr, E. (1970). *Populations, species and evolution.* Cambridge, MA: Belknap Press.

Mead, M. (1977). Letters from the field, 1925–1975. New York: Harper & Row.

Meier, J. H. (1976). *Developmental and learning disabilities: Evaluation, management and prevention in children.* Baltimore: University Park Press.

Meier, J. H. (1978a). Current status and future prospects for the nation's children and their families. In H. Z. Lopata (Ed.), *Family factbook.* Chicago: Marquis Press.

Meier, J. H. (1978b). *A multifactorial model of child abuse dynamics* (Monograph No. 3:4/83). Beaumont, CA.: Research Division, CHILDHELP U.S.A./INTERNATIONAL.

Meier, J. H. (1982a). CHILDHELP U.S.A./INTERNATIONAL: A Comprehensive approach to the treatment and prevention of assault against children. (Monograph No.6:7/83). Beaumont, CA.: Research Division, CHILDHELP U.S.A./INTERNATIONAL.

Meier, J. H. (1982b). Corporal punishment in the schools. *Childhood Education, 58*(4), 235–237.

Meier, J. H., and associates. (1983). Research division progress report. Beaumont, CA: Research Division, CHILDHELP U.S.A./INTERNATIONAL.

Meier, J. H. (in press). Assault against children: Causes, consequences, treatment and prevention. Baltimore: University Park Press.

Meier, J. H. and Sloan, M. P. (1982). Acts of God versus rites of families. Accidental versus inflicted child disabilities (Occasional paper). Beaumont, CA: Research Division, CHILDHELP U.S.A./INTERNATIONAL.

Meyers, R. J. (1980). Attitudes of parents of institutionalized mentally retarded individuals toward deinstitutionalization. American Journal of Mental Deficiency. 85, 184–187.

Newberger, C. (1978). Parental conceptions of children and child rearing: A structural-developmental analysis. Unpublished doctoral dissertation, Harvard University, Boston. Available from University Microfilms, Inc.: Ann Arbor, MI.

O'Connor, R. J. (1978). Brood reduction in birds: Selection for fratricide, infanticide, and suicide. Animal Behavior, 25, 79–96.

Schilling, R. F., Schinke, S. P., Blythe, B. J., & Barth, R. P. (1982). Child maltreatment and mentally retarded parents: Is there a relationship? Mental Retardation, 20, 201–209.

Scholz, J. P., & Meier, J. H. (1983). Conpetency of abused children in a residential treatment program. In J. E. Leavitt (Ed.), Child abuse and neglect: Research and innovation (NATO Advanced Sciences Series). The Hague: Nijhoff.

Sloan, M. P., & Meier, J. H. (1983). Parent typology of abused children in a residential treatment program. Child Abuse and Neglect, 7, 443–450.

Sociobiology: A new theory of behavior. (1977, August 1). Time, pp. 54–58, 63.

Starr, R. H . (1979). Toward the prevention of child abuse. Paper presented at the International Workshop on the "At Risk" Infant, Tel-Aviv. Available from author, Department of Psychology, University of Maryland, Baltimore, MD 21201.

Steele, B. (1976). Experience with an interdisciplinary concept. In R. Helfer & C. H. Kempe (Eds.), Child abuse and neglect: The family and the community. Cambridge, MA: Ballinger.

Svejda, M. J., Campos, J. J., & Emde, R. N. (1980). Mother-infant "bonding": Failure to generalize. Child Development, 51, 775–779.

Tinbergen, N. (1951). The study of instinct. New York: Oxford University Press.

Tomlinson, R., & Peters, P. (1981). An alternative to placing children: Intensive and extensive therapy with "disengaged" families. Child Welfare, 60, 95–103.

Trivers, R. (1974). Parent-offspring conflict. American Zoologist, 14, 249–264.

U.S. Department of Health, Education, and Welfare. (1973). Child Abuse Prevention and Treatment Act (Public Law 93–247). Washington, D.C.

van den Berghe, P. L. (1979). The human family: A sociobiological look. In J. S. Lockard (Ed.). The evolution of human social behavior. New York: Elsevier.

Ward, M. (1981). Parental bonding in older child adoptions. Child Welfare, 60, 24–34.

Warden, J. C. (1927). The historical development of comparative psychology. Psychology Review, 34, 57–85, 135–158.

Williams, G. C. (1966). Adaptation and natural selection. Princeton, NJ: Princeton University Press.

Wilson, E. O. (1975). Sociobiology: The new synthesis. Cambridge, MA: Harvard University Press.

Wilson, M., Daly, M., & Weghorst, S. (1980). Household cooperation and the risk of child abuse and neglect. Journal of Biosocial Science, 12, 333–340.

Zigler, E. (1980). Controlling child abuse: Do we have the knowledge and/or the will? In G. Gerbner, C. Ross, & E. Zigler (Eds.), Child abuse: An agenda for action. New York: Oxford Univ. Press.

PART III

Family Involvement in the Educational Process

Clinical Research and Policy Issues in Parenting Severely Handicapped Infants*

Crystal E. Kaiser
Alice H. Hayden

Introduction

The world of the severely handicapped infant represents a fascinating new expanse of provocative research questions, which both challenge and support current clinical practices. No single discipline can claim this area as its sole academic domain. Almost by definition, any comprehensive literature review of this topic must span the literatures of multiple fields of professional study. In conducting such a review, we found that several interesting patterns emerged.

First, the study of the severely handicapped infant is not confined to a single study, but is a constellation of questions from many disparate perspectives grounded in fundamentally different bases of literature. In

*Portions of this research were done by Crystal E. Kaiser within the Department of Psychiatry at Dartmouth Medical School, Hanover, NH.

275

some cases, parallel work in complementary domains could be examined for fruitful comparison. In other cases, studies have occurred sporadically, without building upon past work, so that they appear almost random and disjointed.

Much of the work in special education has been categorical in nature, with individual strands of research developing around individual categories of handicaps, many of which have spanned all severity levels within a category. Related work in special education with preschool handicapped children has some limited transference value, as does work with older severely handicapped populations. Extrapolation in both cases deserves the utmost in caution. The relevant medical, psychiatric, and social work literature has tended to be largely anecdotal in character, centering primarily on (1) nursing articles about the care of parents of premature or intensive care infants or (2) articles by physicians on the counseling of families with regard to either the initial announcement of the diagnosis or prognosis or the presentation of critical care decision options, which may be surgical or placement-related. Another category of article appearing largely in the nursing journals is the "one mother's story" paradigm—often a bit of a horror story told by a parent of a handicapped infant who is also a nurse, who was treated somewhat callously by the medical establishment, and who has some suggestions for the future care of new parents in similar situations.

Another important point of departure in these readings is the extent to which the focus is on the infant as opposed to the care givers. The research on infants, coming primarily from special education and developmental psychology, has tended to be either clinical (in which a specific developmental or therapeutic assessment or intervention program is evaluated for specific outcomes) or basic (in which a specific element of normal development is differentially studied in a specific categorical population of severely handicapped infants). Further complexity in synthesizing such data arises from the fact that many such studies have considered "handicapped infants" as their population, summing the data not only over variants in type of handicap and age level defined as "infant", but over all levels of severity, including, at perhaps the farthest extreme, the population referred to as "high risk," which may include both disadvantaged and premature infants, among others.

Even when the research population is specified to be "severely handicapped infants," many unresolved issues remain. What distinctive features characterize the population we refer to as severely handicapped infants? What is the chronological age range represented by the term *infant*? Should it include subjects who are developmentally functioning in the infant range, regardless of chronological age? What do autistic, mentally retarded, and deaf–blind infants have in common? Should they be regarded as separate research populations for certain types of studies? Can they be "summed" for other types of research? We need to address such issues before these important lines of research proceed in such a way as to confound any possibility of future comparison statements, both across studies and across disciplines. There is a fundamental need for cross-disciplinary coordination and communication toward the systematic development of this critical knowledge base.

There are, however, certain emerging issues common to professional study across the range of disciplines. There is continuing interest in the concepts of bonding and attachment and the newer, related issues of bonding risk. Societal changes in adult role definitions are stimulating new questions of father involvement in the infant caregiving process. Innovative clinical ideas from the medical community are emerging as preliminary responses to existing data on the care of families. Though many of these ideas are being reported anecdotally in the literature, they provide an important informational source of current clinical practice and future research challenge. In the absence of more systematic investigations, it is the only documentation we have on certain topics.

To provide a literal compilation of all remotely related literature, both research and anecdotal, across the fields of special education, developmental psychology, child psychiatry, social work, counseling and rehabilitation, occupational and physical therapy, medicine, nursing, and early education, would be neither feasible nor desirable in this single chapter. Consequently, more modest goals have been attempted.

While drawing from a wealth of data culled from many professional spheres, this chapter has been organized around a series of current clinical research and policy issues for those working with severely handicapped infants and their families. Such issues include models for working with parents of severely handicapped infants in the context of infant intervention programs, developing bridges between the educational and medical communities around such families, responding to important new questions of bonding risk, and developing means of providing balanced clinical support to families.

It is hoped that this review and the interpretations offered will stimulate a consolidated approach to supporting the family system of the severely handicapped infant through systematic cross-disciplinary empiricism targeted at provocative clinical issues.

Bonding Risk as Developmental Risk

Contemporary infant interventionists have cross-disciplinary concerns. Research from a wide variety of disciplines now focuses on handicapped infants and their families. Each perspective is valued for its unique contribution to our knowledge and understanding. With this in mind we explore a concept of developmental risk that has, until recently, received little attention: the effects of bonding risk on development.

Normal Bonding and Attachment

There is a very special bond, or attachment, that develops between a newborn and his or her primary care givers. Since the 1970s, the literature on mother–infant bonding has expanded rapidly. This literature has focused largely on the special dyadic relationship between mother and infant. (For excellent reference volumes on this topic, see Klaus & Kennell, 1976, and Tronick, 1982).

Parallel research efforts (Brazelton, 1974; Korner, 1974) have sought specifically to analyze the infant's role in this fascinating process. As it turns out, the infant's behavior is a far greater factor in affecting the adult's behavior than might have ever been imagined (Lewis & Rosenblum, 1974). Korner (1974, p. 53), for example, cited an earlier study by Moss and Robson (1968) with 1-month-old babies, which reported the following unexpected results: "In roughly four out of five instances, it was the infant who initiated the exchange" between mother and infant. In other words it is the infant, not the adult, who initiates most interactions. As also noted in Chapter 1 of this volume (Blacher), it is interesting to speculate on the implications of such findings for the interactions between severely handicapped infants and their care givers. If it is the severely handicapped infant who must initiate social interaction with the parent, one might expect seriously reduced or disrupted interactions to result, given the infant's limited mechanisms for doing so.

Fathers' Attachment

More recently, the topic of father–infant bonding has begun to be explored in the research literature. In one of the earlier writings on this topic, Wortis (1971) noted, "It is scientifically unacceptable to advocate the natural superiority of women as child-rearers and socializers of children when there have been so few studies of male-infant or father-infant interaction on the subsequent development of the child" (p. 739).

Such studies soon began to emerge (Greenberg & Morris, 1974), and the preliminary findings were fascinating. In one of the first such studies, Pederson and Robson (1969) wrote: "It causes ... great embarrassment to report that the actual data on father participation were secured by interviewing the mothers" (p. 467). Despite that setback, they reported that approximately three-fourths of their infant sample (ages 8–9.5 months) demonstrated attachment behaviors toward the father.

The more recent research of Parke and Sawin (1977) suggested that we should stop talking of dyads (mother–infant) and begin talking in terms of triads, due to the active participation of many contemporary fathers as early as the first few months of life. One researcher (Earls, 1976) has gone so far as to say: "Ignoring, or minimizing the importance and influence of fathers may not only pose a barrier to effective treatment, but may even exacerbate the stresses found in a young family" (p. 209).

Implications for Infant Programs

This literature is relevant to the study of parents and severely handicapped infants, although it does not typically appear in special education journals. The normal course of bonding and attachment must be fully understood so that the greater complexities involved in the bonding process for handicapped infants and their families can be recognized. In addition, the bonding outcome may have even farther-reaching effects for the unique developmental problems of special needs infants. Waechter (1977) has put it very strongly: "The period immediately following birth is critical for the formation of a bonding relationship between mother and child; in fact, the child's subsequent progress in all developmental areas is dependent on forming a strong attachment with a parenting figure during this time" (p. 298).

Demos (1982) referred to the increasing number of investigators involved in the microanalysis of infant–parent interactions. She suggested that affective expression may well be the only primary communication means available to the infant prior to the development of language and symbolism. Her suggestion increases the relevance of such study with regard to the severely handicapped infant.

A number of fascinating studies are emerging in the area of affective expression in handicapped infants. Cicchetti and Sroufe (1976) found that the median age reported for the onset of laughter in Down's syndrome infants was 10 months, compared to 3–4 months for normal infants. T. Field (1983) was apparently able to determine, through empirical investigation, that high risk infants "have less fun" in their interactions with care givers. R. J. Gallagher, Jens, and O'Donnell (1983) reported that as the degree of muscle tone involvement accompanying an infant's physical disability increases (whether the abnormality is in the direction of hypotonia or hypertonia), the infant's ability to laugh consequently decreases.

The mother of a special needs infant may have multiple reasons for needing the father's participation and relationship with the infant to be as full and as satisfying as possible. The sharing of this important charge, with its greater demands, may be important for her own mental health as well as for the optimal development of the infant. J. J. Gallagher, Cross, and Scharfman (1981) systematically studied stresses in families of young handicapped children with particular emphasis on the father's role in parental adaptation. They found that "traditional father roles" may be "largely diminished or not present at all" (p. 13) in many families with young handicapped children, with alternative roles not yet specified for these fathers. Barnard (1980) reported a rather startling positive correlation between father involvement at 4 months and later developmental problems in the infant. Her interpretation of this finding was that father involvement at that point may be seen as an early index of maternal or family stress.

New means of being responsive to the unique needs of fathers must be explored (Tuck, 1971). Most failures to "get fathers involved" seem to have been attempts to transfer methods developed for a different population (mothers). At present, it seems that the needs and perspectives of fathers are unique enough to suggest that new models may need to be devised that take these variations into account (Hines, 1971: Lamb, 1975; Spelke, Zelazo, Kagan, & Kotelchuck, 1973). M. P. Erickson (1974) described an evening series of group discussions designed specifically for fathers of infants with Down's syndrome. The fathers expressed certain concerns and interpretations of common experiences that did appear to differ somewhat from issues of foremost concern in similar groups of mothers. More recently, Delaney (1979) reported increases in attachment behaviors between fathers and their handicapped infants as a result of a Saturday morning program of support and training specifically designed for fathers.

Higher divorce rates for families with young handicapped children and shifts in child custody rulings have resulted in another new cultural phenomenon with its attendant future challenges: the single-parent father (Keshet & Rosenthal, 1978). At the time of this writing (1984), the first author's clinical experience includes one single-parent father who has two of the twelve trisomy 13 children known in this country, both profoundly handicapped. He is rearing these children at home.

Researchers may be able to play a very critical role in the support of the infant–parent relationship, which, in the case of the severely handicapped infant, may be at great risk. Crawley and Spiker (1982) found, for example, that lower-functioning Down's syndrome infants tend to have significantly fewer positive interactions with their mothers than higher-functioning Down's syndrome infants. While the idea of generally supporting the relationship between parent and handicapped infant is not a new one (Bronfenbrenner, 1975), we researchers have only recently begun to move past the principle to the application of the idea (R. Bromwich, 1981). In addition, we have failed to extend the idea of mother support to parent support and, ultimately, to support of the family system as a whole (Turnbull, 1976).

The next step should perhaps be to question *how* to support parents and families with special needs infants (Beckman-Bell, 1981). Might certain types of support be effective for some families but not for others? Allen, Affleck, McGrade, and McQueeney (1983), for example, found social class differences in the early responses of families to the birth of a handicapped infant. Might certain types of support benefit the infant, but at a cost to the family? How should short-term benefit to one be weighed against long-term benefit to the other? At present, many infant programs base the order of such priorities on their own philosophies or values for lack of empirical data. Research is critically needed to guide these efforts. Within our own field of special education, the work of researchers in the area of disadvantaged infants and their families (Caldwell, Wright, Honig, & Tannenbaum, 1970; Ramey & Smith, 1976; Ramey & Trohanis, 1982) can provide a good beginning, though we may not be able to generalize to other populations of infants and families. Solomon, Wilson, and Galey (1982), for example, embarked on an intervention program designed to improve the quality of interactional patterns between handicapped infants and their parents. Although they were able to demonstrate statistically significant changes as a result of intervention with the at-risk, mild, and moderately handicapped infants, they were not able to do so with their severely handicapped infants.

Affleck, McGrade, McQueeney, and Allen (1982) briefly described a model of what they term "relationship-focused early intervention," which they have used with infants with "severe perinatal complications" or "genetic disorders associated with developmental delay" (p. 260). Preliminary 9-month data on families were reported to show positive changes for both parents and infants, though specific figures were not presented. However, the quoted description of their infant population makes it somewhat difficult to determine whether these are, in fact, severely handicapped infants.

Other helping disciplines (such as clinical psychology and social work) may provide special educators assistance in their efforts. The training of special educators, in most cases, has been with children, not with adults, so the literature and counsel of those who routinely care for adults and families in stress may be welcomed. Could it be that clinicians in this field have inadvertently communicated that they see the infant's well-being as being of greater value than that of the parents or family? To "avoid" making such a value-laden decision may be a decision in itself.

Hayden and Haring (1976) stressed the importance of developing techniques for the application of research findings to support parent–infant interaction. They described a clinical approach used at the University of Washington with parents of infants with Down's syndrome:

> Very often the parents arrive at school holding the baby awkwardly and fearfully.... The staff, from the first, encourage parents to interact with the infant ... to cuddle, to talk to, to hold, and to play with the infant. ... parents who had earlier been somehow frightened of this infant with his "differences" could begin to react to him as they might have reacted automatically to a normal infant. (p. 589)

It should be the ambition of special educators to encourage the development of more programs with the multiple foci of accelerating infant development and providing specific support for the mother–infant and father–infant attachments, while still offering the wide range of alternatives for parent training and support that have been described or recommended by several prominent researchers in our field. Bricker and Casuso (1979), for example, reported that certain family needs (e.g., financial or psychological) must often be met before parents are ready to learn change-agent strategies, and that "parental participation and education must be approached from a comprehensive base" (p. 109). These researchers further suggested a process of individualized assessment, objective setting, intervention, and evaluation in working with parents that parallels our related processes in working with handicapped infants. Karnes (1975) recommended involving parents in the formulation of educational policy with regard to their own child's program and providing a wide range of alternatives for parental involvement. She urged early intervention programs to encourage parents to play an active role in evaluating their own child's program as well as assessing their own contributions to that program. Perhaps most importantly, she suggests helping parents to assess their own readiness for such involvement.

In a more recent review, Schell (1981) suggested that as the severity of the handicap increases, program foci tend to shift from the child to the parents. Handicapped infants, however, are still the group most often identified as the primary target for our intervention efforts. Remarkably, Schell noted, even in intervention programs directed primarily at parents, parent outcomes often remain unmeasured in the program evaluations.

Special Bonding Risks

Severely handicapped infants present special bonding risks of which both researchers and clinicians should be aware. Cohn and Tronick (Tronick, 1982) suggested, for example, that the flip side of "engrossment" in a healthy dyad may be "entrapment" in a troubled dyad. More must be known about the components and sequences of such entrapment. Many of the normal communicative feedback chains may be either broken or severely damaged in the case of a severely handicapped infant. Even if the parent attempts to assume the role of initiator of interactions, are the usual procedures likely to have the desired effect with such an infant? What role does the normal infant have in selectively reinforcing certain care giver responses, and how does this compare with what happens in the case of a severely handicapped infant and his or her care giver? If the "natural" feedback chain results in both diminished initiation of interactions by the severely handicapped infant and a pattern of nonreinforcement of adult initiations, then we might expect to see fewer initiations, and, therefore, fewer interactions from either direction. Beyond quantitative measures, we also need to be able to assess qualitative differences in the interactions that do take place.

In addition, it should be possible to assess the progressive effect of these abnormal patterns of interaction on the care givers. Do parents feel more or less competent over time, for example, on the basis of such interactive patterns? Once such norms are established, can specific intervention techniques reverse a negative pattern or, ideally, prevent such negative patterns from ever beginning? How might the result of such interaction affect the infant? As answers to these provocative questions begin to emerge, the results may dramatically alter the shape of our current intervention efforts with this population.

In a clinical observation (1977) by the first author of a severely involved infant brought to an early intervention program for assessment, a fairly dramatic series of events unfolded. The parents had apparently been concerned that the child might be autistic, as he appeared to react very negatively to any attempts at touching or holding him. In fact, as a parent would draw near, reaching out to pick him up, the baby would rigidly arch his back, and appeared to be trying to move away from the parent's intended embrace. While it was known that the child had severe motor involvement, the precise nature and potential effects of the involvement had never been adequately explained to the parents. When the physical therapist pointed out that this infant was very likely to respond with exaggerated extension in precisely the opposite direction of his intention (e.g., an intention to move *toward* the parent would result in an involuntary move *away* from the parent) a rather dramatic attitudinal change appeared to occur in both parents. The knowledge that their baby was trying to respond positively and to move toward them in such instances made a world of difference. Hard data are needed on such occurrences and the critically important role professionals can play in clarifying potentially confusing early behaviors in the severely handicapped infant that could be otherwise misinterpreted.

Young handicapped children continue to be the nation's primary target of child abuse (Belsky, 1978; Fontana, 1976; Frodi, 1981). How much of this abuse may be triggered by misinterpretations of the meaning of certain infant behaviors? Might a listless infant give the impression of having no interest in a close relationship with the parents? Might a screaming infant indicate general unhappiness or parental failure to meet its needs adequately? The potentially devastating effects of such misinterpretations on the developing parent–infant bond merits our closest attention.

Field's work (1983) has indicated that mothers have an extremely difficult time gauging the right amount and types of stimulation to provide in order to elicit positive responses from their high-risk infants. She has provided a detailed analysis of common counterproductive (yet understandable) parental responses to common misleading and ambiguous cues given by high-risk infants. The usual "logic" which parents of normal infants might apply clearly backfires in these relationships. In her summary of work in this area, Field stated, "researchers know very little about harmonious interactions, less about disturbed interactions, and even less about facilitative techniques" (p. 86).

Bonding risks may not be limited to dyadic or triadic parent–infant relationships, but may even extend into the infant program itself. Is it possible that special educators do, in fact, become "attached" to "their" infants in "their" programs? There are absolutely no data on the existence of this phenomenon, but clinical experience strongly suggests that it may not only exist, but that it may be an important factor well worth investigating for many reasons.

How do "attached" and "unattached" special educators differentially observe, for example, those behaviors in the infant that mitigate both for and against a normal attachment with the parents? Do "attached" special educators make different types of programming or placement decisions? Is their interaction with severely handicapped infants a supporter or a detractor from the developing (and at-risk) infant–parent bond? Are their intervention efforts affected by whether or not (or to what extent) they are "attached" to "their" infants?

When early intervention teachers err, is it in the direction of planning activities that are too high-level or too low-level for the infants they serve? Might a pattern of inappropriately high-level activities reflect a type of professional denial? Might a pattern of inappropriately low-level activities be an indicator of potential problems in the relationship between the professional and the infant? These and related issues have received virtually no attention in the special education literature to date. This attachment process in teachers and therapists of severely handicapped infants is a critical area for further study and may have far-reaching implications for professional training programs.

In a clinical observation (by the first author, 1983) of a severely multiply handicapped child in a well-respected intervention program, the young child's gaze avoidance and unhappy facial expressions were interpreted by the teacher as indicating that this infant "did not like" social contact. A graduate student in training who asked what types of things the infant did seem to like (in an effort to find reinforcers for her) was told that, as far as the teachers and therapists knew, she didn't like much of anything. The apparent effect on the teachers and therapists of these suggestions, and the subsequent circular effects on the child's program, can readily be hypothesized. When further study into this child's medical history and a more detailed observation identified specific physical positions associated with adult contacts that may well have been quite painful for the child, and specific types of adult contact that elicited differential effects (even a rare smile in this child), the attitudes of the care givers (and the nature of the child's program) appeared to change dramatically. More systematic documentation of this type of phenomenon and elaborated paradigms for the study of such changes are needed.

Fraiberg (1974) has given us a moving account of her own gradual realization of differences in her own behaviors and reactions to blind infants in comparison with normal infants. She described how she was able to move from that point of realization to actively searching out the dynamics of such differences. What messages coming from the blind baby were so profoundly influencing the adult care giver? To answer this question, Fraiberg studied the ways in which normal infants seemed to initiate and invite certain interactions. She saw visual regard of faces, eye contact, and facial expressions that seemed to say "I want," "I'm excited," "I'm happy," or "I'm surprised." She saw rewarding smiles elicited at the sound of a familiar voice, the sight of a familiar face, or even a feeding dish. She saw gestures that said "hold me," "pick me up." All these rewarding communicative messages from the infant were virtually absent in blind infants.

Eventually, Fraiberg and her colleagues discovered alternate means of receiving messages from these infants whose nonverbal communication code was so difficult to read. Here is an exerpt:

> We began to read "I want" and intentionality through fleeting, barely-visible motor signs in the hands. Our staff film reviews took on a curious aspect. When we examined mother-child reciprocity, we looked at the mother's face and the baby's hands. (The baby's face told us very little.) When we studied investment in a toy or toy preference, we looked at the baby's hands. When we examined emotional reactions to momentary separation from mother, or toy loss, we looked at the hands. It was—and still is—a bizarre experience for us to read hands instead of faces to read meaning into emotional experience . . . What we ourselves learned from hand language we brought to the mothers of our blind babies. It was most welcome help. (pp. 225, 229)

What a difference such an intervention could make in the developing relationship between a blind infant and his or her parents! Such bonding risks, of course, operate also from the infant's perspective. Bonding is an intricate chain of intimate, nonverbal communication, and a handicap may create critical breaks in that chain for the infant as well as for the care giver. There is evidence that attachment patterns in handicapped infants may differ from normal attachment patterns (Stone & Chesney, 1978). It is also known that Down's syndrome infants exhibit normal (though delayed) attachment patterns (Berry, Gunn, & Andrews, 1980; Cicchetti & Serafica, 1981; Serafica & Cicchetti, 1976). Far more research is needed if the implications of such findings for intervention are to be fully understood.

Some years ago Bowlby (1969) elaborated an attachment model consisting of a series of stages in the development of attachment. These stages suggest certain perceptual and cognitive "prerequisites" that the severely handicapped infant may not have (e.g., using proximity and contact-promoting behaviors, discriminating between familiar persons and responding differentially, active initiation of certain types of behavior, understanding factors that influence caretaker goals and how caretaker's behaviors may be changed). Can (or should) such developmental behaviors be actively assessed in or "taught" to severely handicapped infants in order to facilitate the development of attachment? Systematic studies, as proposed in Blacher and Meyers (1983), are needed to guide our efforts. It can be hypothesized that the infants' need to be understood and to receive messages from their care givers is great. It may be more difficult to hypothesize the positive long-term effects that might come of our taking the time to respond systematically to these central issues as an integral part of research and intervention efforts. To neglect these issues, given the current knowledge base, may even border on irresponsibility.

An excellent study by Emde and Brown (1978) presented sharp challenges to traditional stereotypes about infants with Down's syndrome and their relationships with their parents. This exemplary research has illuminated the major role such infants play in setting the tone for their parent–infant (should it be infant–parent?) relationships. Consider, for example, the implications of an observation made by one of the mothers from the Emde and Brown Study (her infant was 5 months old): "She will only let me have a good smile about twice a week. She mostly smiles when she is just lying there" (p. 316).

The authors noted that this mother began gradually to avoid looking into the baby's face when holding her. The importance this mother had given to smiling is not unusual. The mothers in Frailberg's study (Frailberg, 1974) had similar concerns. The fact that the babies may have initiated this cycle themselves should also not be too surprising, as it has been noted that normal babies, even at the age of 1 month, initiate most of their interactions with care givers (Korner, 1974). Schell (1981) used the term *reciprocity* to describe the often-missing ingredient in such interactions, specifically referring to the ambiguous or diminished feedback many such infants provide their care givers. Teachers and therapists need to find very special ways to support these parents and one another in interactions with such infants.

Bonding Risk and Intervention Efforts

Drezek (1976b) described a situation many special educators will, unfortunately, recognize as not uncommon in the field. In Sesame Street style it might be asked: "What is wrong with this story?"

At a meeting of a parent group, a mother of a 3-month old asked the speaker on language development if there were any sounds she should make to encourage her baby to respond. The speaker answered that she should make any sounds she wants to and to take her cue from the baby as to which he enjoys. At that point the president of the group interrupted to say that she had a book which tells parents how to be teachers which gives a list of three specific sounds to use each month. (p. 4)

What the effects of such an "intervention" might be and whether any negative effects would truly be outweighed by the positive must be questioned. How important is it for parents to feel comfortable and confident in their interactions with their babies? Might some "interventions" inadvertently interfere with this process? Beckwith (1976) found that parents of high-risk infants may be making some natural interventions on their own. Clinicians need to learn more about such interventions and how these relate to their own efforts. In the future, both clinicians and researchers will need to be able to assess the infant's vital role in these interactions as well. According to Brazelton (1974), there may even be a third variable, the interaction itself, which must be separately assessed for a comprehensive understanding of this complex process and its relationship to intervention efforts.

Several models of infant intervention have been developed that have specifically worked to include a systematic focus on supporting special bonding relationships (R. M. Bromwich, 1976; Bryant, Ramey, & Burchinal, 1982; Drezek, 1976a, 1976b; 1982; Roth, 1982). The beautifully elaborated Bromwich model outlines the six-stage Parent Behavior Progression with separate forms for two different child age levels from birth through 35 months. This progression is used as a schema for the assessment of parental behavior in parent–infant interaction as a basis for systematic intervention. At Level I, for example, the parent "enjoys her infant," while at Level VI the parent "independently generates a wide range of developmentally appropriate activities and experiences interesting to the infant, in familiar and in new situations, and at new levels of the infant's development" (R. M. Bromwich, 1976, p. 57). The interactions between parents and infants are viewed as the primary focus of this intervention model, through what Bromwich referred to as a "problem-solving process." Parents are supported in learning to use this problem-solving process on their own, rather than becoming dependent on the experts to determine the "correct" way to respond in a difficult situation involving their own infant. Fifty-three case studies are presented in some detail, organized into the following five domains, shown with examples of situations within quotation marks:

1. Problems in the social-affective area: "The parent did not find it enjoyable to interact with the infant because the infant did not express pleasure" (p. 187).
2. Problems in the cognitive-motivational area: "The infant did not initiate play with materials and was mostly a passive observer" (p. 234).
3. Problems in the language area: "The infant's infrequent and

primitive vocalizations elicited little language from the parent"
(p. 261).
4. Problems in the motor area: "The parent did not value the gross
motor skills of the child that were not common motor milestones
like sitting, crawling, and walking" (p. 274).
5. Problems in parent-care giving: "The parent was so involved
with the infant that she tended to neglect the needs of other family members and her own needs" (p. 285).

Quite detailed information is provided to illustrate how their staff
managed each problem, following a format of empathetic listening, asking relevant questions, discussing important issues, and encouraging the
parent to take certain types of action. Written interaction plans were
prepared every 4 months, and an interesting sample format is provided
incorporating more data in some areas than a more standard Individualized Education Plan (IEP) might include. Bromwich called this
approach the interaction model, and described it as an approach built
on parental strengths and cooperative problem solving. An interesting
component of her book is a chapter describing and analyzing unsuccessful (or partially successful) interventions. It would be interesting to
see evaluation data on the operational use of this model with severely
handicapped infants and their families by diverse infant teams, and to
determine the replicability of these anecdotal but impressive results.

A disturbing yet compellingly important example of the relationship between bonding risk and intervention is the work of investigators
at the University of Washington, who conducted a series of three studies
(Kogan & Tyler, 1973; Kogan, Tyler & Turner, 1974; Tyler & Kogan,
1977).

In their early study (Kogan & Tyler, 1973), mother–infant interaction was compared during play periods for parents of normal infants
and preschool children, those whose children had cerebral palsy, and
those whose children had been diagnosed as mentally retarded. They
found that the mothers of the physically handicapped children were
rated as both "warmer" and "more controlling" than either group of
comparison mothers, while the physically handicapped children
themselves were rated as being more "passive" yet more "assertive and
controlling." At that time, these were interesting findings but they had
many possible interpretations.

In the second study (Kogan et al., 1974), interactional dyads of
parents and their infants or preschoolers with cerebral palsy were
studied over a 2-year period in two situations, play and therapy. The
mothers were all providing physical therapy for their children under the

direction of a staff therapist. In addition, data were also taken on the interactions between professional therapists and the same children.

When the treatment program was just beginning, both mothers and children demonstrated more negative behaviors toward one another in therapy than in play. Staff therapists did not display as many negative behaviors with the children as did the parents. After working with their children in therapy over a period of 2 years, the mothers evidenced a gradual decrease in the warmth and acceptance they demonstrated to the child in therapy. During play, a downward progression was also apparent, suggesting a very negative sort of spillover effect from therapy to play sessions. Surprisingly, the staff therapists themselves demonstrated significant downward changes in affective expression. The authors wrote, "Our anticipation that mothers might become more like therapists as a result of opportunities to model their behavior was not well-supported. Instead, the therapists became more like the mothers" (Kogan *et al.,* 1974, p. 523).

On a somewhat happier note, in a third study (Tyler & Kogan, 1977) an 8-week intervention procedure was partially, though not entirely successful in reducing stressful and conflicted interactions. Ironically, an intervention was required by the same profession that was very likely responsible for the negative findings in the first place by recommending that mothers should provide physical therapy in this way to their own children; yet, of course, this is very similar to what special educators do. This series of studies represents a profound contribution and cannot be dismissed as only applying to physical therapy without calling into question many special education efforts to involve parents in other types of training with their own children.

Wedell-Monnig and Lumley (1980), for example, found that deaf infants and toddlers were also more passive and less involved in interactions than their hearing peers. Mothers of deaf infants were also more dominant in interaction with their children than mothers of hearing infants. Over time, the mothers directed fewer and fewer behaviors toward their deaf infants. Perhaps most disturbingly, while hearing infants and their mothers were somewhat less involved when the infants were younger and more involved over time, the deaf infants and their mothers were less and less involved as time went on. Far more research with different populations is urgently needed, but until more data exist, there certainly are compelling reasons to be cautious.

Barnard (1980) has written of a "super-parent burnout" sequence in which the parent works extremely hard in the early months trying to compensate for the child's handicap through levels of effort "far beyond the endurance of parents of normal children" (p. 90). Such parents were typically burned out before the child's first birthday.

Bonding Risk and Infant Day Care

What happens to attachment patterns when special needs infants go to day care? It is not really known. There is evidence that infant day care does not seem to jeopardize the primary parent–infant attachment with disadvantaged infants (Caldwell *et al.,* 1970). In this study, however, no infant under 6 months of age was in the program; in fact, most were closer to 1 year of age when they began. Perhaps they had had time to develop that important first relationship. Might some special needs infants require even more time to develop their first attachment? Is it more difficult for special needs infants with some handicaps to form such attachments than for others? Are special needs infants able to develop multiple attachments as easily as normal infants?

The only additional data on this point are also from a study of disadvantaged infants (or infants at high risk for developmental retardation) from the Frank Porter Graham Center in North Carolina. Mills (1978) studied the effects of early day care intervention on the parent–infant relationship. Her data indicate that quality of interaction, rather than quantity, seems to be most important for the developing relationship between infant and parent. Is this likely to be true for all types of handicapped infants? How might special education efforts assist in enhancing the quality of these parent–infant interactions? Much more research is needed to guide future intervention efforts.

Bonding Risk and Parental Assumptions

Sometimes it may not be the handicap itself, but rather the meaning of the handicap, that produces difficulty in establishing a normal attachment. If, for example, the parents assume that the handicap is punishment for some wrongdoing of their past, feelings of anger or resentment may be transferred to the infant. Such beliefs may sometimes persist despite objective medical explanations to the contrary (Crocker & Crocker, 1970).

In fact, most expectant mothers worry at some point about the possibility of giving birth to a handicapped child. It is just not possible for them to hear all the warnings about what they should and should not do during pregnancy without considering what might happen if they slip up. The message our society gives to pregnant women is that if they do all the right things, the baby will be fine (Apgar & Beck, 1972; D. W. Smith, 1979). The converse, of course, while rarely stated, is certainly implied. It is not difficult to understand some of the origins of the deep guilt feelings often experienced by such mothers and their intense need to know what caused the handicap. Such feelings of guilt or self-blame can seriously interfere with the development of an attachment for the baby.

In our society, adults (especially mothers) are also expected to "know" automatically (without any specific training) how to be good parents. To this end, they are expected to draw largely from their childhood memories of being parented and to take the rest of their cues from the infant. This system breaks down dramatically in the case of a handicapped baby. T. M. Field (1980) found that mothers who try unusually hard to elicit responses from unresponsive infants may inadvertently overstimulate them, causing gaze aversion. The infant's gaze aversion unfortunately tends to increase the parent's efforts to elicit a response from their infant. Thomas, Becker, and Freese (1978) described an example of one infant who slept (REM sleep) with his eyes wide open, leaving his mother understandably confused about whether he was awake or asleep.

When parents do not automatically know what their baby needs or wants, they may doubt their own adequacy as parents. Special educators must find a way to assure these parents that *no one could reasonably expect them to know precisely how to parent a baby with such divergencies.* Special educators need to help them understand that their baby may not be sending out the same cues as most normal babies do. Eventually they can be helped to see the ways in which they can treat this baby as any other, and the ways in which special techniques (that they could not have known automatically) may be helpful. It may also be necessary to go beyond interpreting interactional patterns involving handicapped infants as either "normal" or "abnormal" and to consider the possibility that certain "abnormal" interactional patterns may well be "normal" for this particular population and circumstance, and to use this information clinically to support parents through such experiences (Goldberg & DiVitto, 1983; Hanson, 1982).

Telling parents their baby's progress was due to their own good work may sound like a good thing to say. But what is the converse? If the baby does not do well, is that then the parent's fault? Well-meaning clinicians may inadvertently perpetuate potential psychological double binds.

Prematurity as a Factor in Bonding Risk

For many parents, psychological preparation for the birth of a child may have involved years of childhood and adolescent fantasies about being a parent and having a family. During the period of pregnancy, such preparation becomes greatly intensified, and every passing month is important in the time it gives for individual and family adjustment and reorganization. In the case of prematurity, however, this important period of preparation is abruptly interrupted.

Not only is the timing of the birth unexpected, but the baby will look very different from the "Gerber baby image" that Barnard has noted parents often anticipate (cited in Klaus & Kennell, 1976). On top of all this, their baby is likely to be whisked away" (Kennell & Klause, 1971) to a neonatal intensive care unit, meaning parents and baby will be separated from the beginning. In addition, the initial care of their infant may need to proceed very differently than the parents are likely to have expected (Iyer, 1981). Prematurity, then, even without other complications, can be a highly disruptive factor for the normal, early development of attachment patterns.

Even mothers of otherwise normal infants often express a deep sense of failure at having prematurely produced such a small, frail baby. Upon seeing her baby in an intensive care unit, the mother may experience additional guilt because of her inability to care for her baby as competently as the nurses in the unit. One mother expressed it this way: "I felt very helpless. It was like you go and visit this baby, and the're taking care of her ... they did most everything for her. It was like their baby" (Klaus & Kennell, 1976, p. 145).

Parents of premature infants may still feel uncomfortable about their ability to care for their own baby even by the time the baby is discharged from the hospital. On this point, responses of mothers and fathers of premature infants were compared with mothers and fathers of full-term infants (Jeffcoate, Humphrey, & Lloyd, 1979). The findings for the mothers included the startling fact that while 91% of control group of first-time mothers were confident about handling their newborn by the time they took the infant home, only 50% of the first-time mothers of premature infants felt this way (despite the fact that a longer time period had elapsed). Although most of the mothers of full-term infants said they had loved their babies immediately (or within a day), fully half of the mothers of premature infants reported that they had not felt affection for their babies for months.

The findings for the fathers were fascinating too. Control group fathers had visual and tactile contact with their babies significantly later than any of their wives, while premature group fathers viewed, touched, and held their babies no later than the mothers. Postnatal depression was reported for only one control group father, but over half of the premature fathers reported feeling unusually depressed. Nearly half of the premature fathers had coped with far more housework and baby care than they had anticipated while no control group father reported any "undue involvement."

Neonatal Critical Illness
and Developmental Ambiguities as Risk Factors

In addition to the special risk factors associated with handicapping conditions and prematurity, some special needs infants may suffer serious illnesses in the neonatal period. Such circumstances pose additional and distinctive threats to the normal parental formation of a loving relationship with their newborn infant. Perhaps most salient of these is the phenomenon known as "anticipatory grief" (Kaplan & Mason, 1960). In anticipation of the possible death of their baby, parents actively (and often consciously) withhold their feelings and attachment so as to protect themselves from a more severe blow should the infant die.

While this may at first sound adaptive, it only works in theory. In fact, the bonds of attachment often begin long before birth, frequently accelerating dramatically with quickening or the first felt movement of the fetus (Klaus & Kennell, 1976). Even when the infant does die, many parents who have held and spoken to their babies treasure these memories, while many who "kept their distance" report that they regret having done so. Most importantly, there is evidence that if the infant does live, parents who have gone through a period of "anticipatory grief" report unusual difficulty in turning that around to develop a normal attachment (Klaus & Kennell, 1976).

In a fascinating study, data were reported comparing what pediatricians say to mothers of newborns who are ill, how the mothers interpret what they say, and what the actual mortality statistics are (Clyman, Sniderman, Ballard, & Roth, 1979). It was found that nearly all the physicians significantly underestimated the infant's actual chances of survival, even to the point of making predictions poorer than statistics from their own hospitals on the survival rate for such infants. To compound the problem, house officers (medical residents and interns) gave even more dire predictions than neonatologists. Finally, in most instances the mother "heard" an even lower chance of survival than the physician had meant to convey. *In every single instance, the mother's expectations for the infant's survival were less than the actual expectations based on statistics from that hospital.* It seems likely from these data that a greater number of anticipatory grief reactions are stimulated in these hospitals than might be the case if more accurate mortality information could somehow be conveyed.

It may also be interesting to consider these data in light of a common clinical observation: the "he'll grow out of it" or "she looks normal to me" pediatric statements to parents that early childhood special educators speak of so disparingly as they mourn the consequent delay of much-needed early intervention and the building of false hopes in the parents they serve. Is it the case that pediatricians are both unrealistically pessimistic about the outcome of neonatal problems but unrealistically optimistic about the outcome of potential problems in older infants and toddlers? Or might it be the case that pediatricians are unrealistically pessimistic about the outcomes of physiological problems and unrealistically optimistic about the outcomes of developmental problems? Another possibility that must be considered is that pediatricians are simply not knowledgeable about early normal developmental milestones, and therefore tend to make honest errors in their assessment of early developmental status. It may be that errors in both directions at the extremes simply indicate inadequate training in either development or prediction. It may also be the case that pediatricians, house officers, and neonatologists do not themselves believe the predictions they share with parents, but are operating on incorrect assumptions about the best way to prepare such parents psychologically for the possibility of unfavorable outcomes. On the other hand, early childhood special educators in the field still report an unfortunate number of "he'll never walk," "she'll never talk," "institutionalize him and forget you ever saw him" pediatric recommendations to parents. Such statements often appear to err in the direction of unrealistically pessimistic predictions of developmental outcomes.

It may be that the failure to acknowledge observed developmental abnormalities is based on inadequate knowledge of the effects of early intervention on subsequent developmental status or inadequate knowledge of local special education resources to whom such cases could reliably be referred. But it may also be the case that pediatricians feel the best thing they can do to facilitate the bonding process and/or the child's development is to encourage the parent to see the child as normal, on the assumption that they will then treat him or her as normal; this, in turn, may help the child to develop normally. While there may be some truth mixed into this thread of assumptions, some considerations have received insufficient attention. What, for example, is the effect on the parent–child relationship if months pass in which the parent believes the child to be normal before the parent must face the "new" information that the child is not, after all, "normal"? More important, how do parents who suspect abnormality, but who are told they are incorrect in that assessment, consequently feel about their own adequacy as parents? Perhaps most seriously, how does such a parent then interpret the strange behavior of an infant he or she has been told is "normal"?

Sometimes the incorrect information given to parents about their babies errs in the opposite direction. Strauss, Utley, & Biglan (1982), noting that up to 90% of the severely handicapped have visual impairments, experimented with several new methodologies for assessing visual acuity in severely handicapped infants. Their research uncovered the startling fact that many infants previously diagnosed as blind (using traditional methodologies) were, in fact, able to see. Some had vision the authors described as "relatively normal." One wonders what changes in care giving patterns and intervention approaches might result from such a marked shift in assessment results and how much damage may have been done through the care givers believing that these infants were blind.

If special educators are to enhance their working relationships with the medical community, it is imperative to embark on systematic studies of the phenomena that have been described above so they can begin to understand what is actually happening. These are problems that teachers in the field of special education have long struggled with clinically, and yet the literature yields surprising little systematic investigation of these topics.

Surely special educators have the motivation to pursue these issues. Researchers must be responsive to the needs of the severely handicapped infants in their care through programs of systematic investigation that are targeted at understanding the underlying patterns and dynamics of such issues. These programs can be the basis for the development of strategies to address such problems, followed by subsequent vigorous evaluation of the effects of related intervention efforts.

Minimizing Bonding Risks: Innovative Approaches
from the Medical Community

Much as special educators might prefer to believe it, they are not always the first providers of early intervention for special needs infants and their families (Miller, 1978). Many hospitals have developed innovative programs and policies designed to facilitate the early bonding process in high-risk cases (Dickson, 1981; Dillard, Auerbach, & Showalter, 1980; Hawkins-Walsh, 1980; Noble & Hamilton, 1981; Schraeder, 1980; Valentin, 1981).

At one New York hospital, for example, a photograph is taken of any newborn about to be transferred to another hospital's intensive care center (Kopelman, Simeonsson, Smaldone, & Gilbert, 1978). This photograph is presented to the mother at the time of transfer, and, according to the mothers themselves, the photos "helped them feel closer to their infants" (pp. 15–16). Four out of five mothers surveyed (only the first five mothers were surveyed) reported looking at the photo for 5 hours per day or more! The lasting effects of the photo idea on parental attachment has also been studied by Kopelman et al. Since it is also known that mothers who are told about a handicap before they have seen their infant generally imagine that it looks much worse than it actually does (Klaus & Kennell, 1976), it might be particularly interesting to try this technique specifically with parents of special needs infants who cannot (for whatever reasons) see their infant immediately.

A nurse has written of the extended telephone support given to a mother who had been separated from her newborn due to the baby's transfer to a regional neonatal high-risk center (Penfold, 1974). Regular observations were shared with the mother, and the mother was able to feel that she was a part of her son's care. Penfold wrote:

> As I described David's responses during eating, being put to sleep, and during comforting, she [the mother] drew from her two isolated experiences of holding him to give me further suggestions: "If you just stroke his leg or rub him he settles down". Her sharing observations of David's responses helped me know how she might mother him at home. Knowing this, I patterned my care measure similarly. (p. 465)

More recently, fathers have been actively involved by hospitals in the "acquaintance process" in an attempt to promote family-oriented care in the special care nursery. Hospital staff are encouraged to remember that many fathers are anxious to touch or cuddle their infants, but are often too embarrassed to suggest it. This approach provides both parents with the same specialized, personal care as the high-risk newborn.

In Illinois, a discharge planning tool has been developed for use with families of high-risk infants (Cagan & Meier, 1979). This assessment allows the nurse to go over all aspects of the baby's home care with the parents systematically and to make observations relevant to the decision that mother and baby are (or are not) ready to go home, based on more than medical data. A copy of this assessment is sent to the agency following the infant and family after discharge (such as an infant program).

Another available tool for assessing high-risk early relationships is the Neonatal Perception Inventory (NPI) (Broussard & Hartner, 1970).[1] By

---

[1] The Neonatal Perception Inventory can be obtained from Dr. Elsie R. Broussard, University of Pittsburgh, Graduate School of Public Health, Pittsburgh, PA 15261.

comparing the parents' perception of the average baby's behaviors with their perception of their own baby's behavior, some indication is given of which parent–infant triads may be at high or low risk for attachment. The Degree of Bother Inventory, also a part of the NPI, can be another very telling indicator that a family or infant warrants further observation (M. L. Erickson, 1976).

Still another interesting idea is the development of a booklet for parents of an infant in a newborn intensive care unit (NICU). The booklet, entitled "A Sign of Hope," introduces parents to the NICU through supportive wording and gentle drawings of what they are likely to see when they visit their baby. The entire text of the booklet and several of the drawings appear in the article describing its usage (Whaley, Gosling, & Schreiner, 1979). In the same article another good idea is described: the "parent care pavilion," a nursing care area designed to include mother and father in their baby's care for a few days prior to going home.

In various modern hospital settings, other helpful techniques are being used to facilitate the most optimal parent–infant relationship: (1) parents may be told about the initial diagnosis together to facilitate coping and to assure that one does not have the onerous task of telling the other; (2) parents may be shown the infant as early as possible, either at the time of birth or, if necessary, in an isolette, (3) any coverings on the infant's eyes may be removed for a few minutes as the parents first try to make contact with their baby; (4) increased opportunities may be provided for handling the baby in the delivery room or isolette; (5) training may be provided by nurses in special handling or feeding techniques that may facilitate the establishment of a closer, warmer relationship; (6) old-fashioned "active listening" may be practiced so that parents' concerns can be heard and supported (Gordon, 1970; Lichter, 1976); (7) parents may be put in touch with parent-to-parent programs (with other parents of infants with respiratory problems, cardiac problems, prematurity, terminal illness, or handicaps); (8) parents may be educated about community resources available to them for follow-up care after leaving the hospital; and (9) regular phone calls may be made to follow up after the parents take the baby home and to ascertain that everything is going well.

Two contrasting models of the parent-to-parent program idea for families of high-risk newborns have been described (Erdman, 1977; Mangurten, Slade, & Fitzsimons, 1979). One such program uses the concept of a "veteran mother" who has been through a similar crisis period with her own child and can now reach out to support a new parent under similar circumstances (Mangurten et al., 1979). Another such program has group meetings wherein the parent-to-parent support comes from other mothers currently going through similar circumstances (Erdman, 1977). These programs are similar in some ways to such programs in the special education field but are available to parents whose infants may have a wider range of high-risk conditions (such as prematurity and illness).

Menolascino and Coleman (1980) have provided a well-differentiated description of their Pilot Parent Program in Omaha, Nebraska, which matches "older" parents of developmentally disabled children with new parents of such infants on 11 criteria, including such sample items as specific handicapping condition, family structure similarities, and parental educational level. Prospective pilot parents are given a formal screening inventory and participate in six weekly 3-hour training sessions. Over 500 families (including single parents) have been served by this program.

Reflections on Parent Involvement

Most current programs make special efforts to involve parents. The prevailing assumption regarding parent involvement in special education seems to have been "the more, the better." There are journal articles offering 50 innovative ways of increasing parent involvement and books describing 101 ways to teach parents to be behavioral scientists. There are very few special education articles on decreasing parent involvement or encouraging parents to be less systematic and behavioral in their interactions with children. Yet most early intervention clinicians have seen many instances of parents' overinvolvement to the extent of risking marriage, mental health, and normal outside social contact. The concept of burnout may well need to be explored as it relates to parents of severely handicapped infants (Hagen, 1981). What relationship is there between extensive parental involvement in the early years and age of institutionalization at a later date? At what point should clinicians consider "giving parents permission" to have some time for themselves, their marriage, their other children, or their friends? Is there a point of no return beyond which additional hours of parental intervention with a severely handicapped infant will not yield enough developmental gain to be worth the level of sacrifice the family has offered in order to facilitate this child's developmental progress? How can training programs address such issues in the future?

In their zealous efforts at bringing all possible forces to bear in accelerating the motoric, cognitive, communicative, and social development of special needs infants, special educators may be losing sight of some very fundamental issues in working with parents. We consider next several such issues and various possibilities of responding with sensitivity to the needs of both fathers and mothers involved in very special parenting.

Parent Involvement as a Means to an End

Many infant programs may try to involve parents primarily as a means to an end—on the assumption that the child will benefit if the parents are involved with the program. Certainly there is a research base for such a strategy (Bronfenbrenner, 1975). But there are only the roughest of guidelines for what type of involvement and how much involvement will result in what sort of developmental progress. Further, it is not known how much findings from work with parents of one infant population can be generalized to another. For example, are research findings with parents of disadvantaged or high-risk infants (e.g., Ramey and Smith, 1976; Ramey & Trohanis, 1982) applicable to parents of infants with Down's syndrome (Hanson & Schwarz, 1978)? Are research findings with parents of infants with Down's syndrome applicable to parents of more severely handicapped infants? It should be noted that some special education infant populations may change over time. With the advent of exemplary early intervention programs for infants with Down's syndrome (Hayden & Haring, 1976), for example, many professionals are no longer routinely considering these infants to be part of the group typically considered severely handicapped.

There is, in fact, documentation (Kogan *et al.*, 1974) of certain negative effects of parent involvement on the infant, on the parent, and on the parent–infant relationship. At what point does encouragement to take on a teacher or therapist role inadvertently risk supplanting the fragile, newly developing parent role, and what may be the ultimate effect of such supplanting on the infant? The special educator's responsibility in giving full weight to these matters cannot be taken lightly. Perhaps most importantly, researchers and clinicians have tended to evaluate only half of the equation: the effects of parent involvement on the infant. Special education research has fallen short in evaluating the effects of such involvement on the parents themselves and on their immediate and extended families.

As part of the research for the *Young & Special* teacher training series in early intervention (Kaiser, 1982), a parent support group for parents of special needs infants was observed. Their children were part of an excellent combination home- and center-based infant program with a good deal of goal-directed activity as well as multiple play groups including siblings, activities for fathers, and a generally broad range of options for parental involvement. Because the atmosphere in this support group was truly open and accepting, several of the parents were able to discuss an issue close to their hearts: parenting time.

Several of the mothers had infants who did not have many "good hours" during the day; one said that her infant was not very likely to have more than one. While there might be other brief "alert, quiet, happy" times, these were very likely to be quickly consumed by the practical need to perform a medically related procedure, clean up an unexpected vomit, or pick up another child from day care.

When faced with the "one good hour" problem, these mothers expressed great conflict. On the one hand, they felt they "should" grab their infant quickly and use that time "to good advantage" by working with him or her on several of the "objectives" set by the project staff. This, however, was clearly described as "work". The mothers' anxiety about accelerating their infant's development and concerns for the future were always somewhat rekindled during such "work" periods.

These mothers often expressed a desire to enjoy their babies through unstructured cuddling and playing. Perhaps this is not as selfish as it might seem. We do not know that learning to roll over several months earlier will be of greater long-term benefit for the infant than a warm and loving relationship with the primary care giver. The parent who first articulated the one good hour phenomenon had a severely multiply handicapped infant who, although not in any known life-threatening danger at the time, died 4 weeks later. Our hope is that the mother gave herself permission to spend some cuddling time and that she was supported by caring professionals who understood her needs and considered that her infant might also have needs that did not appear on the developmental checklists.

Special educators need answers to many questions about parental involvement. What, indeed, does it mean to be the parent of a severely handicapped infant? What commonalities do such parents share with all new parents? What features of this experience are so unique as to thrust such parents into a category that shuts them, as well as their child, out of the mainstream of our society (Blacher & Turnbull, 1983)? Given the realistic prognosis for their infant, is the acceleration of specific developmental milestones of primary importance? How do the individual values of each family interface with societal values for such children and with the values of special infant teachers and therapists? Should parents be supported in the goal of making the infant easier to care for? Under what conditions should keeping the child at home become a cen-

tral program goal? What are the "acceptable" costs to the families of
these children? How can parents be helped to make psychological shifts
in their expectations, not only for their child, but for themselves as
parents of this infant? What are the salient features of the parental role
with a severely handicapped infant? What has been learned from the ar-
ticulate and beautifully documented experiences of families who have
shared feelings, thoughts, and harried sequences of life events that most
professionals could not imagine living through (Featherstone, 1980;
Kupfer, 1982)? How have we changed our clinical practices based on
such important feedback? How can programs adequately accommodate
the wide disparities between the experience of one parent whose severely handicapped infant screams all day and is rigid to the touch, and
the experiences of another whose baby lies listless and quiet for endless
hours, not even signifying hunger or pain? Given the rate of expected developmental progress of such infants, how can we support the parents'
abilities to see and rejoice in the small gains? Are there some parents for
whom this may be an unrealistic or inadviseable goal? How can clinicians differentiate such issues? Some severely handicapped infants,
through no fault of the intervention program, may regress (e.g., as a
result of seizure activity or progressive conditions). Does a case of continued regression call for differential levels or types of parent involvement? What support can be offered to teachers and therapists working
with regressing infants? Data on effective models and strategies for such
situations are needed.

   Blackard and Barsh (1982) compared parental and professional perceptions of the impact of a severely handicapped child on the family.
The parents had severely handicapped children aged 3–18 years, and
the professionals were a multidisciplinary group, all of whom worked
with severely handicapped children (not the same children, however).
Professionals were found to magnify the impact of the handicapped
child on every aspect of family functioning in the questionnaire. Professionals tended to underestimate the home teaching and behavior management abilities of these parents, while parents rated themselves
relatively strongly in these areas. The authors advised that there may
have been methodological problems in this study so the results should be
read with some caution. It may be important, however, to consider that
while it may be the case that professionals have sometimes underestimated the potential impact of a severely handicapped child on the family, it is also possible to overestimate this impact. Data are needed on the
differential effects of such professional perceptions and how such questionnaire data compare with more behavioral measures.

Accommodating the Disparities
in Parental Experience

Some infant programs take the position that their program is really mostly for the parents: The child may benefit indirectly if the parents are well supported. But how much is really known about what types of parental support make the greatest short- or long-term difference? What criteria have been established to determine "success" in working with parents? Perhaps on this topic more has been learned in our direct service to infants than has been applied to work with their parents. For example, one does not intervene with an infant before completing a thorough assessment of current status and needs, but many programs begin their intervention with parents on far less systematic preparation. Similarly, one does not accept as a sole criterion for evaluating work with an infant his or her apparent happiness in the program, yet many programs evaluate their work with parents exclusively through measures of their satisfaction. As noted earlier, R. Bromwich (1981) has provided a beautifully differentiated clinical model for working with parents and infants. Data are needed, however, on the extent to which such models can be operationalized for research purposes (D. Bricker, personal communication, 1981).

Finally, as the clinician explains a program, he or she may say, "All of our parents go through a group training sequence" or ". . . work with their infants one hour a day" or ". . . attend a weekly support group." A special education program might never consider putting all infants through the same intervention program regardless of where they were developmentally, but that is exactly what many programs do to parents.

Disparities between the Experiences
of Parents and Clinicians

Early childhood special educators often love their field and find it gratifying to offer support at a particularly difficult period in the parents' lives—at a time when no other support may be available. It can be thrilling to look at a young infant, regardless of his or her special needs, as a new beginning. Teachers and therapists are often filled with extreme optimism and the hope that, with a given baby, they will surely find the key—the baby seems to be a virtual bundle of unlimited potential. The infant may be a puzzle, but many clinicians are very challenged by such puzzles.

But many teachers and therapists forget that while they chose this type of work, the parent did not. The summer the baby is 3, their work may be over with this child, and they can start fresh with a new baby and more high hopes. For the parent, however, it may be only the end of the first chapter in a very long required reading.

Further, that baby is not a bundle of unlimited potential, much as special educators might wish to believe this. What research has been initiated to monitor the attitudes and stages of acceptance and adaptation evidenced by teachers and therapists? It may not only be parents who need to be studied along these dimensions. There are also overprotective infant teachers and teachers who do not appear to accept fully the severity of an infant's condition. Even in cases of shortened life expectancy, there is often an avoidance of the prognostic realities in program planning. Special educators may need to become more introspective and to be sure their own professional house is in order before embarking on the heady excursion of counseling such families.

Most special educators would object if their program allowed them to spend only 1 year teaching children of each age, so that with each passing year they would be working with progressively older children (the same ones) and by the end of their careers they would be working exclusively with older adults. This analogy between a teacher's situation and that of the parent of a handicapped infant is not exact; after all, teachers get nights and weekends off and, of course, also get paid. Viewing an infant program as a potential first step in long-term management (particularly for the more severely involved infants) is critical if teachers are to provide a strong foundation on which the parents can build future management.

Consider another analogy: that of a couple who, after years of planning and saving, finally are able to purchase their dream house. But when the papers have been signed, they find out a lot they hadn't expected about its condition. There are extremely serious problems involved. Then two utterly implausible things happen: They are told they must live in this house forever and that hiring people to work on the problems (despite the added financial burden) is not enough. They must learn construction, plumbing, carpentry, and electrical work, and participate actively and daily in such efforts. Since the wife first signed the paper, it is the wife who is expected to manage these tasks—the husband is not expected to be very much involved. No matter that she already has a full-time career, two children, and no inclinations whatever in the areas of plumbing, construction, and so forth. Perhaps the analogy is not too far-fetched. There may be serious flaws in the theory that inside every mother is an enthusiastic therapist with time on her hands.

There are many unanswered questions regarding long-term management. What are its salient features? What can be learned in this regard from the experiences of families with older severely handicapped children? Should there be program differences for infants with shortened life expectancies? Should there be differences in the programs designed for the parents of such infants? Is small group home care an acceptable goal for these children? At what age would such a placement be anticipated? What role should teachers and therapists have in advising parents about residential placement options? In our common professional outrage and condemnation of the history of abuses in larger institutions, have value judgments about the potential value of any residential care in any situation inadvertently been made (Kupfer, 1982)? How are our training programs addressing questions of values clarification and ethical issues resolution for new teachers and therapists (Koop, 1976)? What can be learned from other disciplines in these areas, and how can new research be initiated to further guide efforts specific to this population (Grollman, 1980)? What must be known to train teachers and therapists to set developmental priorities based on a long-term management view? What differences might be expected in a program of intervention developed within a long-range management context? Such a knowledge base must be developed and various training models compared to help attain this important objective.

Where are the curricula for severely handicapped infants? The materials currently used with these infants may reflect a failure to acknowledge the long-term management picture. Published curricula (or criterion-referenced instruments in use as curricula) may have been originally designed for use with handicapped infants, but many of these were either designed for substantially higher-functioning infants or profess to be applicable to an unrealistically wide population range. The Vulpe Assessment Battery (Vulpe, 1977), for example, has the sometimes sought-after advantage of an unusually fine breakdown of skills into miniscule component parts and, in addition is designed to be used as a curriculum guide through its criterion-referenced format. The population for which it was intended, however, is described in the introduction (p. v) as "all children with atypical development" (between the ages of birth and five).

Another criterion-referenced tool is the Learning Accomplishment Profile for Infants (Griffin & Sanford, 1975), which designates its population equally broadly as "the handicapped infant." The *Portage Guide to Early Education* (Shearer, Billingsley, Frohman, Hilliard, Johnson, & Shearer, 1976) makes an even broader claim to be appropriate for "children, either handicapped or normal between the mental ages of birth to five years" (p. 1). A guide to early childhood curriculum materials compiled by Technical Assistance Development Systems (TADS) (Mears, 1975) listed only 5 infant curricula, none of which was specifically designed for severely handicapped infants. Another TADS publication dedicated entirely to handicapped infants (Goin, 1975) uncovered 33 infant curricula, but unfortunately none of these was indicated as designed for or particularly appropriate to the severely handicapped either. Bailey, Jens, and Johnson (1983) contributed an important and comprehensive study of curricula for handicapped infants in which 15 infant curricula that met certain specified basic criteria for comparability were thoroughly analyzed. Only 2 curricula were found to provide specific suggestions for adapting or modifying activities for infants with sensory or motor impairment, and only 2 (not the same ones) provided any empirical data on the effectiveness of the intervention strategies recommended in the curricula. This study is highly recommended reading for a thorough analysis of this important area.

Clinicians working with the severely handicapped tend to seek out the curriculum with the smallest steps, which may be an adaptive coping mechanism for the short term. But it must be asked where all these tiny steps are leading. Following some of them far enough reveals that they culminate in a prereading skill or basic mathematical competence. If these end goals are systematically selected for a given child, this may be acceptable. What is not at all acceptable is the reality in many programs that the end goals have not been adequately analyzed in light of the clinical population. Similarly, as noted by Bailey et al. (1983), inordinately detailed curricula can also result in wasting valuable time training items that may be of dubious relevance to the child's eventual developmental outcome. Empirical data on the effectiveness of specific published infant curricula with severely handicapped infants are needed. In an effort to avoid limiting the potential of any young child through self-fulfilling prophesies (Rosenthal & Jacobson, 1968), special educators may have erred in the opposite direction. By so doing they may have failed to support the infants' actual potential in the most efficient manner. Perhaps more seriously, if special educators fail to comprehend the larger picture, they have little hope of helping the parents to see it.

Bailey et al.'s (1983) analysis of comparable infant curricula addressing multiple domains has laid an important foundation for the field; however, it might also be useful to study existing single-domain curricula (e.g., language development programs), as many clinicians do tend to pull from several sources in putting together a program for a given child. Comparability issues might only need to function within and not across domains in such a case. Similarly, curricula for specific subgroups of the severely handicapped infant population (e.g., deaf infants) might be compared within handicap categories and tested for applicability with various combinations of multiple handicaps at the infant level. In other words, until innovative new materials are developed, data offering a better understanding of how to use the existing curricula would be clinically beneficial.

The evaluation of programs for severely handicapped infants and their families must begin to consider cost-effectiveness data collection in light of the current economy and the growing need for social programs to demonstrate such accountability in order to sustain their own existence. While there have been limited studies of cost-effectiveness in which infant intervention programs have been summed and considered to represent a single type of program (Garland, Stone, Swanson, & Woodruff, 1981) and cost-effectiveness studies that consider the case of high-risk infants and families separately (Greenspan, 1983), documentation of the specific figures applicable to programs for severely handicapped infants and their families is still needed. It could be argued that these programs, even more than others in the field of early intervention, have the greatest need to present such data because of the relatively low probability of resultant high percentages of self-supporting adults that may eventually be expected to emerge from these infant programs in the long term. In planning such evaluation studies, relative cost-effectiveness in a greater range of situations than simply intervention versus nonintervention must be considered. Also, the cost-effectiveness of various models of infant and/or infant–parent intervention with the severely handicapped, as well as intervention with various subpopulations of severely handicapped infants and/or their parents, must be taken into account.

Inequalities in the Parent–Clinician Team

A collective consciousness in special education has been raised about the parent–professional partnership and the importance of considering the parent as an equal and full-fledged team member. But related questions arise. In how many programs is it really more the case that parents assist the clinician with the child's program, rather than the converse? Is as much time truly spent in helping the parent in home management techniques as in working to bring classroom activities into the home? Are information and advice from parents solicited as regularly as progress reports and data sheets? Is the parent consulted on the preferred extent of her or his own involvement in a value-free manner?

Is as great an appreciation communicated for the unique perspective and content that the parent can contribute as is communicated for other team members?

Sometimes, when parent involvement is minimal, teachers may feel they have failed. They may feel resentful and that they have kept up their end of the partnership. They may feel that all they seem to be doing, from the parents' perspective, is providing respite care. But even if that were true, perhaps it is not such a small contribution; it may be one way of first meeting the parents' needs so that they, in turn, can become strong enough, through this support, to begin reaching out to their infant (Warren & Dickman, 1981). In fact, this need for respite does not seem to diminish. In one ongoing longitudinal study of the effect of school services for young severely handicapped children on the family (Meyers & Blacher, 1982) families continued to highlight the value of the preschool or school program as respite. The bottom line is that few special education teachers can say they really understand what it is like to be the parent of a special needs infant. Although they may try hard to understand, they have not generally experienced the 24-hour-a-day, 7-day-a-week, lifetime-of-work-ahead-of-them reality.

Clinicians and Physicians

Hospitals and doctors' offices are a primary target for the complaints of many parents. Perhaps special educators have been guilty of listening a little too sympathetically at times. What is their role in supporting the pediatrician's judgment in the child's medical management? It can be confusing and stressful for parents to hear conflicting medical advice, yet special educators offer still additional points of view. Special educators would never support a parent's complaints about a recommendation made by one of their own team members, yet do not take the same care with the physician who may not be considered a direct member of their team.

Special educators may ask for medical records but may not send copies of the child's progress reports. They want the physician to be available to them, yet may not clearly communicate the ways in which they might make themselves available to him or her. Perhaps a noon-hour presentation could be made to a group of nurses and physicians explaining the infant program and inviting visits. Perhaps a list of parents willing to speak with new parents of handicapped babies could be shared in an effort to begin a parent-to-parent program.

The infant's physician might appreciate behavioral data from the classroom demonstrating the apparent effects of certain medications or dosages on the infant's cognitive or communicative performance. A few research articles on the effectiveness of early intervention (e.g., Kaiser & Hayden, 1977) might be helpful additions to the pediatrics department library. The physician could offer patients flyers or brochures on the program. In the concern with a seeming lack of understanding about institutionalization and ethical treatment issues, efforts must be made to evaluate the effects of offering current information on the long-term functional prognosis for various handicaps before an emotionally charged issue comes up regarding a specific child (Ackerman, 1980; Fost, 1981). Special educators must determine what actions can be taken to assure and to evaluate continuity of care, greater understanding, and increased collaboration between education and medicine, for the best interests of parent and child.

Still another way to narrow the communications gap between medicine and special education may lie in the latter's training programs. Graduate students in early childhood special education at Wichita State University, for example, must have a minimum of three semesters of practicum experience, many of which actually represent double and triple placements, providing experiences in the widest possible range of early intervention settings. In addition to spending time in traditional home and center-based infant intervention programs, however, these students also venture into the medical community, bringing their expertise and in the process "selling" their discipline (as they provide free service) to professionals who may be somewhat unsure as to what an early childhood special educator knows or can do in a medical setting. Graduate students' placements include neonatal intensive care nurseries, pediatric intensive care, hospital-based therapeutic nurseries, child protective services placements, and a Ronald McDonald House for families of terminally ill children. In addition to the usual program placements, students routinely apprentice themselves to a person from another discipline (e.g., an occupational or physical therapist, an itinerant teacher for blind infants, or an audiologist). By working with these professionals throughout their day, communication lines are gradually built across disciplines to the ultimate benefit of the families we serve. Data are needed on the effects of such strategies in increasing levels of confidence across disciplines as evidenced by more ready referrals and consultation requests, particularly from the medical to the special education community, but ultimately in both directions.

Occupational and physical therapists and speech–language pathologists in Kansas hospitals have complained (to the first author) that pediatricians do not refer even the most severely handicapped infants to the hospital therapists. The pediatricians, they explain, may see no reason to refer an infant to speech therapy if the child is not even talking yet, to physical therapy if the child is not even walking yet, or to occupational therapy before the child is looking for a job. (They also complain that in the case of the few infants they *do* get as referrals, and with whom they experience some hard-won success, they are then likely to be told by the insurance company that the same child doesn't need speech therapy "because he can talk" nor physical therapy "because he can walk.")

It is easy to be lulled by reading state-of-the-art innovations and assuming them to be representative of actual service delivery levels. The implementation of innovations must be studied with the same scholarly fervor as has been reserved for attempts to move the field of special education ahead with still another creative idea. It has been estimated (M. Mueller, personal communication, 1982) that the average time lapse between innovation and general field usage is 20 years. The families we serve cannot wait that long. The gap between the current knowledge base and current delivery systems must be narrowed.

Closing Thoughts for a New Beginning

The field of infant intervention becomes increasingly interesting and exciting with time and with the influx of new data. As there is more to know, so there is also much more that can be done to help. It is our privilege and responsibility to welcome this progress and rise to this challenge.

Parent involvement must be seen as more than a means to an end. In order to do this, special educators must have the freedom to judge the success of their intervention programs by a wider range of criteria than has previously been accepted. Our enthusiasm at the documentation of long-term positive developmental results of early intervention programs (Lazar, 1979; Lazar & Darlington, 1979) should not result in complacence. If there is still greater benefit to be known, researchers and clinicians must strive together for that greater benefit. If there are potential negative side effects associated with otherwise successful intervention efforts, we must be willing to reconsider those current practices that may be under question in light of the new data.

Special educators must move away from a uniform theory of parent support and training; most have had little formal preparation in the complex area of supporting adults through any sort of psychological stress. Special education training programs must begin to address these areas in the future preparation of infant interventionists. Learning how to train parents may not be enough.

Special educators must appreciate that parenting can be every bit as important and helpful a thing to do as teaching or therapy. The parent role must not be inadvertently disparaged on the basis of its departure from standard professional trappings. A parent's effectiveness must not only be judged through criteria measuring his or her successive approximations to professional therapists and teachers in providing treatment.

Our understanding of the complex bonding phenomenon between infants with special needs and their care givers is still incomplete. Does bonding develop differently in the case of a handicapped baby? Are some handicapped babies at greater bonding risk than others? Does this bonding risk translate into a developmental risk factor that may have been neglected in previous intervention efforts? How does the parent–infant relationship coordinate with the teacher–infant relationship for a special needs baby? What might be the long-term implications of the failure to give our research and clinical attention to these issues?

Continuity is known to be important for infants (Bronfenbrenner, 1975), but there are many implications of the continuity issue for parents that have yet to be explored. How can researchers and clinicians in special education join with other disciplines and programs so that parents of handicapped infants are continuously supported from the time of the infant's birth through enrollment in our infant programs, and eventually in preschool programs, all with very smooth transitions? There will be overlap; contact with the hospital does not end with entrance into an infant program. Preschool entrance should not mean the end of contact with an infant program. More than just "transitions" are needed: Bridges are needed that will stand two-way traffic.

That parents will meet and need to become familiar with a number of professionals may be unavoidable. But at one time it was considered unavoidable for parents to take their children to a number of different people in a number of different programs (with different opinions) to get all the services the child needed. This situation was alleviated by the introduction of the transdisciplinary team with a case manager (Patterson, 1976). As each team member actively trained the others, it was not only the parents who could work primarily through one professional, but also the child. Not only did parent and child benefit, but team members also learned a great deal from one another in a mutually beneficial solution to a very complex problem.

Special educators' success in solving problems of the past should give us confidence and hope that we can also deal successfully with such new problems as have been presented here. In the light of new data, we

must be open to the possibility that our intervention models may need to
be revised in the best interests of those we serve. This does not mean we
were wrong in the past; we proceeded with the best of intentions on the
most current data available. No one could ever ask for more. It is the
responsibility of all special educators to continue that fine tradition and
to meet today's new challenges.

References

Ackerman, T. F. (1980). Meningomyelocele and parental commitment: A policy proposal
    regarding selection for treatment. *Man and Medicine, 5,* 291–310.
Affleck, G., McGrade, B. J., McQueeney, M., & Allen, D. (1982). Relationship-focused early
    intervention in developmental disabilities. *Exceptional Children, 49,* 259–261.
Allen, D. A., Affleck, G., McGrade, B. J., & McQueeney, M. (1983). Characteristics of the
    home observation for measurement of the environment inventory in a sample of
    high-risk/developmentally disabled infants. *Infant Behavior and Development, 6,*
    53–60.
Apgar, V., & Beck, J. (1972). *Is my baby all right?* New York: Simon & Schuster.
Bailey, D. B., Jens, K. G., & Johnson, N. (1983). Curricula for handicapped infants. In S. G.
    Gardwood & R. R. Fewell (Eds.), *Educating handicapped infants.* Rockville, MD:
    Aspen Systems.
Barnard, K. E. (1980). An ecological approach to parent–child relations. In C. C. Brown
    (Ed.), *Infants at risk: Assessment and intervention* (Pediatric Round Table No. 5).
    Piscataway, NJ: Johnson & Johnson Baby Products.
Beckman-Bell, P. (1981). Child-rearing stress in families of handicapped children. *Topics
    in Early Childhood Special Education, 1,* 45–53.
Beckwith, L. (1976). Caregiver-infant interaction and the development of the high risk
    infant. In T. D. Tjossem (Ed.), *Intervention strategies for high risk infants and young
    children.* Baltimore: University Park Press.
Belsky, J. (1978). Three theoretical models of child abuse: A critical review. *International
    Journal of Child Abuse and Neglect, 2,* 37–49.
Berry, P., Gunn, P., & Andrews, R. (1980). Behavior of Down's syndrome infants in a
    strange situation. *American Journal of Mental Deficiency, 85,* 213–218.
Blacher, J., & Meyers, C. E. (1983). A review of attachment formation and disorders of
    handicapped children. *American Journal of Mental Deficiency, 87,* 359–371.
Blacher, J., & Turnbull, A. P. (1983). Are parents mainstreamed? A survey of parent inter-
    actions in the mainstreamed preschool. *Education and Training of the Mentally
    Retarded, 18*(1), 10–16.
Blackard, M. K., & Barsch, E. T. (1982). Parents and professionals perceptions of the handi-
    capped child's impact on the family. *Journal of the Association for the Severely
    Handicapped, 7,* 62–70.
Bowlby, J. (1969). *Attachment and loss* (Vol. 1). New York: Basic Books.
Brazelton, T. B. (1974). Does the neonate shape his environment? In D. Bergsma (Ed.),
    The Infant at Risk. New York: Intercontinental Medical Book Corp.
Bricker, D., & Casuso, V. (1979). Family involvement: A critical component of early inter-
    vention. *Exceptional Children, 46,* 108–116.
Bromwich, R. (1981). *Working with parents and infants: An interactional approach.*
    Baltimore: University Park Press.

Bromwich, R. M. (1976). Focus on maternal behavior in infant intervention. *American Journal of Orthopsychiatry, 46,* 439–446.

Bronfenbrenner, U. (1975). Is early intervention effective? In B. Z. Friedlander, G. M. Sterritt, & G. E. Kirk (Eds.), *Exceptional infant* (Vol. 3). New York: Brunner/Mazel.

Broussard, E. R., & Hartner, M. S. S. (1970). Maternal perception of the neonate as related to development. *Child Psychiatry and Human Development, 1,* 16–25.

Bryant, D., Ramey, C., & Burchinal, M. (1982). Intervention effects on mother-child interactions. *Infant Behavior and Development, 5,* 38. (Special International Conference on Infant Studies issue).

Cagan, J., & Meier, P. (1979). A discharge planning tool for use with families of high-risk infants. *Journal of Obstetric, Gynecologic and Neonatal Nursing, 8,* 146–148.

Caldwell, B. M., Wright, C. M., Honig, A. S., & Tannenbaum, J. (1970). Infant day care and attachment. *American Journal of Orthopsychiatry, 40,* 397–412.

Cicchetti, D., & Serafica, E. C. (1981). Interplay among behavioral systems: Illustrations from the study of attachment, affiliation, and wariness in young children with Down's syndrome. *Developmental Psychology, 17,* 36–49.

Cicchetti, D., & Sroufe, A. (1976). The relationship between affective and cognitive development in Down's syndrome infants. *Child Development, 46,* 920–929.

Clyman, R. I., Sniderman, S. H., Ballard, R. A., & Roth, R. S. (1979). What pediatricians say to mothers of sick newborns: An indirect evaluation of the counseling process. *Pediatrics, 63,* 719–723.

Cohn, Jeffrey F., and Tronick, Edward A. (1982). Communicative rules and the sequential structure of infant behavior during normal and depressed interaction. In E. Z. Tronick (Ed.), *Social interchange in infancy: Affect, cognition, and communication.* Baltimore: University Park Press.

Crawley, S. B., & Spiker, D. (1982). Mother-child interactions and mental development in two-year-olds with Down syndrome. *Infant Behavior and Development, 5,* 54 (Special International Conference on Infant Studies issue).

Crocker, E. C., & Crocker, C. (1970). Some implications of superstitions and folk beliefs for counseling parents of children with cleft lip and cleft plate. *The Cleft Palate Journal, 7,* 124–128.

Delaney, S. W. (1979). Facilitating attachment between fathers and their handicapped infants (Doctoral dissertation, University of Washington, 1979). *Dissertation Abstracts International, 40,* 3229A. (University Microfilms No. 79–27, 768)

Demos, Virginia. (1982). The role of affect in early childhood: An exploratory study. In E. Z. Tronick (Ed.), *Social interchange in infancy: Affect, cognition, and communication.* Baltimore: University Park Press.

Dickson, J. M. (1981). A model for the physical therapist in the intensive care nursery. *Physical Therapy, 61,* 45–58.

Dillard, R. G., Auerbach, K. G., & Showalter, A. H. (1980). A parents' program in the intensive care nursery: Its relationship to maternal attitudes and expectations. *Social Work in Health Care, 5,* 245–251.

Drezek, W. (1976a). *Parenting as a model for infant education: Implications for curriculum.* Austin, TX: Travis County Mental Health—Mental Retardation Center. (ERIC Document Reproduction Service No. ED 132 820) (Also available from Infant-Parent Training Program, 1226 East Ninth Street, Austin, TX 78702)

Drezek, W. (1976b). *Teachers as mothers: An innovative conceptual rationale for program for multiply handicapped infants.* Austin, TX: Travis County Mental Health—Mental Retardation Center. (ERIC Document Reproduction Service No. ED 132 817)

Earls, F. (1976). The fathers (not the mothers): Their importance and influence with infants and young children. *Psychiatry, 39,* 209–226.

Emde, R. N., & Brown, C. (1978). Adaptation to the birth of a Down's syndrome infant. *Journal of American Academy of Child Psychiatry, 17,* 299–323.

Erdman, D. (1977). Parent-to-parent support: The best for those with sick newborns. *The American Journal of Maternal/Child Nursing, 2,* 291–292.

Erickson, M. L. (1976). *Assessment and management of developmental changes in children.* St. Louis: Mosby.

Erickson, M. L. (1974). Talking with fathers of young children with Down's syndrome. *Children Today, 3,* 22–25.

Featherstone, H. (1980). *A difference in the family.* New York: Basic Books.

Field, T. (1983). High-risk infants "have less fun" during early interactions. *Topics in Early Childhood Special Education, 3,* 77–87.

Field, T. M. (1980). Interactions of high-risk infants: Quantitative and qualitative differences. In D. B. Sawin, R. Hawkins, A. Walker, & J. Penticuff (Eds.), *Exceptional infant* (Vol. 4). New York: Brunner/Mazel.

Fontana, V. J. (1976). *Somewhere a child is crying: Maltreatment—Causes and prevention.* New York: New American Library.

Fost, N. (1981). Counseling families who have a child with a severe congenital anomaly. *Pediatrics, 67,* 321–324.

Frailberg, S. (1974). Blind infants and their mothers: An examination of the sign system. In M. Lewis & L. A. Rosenblum (Eds.), *The effect of the infant on its caregiver.* New York: Wiley.

Frodi, A. (1981). Contributions of infant characteristics to child abuse. *American Journal of Mental Deficiency, 85,* 341–349.

Gallagher, J. J., Cross, A., & Scharfman, W. (1981). Parental adaptation to a young handicapped child: The father's role. *Journal of the Division of Early Childhood, 3,* 3–14.

Gallagher, R. J., Jens, K. G., & O'Donnell, K. J. (1983). The effect of physical status on the affective expression of handicapped infants. *Infant Behavior and Development, 6,* 73–77.

Garland, C., Stone, N. W., Swanson, J., & Woodruff, G. (Eds.) (1981). *Early intervention for children with special needs and their families: Findings and recommendations* (WESTAR Series Paper No. 11). Seattle: Western States Technical Assistance Resource.

Goin, K. (Ed.). (1975). *Planning programs and activities for infants and toddlers: A bibliography.* Chapel Hill, NC: Technical Assistance Development Systems.

Goldberg, S., & DiVitto, B. (1983). *Born too soon: Preterm birth and early development.* San Francisco: Freeman.

Gordon, T. (1970). *Parent effectiveness training.* New York: Wyden.

Greenberg, M., & Morris, N. (1974). Engrossment: The newborn's impact upon the father. *American Journal of Orthopsychiatry, 44,* 520–531.

Greenspan, N. T. (1983). Funding for cost-benefit analysis of services for high-risk families and infants. In V. Sasserath (Ed.), *Minimizing high-risk parenting* (Pediatric Round Table No. 7). Piscataway, NJ: Johnson & Johnson Baby Products.

Griffin, P. M., & Sanford, A. R. (1975). *Learning Accomplishment Profile for Infants.* Winston-Salem: Kaplan Press.

Grollman, E. A. (1980). *When your loved one is dying.* Boston: Beacon Press.

Hagen, M. (1981). "Burnout"—Teachers and parents. *Views, 1,* 4–6.

Hanson, M. J. (1982). Issues in designing intervention approaches from developmental theory and research. In D. Bricker (Ed.), *Intervention with at-risk and handicapped infants.* Baltimore: University Park Press.

Hanson, M. J., & Schwarz, R. H. (1978). Results of a longitudinal intervention program for Down's syndrome infants and their families. *Education and Training of the Mentally Retarded, 13*, 403–407.

Hawkins-Walsh, E. (1980). Diminishing anxiety in parents of sick newborns. *American Journal of Maternal/Child Nursing, 5*, 30–34.

Hayden, A. H., & Haring, N. G. (1976). Programs for Down's syndrome children at the University of Washington. In T. D. Tjossem (Ed.), *Intervention strategies for high risk infants and young children*. Baltimore: University Park Press.

Hines, J. D. (1971). Father–The forgotten man. *Nursing Forum, 10*, 177–201.

Iyer, P. (1981, July–August). My baby was premature. *Journal of Obstetric, Gynecologic and Neonatal Nursing*, pp. 304–307.

Jeffcoate, J. A., Humphrey, M. E., & Lloyd, J. K. (1979). Role perception and response to stress in fathers and mothers following pre-term delivery. *Social Science and Medicine, 13A*(2), 139–145.

Kaiser, C. E. (1982). *Young & Special*. Baltimore: University Park Press.

Kaiser, C. E., & Hayden, A. H. (1977). The education of the very very young, (or) But what can you teach an infant? *Educational Horizons, 56*, 4–15.

Kaplan, D., & Mason, E. A. (1960). Maternal reactions to premature birth viewed as an acute emotional disorder. *American Journal of Orthopsychiatry, 30*, 539.

Karnes, M. B. (1975). Mainstreaming parents of the handicapped. In C. Hawkins-Shepard (Ed.), *Making it work*. Reston, VA: The Council for Exceptional Children.

Kennell, J. H. & Klaus, M. H. (1971). Care of the mother of the high-risk infant. *Clinical Obstetrics and Gynecology, 14*, 926–954.

Keshet, H. F., & Rosenthal, K. M. (1978). Single parent fathers: A new study. *Children Today, 7*(3), 13–19.

Klaus, M. H., & Kennell, J. H. (1976). *Maternal-infant bonding*. St. Louis: Mosby.

Kogan, K. L., & Tyler, N. (1973). Mother-child interaction in young physically handicapped children. *American Journal of Mental Deficiency, 77*, 492–497.

Kogan, K. L., Tyler, N., & Turner, P. (1974). The process of interpersonal adaptation between mothers and their cerebral palsied children. *Developmental Medicine and Child Neurology, 16*, 518–527.

Koop, C. E. (1976). *The right to live: The right to die*. Wheaton, IL: Tyndale House.

Kopelman, A. E., Simeonsson, R. J., Smaldone, A., & Gilbert, L. (1978). Does a photograph of a newborn about to be transferred to an intensive care center promote mother-infant bonding? *Clinical Pediatrics, 17*, 15–16.

Korner, A. F. (1974). Individual differences at birth: Implications for child-care practices. *The Infant at Risk, 10*, 51–61.

Kupfer, F. (1982). *Before and after Zachariah*. New York: Delacorte Press.

Lamb, M. E. (1975). Fathers: Forgotten contributors to child development. *Human Development, 18*, 245–266.

Lazar, I. (1979). Does intervention pay off? *D.E.C. Communicator*, Newsletter of the Division for Early Childhood, The Council for Exceptional Children, 6, 1–7.

Lazar, I., & Darlington, R. (1979, September). *Lasting effects after preschool* (Final report, HEW Grant 90C–1311 to the Education Commission of the States) (DHEW Publication No. (OHDS) 79–30179). Washington, DC: U.S. Government Printing Office.

Lewis, M., & Rosenblum, L. A. (Eds.). (1974). *The effect of the infant on its caregiver*. New York: Wiley.

Lichter, P. (1976). Communicating with parents: It begins with listening. *Teaching Exceptional Children, 8*, 66–71.

Mangurten, J. H., Slade, C., & Fitzsimmons, D. (1979). Parent-parent support in the care of high-risk newborns. *Journal of Obstetric, Gynecologic and Neonatal Nursing, 8*, 275–277.

Mears, C. (Ed.). (1975). *Early childhood curriculum materials: An annotated bibliography.* New York: Walker.

Menolascino, F. J., & Coleman, R. (1980). The Pilot Parent Program: Helping handicapped children through their parents. *Child Psychiatry and Human Development, 11,* 41–48.

Meyers, C., & Blacher, J. (1982). *The effect of schooling severely impaired children on the family* (NICHD Grant No. HD14680). UCLA/MRCC Group at Lanterman State Hospital, Pomona, CA.

Miller, C. (1978). Working with parents of high-risk infants. *American Journal of Nursing, 78,* 1228–1230.

Mills, P. J. (1978). *Influence of early intervention on the social relationship between mother and infant.* Chapel Hill: Frank Porter Graham Child Development Center, University of North Carolina. (ERIC Document Reproduction Service No. ED 013 371).

Noble, D. N., & Hamilton, A. K. (1981). Families under stress: Perinatal social work. *Health and Society, 6,* 28–35.

Parke, R. D., & Sawin, D. E. (1977). *The family in early infancy: Social interaction and attitudinal analyses.* Paper presented at the Biennial Meeting of the Society for Research in Child Development, New Orleans. (ERIC Document Reproduction Service No. ED 162 742)

Patterson, G. (Ed.). (1976). *Staff development: A resource for the transdisciplinary process.* New York: United Cerebral Palsy Association.

Pederson, F. A., & Robson, K. S. (1969). Father participation in infancy. *American Journal of Orthopsychiatry, 39,* 466–472.

Penfold, K. M. (1974). Supporting mother love. *American Journal of Nursing, 74,* 464–467.

Ramey, C. T., & Smith, B. J. (1976). Assessing the intellectual consequences of early intervention with high-risk infants. *American Journal of Mental Deficiency, 81,* 318–324.

Ramey, C. T., & Trohanis, P. L. (Eds.). (1982). *Finding and educating high risk and handicapped infants.* Baltimore: University Park Press.

Rosenthal, R., & Jacobson, L. (1968). *Pygmalion in the classroom.* New York: Holt, Rinehart, & Winston.

Roth, C. (1982). Clinical intervention methods for disturbed parent-infant interaction. *Infant Behavior and Development, 5,* 203 (Special International Conference on Infant Studies issue).

Schell, G. (1981). The young handicapped child: A family perspective. *Topics in Early Childhood Special Education, 1*(3), 21–28.

Schraeder, B. D. (1980). Attachment and parenting despite lengthy intensive care. *American Journal of Maternal Child Nursing, 5,* 35–36.

Serafica, F. C., & Cicchetti, D. (1976). Down's syndrome children in a strange situation: Attachment and exploration behaviors. *Merrill-Palmer Quarterly, 22,* 137–150.

Shearer, D., Billingsley, J., Frohman, A., Hilliard, J., Johnson, F., & Shearer, M. (1976). *The Portage guide to early education.* Portage, WI: Cooperative Educational Service Agency 12.

Smith, D. W. (1979). *Mothering your unborn baby.* Philadelphia: Saunders.

Smith, S. (1981). A baby born with a multi-system handicap. *New Zealand Nursing Journal, 74,* 26–28.

Solomon, G. S., Wilson, D. O., & Galey, G. S. (1982). Project DEBT: Attempting to improve the quality of interaction among handicapped children and their parents. *The Journal of the Association for the Severely Handicapped, 7,* 28–35.

Spelke, E., Zelazo, P., Kagan, J., & Kotelchuck, M. (1973). Father interaction and separation protest. *Developmental Psychology, 9*, 83–90.

Stone, N. W., & Chesney, B. H. (1978). Attachment behaviors in handicapped infants. *Mental Retardation, 16*, 8–12.

Strauss, M. S., Utley, B. L., & Biglan, A. (1982). Assessing visual acuity of severely handicapped infants. *Infant Behavior and Development, 5*, 232 (Special International Conference on Infant Studies issue).

Thomas, E. B., Becker, P. T., & Freese, M. P. (1978). Individual patterns of mother-infant interaction. In G. Sackett (Ed.), *Observing behavior: Theory and applications in mental retardation* (Vol. 1). Baltimore: University Park Press.

Tronick, E. Z. (Ed.). (1982). *Social interchange in infancy: Affect, cognition, and communication*. Baltimore: University Park Press.

Tuck, S., Jr. (1971). Working with black fathers. *American Journal of Orthopsychiatry. 41*, 465–472.

Turnbull, H. R., III. (1976). Report of the parents' committee: Families in crisis, families at risk. In T. D. Tjossem (Ed.), *Intervention strategies for high-risk infants and young children*. Baltimore: University Park Press.

Tyler, N. B., & Kogan, K. L. (1977). Reduction of stress between mothers and their handicapped children. *American Journal of Occupational Therapy, 31*, 151–155.

Valentin, L. D. (1981). The problems of grief and separation in the special care baby unit. *Nursing Times, 77*, 1942–1944.

Vulpé, S. G. (1977). *Vulpé Assessment Battery*. Canada: National Institute on Mental Retardation.

Waechter, E. H. (1977). Bonding problems of infants with congenital anomalies. *Nursing Forum, 16*, 298–319.

Warren, R. D., & Dickman, I. R. (1981). *For this respite, much thanks: Concepts, guidelines and issues in the development of community respite care services*. New York: Cerebral Palsy Associations.

Wedell-Monnig, J., & Lumley, J. M. (1980). Child deafness and mother-child interaction. *Child Development, 51*, 744–766.

Whaley, P. A., Gosling, C. G., & Schreiner, R. L. (1979). Relieving parental anxiety: A booklet for parents of an infant in NICU. *Journal of Obstetric, Gynecologic and Neonatal Nursing, 8*, 49–55.

Wortis, R. P. (1971). The acceptance of the concept of the maternal role by behavioral scientists: Its effects on women. *American Journal of Orthopsychiatry, 41*, 733–746.

CHAPTER 9

Intervention with Families with Young, Severely Handicapped Children *

Bruce L. Baker

Introduction

The evidence in this volume is undeniable: Handicapped children do indeed impact on their families, from the moment of discovery and always thereafter. Those who would help have often felt helpless themselves. Friends and relatives have offered platitudes rather than say nothing, and professionals have advised institutional placement in one decade and decried it in the next. Intervening in families with a handicapped child is risky business.

Reviewing interventions is also risky. A myriad of professionals counsel parents, and thousands of agencies seek to help in about as many ways. Any review will of necessity overlook much of value. In keeping with the research orientation of this volume, however, I will

* This chapter was written while the author was on sabbatical at the Judge Baker Guidance Center and Harvard Medical School, Boston, Massachusetts. Preparation was supported in part by Grant 1 R01 HD10962 from the National Institute of Child Health and Human Development.

consider interventions with families of young handicapped children reported in the literature that have at least some empirical foundation.

Program Philosophies

Parent education or parent counseling programs follow two broad philosophies that Tavormina (1974) reviewed as "reflective" and "behavioral." Although reflective counseling programs vary (Auerbach, 1968), Tavormina summarized their common goals as understanding the child's reactions, feelings, and needs at various stages of growth, examining what group members expect of themselves as parents, and focusing on feelings within the parent–child interaction. One example of the reflective approach is the very popular Parent Effectiveness Training (PET), which trains parents in listening techniques, communication skills, and child–parent problem solving (Gordon, 1970).

The focus of reflective programs has been primarily parent attitude change and, sometimes secondarily, child change. Unfortunately, Tavormina's (1974) summary of the evaluations found mixed results on attitude measures and limited actual child change. Rinn and Markle (1977) reviewed 14 available studies of PET since 1970 (noting that only one had been published); after criticizing limitations in scope, design, and analyses, they concluded "the effectiveness of PET as a prevention or intervention strategy was not supported" (p. 95). Moreover, despite the popularity of reflective counseling programs, especially with middle-class families, I found only a few reports of their use with parents of handicapped children. Several of these had dropout rates of 40% or more (Hetrick, 1979; J. H. Miller, 1980). It seems reasonable that the emphasis on verbal communication in this orientation is less applicable to families with a severely handicapped child.

Behavioral programs, viewed broadly, have aimed primarily to change child behaviors and parent–child interactions. Although they are likely to consider some of the concerns addressed by reflective approaches, the main focus of intervention and of evaluation is on teaching the parent to observe, record, and change the child's behavior. I know of only one study that has compared reflective with behavioral intervention for parents of handicapped children. Tavormina (1975; Tavormina, Hampson, & Luscomb, 1976) cleverly included among his outcome measures those often utilized in reflective programs (Hereford Parent Attitude Survey, Missouri Behavior Problem Checklist) and in behavioral programs (behavioral observations, ratings of target behaviors, mother's frequency counts). Trained parents of mentally retarded children generally fared better than those in a delayed training control group, but on every measure where differences were found, the behavioral groups surpassed the reflective ones. On a consumer satisfaction measure, the behaviorally trained mothers also scored higher. This study had several shortcomings, however. Assignment to condition was based on parent's availability rather than being randomized, and, remarkably, no group leader had previous experience with parents of mentally retarded children.

In sum, there are few well-controlled evaluations of reflective approaches, and the question of whether a reflective or behavioral approach best meets the needs of parents with handicapped children has barely been addressed. Therefore I will consider the predominantly behavioral parent-training literature, noting that the empirical literature recounts the more empirical programs and that what is not found therein may have much of value, albeit unproven. Since the majority of programs aim to enhance parents' skills as teachers or therapists, the ways in which implied parent roles and responsibilities have emerged and the particular difficulties that confront any would-be teacher or therapist for a handicapped child will be examined first.

Roles and Responsibilities

Parents of handicapped children occupy diverse roles, some dictated by their children's needs and some by professional practices. Parents are seekers, learners, teachers, advocates. Yet these roles have been too often overlooked and undersupported by professionals who focused instead on the parent's emotional life—who cast parents into the role of patients and offered therapy. Counseling, to be sure, has a valuable place in a continuum of services, especially to help a family over crisis points (e.g., the birth of a disabled child, decisions about schooling, adolescent concerns, planning for a future outside the family). And families of handicapped children are not immune from the psychological distresses that burden the rest of us and that may be lightened by therapy. But the "news" is that at last parents' roles of teacher and advocates are also being validated.

This may not be all good news. Parents have long sought free and appropriate education for their children and with the passage of Public Law 94–142, the Education for All Handicapped Children Act of 1975 (see Turnbull & Winton, Chapter 10 in this volume) they heaved a collective sigh of relief. But with the newly codified rights of children and parents have come increased parental responsibilities to be an informed teacher and decision maker. Shrybman (1982), writing about due process in special education, listed responsibilities of parents, beginning with: "1. Keep written records with copies of all of their letters to and from officials and school personnel" (p. 218) and continuing through 119 items! Turnbull and Turnbull (1982) spoke for many overwhelmed parents in pointing out that some are just not up for all of this. This wide swing of the pendulum from the days when parents were to be silent observers of professional practice threatens to topple parent enthusiasm in its path. Teachers who teach well and administrators who administer well are needed so that generally informed parents can make a meaningful contribution to their child's development without making this their life's focus. One hopes for balance.

Parents as Teachers

Against this backdrop, the parental role of teacher can be examined. To some extent all parents are teachers, but parents of a handicapped child face extra difficulties in whatever teaching they do. Likewise, professionals who seek to help parents in this role need to know more than a few behavioral principles. A severely handicapped child does not have one isolated and obvious target problem, but a plethora of deficiencies and often no clear starting place. Learning will come slowly, and skills must be simplified and then simplified yet further. Presenting a task is often impeded by the child's handicap. For example, the limited effectiveness of verbal control in getting and holding an autistic, retarded, or hearing-impaired child's attention is disconcerting. Parents must learn to rely more on modeling and physical guidance, and these require a more conscious, patient, and well-planned effort.

Moreover, motivating the child to perform a task usually requires imagination and persistence. With multiply handicapped children the problem of finding incentives is compounded. For example, Mira and Hoffman (1974), working with deaf–blind children, noted the frequent failure of social and even food consequences to motivate performance. Finally, the use of firm contingencies and punishment, difficult with any child, is often especially problematic for parents of a handicapped child; they are apt to indulge him or her in ways they would not treat a nonhandicapped child, with predictable consequences in unmanageable behavior. Yet most parents teach their handicapped children a great deal, usually without any professional help. And there have been reports of very successful collaboration when parents have sought guidance in teaching from professionals.

Behavioral Objectives and Interventions

The examination of parent training programs begins with case studies, for here are found the clearest explication of how professionals train parents, how parents intervene with their child, and what specific changes ensue. Subsequently broader service models that incorporate these methods will be examined. Table 9.1 summarizes case studies. It is limited to published reports in which the child was at least 2 years old and handicapped, where parent training was the primary emphasis, and where measurement and design were at least minimally adequate.

Teaching New Skills

The primary focus of intervention for parents of handicapped children needs to be teaching new skills. Table 9.1 cites reports of teaching dressing skills and conversational skills to retarded children, signing and spontaneous conversation to autistic children, prosocial interactions to a child with language delay, sitting, attending, and appropriate use of plurals to severely hearing impaired children, and visual discrimination and arm extension to children with cerebral palsy. Parents were usually taught to break the skill into components, model the steps, prompt and guide as necessary, reinforce successive approximations, fade prompts and reinforcers, and record progress. Some interventions are quite specific, such as Gross, Eduy and Drabman's (1982) two 20-minute sessions to model for parents of physically disabled children how to reinforce arm extension; videotapes demonstrated that with this limited input, parents produced considerable and lasting gains.

An illustration of a more complex program is the teaching of conversational skills to Katie, 15 years old and moderately retarded (Arnold, Sturgis, & Forehand, 1977). Katie frequently interrupted conversations and failed to follow the subject matter. Skills targeted to teach were "encourages" to talk (short verbal introjections to indicate attention and interest in the subject matter) and on-topic questions. In six 1-hour clinic sessions, the authors instructed Katie's mother how to use structured conversations at home each day to teach Katie through imitation, verbal prompting and subsequent fading, immediate feedback, and social reinforcement for correct responding. Audiotaped daily conversations at home showed increases in encourages and then questions after Mrs. M. began teaching each one. The first excerpt is from dialogues during baseline, where Katie demonstrated the tangential speech often heard in

TABLE 9.1

Case Studies of Training with Parents of Developmentally Disabled Children

Authors	Child (age in years); diagnosis	Target behavior	Program	Design	Results; follow-up (FU)
Adubato, Adams, & Budd, 1981	Jay (6), brain damaged	Dressing	Clinic-trained mother who trained father	Multiple baseline	Increase in dressing, eating, and toy use
Arnold, Sturgis, & Forehand, 1977	Katie (15), retarded	Conversational skills	Mother prompt/ reinforcement (6 sessions)	AB	Coded audiotapes showed significant improvement; 2-month FU
Barnard, Christophersen, & Wolf, 1976	Moe (4), retarded; Mark (3), severely mentally retarded with multiple handicaps	Self-injury: head banging, Hand biting	Overcorrection Overcorrection	AB AB	Reduction to almost zero for both 21- and 2-month FU
Brehony, Benson, Solomon, & Luscomb, 1980	Steven (7), severely mentally retarded	Throwing, sitting, compliance	Praise, punishment (6.5 hours training)	Multiple baseline	Considerable change and transfer to restaurant.
Budd, Green, & Baer, 1976	Andrea (3), developmentally delayed	Noncompliance	Differential attention and time out (162 sessions)	Multiple baseline	Eventual success; 4-month FU
Casey, 1978	4 subjects (6–7), autistic	Communication, behavioral problems	Parents taught signing (20 sessions)	Multiple baseline	Significant changes; 2-month FU at school
Forehand, Cheney, & Yoder, 1974	John (7), deaf	Noncompliance	Reinforcement of skills and time out	AB	From 20% to 100% compliance at clinic; 3-month FU

Study	Subjects	Target behavior	Treatment	Design	Results
Fox & Roseen, 1977	T (3.5), phenylkenonuria	Lofenalac refusal	Token economy	ABAB	Increased consumption; maintained at 1 year
Frazier & Schneider, 1975	Boy (3), retarded	Acting-out behaviors	Time out	Multiple baseline	Very effective; 1-month FU
Gerrard & Saxon, 1973	Helen (2.8), deaf, autistic	Screaming, crying; sitting, attending	Team training in clinic		Screaming, crying reduced to zero; increased sitting and attending
Gross, Eudy, & Drabman, 1982	3 subjects (2.8–3.7), physically disabled	Arm extension	Model by physical therapist (40 minutes)	Multiple baseline	Coded videotapes showed good progress; 1-month FU
S. M. Johnson & Brown, 1969	Judy (2.8), developmentally delayed	Mother–child interaction, playing	Modeling (13 sessions)	AB	Change in mother–child behaviors during play
M. R. Johnson, Whitman, & Barloon-Noble, 1978	Girl (4), autistic behaviors	Noncompliance, nonfunctional speech	Positive attention, time out (5 sessions)		Changes in both behaviors
Moore & Bailey, 1973	Girl (4), Autisticlike behaviors	Response to requests	Social reinforcement, punishment (53 sessions)	Multiple baseline	Clear changes
White, 1982	Boy (13), moderately mentally retarded, deaf	Eating for weight gain	Contingency management	ABA	Weight gain; 2-year FU
Wildman & Simon, 1978	Paul (9), autistic	Social interactions	Family tutoring	ABA	Interaction increased during tutoring, not other times
Wiltz & Gordon, 1974	Boy (9), Hyperactive, childhood schizophrenia	Noncompliance, destructive acts	Reinforcement, time out, 5 days in experimental apartment		Good decrease, carried over to home

retarded children, and the second from the eighth session, after teaching was underway for encourages and questions.

> *Mrs. M.* You know, I think we might see if we could get some watermelons or peaches to sell out at the station—have a little stand.
> *Katie.* One time I went to the program for the March of Dimes for crippled children. (p. 271)

> *Mrs. M.* I woke up this morning and the phone was ringing and it was the lady who said your ride wasn't going to go to Athens today.
> *Katie.* Who was it?
> *Mrs. M.* It was Susie's mother. She'd heard a weather report saying the roads were going to be flooded.
> *Katie.* It did?
> *Mrs. M.* They didn't ever flood, but the weather report had said they might, so she was afraid to drive.
> *Katie.* What about tomorrow? (pp. 272–273)

Motivating Behaviors

Often the aim is to motivate the child to use skills that he or she already has. There are examples of increasing spontaneous speech and bead stringing in autistic children, addition and letter writing in a neurologically impaired child, and eating for weight gain in a child moderately retarded and severely deaf from rubella. To motivate skill usage, the primary method has been to teach parents to use reinforcement contingently.

An example is the parent-administered token reinforcement program to increase Lofenalac consumption of a 3.5-year-old boy with phenylketonuria (PKU) (Fox & Roseen, 1977). T was diagnosed as having PKU at the age of 21 days and placed on a phenylalanine-restricted diet to prevent mental retardation; recent intelligence testing revealed normal functioning (IQ = 100). Six months prior to this study T began to refuse Lofenalac; his mother would often spend over 2 hours to get him to drink 3 oz (89 mL), and the required daily intake was 12 oz (355 mL). His parents had tried sending him to his room, withholding toys, refusing him water, spanking, adding chocolate to the Lofenalac, and providing praise and tangible rewards, all to no avail. They noticed changes in other behaviors (i.e., irritability, crying) and, not surprisingly, they noted the problem was having a detrimental effect on their family.

A psychologist helped T's parents to establish a token economy. On a large chart they put five snapshots of T performing desired activities and eight snapshots of backup reinforcers that T could purchase with his tokens. Below each picture they drew a number of tokens to represent the value of that behavior or reinforcer (e.g., drinking 4 oz [118 mL] Lofenalac earned three tokens, dressing earned one; helping mother bake cost three tokens, Saturday cartoons cost nine). As shown in Figure 9.1, consumption increased and remained high for 5 weeks after the token economy was withdrawn, only to plummet suddenly. When the economy was reintroduced for 3 weeks and then faded gradually, however, consumption continued to increase (in keeping with a new criterion established by the nutritionist). Other problem behaviors also improved, and at 1-year follow-up, T was drinking 18 oz (532 mL) of the Lofenalac formula daily.

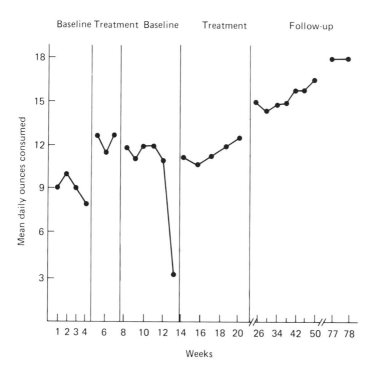

Figure 9.1   Mean daily ounces of Lofenalac T consumed per week; 7 measurements taken each week. (Reprinted with permission from *Journal of Behavior Therapy and Experimental Psychiatry, 8*, Fox, R. A., & Roseen, D. L., A parent administered token program for dietary regulation of phenylketonuria, © 1977, Pergamon Press, Ltd.)

Decreasing Behavior Problems

Despite the importance attached by intervention programs to teaching new skills and motivating existing ones, parents are often most concerned about behavior problems; this includes behaviors that threaten
the child's safety, the family's tranquility, or the child's skill learning or
performance. The most frequent referral complaint, noncompliance,
has been treated in language-delayed, deaf, autistic, and retarded children. There also are case reports of self-injurious head banging and
hand biting, and inappropriate mealtime behaviors of retarded children,
repetitive nonfunctional speech of an autistic child, destructive acts
toward people and property of a schizophrenic child, and screaming and
crying of a child with severe hearing loss and multiple handicaps. Intervention has usually combined contingent positive reinforcement with
punishment, most frequently time out (immediate removal from ongoing
activity to a chair or room for a short period). Sometimes very mild punishments have been successful when parents learned to be consistent.

As an example, consider the training program developed for Steven's
parents, who felt embarrassed and restricted from family outings by their
only child's problem behaviors (Brehony, Benson, Solomon, & Luscomb,
1980). Severely retarded, Steven at the age of 7 also was hyperactive,
with a short attention span and multiple physical disabilities. His parents
attended 12 daily 30-minute sessions at a clinic, to learn under supervision to respond consistently to Steven's problem behaviors with a firm
"no" and to his desired behaviors with praise and gentle touches. Figure 9.2, with a multiple baseline design, shows the changes in Steven's
behavior following the initiation of contingencies for throwing (Session
4), noncompliance (Session 7), and sitting in a chair (Session 10). Of special interest, certainly to Steven's parents, are the triangles on the graph,
denoting Steven's behavior 2 months posttreatment in a restaurant,
when two trained observers posed as customers and recorded the considerably improved target behaviors.

Summary

The programs considered each effectively trained parents in clinic
sessions to carry out specific techniques at home in order to change one
or a few behaviors of special immediate concern. There are only anecdotal reports of the effects of this experience on the family. It does seem
likely that Katie and her mother enjoyed more productive conversations,
that T's whole family were eased the burdens of time, stress, and guilt
imposed by his formula refusal, and that Steven's parents were able to

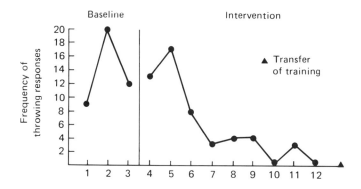

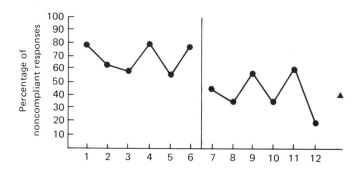

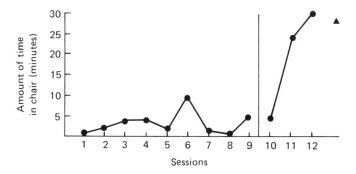

Figure 9.2   Number of throwing responses, percentage of noncompliant behaviors, and amount of time spent in chair during baseline, intervention, and transfer of training sessions. (Source: Brehony, Benson, Solomon, & Luscomb, 1980.)

control his problems enough so that they could engage in their favorite activity, eating out. It is not known, however, whether these parents could go on to apply what they had learned to new teaching or problem management.

Models of Parent Training

Larger-scale parent training programs have incorporated the principles and practices described for the case studies. Exemplary programs to illustrate the prominent training models are next described, organized around the format of training (individual or in groups) and the location (in an agency or at home).

Individual Training

Clinic or School-Based Training

The most common parent training approach involves a series of meetings at a clinic or school (Bricker & Bricker, 1976; Hayden & Haring, 1976). Variations were illustrated in the case studies. Katie's mother attended training sessions alone, bringing audiotapes of conversations with her daughter. Steven's parents brought him for supervised teaching. In both of these cases training was limited, focusing on several target behaviors, and it was brief, only 6 and 12 sessions. Giving parents a more thorough understanding of social learning principles and training them to modify a variety of behaviors can be quite time-consuming in the individual model. The longest report found was 162 sessions to eliminate noncompliance in a 3-year-old with developmental and language delays and, most likely, some stubbornness (Budd, Green, & Baer, 1976).

A related model integrated training into an ongoing residential or day school program (Luterman, 1967). There are examples of parents trained as volunteer aides in the classroom (Benson & Ross, 1972), a live-in school for parents and child (Jelinek & Schaub, 1973), a live-in weekend at a summer camp for group-trained parents (Baker, 1973), and training integrated with 30-day respite care (observed by the author at Delta House, Cambridge, Massachusetts). The 3-week, 90-hour parent training component of the day program at the Judevine Center for Autistic Children (St. Louis, Missouri) is an illustration (O'Dell, Blackwell, Larcen, & Hogan, 1977). Judevine also uses its school to train parents of other children who live out of the state; at the time of O'Dell et al.'s report, parents from 24 states had completed the course. Principles and behaviorally defined skills to be trained are presented through a series of 69 printed modules. Movement through the modules is competency-based—parents must achieve a predetermined skill level before proceeding to the next module. The parent generally learns skills through the written module and a lecture, guided observation in class, co-teaching with a trainer, and teaching independently while the trainer coaches with a "bug in the ear" (a wireless coaching device that allows the trainer to be behind a one-way window). The program has evaluated progress with a written test of knowledge and videotapes of parent teaching. Parents leave training with detailed written suggestions and daily report logs, to be mailed back weekly so the center can monitor progress.

Some school-based training programs regularly monitor parents' home teaching (McClannahan, Krantz, & McGee, 1982). An interesting example is the Lunch Box Data System originated by Teaching Research in Monmouth, Oregon (Fredericks, Baldwin, & Grove, 1974). Parents of handicapped children carry out a teaching program at home for 10 to 30 minutes daily, after aims and procedures have been worked out with the teacher. The key to continuing communication is a data sheet, completed daily by the parent and the teacher and carried between school and home by the child. A short meeting between the parent and teacher each month keeps the program under way, and with such parental teaching the child's rate of progress on target skills doubles.

Home-Based Training

Although many programs include one or a few home visits, regular home visiting over an extended period of time, although costly, is a very popular model of parent training. Levitt and Cohen (1975) noted that while traditionally visits were to the homes of blind, deaf, or physically handicapped children, more recently they have also included families of children with other disabilities. Proponents argue that trainers can instruct and parents can learn best in the "natural" environment. Home-based training is mainly used for early intervention with remote or reluctant cases, such as (1) rural families who have a handicapped infant or preschool child and live far from an agency and (2) disadvantaged families with a high-risk infant who would not otherwise seek help. It has also been increasingly used with families who ask agencies for help with behavior problems in older children—especially in states that rely heavily on private vendors for service, since this model is administratively easy.

Home-Visiting Programs. A number of innovative home-visit projects have been reported. They range from professional programs, such as Fraiberg's (1971; Fraiberg, Smith, & Adelson, 1969) creative work with blind infants to nonprofessional ones, such as the Pilot Parent Program in Omaha, Nebraska, wherein parents of handicapped children offer support and information to new parents (Menolascino & Coleman, 1980). The Portage Project will be described because of its systematic curriculum and extensive replication. It was developed to serve handicapped children between birth and the age of 6 years in south-central rural Wisconsin (Shearer & Shearer, 1972, 1976). It relies entirely on parents as teachers; there is no classroom program. Parents teach for up to 30 minutes each day and record progress.

Home teachers each visit 15 families weekly to (1) assess the child's performance on behaviors targeted for in-home teaching during the previous week, (2) select program steps to be taught the next week (e.g., Billy will name pictures using three word phrases), (3) draw up a home activity chart for recording progress, (4) model the appropriate behavioral teaching techniques, and (5) supervise while the parent tries out the program. Individualized planning is facilitated by an Early Childhood Curriculum Guide consisting of (1) a Developmental Sequence Checklist listing 580 behaviors in five areas: language, self-help, cognition, motor, and social development, and (2) curriculum cards using behavioral objectives to describe each of the 580 skills and suggesting teaching methods. Although the program has reported only limited formal evaluation, it has been successfully exported to many other states and countries because of its clear procedures, focused goals, packaged curriculum guides, lower cost than classroom programs, and proactive efforts at dissemination.

Simulated Home. In this model, an agency furnishes a nearby house so that families can live in for a few days or visit regularly to learn the teaching potential of routine daily activities. A simulated home preserves center-based advantages of having equipment and ancillary services available and eliminating staff travel, while providing the natural interactions, greater range of potential activities, and smoother generalization inherent in the home-based model. Reported programs are almost all for infants and preschool children with severe hearing loss (e.g., John Tracy Clinic, Los Angeles, California; Helen Beebe Speech and Hearing Center, Easton, Pennsylvania; Central Institute for the Deaf, St. Louis, Missouri; University of Kansas Medical Center, Kansas). The Mama Lere Parent Teaching Home at the Bill Wilkerson Hearing and Speech Center in Nashville exemplifies this approach (Horton, 1976, Horton & Sitton, 1970; Knox & McConnell, 1968). Mothers and children under the age of 3 visit a comfortably furnished house on a residential street weekly, to engage with a teacher–counselor in many routine tasks of daily living (e.g., dressing, bathing, making beds, preparing lunch).

The program aims to maximize development of residual hearing through early binaural hearing aid use, and to upgrade the child's auditory and linguistic environment. Parents learn how to orient the child to sounds and speech and to model and reinforce responses. Horton (1976) cited a study by Liff (1973) that found children who had been in the program and wore hearing aids before the age of 3 were later closer in language to their second-grade peers than they were to initially equally hearing impaired children who had not had the early intervention program. In this retrospective study children had not been assigned to Mama Lere or no program at random and, even if gains were valid, it is not known which program components were necessary. But these results certainly suggest that simulated home programs, despite their costs, are worthy of further implementation and study.

Group Training

Parents with a handicapped child are frequently encouraged to join a group. Parent organizations have regular meetings at which information is often presented by guest speakers, and mental health clinics often offer counseling or parent education groups, mainly focused on attitudes or parental adjustment (Lewis, 1972). Behavioral training for parents can also be offered in groups, with some advantages beyond cost-effectiveness. Trainers can use a structured curriculum with mini-lectures, video, modeling, role playing and group problem solving; some of these are cumbersome in individual training, others impossible. Parents can derive support, encouragement for their own efforts, and useful information from other group members. Hence, time-limited groups have become more widely used, especially by persons who desire a more controlled method and larger sample for research.

Independent Groups

Most frequently, training groups stand alone, offering a program to parents who come together just for that purpose. They are supplementary to the family's other services, not integrated with them. Most of the authors represented in Table 9.2 (discussed in a later section) conducted independent groups. Our own cognitive–behavioral Parents as Teachers program in the Project for Developmental Disabilities at the University of California, Los Angeles (UCLA) is an illustration (Baker, 1980, 1983; Brightman, Baker, Clark, & Ambrose, 1982). Aimed at parents of moderately to severely retarded children, aged 3 to 13 years or so, training typically involves an initial assessment followed by 10 2-hour meetings, conducted in groups of about eight families. The first five sessions focus on teaching self-help skills; parents learn assessment and basic teaching methods, such as setting behavioral objectives, breaking skills down into components, and contingent reinforcement, and in one session they teach their child and receive feedback. The next three sessions focus on strategies for behavior problem management and the final two generalize teaching skills to the areas of speech and language and play.

The program emphasizes cognitions as well as behaviors; parents learn to identify interfering thoughts related to teaching and behavior management and to substitute more productive problem-solving thoughts. The program advocates regular formal teaching sessions in the early stages of teaching new skills, and incidental teaching thereafter to incorporate learning experiences into the child's daily routines. Parents conduct about 10 minutes per day of teaching at home, recording their thoughts while teaching and their child's progress. Trainers do only limited didactic presentation; they rely heavily on demonstrations, role playing, videotapes, and consultation with and between parents about progress and problems. To prepare for each session, parents read parts of the *Steps to Independence* series, nine manuals covering skill areas in the curriculum (Baker, Brightman, & Blacher, 1983; Baker, Brightman, Carroll, Heifetz, & Hinshaw, 1978; Baker, Brightman, Heifetz, & Murphy, 1976–1977, Baker, Brightman, & Hinshaw, 1980). The program concludes with a posttraining assessment and several follow-through meetings. Over 300 families had completed the program by 1983 with consistent gains in behavioral knowledge, parent teaching skills, and child gains (Baker, 1980; Baker & Clark, 1983).

All of the programs described have sought to enhance parents' teaching and behavior management skills. An additional program in the UCLA project, Parents as Advocates, conducts seven 2-hour group meetings to teach parents about their child's educational rights and how to insure better that these are realized, especially at Individualized Educational Plan (IEP) meetings. Training involves mini-lectures and video presentations, homework assignments to carry out advocacy-related tasks, and role playing of parent–school advocacy situations. Parents have shown considerable gains in their knowledge of the law and their ability to perform in simulated advocacy situations (Brightman, 1984).

Groups Integrated with Other Programs

Ultimately the most effective model may be one that uses groups for cost-effective training in general knowledge and uses relationships in the natural environment (e.g., parent–teacher) for individualized consulting and maintenance. The Ken Crest Growth and Development Center in Philadelphia, Pennsylvania, used an integrated individual–group–school consultation model (Sandler & Coren, 1981; Sandler, Coren, & Thurman, 1983). Mothers completed four group sessions, based upon the *Steps to Independence* manuals, and then four individual sessions instructing skills on the child's IEP. The core of the continuing school program was a meeting every 6 weeks between mother and teaching team to review and revise objectives and programs; afterwards, the teacher modeled techniques. Of 26 parents surveyed, all valued observing as their child was instructed and 96% valued receiving feedback from the parent trainer on videotapes of their own teaching. Mother and teacher exchanged data sheets (after Fredericks *et al.*, 1974) and met together weekly to coordinate their efforts further. The average parent taught 4.9 days a week for 33 minutes per day. After training, 95% reported feeling more competent in their role as parent of a special child and 100% felt better able to advocate for educational needs and participate with professionals. Although this program seems to have made rather heavy demands on parents, at least in these families of preschoolers it was quite positively regarded.

Evaluating Outcome

Methodological Issues in Evaluating Outcome

The case reports suggest general conclusions. Through individualized training, parents of developmentally disabled children learned specific behavioral techniques, such as contingent attention and time out. Further, these parents applied the techniques at home, with resulting increases in their childrens' adaptive behaviors and decreases in maladaptive behaviors. Most of these case reports have had reliable enough measures and appropriate single-subject designs, so it is safe to conclude a relationship between the intervention and the outcome. There are limitations in single-subject reports, though; larger samples will clarify whether the single-case results are idiosyncratic. The consideration of larger samples confronts a number of methodological concerns. Many of these haunt all intervention research, and the intent is not to rehash methodological points that have been made well elsewhere (Campbell & Stanley, 1966). Rather, some of the most serious difficulties encountered in the parent training literature will be briefly highlighted.

First, the risk of generalizing from populations and interventions that are most frequently encountered in the parent training literature should be noted. The vast majority of reports recount programs for families with nonhandicapped children who have behavior problems. Noncompliance in one form or another—what Bernal has called the "brat syndrome"—is the chief target. Most of the major centers for parent training research in the United States exclude developmentally disabled children from their studies. This review of cases and programs is limited to those with developmentally disabled children, but the discussion of other issues will, from time to time, look in on this broader literature. There is little basis for knowing the extent to which such findings are generalizable to training families of handicapped—especially severely handicapped—children. Moreover, some of the controlled studies can be regarded as analogues to genuine clinical service issues. It is common to recruit and pay volunteers to participate in brief training, sometimes lasting only one session. These studies are heuristic at best, and caution must be exercised in drawing from them to understand intervention with families of severely handicapped children.

Sampling

Even reports with parents of handicapped children have sampling restrictions that signal caution in generalizing. The sample reported is biased by (1) which programs publish their results, (2) which parents join these programs, and (3) which parents complete training and measures. The majority of service programs that offer parent training have not evaluated and published their results. Moreover, many published reports are narrative descriptions with no outcome data. Regarding data-based reports, parents who enter training are unlikely to be representative of others with a handicapped child. Only a small proportion of families invited to join training accept and begin (Hetrick, 1979; McConkey & McEvoy, 1982; Morris, 1973). One program offered group parent training to all 74 families with a moderately or severely retarded child in a special school; 18 joined. Compared to nonjoiners, parents who joined were more educated and more involved in school activities; their children were more retarded with greater behavior problems (Baker, Clark, & Yasuda, 1981). In addition, not all parents complete training. Reported dropout rates have differed widely, from under 10% to over 50%, and there is evidence that dropouts differ from stayers in important respects. For example, in the UCLA group program single parents have dropped out more frequently than married ones (Clark & Baker, 1983). In short, the selectivity of samples that eventually find their way into the literature restricts and beclouds the generalizability of published results.

Focus of Evaluation

Evaluation reports vary in the authors' choice of focus: Whom (parent, child), where (clinic, home), what (feeling, knowing, doing), and how (questionnaire, observation) do they measure? The reader is spared a treatise on each combination of these measurement decisions in favor of several general points. First, every measure has some reactivity. This is obvious for measures of parents' feelings, attitudes, assessment of improvement, or satisfaction, and hence these have been out of vogue in more empirical quarters. Walter (1971), for example, found that parents consistently answered "yes" to the question "Has your child improved?" regardless of whether behavioral observation had indicated a decrease or an increase in targeted child problem behavior. Parent recording of discrete events is more accurate, but such measures call for independent corroboration. Some investigators have observers visit the home, yet one wonders whether the dubious gains in objectivity (from observers who often know what changes are sought) are offset by the unnaturalness of the situation.

Audio recording in the home, while intrusive, is less reactive (S. M. Johnson, Christensen, & Bellamy, 1976). Families agree, for instance, to have microphones placed in their dining and living rooms and activated at random times during predefined intervals (e.g., evening) each day during pre- and posttreatment weeks. Coded audiotapes have shown improvement in interaction patterns for conflictful families with nonhandicapped children. However, a pilot study by this author and Andrew Christensen, recording in four families with moderately retarded children, failed to show consistent changes following group training in parents' verbal behavior (e.g., praise, attention to misbehavior). This may reflect limitations in a measure developed for more verbal conflicts or limits in the generalized benefits of our parent training.

Additionally, measures used with handicapped children are often too broad or too narrow. Many severely handicapped children learn very slowly. They may master only one or a few new skills during even a lengthy training program. However, rather than consider just gains in targeted skills, researchers often use a broader standardized measure. This author has contributed to the problem, for example, by assessing self-help gain in retarded children on the Performance Inventory of 36 self-help skills when parents had taught only two or three skills (Baker, 1980). Others have used even more general tests of development (Clements, Evans, Jones, Osborne, & Upton, 1982) or intelligence (Doernberg, 1971). Not surprisingly, children often do not show greater progress on these measures than controls, and the beneficial effects of programs may be masked. On the other hand, many severely handicapped children do not generalize what they have learned well, and it would be informative to measure related behaviors and/or the target behavior in other settings. For example, can Katie's mother in the case study discussed earlier now teach other skills to Katie, or can Katie have better conversations with her peers? Studies often omit measures that would allow evaluation of the "real life" impact of training.

Finally, taking into account these reservations about the validity and scope of measures, the best procedure is to use multiple measures of outcome. This seems especially wise since the lack of well-standardized measures for severely handicapped children leads many programs to develop their own, with limited reliability and validity information. Moreover, outcome measures show surprisingly little interrelationship. Measures of parents' behavioral knowledge, teaching skill, and child behavior may all show significant changes, but these have been found to be uncorrelated (Flanagan, Adams, & Forehand, 1979; Forehand, Griest, & Wells, 1979). This is less a difficulty with evaluating overall benefits to a group of families than in designating improvement in each family for prediction purposes.

Design and Ethical Considerations

A basic problem with parent intervention research is that samples are often too small to allow for adequate controls or meaningful statistical analyses. The analogue studies are among the best designed because researchers can escape the clinical demands that limit sample size and some ethical dilemmas inherent in genuine treatment research. There are several common difficulties in researching intervention with parents of handicapped children. All children are legally entitled to an appropriate education, so a genuine no-intervention control group, in which the child gets no educational services, is impossible except for very young children in some states. Moreover, there is sufficient evidence that parent training is helpful to make it unethical to keep a family in a no-training group for a long period. Such controls are acceptable and sometimes pragmatically necessary for a few weeks or even months, but the obligation to provide services limits control in follow-through comparisons. For much the same reason, training has rarely been compared with an attention placebo control, so the extent to which nonspecific aspects of being in treatment (e.g., the therapist's attention) account for observed effects is not known. Some authors eschew group studies in favor of single-subject ones, and some designs, such as the multiple baseline, have been employed convincingly. The more traditional reversal design, however, has serious ethical drawbacks (Sapon-

Shevin, 1982). With these caveats and misgivings, the discussion turns to
the outcome literature.

Short-Term Outcome

Table 9.2 summarizes group studies of intervention with parents of
developmentally disabled children. Table 9.2 is limited to published
studies that include at least four families and that have met at least
minimal standards for design and measurement. Inclusion is generally
limited to studies with children at least 2 years old, although there are
several exceptions. Infant intervention is discussed in Kaiser and Hayden (Chapter 8 in this volume).

Parent Knowledge and Teaching Skill

Each of the 11 studies in Table 9.2 that measured parents' knowledge of behavioral teaching principles found significant gain from pre-to
posttraining. Seven reported gains on the Behavioral Vignettes Test,
which presents 20 written vignettes involving a teaching or behavior
management situation with a retarded child and asks the parent to select
the best of four alternative responses for each (Baker & Brightman, in
press; Baker & Heifetz, 1976; Baker & McCurry, 1983; Brightman, Ambrose, & Baker, 1980; Brightman et al., 1982; Feldman, Manella,
Apodaca, & Varni, 1982; Feldman, Manella, & Varney, 1983). In the
seven studies where a comparison was made, trained parents gained in
knowledge on various measures relative to no-training controls (Table
9.2, Parts II and III). The two studies that reported advocacy training
demonstrated increased knowledge of advocacy-related information
posttraining relative to controls (Baker & Brightman, in press; Brightman, 1984).

Nine studies in Table 9.2 directly assessed parents' skill in teaching
their children. All found improvements after training in at least some of
the parent behaviors being coded. Several authors observed unstructured play settings, where the parents were coded for appropriate interactions rather than teaching per se (Diament & Colletti, 1978; Sandler
et al., 1983), and trained parents surpassed controls. Hudson (1982) used
a teaching checklist that gives parents points for each behavioral technique employed; the condition that had employed modeling and role
play in training surpassed controls. The UCLA group has developed the
Teaching Proficiency Test (Clark & Baker, 1984), a videotaped session
wherein teaching techniques are not simply tallied but also scored for
their appropriate use with a given task and child. In the four studies that

TABLE 9.2

Studies of Training with Parents of Developmentally Disabled Children

Authors	N	Child Diagnosis; age (years)	Program	Measures	Results	Results; follow-up (FU)
I. Single group pre–post						
Baker & McCurry, 1983	20	Mentally retarded; 9.2	School-based for low SES (6 half days)	Parent knowledge (Behavioral Vignettes Test), skills, & home teaching	Significant improve pre–post on all measures	Home teaching not maintained; 6-month FU
Feldman, Manella, Apodaca, & Varni, 1982	4	Spina bifida; 8	9 group meetings	Knowledge, child skills; marital inventories	Multiple baseline: significant gains on both; no change marital adjustment	Continued child gain; maintenance of knowledge; 3-month FU
Feldman, Manella, & Varni, 1983	4	Physically handicapped; 4–10	10 group meetings, single parents	Knowledge, child skills	Multiple baseline: significant gains on both	None
Harris, Wolchik, & Weitz, 1981	11	Autistic; 3.9	10 group meetings and 6 home visits	Language skill hierarchy	Significant improvement pre–post; No change pre-1 to pre-2	Continued progress; 2-, 4- & 13-month FU
Rose, 1974b	33	Mentally retarded; 3–8	7–10 small group meetings and home visits	Parent frequency counts	82% modified 1 or more child behavior to their satisfaction	20 of 21 maintained gains; 3–6-month FU
Salzinger, Feldman, & Portnoy, 1970	15	Brain injured; 3–12	Individual or group training	Success of child program	8 fully or partially carried out program and produced change	None

340

Study	N	Population	Format	Measures	Results	Follow-up/comments
Sebba, 1981	5	Profoundly mentally retarded with multiple handicaps	28 individual sessions	Bailey Scales of Infant Development	No significant improvement pre–post	None
Uditsky & MacDonald, 1981	64	Developmentally delayed	8 group and home visits; 3-month tapered FU	Interview post vs. 3-month, 1-year, or 2-year FU		Cross-sectional design; 3 FU groups similar, 75% or more in each condition maintained or improved target behavior

II. Studies with a no-training control group

Study	N	Population	Format	Measures	Results	Follow-up/comments
Bidder, Bryant, & Gray, 1975	16	Mentally retarded, Down's syndrome; 1–3	12 group meetings	Griffiths Mental Development Scales	T > C on Language and Performance Scales	None
Brightman, Ambrose, & Baker, 1980	16	Mentally retarded; 2.5–13	School-based, 3 or more days	Parent knowledge, skill; home teaching	Trained > matched comparison group on all	None
Clements, Evans, Jones, Osborne, & Upton, 1982	20	Mentally handicapped; 6.5	Biweekly home visits for 18 months (Portage model)	Reynell Developmental Language Scales	T improved significantly, but T = C; note: T, C not randomly assigned	None
Diament & Colletti, 1978	22	Learning disabled; 7	8 group meetings, groups of 5, 6	Observing mother–child play, parent ratings, Adjective Checklist (ACL)	T > C Mother praise-child attend and ACL conduct; T = C parent ratings	Maintained gains; 3-month FU
Hirsch & Walder, 1969	30	Severely disturbed and mentally retarded;	9 group meetings	Knowledge, behavior rating; anxiety–depression	T > C on knowledge, behavior rating; no change in anxiety, depression	None

341

(Continued)

TABLE 9.2 (Continued)

Authors	N	Child Diagnosis; age (years)	Program	Measures	Results	Results; follow-up (FU)
Prieto-Bayard & Baker, in press	20	Mentally retarded; 6.7	10 group meetings in Spanish with child group	Parent knowledge, skills; home teaching; child self-help, behavior problem	T significant gain on all; T > C except for teaching skill and self-help	Home teaching gains only partly maintained; 6-month FU
Sandler, Coren, & Thurman, 1983	21	Mentally retarded; 3.8	4 group and 4 individual meetings	Parent-child interaction; knowledge, attitude; Dvp checklist	T > C interaction and knowledge; no change on attitude and child development checklist	None
III. Studies with two or more experimental groups						
Baker & Brightman, in press	15	Mentally retarded; 5.7	Group training (N = 8) or advocacy (N = 7)	Teaching knowledge, skill; advocacy knowledge, skill	Generally, each group improved on measures specific to its training	None
Baker & Heifetz, 1976; Baker, Heifetz, & Murphy, 1980; Heifetz, 1977	160	Mentally retarded; 7.2	Training by manuals (N = 32), phone consultation (N = 32), groups (N = 32), groups and visits (N = 32), or no training (N = 32)	Parent knowledge; child self-help skills	Training conditions had equivalent outcome, but each surpassed controls	Parent-child gains maintained; further teaching equal across conditions; 1-year FU

Study	N	Population; mean age	Conditions	Measures	Results	Follow-up
Brightman, Baker, Clark, & Ambrose, 1982	66	Mentally retarded; 6	Individual (N = 16), group (N = 37), or control (N = 13)	Parent knowledge, skills; self-help, behavior problems	I = G > C except self help (I = G = C)	Home teaching; I = G; 6-month FU
Hudson, 1982	40	Mentally retarded; 0.3–3.5	Group training: Didactic (D), D with behavioral principles, D with modeling and role play, or control (N = 10@)	Parent knowledge and skill; home tasks completed; Denver Developmental Screening Test (DDST)	Knowledge, DDST, T > C, D = DB = DM; skills, DM > C; home tasks DM > D = DB	None
O'Dell, Flynn, & Benlolo, 1977	40	Mentally retarded; 8.2	Group training after pretraining (N = 14), placebo pretraining (N = 13), or no pretraining (N = 13)	Parent knowledge, skills; attitudes; home implementation	Outcome did not differ on any measure across pretraining conditions	Conditions not different in implementation; 1-month FU
Sandow & Clarke, 1978	32	Severely mentally retarded; 2.5	2 years' home visits, biweekly (N = 16) or bimonthly (N = 16)	Cattell Infant IQ	Biweekly, rise in year 1 and then decrement; bimonthly, opposite	None
Tavormina, 1975; Tavormina, Hampson, & Luscomb, 1976	51	Mentally retarded; 6.7	Behavioral (N = 19) vs. reflective (N = 19) vs. control (N = 13)	Hereford Parent Attitude Scale; Behavior observation, parent ratings; Missouri Behavior Problem Checklist	B > R > C on Hereford causation scale. behav. obs. and par. ratings; B = R > C on several subscales of BPC	Assessed satisfaction with training; B > R; 1-year FU

344   Bruce L. Baker

compared trained families with controls on this measure, trained families showed significantly greater benefits in two (Brightman, Ambrose, & Baker, 1980; Brightman et al., 1982) but their advantage failed to reach significance in two others (Baker & Brightman, in press; Prieto-Bayard & Baker, in press).

To summarize, there is compelling evidence that parents who have participated in training increase their knowledge of teaching principles and their skill in applying these with their child. The question arises whether gains in parent knowledge and skills are specific to training program content or derive from nonspecific factors, such as trainer's attention and encouragement. Baker and Brightman (in press) randomly assigned 15 families to either the Parents as Teachers or the Parents as Advocates course (described in the section "Independent Groups"), and administered measures of teaching (knowledge and skill) and advocacy (knowledge and skill) to all parents pre- and posttraining. On three of the four measures, parents demonstrated gains that were specific to their training condition; on the fourth, teaching skill, parents trained as teachers gained more but the difference failed to reach significance. The authors concluded that the effects of nonspecific factors on these indices were minimal.

Parent Attitudes

There is little substantive to be said about the impact of intervention programs on parent attitudes and adjustment, in part because the better-executed studies have not usually included this type of measure. While there are uncontrolled studies that show pre–post attitude changes after some form of intervention, the controlled studies are less positive. Three studies in Table 9.2 that contrasted trained parents with waiting list controls found no differential attitude change (Baker & Heifetz, 1976; Hirsch & Walder, 1969; Sandler et al., 1983). Two others found trained families gained more than controls, but these were limited to just one subscale of the Bipolar Adjective Checklist (Diament & Colletti, 1978) and of the Hereford Parent Attitude Survey (Tavormina, 1975).

Studies with families treated for child noncompliance are informative. One found improvements in parental attitudes and perceptions of child behavior almost to the level of non-clinic-referred children (Forehand & King, 1977). Another found equal changes in marital adjustment and child self-esteem following a parent counseling program or a didactic training program (Scovern, Bukstel, Kilmann, Laval, Busenmeyer, & Smith, 1980), while yet another found the parents perceived the family as more cohesive after training (Karoly & Rosenthal, 1977). These and similar studies suggest a positive spiral effect following training that is focused on a particular child problem. However, similar controlled research on how training affects families with a handicapped child is needed.

Child Gains

Several evaluations of training have cited the proportion of parents successfully implementing change programs with their child. In an early paper, Salzinger, Feldman, and Portnoy (1970) reported only 53% of 15 families implemented a program to successful completion, but O'Dell, Flynn, & Benlolo (1977) found 68% completed one full modification project and Rose (1974b) found that 82% of parents modified at least one child behavior "to their own satisfaction." It would be helpful if more programs included this type of measure, as it further enlightens group statistics.

Standard measures have consistently shown significant child gains when they were directly related to the content of training, such as tests of reading (Fry, 1977), language skills (Harris, Wolchik, & Weitz, 1981), arm flexion (Gross et al., 1982), or self-help skills (Baker & Heifetz, 1976; Baker & McCurry, 1983; Brightman et al., 1982; Feldman et al., 1982; Feldman et al., 1983; Prieto-Bayard & Baker, in press) or behavior problems (Brightman et al., 1982; Tavormina, 1975). Moreover, gains have been shown to be related to training by a time series design (Harris et al., 1981), multiple baseline (Feldman et al., 1982, 1983), an ABA design (Fry, 1977), and waiting list controls (Baker & Heifetz, 1976; Brightman et al., 1982; Tavormina, 1975). In two studies with a measure of 36 child self-help skills trained children did not significantly surpass controls (Brightman et al, 1982; Prieto-Bayard & Baker, in press). In these latter studies control groups were small (N = 13 and 11, and respectively) and unstable, but, more importantly, the measure was much broader than the two or three self-help skills a family actually taught during training.

When studies have used even broader measures, the outcome results have been more mixed. Five studies in Table 9.2 used developmental scales with very young children. Two failed to find significant changes after 8 training sessions (Sandler et al., 1983) and 28 training sessions (Sebba, 1981). Another (Clements et al., 1982) found changes after 18 months, but control children gained as much. Two studies did find significant gains in development relative to controls (Bidder, Bryant, & Gray, 1975; Hudson, 1982). It can be generally concluded that parent training programs affect child gains in the specific behaviors targeted, but the extent to which more generalized improvement results is not known.

Generalization

Immediate training program outcomes are as hoped for—parents and children alike learn new skills. But to see if something meaningful has been accomplished, a wider-angle lens is needed: generalization. Forehand and Atkeson (1977) have noted four kinds of potential generalization: to other settings, over time, to other behaviors, and to other children within the family. This discussion concentrates on the first two of these, setting and temporal generalization, which reveal the extent to which any behavior change has become meaningfully incorporated into the child's repertoire. The third, generalization to other behaviors, has received little research attention. One would expect generalization to behaviors in the same general class as the target behavior; for example, Baker and Heifetz (1976) targeted self-help skills and found generalized improvement in nonprogrammed self-help skills. One would also expect that teaching one behavior or reducing one behavior problem would make other behaviors yield more quickly to a modification program, but such sequential data are not available. The fourth, generalization to other children, has also been little studied, although it is not uncommon in the experience of parent trainers to hear "You know, this works with my other kids too."

Setting Generalization

Katie, in the case study, learned to talk more sensibly with her mother, but how did she talk with her teacher and her friends? And though Steven behaved more like a gentleman in a restaurant, did his increased sitting without crying carry over into his classroom? The common wisdom is that behavior changes do not generalize much to a new setting unless this is intentionally programmed for. S. J. Miller and Sloane (1976), for example, found that home training of vocalizations in nonverbal children produced no changes when they were in the school setting. Unfortunately, most of the parent training studies of setting generalization with handicapped children have used autistic children, perhaps because generalized responses are so difficult for these children. The information-processing deficits and concreteness in autism render natural generalization especially unlikely. I would expect much better generalization in other handicapped children with better verbal skills.

A well designed study with autistic children that enlightens the generalization question looked at generalization from home to school and vice versa (Zifferblatt, Burton, Horner, & White, 1977). Six children, already accustomed to a token economy, were reinforced at home for two behaviors (wiping bottom, sharing toys) and at school for two other behaviors (washing hands, following instructions). Six additional children were similarly trained at home and school, with the pairs of behaviors reversed (e.g., wiping bottom, sharing toys were reinforced at school). All four behaviors were measured in each setting.

The results were quite consistent. Each behavior increased in that setting where it was treated and, simultaneously, in the generalization setting. This very good generalization may be attributable both to the children having the opportunity to perform the skills in the generalization setting and to the existence of a token economy in both settings. The tokens, although not given for the generalization behaviors, may have helped to make the two settings more similar. This is a nice demonstration of the advantage of having both school and home involved in systematic teaching, using the same methods even if not the same target behaviors. The generalization from each may be enhanced. The key to setting generalization appears to be consistency and a similarity in characteristics of the two settings, especially in contingencies. Many parent training programs promote this by having trainers in clinic-based programs visit the home or having teachers sit in on group sessions.

Temporal Generalization

Finally, and in some ways most importantly, it must be known whether there is a lasting impact of intervention programs. First, do child behavior changes persist? If the children in the case studies were looked in on a year later, would Katie and Steven still be talking and sitting well? It is known that T was still eating well because a follow-up was included. In their review of generalization, Forehand and Atkeson (1977) noted that only 12% of 146 behavioral studies reviewed had reported temporal generalization, although since that time studies have been more likely to take follow-up measures. Nine case studies in Table 9.1 reported a follow-up of at least 1 month and all found maintenance of gains or even further improvement. Several studies followed the family for 1 year or more (Barnard, Christophersen, & Wolf, 1976; Fox & Roseen, 1977; White, 1982).

The six studies in Table 9.2 that followed up child skills found maintenance and some reported further improvement. Learning disabled children were still attending to task better 3 months after their parents completed training (Diament & Colletti, 1978), autistic children showed continued language progress 13 months after training (Harris *et al.*, 1981), physically handicapped children showed continued skill gains after 3 months (Feldman *et al.*, 1982) and retarded children maintained and improved upon gains in follow-ups from 3 months to 2 years later (Baker, Heifetz, & Murphy, 1980; Rose, 1974b; Uditsky & Mac-

Donald, 1981). It seems reasonable that skill gains will be maintained if the environment provides opportunity, encouragement, and reinforcement for practicing them—and the evidence bears this out. Less is known about maintenance of behavior problem improvement, though programs that work with noncompliant nonhandicapped children have reported very encouraging long-term results (Patterson & Fleishman, 1979; Strain, Steele, Ellis, & Timm, 1982). Strain and colleagues did an ambitious and creative 3–9 year follow-up, locating 40 formerly noncompliant children in their schools and then including them and four randomly selected same-sex and same-age classmates in a study of "school adjustment." Hence, teachers were blind to the relationship of the measures to some children's former treatment. On observations of teacher and child behaviors and teacher-completed behavior problem checklists, former clients were indistinguishable from their peers.

Yet the aims of intervention with families of handicapped children are of necessity broader than with families of nonhandicapped children who have behavior problems. The few skill gains or behavior problem changes accomplished during training are but a beginning—there will always be a great deal more to teach. Accordingly, follow-up evaluations must examine continued parental skills and new parental teaching as well as the maintenance of original child behavior change. And here the data are more limited. The largest follow-up reported has been Baker, Heifetz, and Murphy's (1980) 14-month posttraining assessment of 95 families who completed a training program aimed at self-help teaching and behavior problem management (see Baker & Heifetz, 1976, and p. 350, this chapter). Parents had maintained knowledge of principles, but a discouragingly low 16% of families had done formal teaching of a new skill and only 22% had carried out a program for behavior problem management. Follow-up performance was considerably better when the authors considered incidental teaching—incorporating behavioral principles into daily routine as the occasion arises, but without formal teaching sessions. Fully 76% reported incidental teaching, with specific goals and good behavioral teaching for at least a month's duration. Uditsky and MacDonald (1981) found very similar results when they assessed three groups of families with a developmentally disabled child 3, 12, and 24 months after group training. Likewise, Ambrose and Baker (1979) interviewed 88 families 6 months after the UCLA program, with very similar results. Based on the extent of programming reported as well as the appropriateness of the behavioral techniques used, this sample classified 25% as low follow-up, with little or no productive teaching.

A difficulty with all of these studies is the absence of an untreated control group, so how much teaching families would have been doing without training cannot be known; for practical and ethical reasons, most programs have not continued a waiting list control group through follow-up. An alternative, though certainly not ideal, approach is a time series. The UCLA project has devised an interview that asks parents about the teaching and behavior problem management that they have done during the past 3 months, and administers pretraining at the end of the 3-month training and at one or more 3-month follow-up intervals. Not unexpectedly, scores of both the extent of teaching and the behavioral sophistication with which it is done have increased from pretraining to posttraining. However, the extent of teaching scores drop off at follow-up. This seems especially a problem in lower-socioeconomic families whose extent of teaching scores attained by 6 months after training have returned to pretraining levels (Baker and McCurry, 1983; Prieto-Bayard & Baker, in press). Hence, a primary question that needs considerably more study is how best to promote continued application of skills learned in training to new teaching areas once training has ended.

Enhancing Outcome

Thus far family intervention models have been described and their overall effectiveness recounted. This and the next section look more closely at correlates of outcome. First components of training are considered to see how a choice of training model, focus, or procedures might affect outcome. Next family predictors of outcome and possible training modifications to accommodate less-successful families are examined. First, a caveat: The most clinically meaningful answers to questions about correlates of outcome would be expressed as interactions ("For parents of type a, and a child of type b, a model of type c, with focus of type d, will maximize results in area e if . . .") or multiple regressions ("From among characteristics of the model and program and family and child, the best predictors of parent implementation are . . ."). Practically all available studies, however, examine only main effects and univariate relationships, with inherent problems of confounding.

Models of Training

Outcomes have been considered without reference to the training model. Studies that have compared models have primarily contrasted clinic-based individual to group training models. Two studies with methodological problems reported better outcome with individual training (Eyberg & Matarazzo, 1980; Mira, 1970). However, comparisons with parents of developmentally delayed (Kogan & Tyler, 1978) and mentally retarded children (Salzinger et al., 1970), as well as emotionally disturbed (Thomas, 1977) and nonhandicapped behavior problem (Christensen, Johnson, Phillips, & Glasgow, 1980) children have found no difference between the two models on measures such as programs completed, parent perception of child problems, parent behavior in play sessions with the child, or observational data from audio recordings made in the home. Brightman et al. (1982) randomly assigned parents of retarded children to waiting list control ($N = 13$), individual ($N = 16$), or group ($N = 37$) training in the 10-session Parents as Teachers program. Two results were consistent. First, trained parents and children showed gains relative to controls. Second, the two training conditions produced almost identical results. However, group training was conducted at half the cost per family. It seems reasonable to conclude that group training is generally more cost-effective than individual training.

   Another comparison of interest is clinic- versus home-based individual training, since proponents of the latter argue that its advantages are worth the increased cost. Unfortunately, comparisons of these models could not be found. The closest are two studies that examined whether additional benefits accrued when group training was supplemented with a series of home consultations. Worland, Carney, Milich, and Grame (1980) found that adding four home consultations to an 8-week group training program for parents of hard-to-manage children produced no additional gains. Baker and Heifetz (1976) randomly assigned 160 families with mentally retarded children to one of five conditions for the Parents as Teachers program: (1) waiting list control, (2) training by manuals only, (3) manuals and phone consultation, (4) manuals and eight group meetings, (5) manuals, eight group meetings, and six home visits. Families in each training condition were superior to controls on measures of knowledge of behavioral principles and child self-help skills. However, the training conditions differed little from one another. Of particular interest here is the comparison of conditions (4) and (5); although the trainers and parents felt that the home visits were useful, there were no discernible differences on the available measures of participation or outcome. This study did not, however, directly observe parents teaching, and it would seem that a few individual sessions (clinic or home) might be useful to enhance application of principles learned in the group to actual teaching.

   A related study addressed the question of how many home visits are optimal. Sandow and Clarke (1978) visited families of severely subnormal children either every 2 weeks or every 8 weeks. In the first year child gains were greatest in families visited more frequently, but in the second year the outcome was reversed. The authors noted that parents related to the frequent visitor more as a friend and babysitter, and apparently had assumed less responsibility themselves for training.

Any definitive conclusion about the relative merits of training models must await more study. Especially needed are direct comparisons of individual clinic- and home-based training. The available research does, however, produce one caution: More is not always better. There is neither evidence that more costly individual training improves on group training nor that time-consuming home visits enhance treatment outcome.

Focus of Training

Intervention programs range from brief consulting directed toward change in a very specific child behavior to continuing programs that intervene much more broadly. Two questions are of particular interest. First, is outcome enhanced when intervention goes beyond training to include consideration of other family issues and ills? Second, is the outcome of training itself enhanced when the program imparts general principles rather than just specific prescriptions? The first question has received very limited empirical attention, although a number of programs report having combined reflective and behavioral methods. Griest, Forehand, Rogers, Briener, Furey, and Williams (1982) have developed Parent Enhancement Therapy, which adds to basic behavioral consultation for parents of noncompliant children treatment related to parents' personal adjustment, marital adjustment, extrafamilial relationships, and perception of their child's behavior. At 2-month follow-up observations, the parent enhancement therapy together with a parent training condition had maintained better parent behavior management and greater child compliance than behavior consultation alone. Clearly this broader focus, drawing on both parent training and other forms of psychological intervention, deserves further study.

The second question asks whether it is desirable to teach general principles so that parent's will understand the rationale for programs they are implementing and be equipped to initiate new intervention after training has ended. Four studies that have compared specific with general training leave this issue unsettled. Two studies (Glogower & Sloop, 1976; McMahon, Forehand, & Griest, 1981) reported enhanced treatment effects when they included the teaching of principles in their training programs for parents of noncompliant children. On the other hand, two studies for parents of retarded children (Hudson, 1982; O'Dell, Flynn, & Benlolo, 1977) found no added benefits of training in general principles. O'Dell, Flynn, and Benlolo conducted 6 sessions of group training, preceded by 3 sessions of didactic pretraining in general principles, 3 sessions of placebo control pretraining, or no pretraining. Hudson compared 10 sessions of "specific focus" training with 10 sessions that added lectures about principles to the former. The two studies used a number of measures of knowledge, behavioral skills, attendance, attitudes, implementation, and child change. It is surprising that general principles did not enhance outcome, especially with parents of retarded children where there is not just one isolated target behavior to treat. It may be that benefits of broader knowledge show up over time; these studies had 1-month and no follow-up, respectively. Also, teaching by lengthy didactic lectures may not be the best way to impart knowledge of principles, as discussed in the next section.

Methods of Training

Modeling, Role Play, and Rehearsal

Although didactic presentation—lecturing, as in a course—has been a natural approach for parent trainers, there are compelling reasons to utilize modeling techniques, role playing, and/or rehearsal with the child. Watson and Bassinger (1974) used both approaches with parents of retarded children, finding parents acquired information well with a didactic approach. However, ability to apply teaching methods increased only when techniques were modeled and role played. Two more recent studies with severely handicapped children underscored the advantage of training by modeling, role play, and rehearsal. Fabry and Reid (1978) trained foster grandparents to teach profoundly retarded, multiply handicapped institutionalized adolescents. While lectures had produced no change in foster grandparent behavior, modeling by the trainer and then practice with feedback were accompanied by increased teaching activity. In Hudson's (1982) study, considered earlier, a modeling and role-playing condition where parents rehearsed with their own children in some sessions proved superior to either verbal instruction alone or the verbal instruction and general principles condition.

A natural extension of training through modeling is the use of video models. Film or videotape can show a wider range of examples more easily than modeling with group members' children (and with more predictable results). For program evaluation, video is more consistent, and for dissemination, more cost-effective and exportable. Unfortunately, most studies of video modeling have used brief programs to teach one behavioral technique (e.g., time out) to volunteer parents of nonhandicapped children. Measures have included knowledge of principles, role playing, or teaching the parents' own child at home. These studies found video modeling superior to didactic lectures (Flanagan, Adams, & Forehand, 1979; Nay, 1975) and as good as or better than live modeling and role playing (Flanagan *et al.*, 1979; Nay, 1975; O'Dell, Krug, Patterson, & Faustman, 1980; O'Dell, Mahoney, Horton, & Turner, 1979; O'Dell, O'Quin, Alford, O'Briant, Bradlyn, & Giebenhain, 1982).

Video Training Packages

The several attempts to use media in a more complete program have been encouraging (Hofmeister & Latham, 1972; Webster-Stratton, 1981, 1982). The most compelling illustration of video training's promise is the program developed for parents of severely handicapped children by McConkey and colleagues in Dublin, Ireland (McConkey & O'Connor, 1982). A video course (composed of five 25–34-minute video programs, a handbook, and a series of specific homework exercises) focuses on one point in language development (putting two words together). Small groups of parents meet with two trainers, who run the videotape and lead discussions. Of 20 families invited to participate in a first trial of the video course, 19 accepted and 18 completed (including 15 fathers). Fourteen children had Down's syndrome and four had an unspecified handicap. Parents subsequently rated the program quite enthusiastically, and audiotapes made by the parents at home indicated changes in the way parents talked to their children and gains in their childrens' language with further gains at a 4-month follow-up.

On the basis of these findings, the course was revised and disseminated (McConkey, 1982). All major services for mentally handicapped people in the Republic of Ireland (N = 20) were invited to nominate two people to be prepared as course tutors. Seventeen services sent 31 people for a 12-hour workshop to experience the video course and prepare to run their own courses. At the time of the report, 12 centers had conducted the course for parents and 3 had active plans to do so. Of 73 families invited, an incredible 71 (97%) accepted. Here, too, parents evaluated the experience very highly, although less-educated parents were more likely to rate the material as difficult to follow.

Manuals

Another approach to cost-effective dissemination of information is through written media. Some form of written handout, pamphlet, or manual is used in almost every parent training program. An example of a manual-based training program is the 1-year correspondence course program offered by the John Tracy Clinic for parents of deaf children; it has been translated into 17 languages and by 1979 had enrolled an impressive 48,637 families of young deaf children in 129 countries (Lowell, 1979). However, when Bernal and North (1978) surveyed 26 commercially available parent training manuals they concluded as others have (Glasgow & Rosen, 1978; McMahon & Forehand, 1980) that sound empirical evaluation has lagged behind production.

The most extensive evaluation of training by manuals was the study by Baker and Heifetz (1976; Baker, Heifetz, & Murphy, 1980; Heifetz, 1977) described in the section "Models of Training." Parents in the manuals-only condition attended a large orientation meeting and then were sent a self-help and later a behavior problem manual. Four months later, they had gained as much in knowledge of behavioral principles and child self-help skills as those trained in more costly professional conditions. The manuals-only families intervened with fewer behavior problems and finished the program less confident about their teaching than families in the other conditions; moreover, they were doing somewhat less teaching 1 year later than parents in the other three conditions combined. Despite these shortcomings, training by manuals only was certainly the most cost-effective of the approaches evaluated. These manuals and others were subsequently published as the *Steps to Independence* series (see the section "Independent Groups"); almost 100,000 were in circulation by 1984.

Computers

Tawney and colleagues (Tawney, Aeschleman, Deaton, & Donaldson, 1979) have piloted a telecommunications approach to reach severely handicapped children in remote areas. Programs to teach visual discriminations and motor responses were transmitted by telephone between a central computer and home-based teaching machines. The project found its low-socioeconomic-status (SES) rural families accepted the placement of equipment in their homes and that their children interacted with and learned from the automated devices. Parents were taught to use the system, but there was no further training. At present, such methods seem expensive, plagued by technical difficulties, and limited in program content—but there is unique service delivery promise here, and a future review might report intriguing results from this most modern approach.

Incentives in Training

Even the most compelling training program must compete with other demands for parents' attention on a given meeting night. And even parents' most carefully designed and conscientiously executed home teaching programs with severely handicapped children are likely to produce progress that is uneven and sometimes painfully slow. Indeed, "seeing progress" cannot be counted on as sufficient to sustain parent performance. Many programs have remembered the law of effect in designing their intervention, and have included incentives to motivate desired parent behaviors. And for once there is almost universal agreement in the literature: incentives work.

Incentives can be grouped into four types, although they follow the same principles and many programs combine several types. First, all programs include some *social pressure and social support.* Trainers make clear performance contracts with parents, sometimes in writing, and trainers and group members alike praise a parent's accomplishments. A second type of incentive is *family members' reinforcement of each other.* The trainer can encourage spouses to support one another's efforts and can help arrange family agreements wherein a specified amount of parent effort and/or child gain will earn a reward: The whole family goes swimming, mother gets breakfast in bed—the possibilities are limitless and need not cost anything. A third class of incentives involves *contingent professional resources,* such as extra training time, a toy-lending library, or reference books (Donahue, 1973). All these three types of incentives have the advantage of utilizing available reinforcers in the parents' or professionals' natural environment.

The most studied type of incentives however, is use of *tangible reinforcers.* One desperate daytime program sought to reduce nonattendance by giving weekly synopses of soap operas missed during meeting time to mothers who attended (Rickel, Dudley, & Bermon, 1980)! The more common tangible reinforcer, however, is money. In some programs a contract deposit is required from families and refunded according to certain performance criteria. Hirsch and Walder (1969), for example, refunded a $50 deposit in its entirety if all nine sessions were attended, with no refund at all otherwise (remarkably, all 30 mothers maintained perfect attendance). Modifications of this strategy have refunded according to a schedule of points earned for attendance, participation in group meetings, and/or completed assignments (Benassi & Benassi, 1973; Rinn, Vernon, & Wise, 1975). Eyberg and Johnson (1974) combined a refundable contract deposit, contingent telephone time, and contingent training time (parents could not attend a consultation session without data). Parents in the incentive condition completed more data recording, treated a greater number of child problems, and received a higher cooperation rating from the staff than parents in the no-incentive condition.

In some programs, parents are paid for successful performance. One clever strategy is a lottery, wherein parents earn tickets toward prizes (Ambrose, Hazzard, & Haworth, 1980; Muir & Milan, 1982). In my experience parents who earn tickets for attending, coming on time, and completing homework enjoy the element of chance, and one relatively inexpensive reinforcer (e.g., houseplant, stuffed animal, canned ham) can motivate a whole group. There is some evidence that incentive programs may make more difference with lower-SES families. Fleischman (1979) paid a $1 parenting salary for each day that parents of "acting out" children carried out prescribed programs. For middle-SES families the cooperation rate was 92%, quite high and unaffected by the salary. For lower-SES and/or single-parent families, however, four with the parenting salary completed 85% while four with no salary completed only 50% and, in fact, all dropped out.

It seems well established that incentives for parents promote greater participation. Quite apart from the inherent desirability of the incentives themselves, their provision may impress upon parents the expectations held for them and concretize an agreement with the trainers. There are, however, virtually no follow-up data reported in studies that have increased participation through incentives. This seems particularly important with tangible incentives. To the extent that greater participation leads to greater mastery of content, parents may follow through better than those who have not received incentives. On the other hand, if parents attribute their increased involvement to the tangible reinforcers, it seems possible that they could drop to lower levels of teaching following training than parents who performed without tangible reinforcers and attributed their involvement entirely to their own interest.

Predicting Outcome: Implications for Intervention

The relationships among parent, child, and family characteristics and intervention outcome have received only limited attention, especially in programs for parents of handicapped children. An adequate approach to this question would involve measuring a wide range of variables, utilizing a large sample, and employing multiple regression analysis to determine the unique contribution of each variable. Only a few studies have done this (Baker and Clark, 1983, in press; Blechman et *al.*, 1981; Clark & Baker, 1983; Clark, Baker, & Heifetz, 1982; Sadler Seyden, Howe, & Kaminsky, 1976). Nonetheless, in this section the available evidence is considered and the implications of predictor relationships for program innovation are explored.

Socioeconomic Status

Socioeconomic status (SES) is considered separately, since it has received the most attention as a correlate of outcome. Two definitional problems are encountered immediately. First, indices of SES vary. Some studies have followed Hollingshead (1957) in combining father's education and occupation, others use mother's education or reading level, and still others use income. Second, cutoff points vary. In some studies low SES means below an absolute cutoff on one dimension (e.g., receiving welfare payments) while in others it only means that families are low relative to others in the sample.

Lower-SES families, by most definitions, have been underrepresented in parent education or training programs (Hargis & Blechman, 1979). Whether this is by exclusion or by choice is unknown. The examination of intervention models for this review revealed potential mismatches. Regular attendance at agency training may be difficult, given child-care needs and lack of transportation. Group curricula, homework, and written manuals may be too much like school to appeal to parents with limited education.

Lower-SES parents who do join training programs generally have been reported to fare less well than middle-class families. Studies of program completion have been mixed, with some reporting a relation to SES (McMahon, Forehand, Griest, & Wells, 1981; Sadler *et al.*, 1976) and some reporting no relationship (Clark & Baker, 1983; Worland *et al.*, 1982). The relationship of SES to outcome is much more consistent. In families with child conduct disorders, Rinn *et al.* (1975) found that lower-income parents attended fewer group sessions and attained fewer goals; Sadler *et al.* (1976) and Patterson (1974) found that families with low education and SES (respectively) produced less reduction in deviant child behavior following individual training. In families with a retarded child, Rose (1974a) found that mothers on welfare trained in groups took longer than middle-class mothers to carry out programs and hence completed fewer, and Brassell (1977) reported father's education correlated with childrens' mental growth rate during training.

Duncan Clark and I have studied outcome predictors in two samples of parents with retarded children. In the primarily self-referred development sample (N = 103), we related a number of SES, parent, child, and family characteristics to short- and long-term outcome (Clark & Baker, 1983). In an agency-referred validation sample (N = 44) we replicated the procedure (Baker & Clark, in press). The most consistent finding was that SES variables (income, mother's education, and the Hollinghead's SES index) related to measures of short-term outcome—how well parents understood behavioral principles and taught their retarded children. Moreover, in discriminant analyses to predict posttraining high-proficiency (versus low proficiency) families, SES components entered the equation. The relationship of SES to long-term implementation at home was less consistent.

The obvious clinical question is how training can be altered to attract low-SES parents, to keep them in the program, and to increase their gains. The UCLA project has explored several alternatives to group training in order to make training more accessible and beneficial for lower-SES families. The UCLA staff conducted meetings at central and familiar locations and counselors recruited families with whom they had a personal relationship. The project provided child care, provided or reimbursed transportation, included a lottery, with tickets earned for attendance and homework, and gave diplomas upon program completion. The major curriculum change was to supplement group meetings with modeling and supervised child teaching, as is done in school or home-based programs.

We conducted two summer mini-camps, one for parents who had shown only limited benefits from group training (Brightman et al., 1980) and one for parents predicted to be low-proficiency based on Clark and Baker's (1983) predictors (Baker & McCurry, 1983). In both school-based programs, parents were actively involved in observing children being taught and then teaching their own child and others, with videotaped and staff feedback. These parents gained significantly in their knowledge of principles and teaching abilities. In the Brightman et al. study, mini-camp-trained parents scored significantly higher than a comparison group who did not attend. We have also developed a program for parents who speak only Spanish. In one study, where parents' education level averaged only the fifth grade, parents and children showed significant gains relative to waiting list control families (Prieto-Bayard & Baker, in press; Prieto-Bayard, Huff, & Baker, 1981). There is one potential drawback, however, to programs with homogeneously lower-SES families. Rose (1974a) reported that mothers on welfare in mixed groups with middle-class mothers completed twice as many programs as those in groups of all mothers on welfare.

These successes in using a combination of group- and school-based models suggest other alternatives. It is widely believed that home-based training is superior with lower-SES families, in part because dropping out of this model involves a more active response. Another inclination is to use individual clinic-based training. Yet two studies with parents of developmentally disabled children found no interaction between education and format (individual versus group)—families with lower education did equally less well than those with higher education when trained individually or in groups (Baker, Prieto-Bayard, & McCurry, 1984; Thomas, 1977).

Two exceptions to the SES–outcome relationship suggest fruitful variations. In a program of individual training for mothers with noncompliant children, Rogers and colleagues (Rogers, Forehand, Griest, Wells, & McMahon, 1981) found that SES did not relate to pre or change scores of child behavior, parent behavior, or maternal perception of the child. In this program, training was individualized and competency-based, requiring parents to master each step before moving on. Hence different families moved through at different rates. Unfortunately the authors did not report whether the number of sessions differed with SES, but this self-paced, criterion-based program offers one alternative. A second exception is the report of no SES–income relationship in programs training through video media (McConkey & O'Connor, 1982; O'Dell et al., 1982). In sum, in designing a program to accommodate lower-SES families better, there are reasonably simple changes that might serve to increase accessibility (e.g., child care), understanding (e.g., self-pacing, video), and motivation (e.g., incentives).

Child Characteristics

Few studies have examined the relationship of child characteristics to outcome. The UCLA project has related characteristics of retarded children to their parents' behavior, with unexpected results. No child characteristic—sex, age, level of functioning, extent of behavior problems, or diagnosis—was significantly related to either parent short-term gains or long-term implementation in any of the three samples studied (Baker & Clark, in press; Clark & Baker, 1983; Clark et al., 1982).

Other studies that have considered child characteristics have trained parents of very young children and considered the child's developmental progress. Brassell (1977) conducted weekly home visits for 10 months to families of 73 retarded children (mean age, 21 months). Barna, Bidder, Gray, Clements, and Gardner (1980) used the Portage Project weekly home visit model (Shearer & Shearer, 1976) in Wales for an average of 1 year with families of 35 retarded children (mean age, 24 months). Sex differences were found by Brassell (girls gained more than three times as much as boys) but were not considered by Barna et al. The age that children entered the program did not relate in either study, while severity of retardation related to progress in both studies. Barna et al. found the slowest rate of progress in infants with cerebral palsy or visual impairments. At this point, although many assumptions are made about the relationship between child characteristics and intervention success, there is little empirical basis for them.

Parent Characteristics

Common clinical wisdom would suggest that parents who are themselves more capable and better adjusted would do best in any intervention program. Yet parent characteristics, such as intelligence, prior related skills and experience, psychological adjustment, or expectancies have received little attention in prediction studies. Once again, most studies have spoken to only single variables, leaving results potentially confounded. In the only study to measure mother's IQ, Hirsch and Walder (1969) reported no relationship with outcome; however, this upper-middle-class group no doubt had a very constricted range. It seems likely that an IQ–outcome relationship would emerge with a broader population, althought it would be confounded with social class. The UCLA project examined pretraining related experience and skills, finding that these were greater for parents who subsequently achieved high proficiency. In turn, higher posttraining proficiency predicted implementation during follow-through (Clark & Baker, 1983; Clark et al., 1982).

Two studies with conduct-disordered children have found mother's adjustment was related to her behavior during and after training. Miller and Gottleib (1974) reported that Minnesota Multiphasic Personality Inventory profiles predicted the pattern of follow-through, but they did not report the combination of scales. McMahon, Forehand, Griest, and Wells (1981) found that dropouts from training scored as more depressed on the Beck Depression Inventory. It is premature to base clinical decisions on these results, but should relationships between adjustment and performance hold up, more empirical ways to decide when to recommend therapy and when to recommend training may be developed.

Parents' expectations were also predictive in Clark and Baker's (1983) study. Parents who forsaw more obstacles and felt they had less ability to overcome them indeed were less proficient when training ended. Role expectations were also studied by Strom, Rees, Slaughter, and Wurster (1980), who administered their Parent As A Teacher Inventory before a home-based language intervention program. Although they did not report quantified results, they noted that scores at the upper or lower extremes served as an excellent guide for identifying those who would be most and least successful as teachers. It would be interesting to see if this test of parental role expectations in childrearing would be predictive with other characteristics (e.g., intelligence, social class) partialled out. Fortunately, parent expectations are amenable to change. Initial results of a cognitive–behavioral program that aims to alter maladaptive thought patterns as well as teach skills are encouraging (Ambrose *et al.*, 1980; UCLA Project for Developmental Disabilities, 1982).

Family Characteristics

The family's socioeconomic context and characteristics of its individual members have been examined, but so far the family itself has not been looked at directly. Two questions about the family are particularly of interest in considering outcome predictors. First, who in the family participates in the intervention program? Most "parent" programs have only involved mothers, raising questions about involvement of, and impact on, the broader family—questions about single parents, fathers, and siblings. Second, how do family relationships relate to receptivity toward and success of intervention?

Family Participants

Single parents have been less likely to complete training programs (Hall & Nelson, 1981; Strain, Young, & Horowitz, 1981). Moreover, those who have completed training were less likely to demonstrate lasting benefits. In a follow-up study of 83 families with retarded children, the likelihood that a parent who began training completed the program, attained proficiency, and followed through some during the subsequent 6 months was only 14% for single parents compared to 59% for parents with intact marriages (Baker & Clark, in press). While having a spouse is predictive of success, it does not seem to matter whether he or she is involved in the intervention program, a finding that seems at odds with theories of family process. There are several studies on father involvement, all with parents of nonhandicapped children. Behrendt (1978) found that families with child management problems did equally well on all measures of outcome after parent training whether or not father participated. Moreover, in studies where father participation was controlled by the researcher—who assigned some families to mother-only and some to mother-and-father conditions—father involvement made no difference (Adesso & Lipson, 1981; Firestone, Kelly, & Fike, 1980; Martin, 1977).

Adubato, Adams, and Budd (1981) demonstrated that a mother who had completed training was then able to train her husband, so that in a few sessions he too was an effective teacher for their severely developmentally disabled child. Perhaps interested fathers in these studies learned new teaching methods from their wives, even though they did not directly participate. Sandler et al.'s (1983) data cast doubt here, though; fathers were not involved in training and their knowledge of principles did not change. It does seem possible, nonetheless, that there are unmeasured delayed benefits of having both spouses involved, if only to prevent such a strong alliance between the teaching parent and handicapped child that the rest of the family is excluded (Minuchin, 1974).

In this regard, intervention with siblings should be mentioned. There are a few empirical reports demonstrating that siblings can effectively teach the handicapped child (Bennett, 1973; Colletti & Harris, 1977; Lavigueur, 1976; Schreibman, O'Neill, & Koegel, 1983); however, the narrow focus and short-term measurement does not inspire confidence that any basic change has been made in the way the siblings live with one another. More promising are reports of group therapy with adolescent siblings (Grossman, 1972) and an intensive training program emphasizing teaching but also information and attitudes (Pasick, 1975). Adolescents in the latter program increased their productive involvement with their younger retarded sibling compared to controls. Clearly there is a great deal more to learn about how fathers and siblings are naturally involved with handicapped children and how best to build upon that involvement. (See Skrtic, Summers, Brotherson, and Turnbull, Chapter 6 in this volume, for a more detailed review of the effect of a handicapped child on siblings.)

Family Relationships

A number of authors have reported poorer short- and long-term outcomes when there was marital discord in the parents of conduct-disordered children, although none directly measured marital discord (Bernal, Williams, Miller, & Reogor, 1972; Patterson, 1974; Reisinger, Frangia, & Hoffman, 1976). Cole and Morrow (1976) noted that when marital conflicts disrupted parent roles, there was an inability to agree on target child behaviors and on modification procedures, as well as a failure to follow through with agreed-upon procedures. The only study relating marital discord to outcome in families with a handicapped child (Baker & Clark, 1983) was consistent, finding that parents who scored low (below 100) on the self-report Marital Adjustment Test (Locke & Wallace, 1959) were less likely to follow through after training.

Cole and Morrow (1976) also considered a characteristic of parenting style—insensitive authoritarian coerciveness toward children—as related to intervention failure. They noted that this may be manifested as emphasis on rigid, punitive standards or as insistence on youngsters' submission to personal adult dictation. They summarized:

> The identifying characteristics of these rigid, punitive parents appeared to include; pervasive negative scanning and negative labeling of the child's behaviors, resistance to positive scanning, setting unrealistically high criteria for reinforcement, impatience for fast results, reluctance to give praise and other reinforcers for small steps of progress, severe punishment for child failure to meet parental performance criteria, a tendency to convert positive reinforcement programs into punitive programs, and, possibly, exaggerated fear of other's criticism. (p. 166)

These observations about rigid, punitive parents are consistent with our own clinical experience of treatment failures, especially in working with child abusive families, and are certainly worthy of empirical study.

Wahler and colleagues have also noted the negative scanning of child behavior, with global, blame-oriented descriptions, by parents who fail (Wahler & Afton, 1980). They took a perspective on interactions that looked beyond the immediate family in an attempt to explain the poorer outcomes of poverty-level, poorly educated parents (Wahler, 1980; Wahler, Leske, & Rogers, 1979). These parents were found to report many problems with persons outside the family; they felt cut off from social contact and the contacts they did experience were viewed as unsolicited and often negative in valence. While successful families reported a high frequency of social contact, which was with friends and was rewarding, the failures "identified their limited and sometimes aversive contacts as kinfolk and helping agency representatives" (Wahler, 1980, p. 208). Wahler called this phenomena insularity, and went on to theorize from a social exchange perspective about how narrow and negative interpersonal relationships can lead to intrenched behavior patterns. Wahler's insular families appeared to be of lower SES while noninsular families were of middle SES; it remains to be seen whether insularity is simply synonymous with lower socioeconomic status. Even so, it still may help to understand the social status and outcome relationship already described.

Since in recent years the mental health professions have embraced the family for theory and therapy, increased study of how family attributes relate to outcome can be expected. Family systems theorists have implicated the entire family in the etiology and maintenance of the target child's problem (Minuchin, 1974; Minuchin, Rosman, & Baker, 1978). While in the etiological sense this does not fit well when the problem is a developmental disability that was present at birth or soon thereafter, is physical in origin, and is to some degree permanent, throughout this volume it has been shown that a disabled child has a continuing influence on family roles and relationships. Future programs can be expected to combine skills training for parents with greater attention to family decision making and relationships (Berger & Fowlkes, 1980).

Implications for Families of Severely Handicapped Children

What does all of this mean for families of severely handicapped children? Several general conclusions can be drawn about intervention programs. Parent involvement in educational programs for their handicapped children is now an explicit right and an implicit responsibility. An enticing variety of program models have demonstrated some applicability with families who have severely handicapped children. Parents who participate in these programs become more knowledgeable and skillful in the teaching role, and their children demonstrate convincing changes in those behaviors where training efforts are concentrated. Between the lines of these conclusions, however, lurk a number of continuing questions. Little firm evidence has been found to guide the countless administrative and clinical decisions involved in executing a program of intervention. Little is known about whether intervention programs have generalized effects on other child behaviors, parent attitudes, or family adjustment. Long-term benefits are uncertain; although initial child changes are generally maintained, it is unclear how much parents use procedures they have learned for new interventions. Not all parents benefit equally, but there is little basis for predicting which families will benefit in a particular program.

Nonetheless, enough is known already about intervention with families that more of it could be done. Lest this review of what has been tried give a distorted picture of what is available, the present shortage of help for parents must be underscored. Any particular family with a young severely handicapped child would read this review perhaps with interest but certainly with frustration, wondering where they can find for themselves the individual help given to Katie's, T's, and Steven's families or the home consultation, group training, or advocacy classes described.

The truth of it is that in any given place resources are still quite limited and much of what is available falls short of the carefully designed and monitored programs reviewed. Berlin and Baker (1983) recruited staff from 24 agencies serving retarded children in Los Angeles, California, and conducted workshops on implementing parent training. Despite good participation and good intentions about initiating programs, a 3-month follow-up found only six agencies doing productive parent training and a 2-year follow-up found only one agency offering a well-conceived, systematic program. Hence, a primary recommendation must be that the service system pay greater attention to, and act upon, what is already known. Parents of severely handicapped children, especially, require informed and thoughtful help with their child's development, from specialists who understand their child's difficulties, who are proficient in behavior change methods, and who know how to communicate these to families.

This review suggests additional implications for intervening with families of severely handicapped children. Four interrelated points will be noted. First, a primary concern must be choosing specific child behaviors to modify and monitoring the progress of these. Not unexpectedly, child gains have been shown to be less as the level of handicap is greater. Moreover, gains from parent training in young children often do not register on general developmental scales. For a program to use its time wisely, to document its successes, and to sustain parental motivation, then, it must be focused in its intervention and measurement. Second, it is likely that the most helpful program for parents will be integrated with the child's ongoing school, and draw on related professionals for consultation about objectives and techniques. Given the early identification, special problems, and chronicity of severe handicaps, the family will need more than a brief intervention imparting general teaching principles. The advantages of group training can still be maintained in programs such as Sandler and colleagues described (1983), where group and individual training precede an ongoing involvement with the child's school.

Third, although intervention with children should be focused on specific skills, intervention with parents might be productively broadened. Parents of severely handicapped children are likely to need more support and information than those where the disability is milder. The role of teacher is only one of many that a parent assumes, and should not obscure other needs, such as family stress reduction, advocacy training, medical information, advice about respite services, or support for siblings. It is not so much that a family intervention program should offer everything but that staff should appreciate a family's multiple needs and help them find other ways to fulfill these. Fourth, families should have a choice about their level of involvement. There must not only be greater services but also greater options (Turnbull & Turnbull, 1982). Simply because persons suddenly find themselves in the roles of parents of a handicapped child does not mean they should be required to participate a half-day every week in a school program or any other involvement.

It seems important to close with a plea for continued study, for there is still much that is not known about how to intervene most sensitively and effectively with families of young severely handicapped children. This review has suggested many directions for research; four of these will be highlighted. First, most studies use small samples and examine a particular program; much could be learned from multisite investigations with an increased data base, better designs, and standardized measures. Second, ecological studies of families who cope well with severely handicapped children and those who do less well (such as Blacher and Meyer's, described in Blacher, Chapter 1 in this volume) would help designers of intervention programs to choose appropriate aims. Third, studies of the broader impact of parent training on parent and family adjustment are very much needed, especially given the empirically unsupported argument often advanced that the demands of parent programs increase family stress. And finally, studies that consider the cost-effectiveness of intervention approaches could help provide a sounder basis for programmatic decision making. Studies especially of long-term benefits might strengthen the case for early and effective intervention with families of severely handicapped children.

References

Adesso, V. J., & Lipson, J. W. (1981), Group training of parents as therapists for their children. *Behavior Therapy, 12,* 625–633.
Adubato, S. A., Adams, M. K., & Budd, K. S., (1981). Teaching a parent to train a spouse in child management techniques. *Journal of Applied Behavior Analysis, 14,* 193–205.
Ambrose, S. A., & Baker, B. L. (1979, September). *Training parents of developmentally disabled children: Follow-up outcome.* Paper presented at the American Psychological Association 87th Annual Convention, New York.
Ambrose, S., Hazzard, A., & Haworth, J. (1980), Cognitive-behavioral parenting groups for abusive families. *Child Abuse and Neglect, 4,* 119–125.
Arnold, S., Sturgis, E., & Forehand, R. (1977), Training a parent to teach communication skills. *Behavior Modification, 1,* 259–276.
Auerbach, A. B., (1968). *Parents learn through group discussion: Principles and practices of parent group education.* New York: Wiley.
Baker, B. L. (1973). Camp Freedom: Behavior modification for retarded children in a therapeutic camp setting. *American Journal of Orthopsychiatry, 43,* 418–427.

Baker, B. L. (1980). Training parents as teachers of their developmentally disabled children. In S. Salzinger, J. Antrobus, & J. Glick (Eds.), The ecosystem of the "sick" child. New York: Academic Press.

Baker, B. L. (1983). Parents as teachers: Issues in training. In J. A. Mulick & S. M. Pueschel (Eds.), Parent-professional partnerships in developmental disability services. Cambridge, MA: Ware Press.

Baker, B. L., & Brightman, R. P. (in press). Training parents of retarded children: Program specific outcomes. Journal of Behavior Therapy and Experimental Psychiatry.

Baker, B. L., Brightman, A. J., & Blacher, J. B. (1983). Steps to independence series: Play skills. Champaign, IL: Research Press.

Baker, B. L., Brightman, A. J., Carroll, N. B., Heifetz, B. B., & Hinshaw, S. P. (1978) Steps to independence series: Speech and language, level 1 and level 2. Champaign, IL: Research Press.

Baker, B. L., Brightman, A. J., Heifetz, L. J., & Murphy, D. (1976–1977). Steps to Independence series: Behavior problems, early self-help skills, intermediate self-help skills, advanced self-help skills, toilet training. Champaign, IL: Research Press.

Baker, B. L., Brightman, A. J., & Hinshaw, S. P., (1980). Steps to independence series: Toward independent living. Champaign, IL: Research Press.

Baker, B. L., & Clark, D. B. (1983). The family setting: Enhancing the retarded child's development through parent training. In K. T. Kernan, M. J. Begab, & R. B. Edgerton (Eds.), Settings and the behavior and study of retarded persons. Baltimore: University Park Press.

Baker, B. L., & Clark, D. B. (in press). Intervention with parents of developmentally disabled children. In S. Landesman-Dwyer, & P. Vietze (Eds.), The impact of residential environments on retarded persons and their careproviders. Baltimore: University Park Press.

Baker, B. L., Clark, D. B., & Yasuda, P. M. (1981). Predictors of success in parent training. In P. Mittler (Ed.), Frontiers of knowledge in mental retardation. Baltimore: University Park Press.

Baker, B. L., & Heifetz, L. J. (1976). The Read Project: Teaching manuals for parents of retarded children. In T. D. Tjossem (Ed.), Intervention strategies for high risk infants and young children, Baltimore: University Park Press.

Baker, B. L., Heifetz, L. J., & Murphy, D. (1980). Behavioral training for parents of retarded children: One year follow-up. American Journal of Mental Deficiency, 85, 31–38.

Baker, B. L., & McCurry, M. C. (1983). School-based training for predicted low gain parents. Manuscript submitted for publication.

Baker, B. L., Prieto-Bayard, M., & McCurry, M. (1984). Lower socioeconomic status families and programs for training parents of retarded children. In J. M. Berg (Ed.), Perspectives and progress in mental retardation. Baltimore: University Park Press.

Barna, S., Bidder, R. T., Gray, O. P., Clements, J., & Gardner, S. (1980). The progress of developmentally delayed pre-school children in a home-training scheme. Child: Care, Health and Development, 6, 157–164.

Barnard, J. D., Christophersen, E. R., & Wolf, M. M. (1976). Parent-mediated treatment of children's self-injurious behavior using overcorrection. Journal of Pediatric Psychology, 1, 56–61.

Behrendt, W. M. (1978). The effects of preparation for training and parental characteristics on the outcome of a behavioral parent training program. Unpublished doctoral dissertation, Washington, University, St. Louis.

Benassi, V. A., & Benassi, B. (1973). An approach to teaching behavior modification principles to parents, Rehabilitation Literature, 34, 134–137.

Bennett, C. W. (1973). A four-and-a-half year old as a teacher of her hearing impaired sister: A case study. *Journal of Communication Disorders, 6,* 67–75,

Benson, J., & Ross, L. (1972). Teaching parents to teach their children. *Teaching Exceptional Children, 5,* 30–40.

Berger, M., & Fowlkes, M. A. (1980, May). Family intervention project: A family network model for serving young handicapped children. *Young Children,* pp. 22–32.

Berlin, P. H., & Baker, B. L. (1983). *Role conflict and organizational climate as predictors to implementation of a parent training program.* Manuscript submitted for publication.

Bernal, M. E., & North, J. A. (1978). A survey of parent training manuals. *Journal of Applied Behavior Analysis, 11,* 533–544.

Bernal, M. E., Williams, D. E., Miller, W. H., & Reogor, P. A. (1972). The use of videotape feedback and operant learning principles in training parents in management of deviant children. In R. Rubin, H. Fensterheim, J. Henderson, & L. Ullman (Eds.), *Advances in behavior therapy.* New York: Academic Press.

Bidder, R., Bryant, G., & Gray, O. P. (1975) Benefits to Down's syndrome children through training their mothers. *Archives of Disease in Childhood, 50,* 383–386.

Blechman, E. A., Budd, K. S., Szykula, S., Embry, L. H., O'Leary, K. D., Christopherson, E. R., Wahler, R., Kogan, K., & Riner, L. S. (1981). Engagement in behavioral family therapy: A multisite investigation. *Behavior Therapy, 12,* 461–472.

Brassell, W. R. (1977). Intervention with handicapped infants: Correlates of progress. *Mental Retardation. 15,* 18–22.

Brehony, K. A., Benson, B. A., Solomon, L. J., & Luscomb, R. L. (1980). Parents as behavior modifiers: Intervention for three problem behaviors in a severely retarded child. *Journal of Clinical Child Psychology, 9,* 213–216.

Bricker, W. A., & Bricker, D. D. (1976). The infant, toddler, and preschool research and intervention project. In T. D. Tjossem (Ed.), *Intervention strategies for high risk infants and young children.* Baltimore: University Park Press.

Brightman, R. P. (1984). Training parents as advocates of their developmentally disabled children. In J. M. Berg (Ed.), *Perspectives and progress in mental retardation.* Baltimore: University Park Press.

Brightman, R. P., Ambrose, S. A., & Baker, B. L. (1980). Parent training: A school-based model for enhancing teaching performance. *Child Behavior Therapy, 2,* 35–47.

Brightman, R. P., Baker, B. L., Clark, D. B., & Ambrose, S. A. (1982). Effectiveness of alternative parent training formats. *Journal of Behavior Therapy and Experimental Psychiatry, 13,* 113–117.

Budd, K. S., Green, D. R., & Baer, D. M., (1976). An analysis of multiple misplaced parental social contingencies. *Journal of Applied Behavior Analysis, 9,* 459–470.

Campbell, D. T., & Stanley, J. C. (1966). *Experimental and quasi-experimental designs for research.* Skokie, IL: Rand McNally.

Casey, L. (1978). Development of communicative behavior in autistic children: A parent program using signed speech. *Devereux Forum, 12,* 1–15.

Christensen, A., Johnson, S. M., Phillips, S., & Glasgow, R. E. (1980). Cost effectiveness in behavioral family therapy. *Behavior Therapy, 11,* 208–226.

Clark, D. B., & Baker, B. L. (1983). Predicting outcome in parent training. *Journal of Consulting and Clinical Psychology, 51,* 309–311.

Clark, D. B., & Baker, B. L. (1984). *The Teaching Proficiency Test: A measure to assess teaching skills of parents of developmentally disabled children.* Manuscript submitted for publication.

Clark, D. B., Baker, B. L., & Heifetz, L. J. (1982). Behavioral training for parents of retarded children: Prediction of outcome. *American Journal of Mental Deficiency, 87,* 14–19.

Clements, J., Evans, C., Jones, C., Osborne, K., & Upton, G. (1982). Evaluation of a home-based language training programme with severely mentally handicapped children. *Behaviour Research and Therapy, 20,* 243–249.

Cole, C., & Morrow, W. R. (1976). Refractory parent behaviors in behavior modification training groups. *Psychotherapy: Theory, Research, and Practice, 13,* 162–169.

Colletti, G., & Harris, S. L. (1977). Behavior modification in the home: Siblings as behavior modifiers, parents as observers. *Journal of Abnormal Child Psychology, 5,* 21–30.

Diament, C., & Colletti, G. (1978). Evaluation of behavioral group counseling for parents of learning-disabled children. *Journal of Abnormal Child Psychology, 6,* 385–400.

Doernberg, N. J. (1971) *The differential effect of parent-directed and child-directed part-time educational intervention on the level of social functioning of young mentally ill children on waiting lists.* Unpublished doctoral dissertation, New York University, New York.

Donahue, M. J. (1973). *Home stimulation of handicapped children: Parent guide.* (ERIC Document Reproduction Service No. ED 079 921).

Eyberg, S. M., & Johnson, S. M. (1974). Multiple assessment of behavior modification with families: Effects of contingency contracting and order of treated problems. *Journal of Consulting and Clinical Psychology, 42,* 594–606.

Eyberg, S. M. & Matarazzo, R. G. (1980). Training parents as therapists: A comparison be-tween individual parent-child interaction training and parent group didactic training. *Journal of Clinical Psychology, 36,* 492–499.

Fabry, P. L., & Reid, D. H. (1978). Teaching foster grandparents to train severely handi-capped persons. *Journal of Applied Behavior Analysis, 11,* 111–123.

Feldman, W. S., Manella, K. J., Apodaca, L., & Varni, J. W. (1982). Behavioral group parent training in spina bifida. *Journal of Clinical Child Psychology, 11,* 144–150.

Feldman, W. S., Manella, K. J., & Varni, J. W. (1983). A behavioral parent training program for single mothers of physically handicapped children. *Child: Care, Health, and De-velopment, 9,* 157–168.

Firestone, P., Kelly, M. J., & Fike, S. (1980), Are fathers necessary in parent training groups? *Journal of Clinical Child Psychology, 9,* 44–47.

Flanagan, S., Adams, H. E., & Forehand, R. (1979). A comparison of four instructional techniques for teaching parents to use time out. *Behavior Therapy, 10,* 94–102.

Fleishman, M. J. (1979). Using parenting salaries to control attrition and cooperation in therapy. *Behavior Therapy, 10,* 111–116.

Forehand, R., & Atkeson, B. M. (1977). Generality of treatment effects with parents as therapists: A review of assessment and implementation procedures. *Behavior Therapy, 8,* 575–593.

Forehand, R., Cheney, T., & Yoder, P. (1974). Parent behavior training: Effects on the non-compliance of a deaf child. *Journal of Behavior Therapy and Experimental Psychi-atry, 5,* 281–283.

Forehand, R., Griest, D. L., & Wells, K. C. (1979). Parent behavioral training: An analysis of the relationship among multiple outcome measures. *Journal of Abnormal Child Psy-chology, 7,* 229–242.

Forehand, R., & King, H. E. (1977). Noncompliant children: Effects of parent training on behavior and attitude change. *Behavior Modification, 1,* 93–108.

Fox, R. A., & Roseen, D. L. (1977). A parent administered token program for dietary regula-tion of phenylketonuria. *Journal of Behavior Therapy and Experimental Psychiatry, 8,* 441–443.

Fraiberg, S. (1971). Intervention in infancy: A program for blind infants. *Journal of American Academy of Child Psychiatry, 10,* 381–405.

Fraiberg, S., Smith, M., & Adelson, E. (1969). An educational program for blind infants. *Journal of Special Education, 3,* 121–139.

Frazier, J. R., & Schneider, H. (1975). Parental management of inappropriate hyperactivity in a young retarded child. *Journal of Behavior Therapy and Experimental Psychiatry, 6,* 245–247.

Fredericks, H. D., Baldwin, V. L. & Grove, D. (1974). A home-center based parent training model. In J. Grim (Ed.), *Training parents to teach: Four models* (Vol. 3). First Chance for Children. Chapel Hill, NC:

Fry, L. (1977). Remedial reading using parents as behaviour technicians. *New Zealand Journal of Educational Studies, 12,* 29–36.

Gerrard, K. R., & Saxon, S. A. (1973). Preparation of a disturbed deaf child for therapy: A case description in behavior shaping. *Journal of Speech and Hearing Disorders, 38,* 502–509.

Glasgow, R. E., & Rosen, G. M. (1978). Behavioral bibliotherapy: A review of self-help behavior therapy manuals. *Psychological Bulletin, 85,* 1–23.

Glogower, F., & Sloop, E. W. (1976). Two strategies of group training of parents as effective behavior modifiers. *Behavior Therapy, 7,* 177–184.

Gordon, T. (1970). *P.E.T.: Parent effectiveness training.* New York: Wyden.

Griest, D. L., Forehand, R., Rogers, T., Briener, J., Furey, W., & Williams, C. A. (1982). Effects of parent enhancement therapy on the treatment outcome and generalization of a parent training program. *Behaviour Research and Therapy, 20,* 429–436.

Gross, A. M., Eudy, C., & Drabman, R. S. (1982). Training parents to be physical therapists with their physically handicapped child. *Journal of Behavioral Medicine, 5,* 321–327.

Grossman, F. K. (1972). *Brothers and sisters of retarded children.* Syracuse, NY: Syracuse University Press.

Hall, M. C., & Nelson, D. J. (1981). Responsive parenting: One approach for teaching single parents parenting skills. *School Psychology Review, 19,* 45–53.

Hargis, K., & Blechman, E. A. (1979). Social class and training of parents as behavior change agents. *Child Behavior Therapy, 1,* 69–74.

Harris, S. L., Wolchik, S. A., & Weitz, S. (1981). The acquisition of language skills by autistic children: Can parents do the job? *Journal of Autism and Developmental Disorders, 11,* 373–384.

Hayden, A. H., & Haring, N. G. (1976). Early intervention for high risk infants and young children: Programs for Down's syndrome children. In T. D. Tjossem (Ed.), *Intervention strategies for high risk infants and young children.* Baltimore: University Park Press.

Heifetz, L. J. (1977). Behavioral training for parents of retarded children: Alternative formats based on instructional manuals. *American Journal of Mental Deficiency, 82,* 194–203.

Hetrick, E. W. (1979). Training parents of learning disabled children in facilitative communicative skills. *Journal of Learning Disabilities, 12,* 275–277.

Hirsch, I., & Walder, L. (1969). Training mothers in groups as reinforcement therapists for their own children. *Proceedings of the 77th Annual Convention of the American Psychological Association,* 561–562.

Hofmeister, A. M., & Latham, G. (1972). Development and validation of a mediated package for training parents of preschool mentally retarded children. *Improving Human Performance: A Research Quarterly, 1,* 3–7.

Hollingshead, A. B. (1957). *Two-factor index of social position.* Unpublished manuscript, Yale University, New Haven, CT.

Horton, K. B. (1976). Early intervention for hearing impaired infants and young children. In T. D. Tjossem (Ed.), *Intervention strategies for high risk infants and young children.* Baltimore: University Park Press.

Horton, K. B., & Sitton, A. B. (1970). Early intervention for the young deaf child. *Southern Medical Bulletin, 58,* 50–57.

Hudson, A. M. (1982). Training parents of developmentally handicapped children: A component analysis. *Behavior Therapy, 13,* 325–333.

Jelinek, J. A., & Schaub, M. T. (1973). A model of parent involvement in programming for communicatively handicapped children. *Rehabilitation Literature, 34,* 231–234.

Johnson, M. R., Whitman, T. L., & Barloon-Noble, R. (1978). A home-based program for a pre-school behaviorally disturbed child with parents as therapists. *Journal of Behavior Therapy and Experimental Psychiatry, 9,* 65–70.

Johnson, S. M., & Brown, R. A. (1969). Producing behaviour change in parents of disturbed children. *Journal of Child Psychology and Psychiatry. 10,* 107–121.

Johnson, S. M., Christensen, A., & Bellamy, G. T. (1976). Evaluation of family intervention through unobtrusive audio recordings: Experiences in "bugging" children. *Journal of Applied Behavior Analysis, 9,* 213–219.

Karoly, P., & Rosenthal, M. (1977). Training parents in behavior modification: Effects on perceptions of family interaction and deviant child behavior. *Behavior Therapy, 8,* 406–410.

Knox, L. L. & McConnell, F. (1968). Helping parents to help deaf infants. *Children, 15,* 183–187.

Koegel, R. L., Glahn, T. J., & Nieminen, G. S. (1978). Generalization of parent-training results. *Journal of Applied Behavior Analysis, 11,* 95–109.

Kogan, K. L., & Tyler, N. B. (1978). *Comparing ways of altering parent-child interaction.* (ERIC Documentation Reproduction Service No. ED 161 558).

Lavigneur, H. (1976). The use of siblings as an adjunct to the behavioral treatment of children in the home with parents as therapists. *Behavior Therapy, 7,* 602–613.

Levitt, E., & Cohen, S. (1975). An analysis of selected parent intervention programs for handicapped and disadvantaged children. *Journal of Special Education, 9,* 345–365.

Lewis, J. (1972). Effects of a group procedure with parents of mentally retarded children. *Mental Retardation, 10,* 14–15.

Liff, S. (1973). *Early intervention and language development in hearing impaired children.* Unpublished master's thesis, Vanderbilt University, Nashville.

Locke, H. J., & Wallace, K. M. (1959). Short marital-adjustment and prediction tests: Their reliability and validity. *Journal of Marriage and Family Living, 21,* 251–255.

Lowell, E. L. (1979). Parent-infant programs for preschool deaf children: The example of John Tracy Clinic. *The Volta Review, 81,* 323–329.

Luterman, D. M. (1967). A parent-oriented nursery program for preschool deaf children. *Volta Review, 69,* 515–520.

Martin, B. (1977). Brief family intervention: Effectiveness and the importance of including the father. *Journal of Consulting and Clinical Psychology, 45,* 1002–1010.

McClannahan, L. E., Krantz, P. J., & McGee, G. G. (1982). Parents as therapists for autistic children: A model for effective parent training. *Analysis and Intervention in Developmental Disabilities, 2,* 223–252.

McConkey, R. (1982, July). *Videocourses for parents: A model of systematic dissemination.* Paper presented at the Tenth International Association for Child and Adolescent Psychiatry and Allied Professions, Dublin, Republic of Ireland.

McConkey, R., & McEvoy, J. (1982). *Parental involvement courses: Contrasts between mothers who enroll and those who don't.* Paper presented at the Sixth International Congress of the International Association for the Scientific Study of Mental Deficiency, Toronto, Canada.

McConkey, R., & O'Connor, M. (1982). A new approach to parent involvement in language intervention programmes. *Child: Care, Health and Development, 8,* 163–176.

McMahon, R. J., & Forehand, R. (1980). Self-help behavior therapies in parent training. In B. B. Lahey & A. E. Kazdin (Eds.), *Advances in clinical child psychology* (Vol. 3). New York: Plenum Press.

McMahon, R. J., Forehand, R. & Griest, D. L. (1981). Effects of knowledge of social learning principles on enhancing treatment outcome and generalization in a parent training program. *Journal of Consulting and Clinical Psychology, 49,* 526–532.

McMahon, R. J., Forehand, R., Griest, D. L., & Wells, K. C. (1981). Who drops out of treatment during parent behavior training? *Behavioral Counseling Quarterly, 1,* 79–85.

Menolascino, F. J., & Coleman, R. (1980). The Pilot Parent Program: Helping handicapped children through their parents. *Child Psychiatry and Human Development, 11,* 41–48.

Miller, J. H. (1980). Structured training with parents of exceptional children. *Dissertation Abstracts International, 40*(08), 3908B.

Miller, S. J., & Sloane, H. N. (1976). The generalization effects of parent training across stimulus settings. *Journal of Applied Behavior Analysis, 9,* 335–370.

Miller, W. H. & Gottlieb, F. (1974). Predicting behavioral treatment outcome in disturbed children: A preliminary report of the Responsivity Index of Parents (RIP). *Behavior Therapy, 5,* 210–214.

Minuchin, S. (1974). *Families and family therapy.* Cambridge, MA: Harvard University Press.

Minuchin, S., Rosman, B., & Baker, L. (1978). *Psychosomatic families: Anorexia nervosa in context.* Cambridge, MA: Harvard University Press.

Mira, M. (1970). Results of a behavior modification training program for parents and teachers. *Behaviour Research and Therapy, 8,* 309–311.

Mira, M., & Hoffman, S. (1974). Educational programming for multihandicapped deaf-blind children. *Exceptional Children, 40,* 513–514.

Moore, B. L., & Bailey, J. S. (1973). Social punishment in the modification of a pre-school child's "autistic like" behavior with a mother as therapist. *Journal of Applied Behavior Analysis, 6,* 497–507.

Morris, R. J. (1973). *Issues in teaching behavior modification to parents of retarded children.* Paper presented at the 81st Annual Meeting of the American Psychological Association, Montreal, Canada.

Muir, K. A., & Milan, M. A. (1982). Parent reinforcement for child achievement: The use of a lottery to maximize parent training effects. *Journal of Applied Behavior Analysis, 15,* 455–460.

Nay, W. R. (1975). A systematic comparison of instructional techniques for parents. *Behavior Therapy, 6,* 14–21.

O'Dell, S. L., Blackwell, L. J.; Lareen, S. W., & Hogan, J. L. (1977). Competency-based training for severely behaviorally handicapped children and their parents. *Journal of Autism and Childhood Schizophrenia, 7,* 231–242.

O'Dell, S., Flynn, J., & Benlolo, L. (1977). A comparison of parent training techniques in child behavior modification. *Journal of Behavior Therapy and Experimental Psychiatry, 8,* 261–268.

O'Dell, S. L., Krug, W. W., Patterson, J. N., & Faustman, W. O. (1980). An assessment of methods for training parents in the use of time-out. *Journal of Behavior Therapy and Experimental Psychiatry, 11,* 21–25.

O'Dell, S. L., Mahoney, N. D., Horton, W. G., & Turner, P. E. (1979). Media assisted parented training: Alternative methods. *Behavior Therapy, 10,* 103–110.

O'Dell, S. L., O'Quin, J., Alford, B. A., O'Briant, A. L., Bradlyn, A. S., & Giebenhain, J. E. (1982). Predicting the acquisition of parenting skills via four training methods. *Behavior Therapy, 13,* 194–208.

Pasick, R. S. (1975). *Inclusion of siblings of the retarded in a family training program in behavior modification.* Unpublished doctoral dissertation, Harvard University, Cambridge, MA.

Patterson, G. R. (1974). Interventions for boys with conduct problems: Multiple settings, treatments, and criteria. *Journal of Consulting and Clinical Psychology, 42,* 471–481.

Patterson, G. R., & Fleishman, M. J. (1979). Maintenance of treatment effects: Some considerations concerning family systems and follow-up data. *Behavior Therapy, 10,* 168–185.

Prieto-Bayard, M., & Baker, B. L. (in press). *Behavioral parent training for Spanish-speaking families with a retarded child. Journal of Community Psychology.*

Prieto-Bayard, M., Huff, R. C., & Baker, B. L. (1981). *Parent training for Spanish-speaking families with developmentally disabled children.* Paper presented at the annual meeting of the Western Psychological Association, Los Angeles.

Reisinger, J. J., Frangia, G. W., & Hoffman, E. H. (1976). Toddler management training: Generalization and marital status. *Journal of Behavior Therapy and Experimental Psychiatry, 7,* 335–340.

Rickel, A. U., Dudley, G., & Bermon, S. (1980). An evaluation of parent training. *Evaluation Review, 4,* 389–403.

Rinn, R. C., & Markle, A. (1977). Parent effectiveness training: A review. *Psychological Reports, 41,* 95–109.

Rinn, R. C., Vernon, J. C., & Wise, M. J. (1975). Training parents of behaviorally-disordered children in groups: A three years' program evaluation. *Behavior Therapy, 6,* 378–387.

Rogers, T. R., Forehand, R., Griest, D. L., Wells, K. C., & McMahon, R. J. (1981). Socioeconomic status: Effects on parent and child behaviors and treatment outcome of parent training. *Journal of Clinical Child Psychology, 10,* 98–101.

Rose, S. (1974a). Group training of parents as behavior modifiers. *Social Work, 19,* 156–163.

Rose, S. (1974b). Training parents in groups as behavior modifiers of their mentally retarded children. *Journal of Behavior Therapy and Experimental Psychiatry, 5,* 135–140.

Sadler, O. W., Seyden, T., Howe, B., & Kaminsky, T. (1976). An evaluation of "Groups for Parents": A standardized format encompassing both behavior modification and humanistic methods. *Journal of Community Psychology, 4,* 157–163.

Salzinger, K., Feldman, R. S., & Portnoy, S. (1970). Training parents of brain injured children in the use of operant conditioning procedures. *Behavior Therapy, 1,* 4–32.

Sandler, A., & Coren, A. (1981, October). Integrated instruction at home and school: Parents' perspective. *Education and Training of the Mentally Retarded,* pp. 183–187.

Sandler, A., Coren, A., & Thurman, S. K. (1983). A training program for parents of handicapped preschool children: Effects upon mother, father, and child. *Exceptional Children, 49,* 355–358.

Sandow, S., & Clarke, A. D. (1978). Home intervention with parents of severely subnormal, pre-school children: An interior report. *Child: Care, Health, and Development, 4,* 29–39.

Sapon-Shevin, M. (1982). Ethical issues in parent training programs. *Journal of Special Education, 16,* 341–357.

Schreibman, L., O'Neill, R. E., & Koegel, R. L. (1983). Behavioral training for siblings of autistic children. *Journal of Applied Behavior Analysis, 16,* 129–138.

Scovern, A. W., Bukstel, L. H., Kilmann, P. R., Laval, R. A., Busemeyer, J., & Smith, V. (1980). Effects of parent counseling on the family system. *Journal of Counseling Psychology, 27,* 268–275.

Sebba, J. (1981). Intervention for profoundly retarded mentally handicapped children through parent training in a preschool setting and at home. In P. Mittler (Ed.), "Frontiers of knowledge in mental retardation: Vol. 1, Social educational and behavioral aspects. Baltimore: University Park Press.

Shearer, M. S., & Shearer, D. E. (1972). The Portage Project: A model for early childhood education. Exceptional Children, 39, 210–217.

Shearer, D. E., & Shearer, M. S. (1976). The Portage Project: A model for early childhood education. In T. D. Tjossem (Ed.), Intervention strategies for high risk infants and young children. Baltimore: University Park Press.

Shrybman, J. A. (1982) Due process in special education. Rockville, MD: Aspen.

Strain, P. S., Steele, P., Ellis, T., & Timm, M. A. (1982). Long-term effects of oppositional child treatment with mothers as therapists and therapist trainers. Journal of Applied Behavior Analysis, 15, 163–169.

Strain, P. S., Young, C. C., & Horowitz, J. (1981). Generalized behavior change during oppositional child training. Behavior Modification, 5, 15–26.

Strom, R., Ress, R., Slaughter, H., & Wurster, S. (1980). Role expectations of parents of intellectually handicapped children. Exceptional Children, 47, 144–147.

Tavormina, J. B. (1974). Basic models of parent counseling: A critical review. Psychological Bulletin, 81, 827–835.

Tavormina, J. B. (1975). Relative effectiveness of behavioral and reflective group counseling with parents of mentally retarded children. Journal of Consulting and Clinical Psychology, 43, 22–31.

Tavormina, J. B., Hampson, R. B., & Luscomb, R. L. (1976). Participant evaluations of the effectiveness of their parent counseling groups. Mental Retardation, 14, 8–9.

Tawney, J. W., Aeschleman, S. R., Deaton, S. L., & Donaldson, R. M. (1979). Using telecommunications to instruct rural severely handicapped children. Exceptional Children, 46, 118–125.

Thomas, C. A. (1977). The effectiveness of two child management training procedures for high and low educational level parents of emotionally disturbed children. Dissertation Abstracts International, 37, A12.

Turnbull, A. P., & Turnbull, H. R., III. (1982). Parent involvement in the education of handicapped children: A critique. Mental Retardation, 20, 115–122.

UCLA Project for Developmental Disabilities. (1982). Parents as Teachers curriculum guide. Mimeograph, Department of Psychology, University of California, Los Angeles.

Uditsky, B. & MacDonald, L. (1981). Behavioral training for parents of developmentally-delayed children: A two year follow-up. Journal of Practical Approaches to Developmental Handicap, 5, 5–8.

Wahler, R. G. (1980). The insular mother: Her problems in parent-child treatment. Journal of Applied Behavior Analysis, 13, 207–219.

Wahler, R. G., & Afton, A. D. (1980). Attentional processes in insular and noninsular mothers: Some differences in their summary reports about child problem behaviors. Child Behavior Therapy, 2, 25–41.

Wahler, R. G., Leske, G., & Rogers, E. S. (1979). The insular family: A deviance support system for oppositional children. In L. A. Hamerlynck, (Ed.), Behavioral systems for the developmentally disabled: I. School and family environments. New York: Brunner/Mazel.

Walter, H. (1971). Placebo versus social learning effects in parent training. Unpublished doctoral dissertation, University of Oregon, Eugene.

Watson, L. S., & Bassinger, J. F. (1974). Parent training technology: A potential service delivery system. Mental Retardation, 12, 3–10.

Webster-Stratton, C. (1981). Modification of mothers' behaviors and attitudes through videotape modeling group discussion program. *Behavior Therapy, 12,* 634–642.

Webster-Stratton, C. (1982). The long-term effects of a video-tape modeling parent-training program: Comparison of immediate and 1-year follow-up results. *Behavior Therapy, 13,* 702–714.

White, A. J. R. (1982). Outpatient treatment of oppositional non-eating in a deaf retarded boy. *Journal of Behavior Therapy and Experimental Psychiatry, 13,* 251–255.

Wildman, R. W. & Simon, S. J. (1978). An indirect method for increasing the rate of social interaction in an autistic child. *Journal of Clinical Psychology, 34,* 144–149.

Wiltz, N. A., & Gordon, S. B. (1974). Parental modification of a child's behavior in an experimental residence. *Journal of Behavior Therapy and Experimental Psychiatry, 5,* 107–109.

Worland, J., Carney, R., Milich, R., & Grame, C. (1980). Does in-home training add to the effectiveness of operant group parent training? A two-year evaluation. *Child Behavior Therapy, 2,* 11–24.

Worland, J., Carney, R. M., Weinberg, H,, & Milich, R. (1982). Dropping out of group behavioral training. *Behavioral Counseling Quarterly, 2,* 37–41.

Zifferblatt, S. M., Burton, S. D., Horner, R., & White, T. (1977). Establishing generalization effects among autistic children. *Journal of Autism and Childhood Schizophrenia, 7,* 337–347.

CHAPTER 10

Parent Involvement Policy and Practice: Current Research and Implications for Families of Young, Severely Handicapped Children

Ann P. Turnbull
Pamela J. Winton

Introduction

Parent involvement policy and practice are integral features of providing services to young severely handicapped children. This chapter
provides an analysis of policy requirements that have shaped parent involvement practices in educational programs, reviews research on the
nature and degree of parent involvement, and suggests future directions
for adapting parent involvement practices to the individual needs of
families.

Evolution of Parent Involvement Policy

Policies for involving parents of handicapped children in educational programs and decision making have shifted dramatically since

the early 1900s. A historical perspective of this evolution is helpful in clarifying current practices and providing insight for future directions.

From the early to mid-1900s, a predominant practice was to institutionalize severely handicapped children. This practice was based on the premise that the care and nurturance of these children presented an insurmountable burden for their parents. Wolfensberger (1970) described this viewpoint, based on a paper by Aldrich (1947):

> When the physician attending at birth recognizes the baby as mongoloid, the baby is withheld from the mother under the pretext that it is weak. In the meantime, the physician marshals the father and other relatives, instructing them that the baby should be institutionalized immediately. After father and relatives have agreed to this, the mother is then told about the baby and informed of the decision which was made without her having been consulted. All this is done because a mongoloid child is seen as having a destructive impact upon the family, because the mother is considered incapable of making a sensible decision, and because the child is presumably much better off and happier in an institution. This model for "instant institutionalization" (Grant, 1965) and for handling parents of mongoloid children is offered as an example of good preventive medicine. (p. 369)

This passage suggests that institutionalization as a form of treatment was recommended to promote positive outcomes for the family (e.g., "a mongoloid child is seen as having a destructive impact upon the family") as well as positive outcomes for the child (e.g., "the child is presumably much better off and happier in an institution"). Furthermore, the role of parents was clearly to adhere to the recommendation of the physician rather than to participate in the decision-making process.

A major force causing the pendulum to swing in support of public school programs in community settings and the participation of parents in decision making was the political advocacy of parent groups, particularly the National Association for Retarded Citizens (NARC). An educational bill of rights for the retarded child was published as a policy statement by the NARC in 1954 (Boggs, 1978). This statement clearly sets forth the role of parents of retarded children as active decision makers on issues pertaining to care, treatment, and training:

An Educational Bill of Rights for the Retarded Child

Every child, including every retarded child, is important and has the right to:
1. Opportunities for the fullest realization of his potentialities, however limited, for physical, mental, emotional, and spiritual growth;
2. Affection and understanding from those responsible for his care and guidance during his years of dependence;
3. A program of education and training suited to his particular needs and carried forward in the environment most favorable for him, whether in the public schools, a residential center, or his own home;
4. Help, stimulation and guidance from skilled teachers, provided by his com-

munity and state as part of a broadly conceived program of free public education.
And his parents have the right to determine for themselves, on the basis of competent advice, the course of care, training, and treatment, among those open to them, which they believe best for their family; and to have their decisions respected by others. (National Association for Retarded Children, 1954, cited in Boggs, 1978, p. 60)

As the NARC and other activist groups were exerting pressure in judicial and legislative arenas to have their preferences for the active involvement of parents undergirded by law, a concomitant force in shaping both policy and practice was compensatory education programs for economically disadvantaged children. A primary component of compensatory education programs of the 1960s was parent involvement. Two perspectives of parent involvement were prevalent in these programs. In retrospect, it is clear that these perspectives served as precursors to current policy for involving parents of handicapped children in educational programs.

The first perspective was rooted in a cultural deficit model: Parents were seen as being in need of remediation (knowledge and skills) in order to improve the child's environment. The goal of such intervention was described by Hunt (1971) as being a strategy for societal integration of poor families. The parent's role was that of learner, and professionals decided on the structure and content of such learning. Those espousing the second perspective, which might be called the political perspective, looked on parent involvement as being important for very different reasons than those operating from a deficit model. From the political perspective, poor parents were viewed as being disenfranchised and in need of opportunities to increase their decision-making power and political advocacy.

The design of the Head Start Program was based upon a synthesis of these two perspectives. Federal legislation—Public Law (PL) 89–794—required parents to participate not only as learners and as teachers, but also as decision makers. This legislation was the first to reflect a policy of parent involvement (Wiegerink, Hocutt, Posante-Loro, & Bristol, 1980).

In 1968 Congress passed PL 90–538 authorizing the Handicapped Children's Early Education Program (HCEEP). Influenced by the early reported successes of the Headstart Program, this legislation created a program of demonstration projects designed to develop a variety of methods and techniques to assist handicapped preschoolers (Harvey, 1977). Furthermore, a major intention of the legislation, as stated by Congressman Dominick V. Daniels, the chairman of the Select Committee on Education, was to enlist the active involvement of parents. Lavor and Krivit (1969) cited Daniels's testimony as follows:

Few parents are prepared to take care of a child who looks different, behaves in grossly unacceptable ways or fails to respond even to the sound of a mother's voice. Parents of handicapped children may have fears and are often frustrated and bewildered. They need help in understanding their child's disability. They need help in working with their handicapped child.

This bill will bring us into a new era of educating handicapped children. In addition, it is anticipated that this legislation will enlist the help of the parents as allies and associates of educators to provide a total program. (p. 381)

To translate this policy emphasis of parents as learners and decision makers into procedural guidelines, federal regulations specified the following modes for parent involvement:

1. parent assistance in the planning, development, operation and evaluation of a project;
2. parent training as a project component;
3. parent participation in educational and therapeutic components of the project; and
4. opportunity for parents to advise and assist in information dissemination concerning the project.

Legislation in the 1970s emphasized the role of parents as decision makers and further empowered them as advocates to ensure their handicapped children received the services to which they were entitled. An intent of the Developmental Disabilities Assistance and Bill of Rights Act (Public Law 95–602) was to provide opportunities for parents to share in the responsibility for the provision of services for handicapped persons at the state level. For the first time the parent's role as a co-partner in the assessment of needs and planning of services at a state level was recognized publicly (Wiegerink et al., 1980). The Buckley–Pell amendments, passed in 1974, allowed parents of handicapped and nonhandicapped children to have access to their children's school records.

Unquestionably, the revolutionary legislation granting decision-making rights to parents of handicapped children was PL 94–142, the Education for All Handicapped Children Act of 1975. The specific decision-making rights afforded to parents by PL 94–142 are outlined in the following:

Key Requirements of P.L. 94–142 Regarding Parent Rights

1. The local school system must provide an appropriate special education including related services to each handicapped child at no cost to the parent.
2. Prior to an initial evaluation being administered to their child, parents must be provided with a written notice describing the proposed action and voluntarily give their consent for the evaluation.
3. Parents are entitled to receive an explanation of all evaluation results and an explanation of any actions proposed or rejected in regard to evaluation results.

4. Parents must receive a notice of the IEP [individualized education program] meeting that includes the following information: purpose, time, location, and persons attending.
5. Parents have the right to participate in their child's IEP conference as an equal decision-maker with educators.
6. The IEP conference may be held without the parent in attendance only when the school has documentation of their attempts to involve the parents and the parents' unwillingness to attend the conference.
7. Parents have the right to request an independent evaluation (conducted by someone not employed by the school) and have the results considered in discussions regarding the school placement of their child.
8. Parents may inspect all educational records maintained on their child and request explanations of information contained in the records. They may also request that the information be amended if they do not agree with it.
9. The privacy of all school records must be maintained. Parents may request copies of their child's school records. Furthermore, they may obtain information from school personnel concerning the particular individuals who are allowed to see their child's records.
10. Parents have the right to request an impartial hearing (due process hearing) at any time when they disagree with the proposed procedures for evaluation and/or placement of their child. At the hearing they may have legal counsel, present evidence, cross-examine witnesses, and obtain written findings of the proceedings. If they are deaf or normally communicate in a language other than English, the hearing must be conducted so that all communication is completely understandable to them. (Turnbull, 1984, p. 110)

Based on their review of the legislative history of the parent involvement policy of PL 94–142, Turnbull, Turnbull, and Wheat (1982) speculated that Congress believed that parents could make no assumptions concerning the education of their handicapped children. This no-assumptions perspective emanated from the fact that Congress could not guarantee that schools would, indeed, provide an appropriate education to handicapped students unless they were held accountable by empowered agents.

The role of empowered agents to increase the schools' accountability was legislatively conferred on parents. During the PL 94–142 hearing, the New Jersey Commissioner of Education attested to this parental expectation in his congressional testimony that the provisions for parental involvement and due process "will serve as the most effective remedy [Congress] could design to protect the rights of handicapp᷏ children . . . such as excessive or mistaken labelling . . . and [plac᷏ in inappropriate educational programs" (Turnbull et al., 19ᵖ

The conference to develop the handicapped child's ˙ education program (IEP) was viewed by Congress aᶜ parents to exert their decision-making role in ˈ countable for providing an appropriate educa᷏   ᴄ issued in the Federal Register of August 23, 1977, specify parents as required participants in the IEP conference, although the nature of their participation or the degree of their expected decision making was not described. The intent of this requirement, however, was embellished in the policy clarifications issued in the Federal Register of January 19, 1981. This intent was stated as follows: "The IEP meeting serves as a communication vehicle between parents and school personnel, and enables them as equal participants to, jointly decide what the child's needs are, what services will be provided to meet those needs, and what the anticipated outcomes will be" (Federal Register, 1981, p. 5462). Equal participation in educational decision making represents a strong expectation for parental involvement.

The role of parents as decision makers is clearly the predominant one specified by PL 94–142. It is important to recognize, however, that PL 94–142 also addresses the role of parents as learners. Parent training is a required related service when such training is needed to ensure that handicapped children will benefit from special education. Furthermore, parents are specifically mentioned in the PL 94–142 regulations as a target group for the Comprehensive System for Personnel Development that the state educational agency is responsible for providing. The implementation of these policy requirements in involving parents as learners has to date been negligible (Turnbull, 1984).

In applying these policies to the parents of young, severely handicapped children, it is important to consider the types of educational programs in which these children are likely to be educated. These programs included (1) mandated and permissive public school services required by PL 94–142 and state legislation—approximately 232,000 preschool (chronological age 3–5 years) handicapped children were educated in these programs during the 1979–1980 school year (*To Assure Free Appropriate Public Education of Handicapped Children*," 1980); and (2) HCEEP projects—90 projects served approximately 3316[1] handicapped children (chronological age 0–8 years) during the 1981–1982 year (Assael & Waldstein, 1982).

The type of program in which a severely handicapped child is educated determines to a large extent the expected role of parents as set forth in policy. As previously discussed, the policy expectations in public school programs are for parents to be active, albeit equal, decision makers in determining the nature of the child's educational program (e.g., goals and objectives), placement, and related services. The

---

[1] This figure is an estimate based on 76 of the 90 projects who submitted information the 1981–1982 directory on numbers of children served.

role of parents as learners is a secondary policy requirement that has not been emphasized. A broader policy of parent involvement has occurred in HCEEP projects covering activities that place parents in roles of both learner and decision maker.

The evolution of parent involvement policies has created expectations for parents to assume tremendous educational roles—to make *informed* decisions about the precise development and implementation of their child's program, to increase their skills in order to teach their child, and to participate actively in the administration and delivery of educational programs. These policies have shifted dramatically from the frequent practice in the not-too-distant past of urging parents to institutionalize their child at birth and to abdicate their parental responsibilities in favor of professional control. This policy has largely been influenced by political factors rather than theoretical or empirical evidence.

Current Implementation of Policy

In light of the pervasive policy expectations for parents of handicapped children to be involved in educational programs, there is an appalling lack of research and evaluation on the actual extent and outcomes of these practices. This section, however, reviews the data that are available.

Parent Involvement in Handicapped Children's Early Education Program Projects

Hocutt and Wiegerink (in press) surveyed third-year HCEEP programs to document the actual nature of parent involvement practices. Their results indicated that involvement was greatest in the more passive activities (e.g., parents receiving information and services from the project) as contrasted to more active decision-making roles.

The extent of parent involvement in a 3-year model program for severely handicapped children was investigated as part of a larger program evaluation by Bricker and Dow (1980). Parent involvement in this program covered the areas of educational training, social services, and counseling. The extent of involvement was assessed by having teachers and parent interventionists rate parents on a 4-point scale (e.g., 1 = no participation; 4 = active participation) regarding the amount of their direct participation in the child's programming and the amount of participation in parent education meetings and quarterly parent meetings. The mean rating for these two activities was 2.31, indicating a moderate degree of involvement. It is paradoxical that the program description stated that parent involvement was individualized; however, the evaluation of parent involvement implied normative criteria.

Parent Involvement in Public Schools

There is a growing, yet still small, body of literature on the degree of parents' participation in IEP conferences. Goldstein, Strickland, Turnbull, and Curry (1980) observed IEP conferences pertaining to mildly handicapped, elementary-school-aged students. This observational analysis revealed that parental contributions accounted for less than 25% of the total conference contributions. The typical conference communication was characterized as professionals describing an already developed IEP to the parents (typically only the mother attended the conference). Parents were passive recipients of information rather than active decision makers.

These findings were corroborated by McKinney and Hocutt (1982) in a survey of parents of learning disabled students also at the elementary school level. Based on the responses of parents in their sample, 43% indicated that they did not participate fully in the development of their child's IEP. Approximately one-third of the parents indicated that they had helped to write the IEP and only 16% of these parents could recall the actual contribution they had made. Parents reported the major barriers to assuming a more active role were their work and home responsibilities.

One of the largest studies on parent involvement reported in the literature to date was conducted with 400 parents representing mildly and severely handicapped children ranging in age from 4 to 20 years (Lynch & Stein, 1982). The findings of this study pertaining to the parental perceptions of their participation in the IEP meeting are as follows:

> Nearly three fourths (71%) of the families interviewed felt that they were actively involved in the development of their child's IEP, but when asked how they were involved, parents generally gave responses that do not connote active involvement. When asked why they felt they were active participants, parents frequently indicated that they had expressed opinions and made suggestions (14.6%); they had worked with, helped, and trusted the professionals who had set up the programs and goals (11.2%); they had listened and agreed to the teacher's recommendations (7.5%); and they understood everything that was going on because it was explained clearly and in detail (6.3%). (pp. 60–61)

A note of caution is in order on the population of students and parents represented in the IEP studies. These studies primarily focused on IEP conferences of mildly handicapped students at the elementary school level. Thus, generalizations to young, severely handicapped children cannot automatically be assumed. There is no empirical evidence to suggest whether parent involvement is more or less important for parents of severely handicapped youngsters.

Data on the precise nature of the involvement of severely handicapped children's parents in educational decision making are currently unavailable. The involvement of parents in programs for these youngsters is recognized in policy and in program descriptions as a major intervention strategy. There is a critical need for professionals to direct time and effort to systematic inquiry regarding parent involvement. All too frequently professionals have extolled the virtues of the parent involvement concept; however, how the concept is implemented and with what results for which of the involved parties is largely a matter of conjecture.

Contradictions between Policy Principles and Implementation

An obvious contradiction exists between the active role ascribed to parents in policy and the passive roles that appear to characterize implementation. Considering that the congressional intent was for parents to be empowered agents in order to ensure the accountability of the school, it is important to examine the reasons for the discrepancy. Research conducted on professional and parent attitudes toward involvement sheds light on this issue.

Regarding professional perspectives, Hocutt (1980) conducted a Delphi study with a select panel of experts to clarify how the HCEEP parent involvement policy should be implemented. The panel of experts consisted almost exclusively of professionals. The results of the survey indicated high priority given to the passive parental roles (e.g., learner and audience) and low priority to parent involvement in decision-making functions and activities. The panel of experts perceived the primary goal of involvement to be improved child functioning. Thus, parent involvement was viewed as a strategy for improving child outcomes, rather than parent outcomes.

A number of other studies have indicated that professionals do not agree with the assumption that parents should be active decision makers (Morgan & Rhode, 1980; Safer, Morrissey, Kaufman, & Lewis, 1978; Yoshida, Fenton, Kaufman, & Maxwell, 1978). These studies have been reviewed elsewhere by Turnbull (1984).

Parent perspectives on preferred roles for decision makers were investigated by Lusthaus, Lusthaus, and Gibbs (1981). They surveyed the parents of handicapped students on their present and desired levels of participation in nine different types of educational decisions. Three categories were used to classify roles: no involvement, giving and receiving information, and having control over decisions. It is interesting that the PL 94–142 policy preference of *equal* participation was not included in these categories. In terms of their present level of participation, the most frequent role reported by parents in this study was giving and receiving information, the second most frequent role was no involvement, and the role ranked third was having decisional control. In six of the nine areas, 50% or more of the parents reported their desired level of participation to be an informational role. These areas included discipline, class placement, evaluation, instructional grouping, transportation, and special resources. Preference for control over three types of decisions (types of records, medical services, and transfers to other school) was expressed by a majority of parents.

Winton and Turnbull (1981) interviewed parents of preschool, mildly and moderately handicapped children on their preferences for parent activities. Of these parents, 65% indicated that they most preferred informal contact with teachers. The two major characteristics of informal contact mentioned by parents were the importance of frequency (e.g., at drop-off and pick-up times) and openness of communication shared in a relaxed, give-and-take fashion. The parents in this sample rated informal contact as a preferred activity substantially higher than more active roles such as volunteering time at the preschool, serving on policy boards, and participating in training or counseling sessions.

Parents in this study were also asked to identify factors responsive to their own needs in selecting a preschool for their child, 65% of the parents described the importance of finding competent professionals so they could take a break from the educational responsibility for their child as being a factor in their choice of a preschool. One could speculate that the needs of parents of mildly and moderately handicapped children for a break may not be as great as the needs of parents of severely handicapped children (MacMillan & Turnbull, 1983). In may be that parents needing time for themselves away from the special problems of their children are likely to prefer a more passive level of involvement with program activities connected with their children, but they may prefer involvement that provides them with emotional support.

In a study conducted by Turnbull, Winton, Blacher, and Salkind (1982), parents of 50 mildly handicapped and 50 nonhandicapped children were surveyed to ascertain their perspectives on their child's kin-

TABLE 10.1

Percentage of Parents of Handicapped and Nonhandicapped Children
Responding to Questionnaire Items Regarding Characteristics
of Kindergarten Important for Parents

Characteristics of kindergarten	Percentage of parents of handicapped children	Percentage of parents of nonhandicapped children
Day care is provided after school as part of the school program	4	2
Teachers who have the time are willing to talk with me about my child just about any time	44	34
Programs and workshops for parents, so I can learn about ways to deal with and teach my child	10	14
Chances for me to get information about other community services which may help me	4	4
Chances to meet and to get together with other parents	0	0
Chances to help out in my child's classroom	6	2
Chances to help at school outside of class (drive on field trips, office work, etc.)	0	0
Chances to serve on advisory boards or in decision-making roles in regard to school programs	2	2
Chance to do the things I need to do each day knowing that my child's educational needs are being met in the kindergarten program	31	42

dergarten program. As documented in Table 10.1, both groups indicated that the characteristics of kindergarten programs most important in meeting their needs were (1) informal and frequent communication with teachers, and (2) having an opportunity to relax during the day knowing their child's educational needs were being met by the kindergarten program. The striking similarity between the preferences of parents of handicapped and nonhandicapped children is noteworthy.

A trend found in the research on professional and parent perspectives is that, despite policy requirements for the active role of parents in specified activities and forums for decision making, assigning a more passive role seems to be dominant practice. There is an increasing recognition that parent involvement policy and practice needs to be re-examined (Foster, Berger, & McLean, 1981; Lynch & Stein, 1982; Morgan, 1982; Turnbull & Turnbull, 1982; Winton & Turnbull, 1981; Yoshida, 1982).

The idea of matching services with the needs of handicapped children is not a new one (Karnes & Zehrbach, 1975). Only recently has the need for matching services with the needs of families been widely called for in the literature; this approach is still not systematically implemented. In the previously described study conducted by Hocutt (1980), professionals did not give receipt of an individually planned parent involvement program a high priority. (It was ranked as 18th in importance among 34 other parent involvement activities). Some programs for handicapped children have mandatory parent involvement in order for a child to be served (Flynn, Pelosi, & Wiegerink, 1981). Can the needs of parents of handicapped children best be served by such rigid requirements—particularly if their most pressing need is to have a break from the chronicity of their severely handicapped child's needs? Given the additional daily care needs, health needs, costs, and frustration often imposed by a very severely handicapped child, individualizing for families of this population is a particularly important intervention strategy (MacMillan & Turnbull, 1983).

In some respects, a policy that does not take into account the individual needs, capabilities, and interests of families to be involved has been created; in part, this may be one reason why there is a contradiction between parent involvement policy and the way policy has been implemented. Because there is a group of parents who strongly desire to be actively involved in parent activities and in educational decision making and these parents have been successful in making their needs known (Turnbull & Turnbull, 1982), it has been assumed that all parents share this perspective. Professionals have begun to recognize the need to reassess current parent involvement policy and modify it in ways that reflect a more individual and flexible approach for families.

Future Directions: Needs and Barriers

In reassessing current parent involvement policy and recognizing the importance of individualizing for families, certain needs and barriers must be taken into account that have implications for planning, research, and training.

Needs in Reassessing Parent Involvement

Need to Consider Theory from Other Disciplines

One might assume that individualizing for families would be a simple and easily obtainable goal for programs, given the expertise in individualizing for children that has been developed over the years; however, this is not so. One reason why individualizing for children is easier than individualizing for families is that there are accepted theories of child development that map out expected areas of growth and development in children. Research has guided the development of sound educational practices based on those theories. Training programs for early childhood professionals are typically based on such theories and practices. Where families are concerned, theories of functioning and development are more complicated because of the need to take into account multiple relationships. It is only relatively recently that theories have been developed, primarily by family therapists (Haley, 1973; Minuchin, 1974), that adequately account for the interrelatedness of the family system. These theories have begun to be recognized by early childhood professionals as providing a useful framework for understanding the ways that a handicapped child impacts the family system. Featherstone (1981) has provided a personalized account of how the birth of her severely handicapped son affected their family system, using Minuchin's (1974) framework. The chapter on siblings by Skrtic, Summers, Brotherson, and Turnbull (Chapter 6 in this volume) outlines a comprehensive family system model based on theory from sociology and psychiatry.

Family systems theories also provide a useful framework for examining the ways that intervention affects all family members, even those that are not directly involved in program activities (Foster *et al.*, 1981). For example, if a mother is expected to invest a large amount of time and energy in the education of her handicapped child, this will have an impact on her husband and other children in the family. A mother interviewed as part of the research study by Winton and Turnbull (1981) described earlier made the following comment about parent involvement: "When you're putting in so much time that your family is no longer benefiting from it, then it's time to quit" (p. 17).

Foster *et al.* (1981) have described specifically how key concepts and techniques from family systems theory can be useful in enhancing professionals' understanding of families and the ways that program activities affect family members. Providing specific activities and support for members of the extended family, such as grandparents (Gabel & Kotsch, 1981), is another way in which programs can serve the broader family network. The utilization of existing family systems theories should guide future developments in parent involvement policy, practice, research, and training. In addition, these theories lend themselves to an understanding of other factors that must be taken into account when plotting future directions.

Family Structures Have Changed

Parent involvement activities frequently are focused on mothers and are offered at times when mothers and fathers employed outside the home have difficulty participating. Demographic evidence indicates that the conventional nuclear family with children being raised by a biological mother who stays at home and a biological father who works outside the home is no longer the predominant type of family; 48% of preschool children have mothers working or looking for work (*Report on Preschool Education*, 1982). Of all people now marrying, 40% will end their marriages in divorce, meaning a large increase in the number of young children living in single-parent homes (Foster *et al.*, 1981). Changing family roles mean more men are involved in caretaking roles.

These changes in family structures have implications for parent involvement practice and policy. Early intervention programs should offer services and activities at times when working parents, single parents, and fathers can be involved by arranging flextime work schedules for some of the program's professional staff. It is also important to realize that simply not all parents have the time and energy to be involved—not because they are not interested in the development of their severely handicapped child, but rather because of their families' structural characteristics and competing responsibilities. In addition, there is a need to make available assistance to fathers in alleviating the particular stresses associated with having a handicapped child. For instance, research has shown that fathers typically take on a play-maker role when interacting with their normally developing children (Lamb, 1977). Fathers may need assistance and direction in interacting with a child who may be delayed in developing play skills.

Families Perform Many Functions

A major emphasis has been placed on parents of handicapped children being teachers of their children (Lillie, Trohanis, & Goin, 1976; Turnbull & Turnbull, 1982). While this approach has been documented as successfully affecting child outcome (Baker, Heifetz, & Murphy, 1980; Embry, 1980; Tjossem, 1976), there is a need to consider the possible negative consequences of focusing narrowly on the parent-as-teacher role. As many as nine major family functions have been identified in a literature review (Turnbull, Brotherson, & Summers, 1982) and are outlined in the sibling chapter of this volume (Skrtic et al., Chapter 6). In addition to providing education, families serve individual needs in the economic, physical, rest and recuperation, socialization, ideology, self-definition, affectional, guidance, and vocational areas. Limited time and energy are factors for all families, particularly two-career and single-parent families. The emphasis placed by early intervention programs on parents being educators is likely to result in other important family functions receiving less attention. While the outcome for the handicapped child may be positive in terms of the targeted educational behavior, other important aspects of the child's development may be overlooked or neglected. A quote from a physically handicapped adult reflecting on her childhood illustrates this point:

> Something happens in a parent when relating to his disabled child; he forgets that they're a kid first. I used to think about that a lot when I was a kid. I would be off in a euphoric state, drawing or coloring or cutting out paper dolls, and as often as not the activity would be turned into an occupational therapy session. "You're not holding the scissors right," "Sit up straight so your curvature doesn't get worse." That era was ended when I finally let loose a long and exhaustive tirade. "I'm just a kid! You can't therapize me all the time! I get enough therapy in school every day! I don't think about my handicap all the time like you do!" (Diamond, 1981, p. 30)

An awareness on the part of professionals of the competing time and energy demands on families to function in a multitude of ways should underlie a program's approach to involving families. A major programmatic goal may be to assist the family in maintaining the severely handicapped child in the home setting rather than seeking institutionalization. If home placement is, indeed, the goal, some parents may need less parent involvement in order to have more time to meet their own needs. An assessment of families' preferences and priorities for involvement and their attitudes towards performing in different roles should be part of the development of an individualized approach.

Needs of Families Evolve over Time

An individual family's needs and support are likely to change over time. A mother who participated in the Winton and Turnbull study (1981) made this comment about her changing sentiments towards mother support groups: "It was good at that time, and I think I'll always have a feeling for those mothers because we got so close; but I don't miss it now. I don't feel the need for it. I may when he gets older and there are more problems" (p. 17).

In order to maintain a flexible and individualized approach for families, programs should have built-in mechanisms for reassessing families' needs and preferences for involvement. For example, in the program evaluation study described earlier by Bricker and Dow (1980), parents were assessed on their participation in parent education meetings. It is possible that such meetings would be a source of assistance and support for some parents at one point in time and that they would be unresponsive to some of these same parents' needs at another point in time. When parents do not attend such meetings, it is likely that some of them may feel guilty over their lack of participation or teachers may feel frustrated with parents for not cooperating with program activities. When there is a shift in parent needs, it is important to have a corresponding shift in parent involvement options and expectations.

Utilizing existing theory to predict times when a family's needs are likely to change is a strategy that would help professionals address this issue. For instance, family systems theory suggests that all families undergo certain life cycle transitions, such as birth or death in a family, job changes, or children moving into new stages of development, which will increase stress and will require a reorganization of family roles (Foster et al., 1981). Foster et al. addressed how program activities can be geared to assist families in negotiating these stressful life cycle events.

Having a handicapped individual in the family not only may add to the stress associated with life cycle transitions, but also will create additional stressful events that families must negotiate. Data from a longitudinal study of young mildly and moderately handicapped children and their families have been used to document certain stress points (e.g., obtaining a diagnosis of the child's handicapped condition, seeking services and making transitions from infant to preschool programs) and to describe parents' perspectives on these events (Bernheimer, Young, Winton, & Turnbull, 1980). For instance, this study indicated that having a child whose handicap is ambiguous and subject to varying professional interpretation may increase the stress associated with obtaining a diagnosis and securing appropriate intervention.

A third theoretical framework helpful in understanding the evolving needs of parents is the stage theory of parents' acceptance of a child's handicap. In a review of the literature on stages of parental adjustment, Blacher (in press) discussed the stages of initial crisis reaction, feelings and responses associated with "emotional disorganization," and adjustment and assessment. She advocated taking into account the parents' evolving needs related to adjustment stage when planning educational services for severely handicapped children and their families.

Barriers to Reassessing Parent Involvement

An underlying premise in mapping out future directions for the evolution of parent involvement policy has been that professionals adopt new theories from other disciplines that take into account the complex interrelationships characterizing family systems. If this direction is to be actualized, then certain barriers must be acknowledged and overcome.

Research

The bulk of the early childhood research involving parents has focused on child outcome and has been conducted with mother–child dyads. For the most part, quantitative research methodologies have been employed. If new theories are to be adopted that describe multiple relationships, then new methodologies for conducting research to develop and verify theory must be adopted also. The types of methodologies (such as clinical observation and case study reports) traditionally employed by psychiatry, the field from which family systems theory has emerged, are qualitative ones and are not typically used in early childhood research. Problems, such as transforming qualitative case material into discrete units for systematic and reliable analysis, have been identified by early childhood researchers who have used qualitative methodologies in studies with parents (Winton, 1982). For researchers interested in generating funding from traditional sources and publishing results in peer-reviewed early childhood journals, the selection of nontraditional research methodologies can be particularly problematic. A promising direction for those aspiring to do research with families that is compatible with family systems theory is Guba's (1981) paradigm of "naturalistic" inquiry. This paradigm allows researchers and those evaluating a research methodology to use an alternative set of criteria to assess the acceptance of research proposals for funding and results for publication.

Programming Barriers

An underlying assumption of this chapter is that parent involvement policy should move in a direction that will benefit the family as a whole. This assumption is based on the premise that an optimally functioning family is a critical component for a child's development. It may be unrealistic to assume that program planners share the assumption that helping family members is a strategy for helping the severely handicapped child. Using parents as volunteers and involving them in taking on educational responsibility for their children has been described as a cost-effective way of serving children (Ora, 1973). Farber and Lewis (1975) have suggested that involving parents may be merely a symbolic gesture that ultimately benefits schools, not parents, because involved parents can be held partially responsible for lack of progress on their child's part.

From these perspectives, it may not be realistic to expect programs to offer parents flexibility in selecting roles and ways of participating. Given the financial uncertainty of the times and the emphasis placed on cost effectiveness and efficiency, requiring parents to serve in certain roles may be more important to planners than offering an individualized parent program. Funding cutbacks present an additional barrier in that individualizing for families requires more time and effort on the part of program staff.

Training Barriers

Research conducted on teacher stress has indicated that interactions with parents are a major source of job anxiety (Bensky, Shaw, Gouse, Bates, Dixon, & Beane, 1980). Working with entire families is likely to present an even more stressful and unfamiliar situation for professionals. If parent involvement policy is to evolve in the directions outlined, then there is a need to provide knowledge and skill to early childhood professionals in areas such as family systems theory, group dynamics, and communication skills.

Summary

The literature reviewed makes it clear that a discrepancy exists between the intent of current parent involvement policy and the way it is being implemented on a programmatic level. The reasons for this discrepancy relate to two factors. The first factor is the strong political force that influenced policy and popularized the assumption that all parents want to be actively involved. This force misrepresented the needs of many parents. The second factor is the heavy emphasis on the roles of parents as teachers and decision makers: Just because parents can be trained to teach their children effectively does not mean that all parents should be expected to function in this role; just because early intervention programs with parent components have been shown to be successful does not mean that increased parent involvement is always in the best interests of all parents and children. Professionals are beginning to recognize the need to back away from prescribing a singularly focused parent program, to reassess some of the assumptions underlying our current policy, and to look at ways in which programs can support and assist families in an individualized way. In order to do this, new theories and new methodologies must be adopted by researchers in early childhood fields that take into account factors such as changing family structures, the interrelatedness of family members, life cycle transitions as they affect families of young handicapped children, and the multiple functions families perform in addition to educating their children.

References

Aldrich, A. (1947). Preventive medicine and mongolism. *American Journal of Mental Deficiency, 52,* 127–129.

Assael, D., & Waldstein, A. (Eds.). (1982). *Handicapped Children's Early Education Program: 1981–1982 overview and directory.* Chapel Hill, NC: Technical Assistance Development System.

Baker, B. L., Heifetz, L. J., & Murphy, D. M. (1980). Behavioral training for parents of mentally retarded children: One-year follow-up. *American Journal of Mental Deficiency, 85*(1), 31–38.

Bensky, J., Shaw, S., Gouse, A., Bates, H., Dixon, B., & Beane, W. (1980). Public Law 94–142 and stress: A problem for educators. *Exceptional Children, 47*(1), 24–29.

Bernheimer, C., Young, M., Winton, P., & Turnbull, A. (1980, March). *Coping patterns over time: Parents of young handicapped children.* Paper presented at the Society for Research in Child Development, Boston.

Blacher, J. (in press). Sequential stages of parental adjustment to the birth of a handicapped child: Fact or artifact? *Mental Retardation.*

Boggs, E. M. (1978). Who is putting whose head in the sand or in the clouds as the case may be? In A.P. Turnbull & H. R. Turnbull (Eds.), *Parents speak out.* Columbus, OH: Merrill.

Bricker, D., & Dow, M. (1980). Early intervention with the young severely handicapped child. *Journal of the Association for the Severely Handicapped, 5*(2), 130–142.

Diamond, S. (1981). Growing up with parents of a handicapped child: A handicapped person's perspective. In J. L. (Ed.), *Understanding and working with parents of children with special needs.* New York: Holt, Rinehart, & Winston.

Embry, L. H. (1980). Family support for handicapped preschool children at risk for abuse. In J. J. Gallagher (Ed.), *New directions for exceptional children* (Vol. 4). San Francisco: Jossey-Bass.

Federal Register. (1977, August 23). Washington, DC: U.S. Government Printing Office.

Federal Register. (1981, January 19). Washington, DC: U.S. Government Printing Office.

Farber, B., & Lewis, M. (1975). The symbolic use of parents: A sociological critique of educational research. *Journal of Research Development in Education, 8*(2), 34–43.

Featherstone, H. (1981). *A difference in the family.* New York: Basic Books.

Flynn, C., Pelosi, J., & Wiegerink, R. (1981). *Preschool program for special children and their parents: A guide for public schools.* Chapel Hill, NC: Frank Porter Graham Child Development Center.

Foster, M., Berger, M., & McLean, M. (1981). Rethinking a good idea: A reassessment of parent involvement. *Topics in Early Childhood Special Education, 1*(3), 55–65.

Gabel, H., & Kotsch, L. (1981). Extended families and young handicapped children. *Topics in Early Childhood Special Education*, 1(3), 29–36.

Goldstein, S., Strickland, B., Turnbull, A. P., & Curry, L. (1980). An observational analysis of the IEP conference. *Exceptional Children*, 46(4), 278–286.

Grant, D. K. (1965). Out of the shadows. *American Journal of Disorders of Children*, 110, 2–3.

Guba, E. (1981). Criteria for assessing the trustworthiness of naturalistic inquiries. *Educational Communication on Technology Journal*, 29, 75–92.

Haley, J. (1973). *Uncommon therapy*. New York: Norton.

Harvey, J. (1977). The enabling legislation: How did it all begin? In J. B. Jordan, A. H. Hayden, M. B. Karnes, & M. M. Wood (Eds.), *Early childhood education for exceptional children: A handbook of ideas and exemplary practices*. Reston, VA: Council for Exceptional Children.

Hocutt, A. (1980). *Parent involvement policy and practice: A study of parental participation in early education programs for handicapped children*. Unpublished doctoral dissertation, University of North Carolina at Chapel Hill.

Hocutt, A., & Wiegerink, R. (in press). Perspectives on parent involvement in preschool programs for handicapped children. In R. Haskins (Ed.), *Parent education and public policy*. Norwood, NJ: Ablex.

Hunt, J. (1971). Parent and child centers. *American Journal of Orthopsychiatry*, 41, 13–37.

Karnes, M., & Zehrbach, R. (1975). Matching families and services. *Exceptional Children*, 41, 1–4.

Lamb, M. (1977). Father-infant and mother-infant interaction in the first year of life. *Child Development*, 48, 167–181.

Lavor, M., & Krivit, D. (1969). The handicapped children's early education assistance act, Public Law 90–538. *Exceptional Children*, 35, 379–383.

Lillie, D., Trohanis, P., & Goin, K. (Eds.). (1976). *Teaching parents to teach: A guide for working with the special child*. New York: Walker.

Lusthaus, C. S., Lusthaus, E. W., & Gibbs, H. (1981). Parents' role in the decision process. *Exceptional Children*, 48(3), 256–257.

Lynch, E. W., & Stein, R. (1982). Perspectives on parent participation in special education. *Exceptional Education Quarterly*, 3(2), 56–63.

MacMillan, D. L., & Turnbull, A. P. (1983). Parent involvement with special education: Respecting individual preferences. *Education and Training of the Mentally Retarded*, 18(1), 10–16.

McKinney, J. D., & Hocutt, A. M. (1982). Public school involvement of parents of learning-disabled children and average achievers. *Exceptional Education Quarterly*, 3(2), 64–73.

Minuchin, S. (1974). *Families and family therapy*. Cambridge, MA: Harvard University Press.

Morgan, D. P. (1982). Parental participation in the IEP process: Does it enhance appropriate education? *Exceptional Education Quarterly*, 3(2), 33–40.

Morgan, D., & Rhode, V. (1980). Attitudes of Utah's special education teachers towards IEPs. In *Individualized education programs: A handbook for the school principal*. Logan: Department of Special Education, Utah State University.

National Association for Retarded Children. (1954). *The educator's viewpoint*. New York: Author.

Ora, J. (1973). Involvement in training of parent and citizen workers in early education for the handicapped. In Karnes, M. (Ed.), *Not all little wagons are red*. Reston, VA: Council for Exceptional Children.

Report on Preschool Education. (1982). 14, 7.

Safer, N. D., Morrissey, P. A., Kaufman, M. J., & Lewis, L. (1978). Implementation of IEPs: New teacher roles and requisite support systems. *Focus on Exceptional Children,* 10(1), 1–20.

Tjossem, T. D. (Ed.). (1976). *Intervention strategies for high risk infants and young children.* Baltimore: University Park Press.

To assure the free appropriate public education of all handicapped children: Second annual report to Congress on the implementation of P.L. 94–142: The Education for All Handicapped Children Act. (1980). Washington, DC: U.S. Department of Education.

Turnbull, A. P. (1984). Parent participation in the IEP process. In J. A. Mulick & S. M. Pueschel (Eds.), *Parent-professional participation in developmental disability services: Foundations and prospects.* Cambridge, MA: Ware Press.

Turnbull, A. P., Brotherson, M., & Summers, J. (1982, June). *The family's influence on the development of independence: Rationale, design, and conceptual framework.* Paper presented at the American Association on Mental Deficiency Annual Meeting, Boston.

Turnbull, A. P., & Turnbull, H. R. (1982). Parent involvement: A critique. *Mental Retardation,* 20(3), 115–122.

Turnbull, A. P., Winton, P. J., Blacher, J., & Salkind, N. (1982). Mainstreaming in the kindergarten classroom: Perspective of parents of handicapped and nonhandicapped children. *Journal of the Division for Early Childhood,* 6, 14–20.

Turnbull, H. R., Turnbull, A. P., & Wheat, M. (1982). Assumptions about parental participation: A legislative history. *Exceptional Education Quarterly,* 3(2), 1–8.

Wiegerink, R., Hocutt, A., Posante-Loro, R., & Bristol, M. (1980). Parent involvement in early education programs for handicapped children. In J. J. Gallagher (Ed.), *New directions for exceptional children: Ecology of exceptional children.* San Francisco: Jossey-Bass.

Winton, P. (1982, June). *The use of qualitative methodologies in conducting research with parents of handicapped children.* Paper presented at the American Association on Mental Deficiency Annual Meeting, Boston.

Winton, P., & Turnbull, A. (1981). Parent involvement as viewed by parents of preschool handicapped children. *Topics in Early Childhood Special Education,* 1(3), 11–19.

Wolfensberger, W. (1970). Counseling the parents of the retarded. In A. A. Baumeister (Ed.), *Mental retardation: Appraisal, education, and rehabilitation.* Chicago: Aldine.

Yoshida, R. K. (1982). Research agenda: Finding ways to create more options for parent involvement. *Exceptional Education Quarterly,* 3(2), 74–80.

Yoshida, R. K., Fenton, K. S., Kaufman, M. J., & Maxwell, J. P. (1978). Parental involvement in the special education pupil planning process: The school's perspective. *Exceptional Children,* 44(7), 531–534.

PART IV

Conclusion

Severely Handicapped Children and Their Families: A Synthesis

Regina Yando
Edward Zigler

Introduction

The work presented in this volume represents a major shift in the orientation of psychological inquiry and intervention with severely handicapped children. Questions related to a child's intelligence and achievements are not central to the research reviewed or the models proposed. Instead, the focus is on questions concerning the child's effect on the family and how parents, siblings, and the extended environmental community, including professionals, respond to the child and to each other. The child has been placed in a context, and the problem has been reformulated to allow intervention and change to interact over the course of the development of both the child and the family.

In addition to the original research presented here, the book offers a comprehensive review of the current state of the literature pertaining to severely handicapped children and their families. Necessarily included in all chapters is a considerable amount of research with nonhandicapped children, disadvantaged children, and children who, according to Blacher's guidelines (see Chapter 1), would be classified as only mildly handicapped. Reliance on these data is a dramatic illustration of the fact that until recently severely handicapped children did not receive the attention from developmental and clinical investigators that is necessary both for the purpose of successful intervention and for the formation of social policy.

Given the paucity of research directly related to severely handicapped children and their families, it is not surprising that the topics of inquiry among the chapters in this volume vary considerably. A number of authors are concerned with the application of theory and results from experimental research in child development to the population of severely handicapped children. For example, Blacher (Chapter 1) reviews the Bowlby–Ainsworth model of attachment and suggests its usefulness for examining issues of acceptance or parental rejection, and Kaiser and Hayden (Chapter 8) focus on infant bonding for intervention and study. Research and theory from the literature on child abuse is also reviewed by Blacher and examined in depth by Meier and Sloan (Chapter 7), each applying what has been learned about precursors to child abuse, over the range of children who are its victims, to the population of severely handicapped children. The broader issue of parenting, what researchers think they know about it and what still eludes their grasp, is the subject of the work by Wright, Granger, and Sameroff (Chapter 2). Here, knowledge acquired from work with parents of many different kinds of children is used and suggested as a model for intervention with and study of severely handicapped children.

A second set of chapters deals with specific populations of children. Bristol and Schopler (Chapter 3) provide an informative and thoughtful review of autistic children and their families, making many suggestions for further research and study of families of severely handicapped children. Skrtic, Summers, Brotherson, and Turnbull (Chapter 6) focus on the siblings of handicapped children, an important subsystem of the family also receiving long overdue attention in work with acutely and chronically ill children (e.g., Sourkes, 1980). Finally, Stoneman and Brody (Chapter 5) present a review of theoretical and methodological considerations in doing research with families of severely handicapped children.

A third set of chapters is primarily issue-oriented. Three of them are concerned with training programs for parents of handicapped children (Kaiser & Hayden, Chapter 8; Baker, Chapter 9; Turnbull & Winton, Chapter 10). Each of these presents the issue of professional involvement with the parents and families of handicapped children. Seltzer and Krauss (Chapter 4) present a review, at both the psychological and sociological level, of placement alternatives and decision-making processes.

Although the chapters in this volume can be roughly categorized according to theoretical, population, and intervention issues, it is important to note that all of the authors are struggling with the same task that Blacher outlined in her introduction. That is, can what has been learned in recent research in child development and special education be used to approach more successfully, more objectively, and possibly more effectively, the work with severely handicapped children and their families? The first step is to select, organize, and gather the information available into one volume, accessible to professionals and researchers in the field. That purpose has been accomplished here. The next step is to review the state of current knowledge and point the way to new research and intervention programs. That step is the focus of this chapter as we review the models of inquiry and hypotheses implicit in the work collected here, and then make recommendations for social and professional policy that can take current knowledge and best ideas for the future into account.

The Models of Inquiry

Historically, research on severely handicapped children has focused on the nature and extent of their disability and implications for their functioning as children and adults. Investigators have searched for causes, boundaries of diagnoses, and intervention strategies, all tending to focus on the primary disability or handicap and presumed fixed limitations. Research design has typically been within a single-factor cause-and-effect model, with independent predictive variables such as genetic and environmental disturbance and dependent outcome variables such as physical development, IQ, and socially appropriate behaviors. For many kinds of physical and mental handicaps, progress has been made in identifying specific genetic or metabolic disturbances that were implicated in the conditions. For others, the preponderance of evidence points to as yet unidentified but still physiological determinants of the primary disability.

More recently, research on environmental factors such as parenting, social class, and education has focused on the identification of secondary handicapping conditions—for example, emotional disturbance and retardation as derivative and often preventable effects of the initial handicap. Additionally, as it becomes clear that neither the child nor the child's environment are fixed entities, the research emphasis has shifted from identifying specific environmental independent variables to taking into account the mutual influence of handicapped child and environment. This important change in orientation is reflected in the major model of inquiry and intervention proposed in this volume.

Almost without exception, the chapters collected here make reference to systems theory concepts currently in use both for describing the bidirectionality of effects within interactions,—"transactions"—and for describing the multiple transactions in the environment of a dynamic organism—"systems." Analysis of transactions implies a focus on dyadic interaction, with systems analysis allowing for consideration of a greater multiple of impinging factors. Simply said, systems theory takes the view that cause and effect are not divisable, that organisms both respond to and create their environments by virtue of their response. A systems analysis of change or development also demands a focus on variables in context over time (Bateson, 1972; Hoffman, 1981; Miller, 1978). While it may be possible to focus on particular variables at any given moment in time, a kind of freeze-frame approach, predicting a distant future outcome is extremely difficult because of the multiple unforeseen or uncontrolled events and transactions that inevitably occur. Thus, systems theory does not easily admit a causal, predictive, or "outcome" model of research (Jantsch, 1980); rather, it provides a perspective that allows investigators to make hypotheses about shorter-term transactional probabilities.

Because a systems perspective has been used in the discussion of the research and research proposals presented here, most of the investigators acknowledge the importance of describing severely handicapped children as not only affected by, but also affecting, all parts of their environmental system. In the future, however, investigators need to make more clear what aspects of a system are receiving experimental or theoretical attention, as well as which are being ignored and why. Only in this way can they hypothesize what other factors might explain negative results in their data or changes in outcome across individuals or over time. Perhaps a useful task in synthesizing the reviews and research presented here, then, is to point out what aspects of the system receive attention in the models of inquiry proposed, as well as to identify the causal assumptions implicit in them. There are three possible models that can be identified, and each warrants further discussion.

Attachment

The first model, implicit in the discussions by Blacher (Chapter 1), Kaiser and Hayden (Chapter 8), Meier and Sloan (Chapter 7), and Wright *et al.* (Chapter 2), concerns attachment. In this model, the transactions between handicapped child and parent are focused on and hypothesized to lead to the formation of attachment or its failure. Attachment is causally related to parental acceptance or rejection, which is assumed to determine outcomes for the child such as placement outside the home, retention, and/or child abuse. What is not very well specified in these chapters, or elsewhere for that matter, is how one might *measure* attachment *to* severely handicapped infants. Indeed, in discussion it often seems that the outcome variables become by inference the measure of attachment; and, as Blacher warns, the concept of attachment may risk tautological misuse.

Certainly the first difficulty in assessing attachment with severely handicapped children is defining the type of handicap and, more specifically, what aspect of the condition is most important in affecting specific transactions. In the reviews presented in this volume, the term *severely handicapped* has included a wide variety of conditions, most of which are classified on the basis of the salience of a single dimension of functioning (e.g., severely retarded). The use of single-dimension categories in theorizing and, even more, in research, tends to obfuscate meaning and generate conflicting patterns of results. For example, the importance of the severity of a condition has little weight in measuring maternal stress in the findings reviewed by Wright *et al.* (Chapter 2), whereas Bristol and Schopler (Chapter 3) find that in the population of autistic children, the severity of their disorder is an important factor in parental adaptation.

Research on attachment would benefit if less attention in sampling were given to the category of handicap than to the more specific child characteristics that might influence parental acceptance or rejection. It would be perhaps useful for investigators to assess child characteristics along each of at least three general dimensions of severity: physical appearance and functioning, cognitive functioning, and psychosocial functioning and behavior. Although simple, the combined use of these three broad dimensions of assessment would force attention to the variability among children classified as severely handicapped and acknowledge the importance of child characteristics on our perceptions. This point is alluded to by Blacher (Chapter 1) in her review of research on infant attachment. One can infer from her discussion that the process of attachment might differ greatly for a blind, severely retarded, temperamentally difficult infant and a blind, nonretarded, temperamentally easy infant. Just as the transactional process of these two infants will differ, one could predict that the more difficult (or acting out) adult who is blind and mildly retarded is more vulnerable to placement than is the blind, mildly retarded socially appropriate adult. Despite the obviousness of these examples, little of the research reported in this volume has examined the relationship between multiple salient child characteristics and a variety of specific outcome variables identified as important in the numerous transactions that occur in the life of the severely handicapped child.

Interestingly, the first dimension, physical appearance and functioning, has received less general attention than the other two. Nonetheless, autism is illustrative of the importance of the role of physical characteristics in many of the outcomes under consideration. It is to a great extent because young autistic children often appear to be physically normal and even attractive that ambiguity marks the diagnostic process, despite their low psychosocial and intellectual functioning (Bristol and Schopler, Chapter 3). On the other hand, erroneous assumptions regarding cognitive functioning are often associated with conditions (such as cerebral palsy) that have salient physical characteristics. If the people in the professional and extended environments of these children react so strongly to physical characteristics, surely this variable must be considered when an affective process such as attachment is under study.

The second difficulty confronting investigators who attempt to use the attachment model as it has been defined in the literature with nonhandicapped children concerns the foci of important transactions. That is, the transactional process is assumed to be confined to the infant and his or her immediate family. The development and socialization of severely handicapped children, however, are not solely dependent on the interactions within families. Unlike the nonhandicapped infant whose early caretaking environment is primarily limited to his or her parents and to those individuals in the immediate physical environment, the severely handicapped infant exists in an ever-expanding network of systems responsible for his or her care. So, too, the severely handicapped infant's family is unique in that it must interact frequently with these systems. What is, for the nonhandicapped infant, a check-up with the pediatrician becomes routine visits to various specialists for the severely handicapped. Baby-sitting and day-care services, difficult under normal circumstances, often reach the level of impossible for severely handicapped children. And the educational opportunities and alternatives available to these children are limited by countless factors including the availability of professional expertise and funding. Given this situation, it is almost impossible to consider the transactional process between the severely handicapped infant and his or her parents and family as similar to that of the nonhandicapped infant. The severely handicapped infant, in fact, influences not only his or her parents and siblings but also the many professionals involved with his or her care who in turn affect the family. This means that the characteristics of the parents and other family members as well as the individuals who comprise the service systems involved must be considered as important factors that could influence the transactional process which is central to the attachment model.

While system factors are acknowledged as important by most of the investigators in this volume, that acknowledgment does not always easily translate to experimental design. For example, Wright *et al.* (Chapter 2), who are the major promulgators of the transactional model in this volume, effectively argue that the parents' perceptions, beliefs and developmental understanding will mediate their ability to utilize interventions and support systems that will, in turn, help them to help their child. Note in the research reported, however, the slight change in emphasis away from the parent–child transactions that is of central interest in their discussion. It is the parents' transactions with the service and support systems that are focused upon. And, it is the mothers' anxiety and attitudes about their children that were used as the dependent measures, not the child's behavior or the mother's behavioral interaction with her child. This example points out the need for future researchers to design methods that enable them to analyze the relationship among transactions that occur at various levels of the system defined as influencing the primary transaction of interest—in this case, that of the parent and child.

Finally, whereas much of the attachment research on nonhandicapped infants focuses on the child's attachment to the parent, the work presented in this volume focuses on the parents' attachment to the child. This shift in emphasis, as well as the nature of the population of children referred to, seems to warrant examination and clarification of a basic assumption underlying attachment research with nonhandicapped infants: The quality of infant attachment and the development of the attachment system is related to expectations of mature adult functioning. Positive infant attachment results in a mentally and emotionally mature adult. Given that most severely handicapped children will not achieve either cognitive or affective maturity, as defined for the nonhandicapped population, investigators interested in pursuing the attachment model need to specify the significance of attachment for severely handicapped children and their parents. What, for example, are the behavioral indices, for both child and parent, that positive attachment has been achieved?

Additionally, although the relationship between failures in attachment and placement or abuse is intuitively appealing, whether attachment failure is a necessary and/or sufficient condition for such outcomes also needs further investigation. It is possible to imagine a model of attachment for severely handicapped children that allows for changes in attachment over time, perhaps related to changes in physical appearance or behavior or to parental expectations, all of these in positive or negative directions. The idea would be to allow attachment itself to be subject to change resulting from systemic influences. Investigation of this idea would, in addition, have ramifications for the general theory of attachment.

Stress

The second model of inquiry proposed by many of the contributors to this volume might best be called the stress model (Bristol & Schopler, Chapter 3; Seltzer & Krauss, Chapter 4; Skrtic et al., Chapter 6; Turnbull & Winton, Chapter 10). Here the focus is on the handicapped child's effect on the family, viewed largely in terms of stress and adaptation. In this model, the child is the initial event that affects the social–emotional health of the family. Innumerable other events in family life are perceived to interact with the presence of a handicapped child to produce further stress or facilitate coping and adaptation, again presupposing a bidirectionality of effects between child and family. An increase in family stress to some critical level, presumed to be different for each family, becomes the mediating variable affecting child outcomes. Placement, retention, and abuse are again focused on as the broadly defined outcomes of interest. In this model, attachment or failure of attachment becomes only one of many variables either increasing or decreasing family stress and adaptation. The stress model focuses less on the infant and young child than the attachment model, and it is presented as more able to accommodate the developmental and life cycle changes of handicapped children and their families. Both Bristol and Schopler (Chapter 3) and Skrtic et al. (Chapter 6), for example, emphasize the importance of the stage of the family life cycle when assessing stress.

In this model, stress variables such as income, availability of services, socioeconomic status, illness of family members, and formal and informal resources are not given an independent predictive weight as in linear models of causality. Rather, these variables are assessed only as they affect and are affected by the parent–child or parent–environment transactions. The concept of stress is, as it must be, defined subjectively by parents' reports and by observational data. Here, as in the attachment model, there is nonetheless some risk of defining stress by outcome rather than using it as a mediating variable.

Perhaps the most interesting component of the model, hinted at but not formalized as an area for research by the authors, is the role of professionals in the life of the severely handicapped child and his or her family. When one reviews the history of professional involvement with severely handicapped children, it should become clear that the diagnostic disagreements, mistakes, and labels may have profound effects on families who seek relief, support, and guidance from the profession. The changing ideas about the etiology of such conditions as autism (see Bristol & Schopler, Chapter 3) and schizophrenia, from the environmental to the biological, is a good example. Equally, changes in what is considered appropriate treatment may occur frequently over the course of a family's life cycle leading to guilt, anger, and a lack of faith in professionals.

For example, in the not too distant past, as many of the contributors to this volume note, parents of a Down's syndrome child were often encouraged to institutionalize their child immediately at birth. For a number of reasons, including those related to current social policy, such advice today would be seriously questioned by most workers in the field. What has changed—the child's characteristics or the context in which the child is given the opportunity to develop? To some extent, both. That is, as it was observed that Down's syndrome children develop better at home than in institutions, more community services became available. The additional creation of more favorable learning environments, in turn, has resulted in the recognition that, as a group, these children are able to exceed their previously expected level of development. Given the changes in the behavior of these children, very few are now considered to be severely handicapped. The upper limit for cognitive growth has not changed, but the contexts for expression and the reaching of a fuller potential have. The lesson, of course, is that for many handicapping conditions professionals may prematurely set the notion of what an upper limit of development is. Understanding contextual change as it relates to a child whose impairment cannot be totally eradicated, then, becomes extremely important not only to the definition of the severity of the handicap, but also to the continued provision of environmental opportunities for enhancing a child's development.

An additional danger is unwittingly portraying to parents through the enthusiasm for intervention the notion that if they take on responsibility to become the "best" parents providing the "best" opportunities, "normality" may be the outcome. Several contributors touch on this sensitive topic, particularly Bristol and Schopler (Chapter 3) and Skrtic et al. (Chapter 6). Not only can assumptions about etiology be wrong, as in the case of autism, but also expectations for the long-term effectiveness of early interventions.

Finally, Kaiser and Hayden (Chapter 8) raise the difficult issue of assessing the needs of the handicapped child against a background that includes the whole family. They rightly suggest that professionals may "overvalue" the handicapped infant, who, of course, is the target of professional efforts the way most intervention programs are designed. Other family members and total family health may be ignored in the process. In their discussion of autistic children, Bristol and Schopler (Chapter 3) also note the increase in family stress as the children become adolescents, at which point there is not only a resignation and finality about diagnosis, but also a dramatic drop in services available to these "children" who are now almost adults. If stress on the families of handicapped children is to be reduced, professionals must be sensitive to total family dynamics, family life cycles, and their own unrecognized value judgments when trying to intervene or support.

Coping

The last model can be described by the term *coping*. That is, do interventions such as parent training enable parents better to cope with their severely handicapped child? Both the work of Baker (Chapter 9) and the chapter by Turnbull and Winton (Chapter 10) address this question. Here the focus is on the service system's effect on the parent as measured by parent and child change. The implicit assumption is that parent training affects child–parent interactions, which in turn results in changes in child behavior, which result in more positive child and family outcomes. With reference to the outcomes of central interest in this volume, one could further assume that the child would not be placed out of the home and that family stress would be decreased or better managed.

Baker (Chapter 9) presents a comprehensive review of the parent training literature, offering an objective evaluation of methods and outcomes as well as suggestions for further research. Although Baker does not specifically address the relationship between parent training and placement out of the home, one can hypothesize that the parents' inability to manage their child's behavioral problems might result either in abuse or placement, or in both. Thus, parent training can be viewed as a critical element in preventing such outcomes, the first of which is an unquestionably "bad" outcome and the latter an outcome currently viewed as negative by many professionals and parents. Thus, it is useful to look at the mediating variables in the model, that is, what parent training purports to do to effect desired outcomes. Although a wide range of specific child effects are reviewed by Baker, they can be grouped around the categories of skill acquisition and maintenance and the elimination of inappropriate behaviors. The parent effects focused on are primarily the acquisition of knowledge and teaching skills as well as positive changes in parental attitudes and adjustment. As might be expected, parent training is not equally effective with all families. Families marked by low socioeconomic status and single parents may need additional types or forms of parent training if home-based care is to be considered a viable option. In this case, factors located in the social system, such as in-home services and support networks, need to be examined as possible variables affecting the child and parent outcomes in the parent training model. Baker also suggests that there is a need for greater flexibility in the kinds of parent training offered so that differences in education, marital status, and belief systems will not act as barriers to access to parent training programs.

One of the elements often overlooked in the parent training literature, but well addressed by Turnbull and Winton (Chapter 10), is the effect on parenting roles as parents become teachers of their children. Parents bring many characteristics to the training program, ranging from high motivation for learning skills to fear and low self-esteem. For some, parent training may result in a net increase not only in skills, but also in ability to accept their children or to feel freer to devote needed attention to siblings. For others, participation in a training program may result in feelings of inadequacy, fear of being judged, and rejection of a child who does not respond as hoped to the training. For some family members, then, training may be viewed not as helpful but as an additional burden of time and interfacing with the professional system. The empirical data to support these assertions, however, are not available. Clearly the parental testimony offered by Turnbull and Winton argues that this is an important area for future research.

In summary, it is perhaps useful to return for a moment to the approach employed as a framework for the work presented in this volume. While systems theory has contributed to a growing awareness of the interdependency and interrelatedness of child, family, and extended environmental variables, it is, in the true sense of the word, not a theory but rather a model for describing structure and change. We do not suggest, therefore, that traditional research approaches be tailored to examine the entirety of the severely handicapped child's environment. To do so, research would have to be designed to handle not only multivariate input but also to monitor and analyze the mutual influences and changes in variables over time. For example, given the data accumulated in this

volume, a variety of child, parent, family, and service system variables
would have to be related to the development of parent–child attachment
as well as to the mental health of the whole family. Further, none of these
variables could be isolated from the other or from their reassessment
over the developmental course of the child or the life cycle of the family.
Clearly, this would be an enormous, unwieldly, and perhaps unproduc-
tive task. Given that this possibility is not probable in the near future,
how can a systems perspective be useful? We obviously believe that this
perspective does have value. As can be seen in the work presented here,
the systems model can enhance professionals' ability to define new relationships among variables and to be open to combining a variety of
approaches in the understanding of complex human behavior. Investigators can be conceptually aware of systems, conduct some descriptive "natural history" studies of families over time, and engage in
causal, predictive research that collapses and simplifies those variables
whose contributions to change or outcome appear to be relatively small.
The systems model can inform research, even if it is not likely yet to influence the design of experiments, which, if variable-specific prediction
is to play a part, are by definition outside of a systems orientation. The
caveat, then, is that investigators should choose carefully which child,
family, and extended environmental variables they will look at—bear-
ing in mind that they are overlooking others for the sake of experimental
efficiency—but should not shy away from identifying their concern with
causality and with outcome. That the total system in which the severely
handicapped child is involved cannot yet be explained does not mean
that the relative importance of parts of the system at specific points in
time cannot be examined.

Finally, while the methodological issues may seem overwhelming if
one tries to take into account all of the factors that may affect handicapped children and their parents, it is important to remember that it is
not necessary to know "the answer" before advocating for services to
severely handicapped parents and children, because part of "the
answer" is discovering *with* them what works. There is no static system
to be discovered or described.

Policy Implications

It is difficult to limit a discussion of social policy to severely handicapped children, for society must assess and formulate its commitment
to children across a range of diversity in health and ability. As pointed
out elsewhere (Zigler, in press), there is a well-intended myth that the

United States is a child-oriented society, but the reality is a profound neglect of services for children who are disadvantaged and particularly for children who are mentally and physically handicapped. Among this group, severely handicapped children have been perhaps most neglected because of the greater cost of care and intervention and the relatively smaller amount of professional focus on these children and families.

Efforts have been made since the 1960s, through intensive lobbying, to procure broadly defined services for children. Two major policies have indeed been put into effect that have benefited all disadvantaged children: Medicaid and Public Law (PL) 94–142. The former has made hitherto unobtainable medical and support services available to the poor, while the latter, designed to provide every child with special needs a free and appropriate public education, has given parents of handicapped children legitimate access to a major public system and a potential service network where previously they had none. Legislation, however, does not ensure implementation, nor funding. For example, PL 94–142 demands much but the federal government provides very little of the funds necessary to enact the mandated services (Washington Report, 1978). Already pressed local school systems have been, therefore, responsible for financing PL 94–142, and many, under economic pressures, have cut back services or remained out of compliance with the law. While it is clear that a child's education is critical to his or her functioning as an adult, this society has not been willing to invest in *all* of its children's education. In times of economic strength, social policy decisions tend to result in favorable outcomes for handicapped children. In times of economic constriction, programs and services for handicapped children are cut and commitment to their care is shown to be less firm. This book may provide a basis for renewed professional commitment to helping effect social policy for severely handicapped children by establishing areas of known need and likely cost-effective areas for intervention.

While it is possible to argue that a great deal is known about the kinds of environments that seem to enhance children's cognitive and social–emotional development in general, this book makes it clear that investigators are still struggling with the most basic issues when the child is severely handicapped. It can also effectively be argued that all children should, if possible, be reared by their parents. The research reviewed in this volume, however, raises the possibility that for some children and families, keeping a severely handicapped child in the home may result in considerable stress on the parents and/or siblings and in outcomes such as abuse and neglect for the children themselves. Continual home care may not be a viable option for these families and children. Yet, residential care in institutions has not always been an acceptable alternative, which has led to the movement for deinstitutionalization and community-based care. A difficulty arises if community-based care becomes a code term for reduction in services. In times of federal economic constriction, hard-pressed communities may not be able to provide the level of funding necessary for the comprehensive services needed to keep a child in the home or to design acceptable residential alternatives. Thus, policy efforts should be directed toward ensuring funding for community-based services that are sufficiently comprehensive to allow parents the option to obtain in-home support services or opportunities for short- or long-term placement out of the home.

What is needed at the community level has been described by Larsen (1977) and elaborated on by Seltzer and Krauss (Chapter 4). The essential community-based services are identified as early intervention, public education, community residential services (including respite care, in-home support services, and family counseling), and protective services that include advocacy. Note that although this is a community-based model, it includes residential options, particularly the much-needed respite care for families who are able to keep their severely handicapped child with them but who need periodic time off in order to do so. If such a selection of services were available, a central referral system bolstered by the employment of trained and informed home visitors would be a necessity. Parents of handicapped children spend a lot of time, effort, and money going from professional to professional and agency to agency simply to obtain information about what services are available and where they can be found.

Funding for comprehensive community-based services will of necessity have to be shared by communities with some other funding source. This is an area where public–private cooperation, that is, enlisting the aid of state or community-located industries and businesses in the effort, might be appropriate. This suggestion has been elaborated on by Zigler and Finn (1981). They report that such cooperative services have already begun in various parts of the country and have proven effective. The goal of such programs would be to foster local control and flexibility without limiting funding to also dwindling local public resources.

The value of community-based services, even those that offer permanent residential placement or residential respite care, is that parents may remain involved with their children's programs and give important feedback to the professionals who design interventions. The chapters in this book and the systems model referred to emphasize the need to offer services for severely handicapped children that can take into account the changing needs of these children and families over time. Because knowledge is not yet strong enough to predict what these needs will be for any given family, services instead have to be designed that can respond within a short time to changing needs, incorporate new knowledge, and be varied enough to accommodate different families at various stages of development. Again, community-based programs offer more flexibility for local feedback than those legislated at the federal level, where budgets are locked into providing specific services. Often when a program becomes obsolete, federal funding is withdrawn without substitution of new or more appropriate services. What is ideally needed is a permanent federal funding commitment to severely handicapped children with flexible regional programming and disbursement capacity.

A model of services within a state or region might include multiple local programs for preschool- and school-age children, integrated into the school system much as they are mandated now, with the addition of coordinated parent training and family clinical services available through community agencies such as mental health centers. At the same time, larger regions could share a residential facility offering respite care and full-time care for those who need it. A foster care resource center could be maintained at the residential facility along with an in-house training program for foster parents. For adolescents and young adults, group home situations could again be provided at the regional level, with another set of these facilities available for adults. Families who made use of these facilities could be encouraged to give time to the care of their own members, or to be a regular visiting resource. No further research is needed to show that these kinds of programs and facilities should be available to all severely handicapped children and families. There is a continuum of severity of handicaps and a range of transactional outcomes for children and families. Flexible programming would enable more children to remain members of their families through the provision of services to entire families.

The systems model, implicit and explicit in the work reviewed here, might be seen as so complicated as to make effective social policy impossible. On the contrary, the systems model is a welcome reminder that "the answer" is not needed for planning because there is no one answer, or even a limited set of questions. Rather, professionals must act on what they know, even if they know that knowledge is incomplete, and then evaluate the effects of these actions so as to elaborate new ones. The process is not serendipitous, but rather one in which the importance of the actual effects of professional intervention in transactions with handicapped children and their families is recognized. Professionals' knowledge of child development and parents' knowledge of their own and their families' needs must be used to plan programs together and to undertake constant reevaluation of a dynamic system. Fixed programs, such as institutionalization in large facilities far from the patient's community, that are not able to respond to the changing needs of children and the changing ideas of society are doomed not only to obsolescence but also to causing avoidable trauma to the families and children who need help.

References

Bateson, G. (1972). *Steps to an ecology of mind.* New York: Ballantine Books.

Hoffman, L. (1981). *Foundations of family therapy.* New York: Basic Books.

Jantsch, E. (1980). *The self-organizing universe.* New York: Pergamon Press.

Larsen, L. A. (1977). Community services to program effectively for the severely/profoundly handicapped. In L. W. Sontag (Ed.), *Educational programming for the severely and profoundly handicapped.* Reston, VA: Council for Exceptional Children.

Miller, J. G. (1978). *Living systems.* New York: McGraw-Hill.

Sourkes, B. M. (1980). Siblings of the pediatric cancer patient. In J. Kellerman (Ed.), *Psychological aspects of childhood cancer.* Springfield, IL: Thomas.

Washington report: School systems bitterly complain about education act problems. (1978), *Arise,* 1(6), 4.

Zigler, E. (in press). Handicapped children and their families. In E. Schopler & G. Mesibov (Eds.), *The effects of autism on the family.* New York: Plenum.

Zigler, E., & Finn, M. (1981). From problem to solution: Changing public policy as it affects children and families. *Young Children, 36*(4), 31–32, 55–58.

Author Index

Numbers in italics refer to the pages on which the complete references are cited.

Willer, B., 35, *50*
Williams, C. A., 351, *370*
Williams, D. E., 362, *368*
Williams, G. C., 261, *272*
Williams, S. M., 166, *172*
Wilson, D. O., 281, *316*
Wilson, E. O., 249, *272*
Wilson, M., 249, 250, 262, 263, 264, *270*, *272*
Wiltz, N. A., 325, *375*
Wimberger, H. C., 63, *88*, 101, *137*, 183, 192, 204, *212*
Wind, Y., 186, *211*
Windle, D. R., 58, *87*
Wing, L., 97, *141*
Winton, P., 386, 388, 389, 390, 391, 392, *395*, *397*
Wise, M. J., 355, 357, *373*
Wittig, B. A., 9, 12, *42*
Wolchik, S. A., 194, *214*, 340, 345, 347, *370*
Wolfe, H., 263, *271*
Wolfensberger, W., *397*
Woodruff, G., 307, *314*
Worland, J., 357, *375*
Wortis, R. P., 278, *317*
Wright, B. M., 23, *50*
Wright, C. M., 281, 291, *313*
Wright, J., 63, 64, 65, 66, *90*
Wright, S. W., 145, *175*
Wurster, S., 361, *374*

Wyngaarden, M., 151, 158, 160, 165, 166, 171, *173*, *175*

Y

Yang, E., 108, *135*
Yarrow, M. R., 182, 186, *214*
Yasuda, P. M., 336, *367*
Yeates, K. O., 20, 26, *48*
Yoder, P., 324, *369*
York, R., 6, *49*
Yoshida, R. K., 385, 388, *397*
Young, A., 28, *49*
Young, C. C., 361, *374*
Young, M., 392, *395*
Yule, W., 11, 14, *47*
Yuwiler, A., 97, *139*

Z

Zachofsky, T., 153, 163, *172*
Zahn-Waxler, C., 209, *214*
Zehrbach, R., 388, *396*
Zelazo, P., 280, *317*
Zetlin, A., 157, *174*
Zifferblatt, S. M., 346, *375*
Zigler, E., 193, *214*, 251, *272*, 412, 414, *416*
Zlutnick, S., 6, *50*
Zucker, R. A., 23, *50*
Zuk, G. H., 231, *246*

Subject Index

Child abuse (*cont.*)
child factors, 250, 252–256, 263
and cleft palate children, 250, 263, 269
and clubfootedness in children, 250
and crying, 16, 17, 284
definition of, 251, 253
and developmental handicaps, 247
diagnosis and treatment, 252, 265–269
dynamics of, 15–18, 251–253
ecological factors, 248, 249, 252–256
episodes, 252–256
and handicapping condition, 247–250
identification and reporting, 251, 252, 256
and marital relationships, 248, 249
and nonhuman animal world, 248, 260, 261
parental factors, 248, 250, 252–256, 265, 266
precipitating situations and events, 252–256
primary prevention, 252
and removal from home, 248, 249, 265
and sexual abuse, 251, 262, 266
and smiling, 17, 250
and spina bifida children, 250
and stepchildren and parents, 262, 263
and treatment strategies, 265–269
Child Abuse Prevention and Treatment Act of 1973, 251
Child characteristics
of autistic child, 100–106
and parent–child dynamics, 21–25
Child custody, 280
Child neglect, 17, 248–250, 260, 262
Child rearing
philosophy, 229, 230, 232, 253
practices in other cultures, 253
Child temperament, 22, 24
Chronic sorrow, 54, *see also* Parents' feelings and stages of adjustment
Chronically ill child, 29
Chronological age (CA) match design, 191–194
Cleft palate in children, 55, 250, 263, 269
Clinical
observations, 53–56
psychology, 282
research, 275–312
Clubfoot in children, 55, 250
Cluster analysis, 9

Cognitive functioning, 405–407
Cognitive impairment and language, 24
Communication style, 11, 22, 230, 232, 233, 240, 320, 323, 324, 336
Community acceptance and support, and autism, 129, 133
Community advocacy, 131–133
Community residential facilities, 7, 159, 160, 163, 164, 168, 169, 305, 414, 415, *see also* Placement alternatives
Community-based programs and feedback, 414, 415
Computers as training tools, 354
Concepts of Development Questionnaire, 76, 77
Conflict–harmony continuum, 230, 233, 234
Confusion, feelings of, 28, 78, *see also* Parents' feelings and stages of adjustment
Conversational skills, teaching of, 323, 324
Coping, 28–31, 39, 53, 75, 79, 236, 269, 298
and autistic children, 91–134
and emotional climate, 30, 31
and religion, 126
Coping Health Inventory for Parents, 125, 126
Counseling
parent, 59, 67–69, 71, 72, 129, 320, 321
psychological, 59
sibling, 167
Crisis studies, 27, 321, 392
Criterion-match designs, 194, 195
Critical care decision options, 276
Cross-disciplinary coordination, 277
Crying, 11, 284, 325, 328, 346
caretaking response, 3, 6
and child abuse, 16, 17, 284
and child characteristics, 23, 41
"Cuddleability", 11, 22, 23
Cues, 11, 70, 292
affective expression, 279
and crying, 3, 6, 23, 41
crying and attachment, 11, 284, 325, 328, 346
crying and child abuse, 16, 17, 284
and eye contact, 11, 12, 23, 41, 101, 269, 286, 298
and facial expression, 285, 286

Parent training programs, 62–69, 71–73,
269, 298, 319–366, 380, 382, 402, 410,
411
case studies of, 323–326
and coping, 410, 411
lack of interest in, 65, 66
outcome of, 72, 73
Parental Attitude Research Instrument
(PARI), 57, 58, 75
Parent–child attachment and child abuse,
263, 264
Parent–child dynamics, 4, 18–35, 181
child characteristics, 21–25
and cultural influences, 32–35
and emotional climate in the family,
25–31
and severely handicapped children,
20–35, 181
and social support networks, 31, 32
Parent–child interaction, 22, 63, 266
training, 63, 69–72
Parent–child subsystem, 181, 193, 217,
233, 234
Parent–infant relationships, 281, 282, 287
Parenting role, 39, 182, 184, 411
and clinical research, 275–312
Parenting skills and emotional climate,
25–27
Parents
as advocates, 321, 334, 344, 364, 380,
414
attitudes and emotions, 52, 64
and counseling, 59, 67–69, 71, 72, 129,
320, 321
and counseling programs, 320, 321, 344
and cues, 22, see also Cues
decision makers, 378–386
education, 52, 196, 282, 299, 320, 321,
357, 358, 363, 411
education and autistic children, 118,
128
employment, 200
and intervention programs, 62–73, 344,
345, 360, 361
investment, 261, 262
learners, 379, 383, 385
needs and siblings, 233, 236, 238
neglect, 54, 60, see also Child neglect
options, 366
overinvolvement, 299
overprotection, 58, 68, 69

rejection, 57, 68
skill in caretaking, 22, 182, 232, 277,
280
special needs, 280, 301
studies of cognition, 75–80
therapists, 300, 321
Parents, and clinicians
disparities in experiences, 303–307
disparities of treatment, 276, 295
Parents Anonymous, 267
Parents as Advocates (UCLA), 334, 344
Parents as Teachers (UCLA), 333, 344
Parents' feelings and stages of adjustment
acceptance, 28, 232, 233, 257, 392
adaptation, 55, 59–62, 405
adjustment, 238, 257, 392
affection, 218, 220, 225, 226, 391
aggression, 68
ambivalence, 66, 70
anger, 28, 32, 54, 66, 126, 257, 291, 409
anticipatory grief, 294
anxieties, 54, 56, 59, 73, 78, 79, 84, 341,
407
bewilderment, 380
burnout, 112, 129, 290, 299
chronic sorrow, 54
chronically ill, 29
confusion, 28, 78
coping, 28–31, 39, 53, 75, 79, 236, 269,
298
denial, 27, 28, 32, 66, 238, 257, 269
depression, 28, 66, 70, 101, 121, 181,
293, 341
despair, 28
disappointment, 28
disbelief, 55
embarrassment, 297, 328
fatigue, 66, 183
and autistic children, 113–116
fears, 54, 114, 282, 380, 411
and autistic children, 114
frustration, 54, 70, 269, 380, 388, 392
grief, 28, 238, 257, 269
studies of, 27, 28
guilt, 28, 54, 64, 70, 123, 126, 226, 232,
233, 258, 269, 291, 328, 392, 409
hopelessness, 66
hostility, 68
impatience, 66
inadequacy, 54, 292, 411
incompetence, 66

Siblings (*cont.*)
  and religious belief, 231
  and roles, 182, 227, 228, 234, 235, 238, 243
  self-definition, 224, 225
  and self-report methodology, 185
  and sex roles, 205–207, 235, 236, 242, 243
  and socialization, 223, 224
  and socioeconomic status, 222, 231, 232
  and stress, 149, 150, 221, 222, 231, 238, 413
  task assignment, 219
  and training, 216, 221
Sibling–peer interactions, studies of, 188, 205, 207, 216, 239
Sibships, 217
Signing, as teaching tool, 323, 324
Single parent families, 40, 196, 229, 230, 280, 390, 411
Smiling, 11, 22–24, 41
  and attachment, 11, 12, 22–24, 41, 285–287
  and child abuse, 17, 250
  child characteristics, 22–24
Social isolation and mothers, 25
Social support systems, 22, 31, 32, 39, 52–54, 56–59, 62, 67, 68, 74, 78, 79, 83, 85, 258, 259, 296–299, 411
  and abusive parents, 267–269
  and autistic children, 106, 124, 125, 128–130, 132
  and coping, 59
Social work, 282
Socialization and family functions, 218, 220, 223, 224
Socioeconomic status, 6, 22, 77, 78, 195, 196, 229–232, 408, 411
  and autism, 92, 97, 105, 106, 122
  and caretaking casualty, 80, 81
  and institutionalization, 27
  and intervention programs, 354, 356–359, 361
  and mentally retarded children, 149, 153, 157
  and parent counseling, 69
  and siblings, 222, 231, 232
Special educators and clinical research, 275–312
Speech handicap in children, 258
Spina bifida, 57, 58, 78, 123, 250, 340

Spouse subsystem, 181, 217, 233
Stages of adjustment, *see* Parents' feelings and stages of adjustment
Standardized tests, arguments against, 194
Stanford-Binet IQ test, 19
Step-parenting and child abuse, 262, 263
Steps to Independence Series, 334, 335, 354
Stepwise multiple regression analyses, 9
Stress, feelings of, 29, 53, 59, 75, 77, 78, 236, 237, 242, 280, 282, 310, 328, 392, 405, 408, 410 413, 416
  and autistic children, 91–141, 409, 410
  and child abuse, 413
  degree of, 52, 58, 59, 62, 64, 66, 78
  and emotional climate, 29, 30, 32
  and overeating, 126
  teachers and, 394
  and siblings, 149, 150, 221, 222, 231, 238, 413
  variables, 408
Stressful life events, 22, 27, 38, 53, 56, 73
Subsystems,
  family, 180, 181, 197, 217–219, 229, 230, 233, 234
  parent–child, 181, 193, 217, 233, 234
  sibling, 181, 197, 217, 230, 233, 234, 402
  spouse, 181, 217, 233
Successive adaptation, six phases of, 60–62
Systems model, 411, 412, 414, 415

T

Tantrums, 115
TEACCH, *see* Treatment and Education of Autistic and related Communication handicapped CHildren
Teacher role of parent, 22, 63, 64, 182, 184, 204
Teaching at home, 26, 29, 32, 38
Teaching Proficiency Test, 339
Teaching tools, 354
  audiotaping, 323, 330, 337, 353
  manuals, 353, 354, 357
  signing, 323, 324
  videotaping, 36, 201, 323, 331, 334, 335, 339, 352, 358
Technical Assistance Development Systems (TADS), 306